FEMINISTS
REVISION
HISTORY

FEMINISTS REVISION HISTORY

EDITED BY

ANN-LOUISE SHAPIRO

Rutgers University Press
New Brunswick, New Jersey

Library of Congress Cataloging-in-Publication Data

Feminists revision history / edited with an introduction by Ann-Louise Shapiro.

              p.   cm.
      Includes bibliographical references.
      ISBN 0-8135-2063-9 (cloth)   0-8135-2064-9 (pbk.)
      1. Women—History. 2. Feminist theory. I. Shapiro, Ann-Louise, 1944-
HQ1121.F45   1994
305.4 09—c20   93-21105
                                               CIP

British Cataloging-in-Publication information available

Contents

PREFACE

This collection arises out of the theoretical debates that currently animate scholarship among feminists and historians—and indeed, among feminist historians. It seeks above all to bring the critical challenges of feminist theoretical work to the discipline of history, that is, to rethink the traditional preoccupations and presumptions of historians in terms of critiques posed by feminist scholars. Converging in this project are two separate sets of problems: the first derives from issues related to bringing theory to bear in a discipline that has traditionally defined itself as largely empirical; and the second, from the fact that much of the theoretical apparatus used by feminists has emerged outside the discipline of history, raising questions about boundary crossing and translation. The essays included here sit at the intersection of these two problematics as they reflect on the implications of theory for the writing of history and provide models of new interpretive directions opened by feminist scholarship.

Feminist historians have been particularly concerned to tease out the conditions—cultural and disciplinary, conscious and unconscious, discursive and material—that have informed the construction of the historical narrative. According to what criteria, and through what mechanisms, is evidence selected and preserved? How, and in what terms, are claims of historical "truth" validated and authorized, and what is occluded in the historian's assertion of objectivity? How are assumptions about gender written into the historical record? And how can presumptions preserved in the historian's very categories of analysis be unpacked, interrogated, and transformed? This collection looks closely at the writing of history, uncovering the conceptual and epistemological imperatives embedded in the process and the product.

As contemporary feminist scholarship moves into its third decade, debates among feminist theorists are as much at the center of current research as controversies arising between feminists and their more traditional counterparts. While these essays suggest that there is no single or unifying feminist theoretical position, they also, as a whole, provide specific content to Teresa de Lauretis's claim that there is "an essential difference . . . between a feminist and a non-feminist historical consciousness," a difference that constitutes its critical challenge. From quite different perspectives, then, these essays combine an examination of history-writing-as-genre with a focus on problems that are of interest to feminists across disciplines, including such issues as: the complexities of relations among women as well as between women and men; the problem of adequately theorizing the implications of different kinds of difference; the ways that gender is used to construct, preserve, and subvert relations of power; the significance of cross-national and cross-cultural investigations; and the articulation of gender along multiple axes, including those of race, ethnicity, nationality, class, and sexuality.

The essays collected here are designed to move these issues onto the terrain of historical practice. Each essay was either commissioned for this volume or revised so as to directly address this project. Each thus not only has an explicit theoretical problem at its center, but provides an exemplar of the specific ways that feminist theory invites and realizes a revisioning of traditional histories. Taken together, these essays seek to map out some of the most productive critical insights of feminist research, to generate new questions, and to incite colleagues and students to further reimagine the contours of feminist historical practice.

ACKNOWLEDGMENTS

I would like to thank especially the authors of these essays who responded with enthusiasm to my call for articles that would demonstrate—through theoretical abstraction and concrete example—the challenges and effects of feminist historical work. The coherence of this collection is the result of their attentiveness to the larger goals of the project even as they worked with diverse materials, across centuries and geographical spaces, on quite different problems.

I would also like to acknowledge the support of Brian Fay, executive editor of *History and Theory,* who gave me the opportunity to begin this project as a special issue of the journal, and the assistance of Julie Perkins, administrative editor, whose editorial skills eased the passage of this work into print at every stage.

The following essays appeared first in "History and Feminist Theory," *History and Theory* 31, no. 4 (December 1992):

Ann-Louise Shapiro, "History and Feminist Theory; or, Talking Back to the Beadle"

Bonnie G. Smith, "Historiography, Objectivity, and the Case of the Abusive Widow"

Carolyn Steedman, "*La Théorie qui n'en est pas une;* or, Why Clio Doesn't Care"

Regina Morantz-Sanchez, "Feminist Theory and Historical Practice: Rereading Elizabeth Blackwell"

Marilyn A. Katz, "Ideology and 'The Status of Women' in Ancient Greece"

Sylvia Schafer, "When the Child is the Father of the Man: Work, Sexual Difference and the Guardian-State in Third Republic France"

Vron Ware, "Moments of Danger: Race, Gender, and Memories of Empire"

An earlier version of Judith M. Bennett's "Medieval Women, Modern Women: Across the Great Divide" was originally published in *Culture and History, 1350–1600: Essays on English Communities, Identities and Writing,* ed. David Aers (London: Harvester Wheat-sheaf and Detroit: Wayne State University Press, 1992).

Portions of Nell Irvin Painter's essay appeared in slightly dif-ferent form in: "Of *Lily,* Linda Brent, and Freud: A Non-Exceptionalist Approach to Race, Class, and Gender in the Salve-holding South," *Georgia Historical Quarterly* (Summer 1992); and in her introduction to *The Secret Eye: The Diary of Ella Gertrude Clanton Thomas,* ed. Virginia Ingraham Burr (Chapel Hill: University of North Caro-lina Press, 1990).

Carolyn Steedman published a version of her essay in this volume in her monograph *Childhood, Culture and Class in Britain: Margaret McMillan, 1860–1931* (New Brunswick: Rutgers Univer-sity Press, 1990).

An earlier version of Jennifer Terry's essay "Theorizing Deviant Historiography" appeared in *differences* vol. 3 (Summer 1991).

Feminists Revision History

History and Feminist Theory; or, Talking Back to the Beadle

ANN-LOUISE SHAPIRO

It was thus that I found myself walking with extreme rapidity across a grass plot. Instantly a man's figure rose to intercept me. Nor did I at first understand that the gesticulations of a curious-looking object, in a cut-away coat and evening shirt, were aimed at me. His face expressed horror and indignation. Instinct rather than reason came to my help; he was a Beadle; I was a woman. This was the turf; there was the path. Only the Fellows and Scholars are allowed here; the gravel is the place for me.
— *Virginia Woolf,* A Room of One's Own, *1929*

In the past two decades feminist scholars have come a long way toward vindicating Virginia Woolf's fictional alter ego who was, in 1929, so peremptorily deterred in her approach to a "famous university library" by an indignant Beadle guarding male academia against the intrusion of a female interloper. Women have indeed entered the academy in the past twenty years, and feminist theorists have set out to transform conceptual categories and institutional practice. Emerging in conjunction with the feminist movement of the late 1960s, academic feminism, across and within disciplines, has defined itself as a theoretical/political enterprise that challenges what it sees as the fundamentally male-centered bias of traditional scholarship. In its broadest outlines, feminist work seeks to produce a set of destabilizing questions that generate a reexamination of the content, methods, and epistemology of existing academic paradigms as it theorizes the meaning of sexual difference.[1]

Feminist theory points simultaneously to the ways in which the exclusion of women has shaped professional practices and to the effects, within the knowledges of each discipline, of socially and historically constructed gender identities. Although feminists in the academy have attempted to refocus attention on the lives of women and to recover lost stories and alternative experiences, the goals of feminist theoretical work are considerably more far reaching. Feminist theorists have called upon scholars to examine the way that knowledge is constituted: to unpack the processes that select and preserve evidence, to decenter the narrative, recognizing that the neglected or invisible people on the margins have, in fact, defined the center; to interrogate the categories of analysis within each discipline; to demonstrate the way that gender works to legitimize structures of power.[2]

For historians, feminist theory is both a powerful tool of (re)vision and (re)writing and a problematic that continues to unsettle familiar modes of explanation. Theory has often been held suspect in a discipline that is conventionally empirical, grounded in archival sources, and legitimized by its claim to tell the truth of the past. And much of feminist theory has not been written by historians, but rather has emerged in arenas, especially literary criticism and psychoanalytic thought, that have not been particularly hospitable to historical analysis nor responsive to the historian's concern to explain change over time. Yet, Teresa de Lauretis has argued, rightly I think, that there is "an essential difference . . . between a feminist and a non-feminist historical consciousness." In spite of the diverse positions occupied by feminists—positions suggested by the hyphenated labels of cultural-, radical-, liberal-, socialist-, or post-structuralist-feminism—their work proceeds, she claims, within a recognizable framework of theoretical suppositions that constitute its critical challenge.[3]

It is the purpose of this collection to explore the intersections of feminist theory and history. By presenting models of feminist historical work that exemplify a range of practices and perspectives, it suggests some of the components of a theoretically informed feminist historical consciousness. Contributors were invited to reflect on the ways that feminist theory matters in doing history, to demonstrate the effects of bringing the more speculative work of feminist theorists to a traditionally empirical discipline. What are, for example, the new directions/interpretations suggested by feminist theories? What kinds of methodological challenges do feminist theories pose? Are there disciplinary incompatibilities between history and feminist theory? And what would the (re)visioned, (re)written history look like? It has been particularly important to explore the relation between feminist theory and the history of women and to identify some of the theoretical and substantive issues that continue to provoke heated debate. The essays that follow not only address these issues, but collectively lay out a broader agenda.

Bonnie G. Smith and Regina Morantz-Sanchez, in quite different arguments, together call attention to histories not written, promoting, above all, the return of the repressed. Describing the way that historiography has been inflected by "gendered fantasy, passion, and outrage," Smith points to the need to rethink the definition of an author, and more particularly, to remake the identity of the professional historian that has, she argues, been gendered male. Similarly, Morantz-Sanchez demonstrates how medicine and natural science developed in ways that reinforced the subordination, exclusion, and marginalization of women, a pattern mirrored in the *writing* of the history of medicine and science. By looking closely at the needs, values, and circumstances that shaped ostensibly neutral historical accounts, both propose a revaluation of objectivity as they provide alternative stories.

Carrying this critique of the writing of history into the field of women's history, Judith M. Bennett and Carolyn Steedman argue that feminist historians must move beyond existing paradigms in the history of women, beyond even feminist concerns to demonstrate the artificiality of the divide between histories of public and private life. As women's history moves into its third decade, they call not only for a reformulation of its subject matter, but for a new historiography, one that refuses the constraints imposed by traditional periodization and by established conventions of the genre of history writing.

The essays of Marilyn A. Katz, Ava Baron, and Sylvia Schafer all seek to rethink and revise traditional categories of analysis as they suggest new models to reorient research in their respective fields. Katz encourages scholars of the ancient world to abandon their nearly two-hundred-year investigation of the status of "woman"; Baron insists on the need to replace the ungendered male subject of labor history with studies of the varied meanings and uses of masculinity; while Schafer seeks to discard the concept of *raison d'état,* substituting a gendered *imaginaire d'état* as a means to understand administrative decisions and social policy.

As part of a larger project to produce more interactive models to express the articulation of race, class, sexuality, and gender, Nell Painter and Vron Ware focus on images of black and white womanhood and their cultural effects. Both deconstruct assumptions about "blackness" and "whiteness" by exploring contacts across the color line, revealing the complexity of relationships between women. Pursuing further this more nuanced perspective on difference, Mrinalini Sinha and Jennifer Terry call into question unexamined assumptions about identity, experience, authenticity, and agency. Both Sinha's discussion of "authentic voice" and Terry's study of deviant subjectivity suggest ways to account for individuals as both subjects and objects in history.

All of these authors provide theoretical insights that undermine conventional historical inquiry, writing, and understanding; and all offer alternative models. We need, then, to understand the ground for such provocative subversion.

Feminist scholars have made extensive use of the interpretive possibilities opened by Foucault's coupling of power and knowledge, his concept of "subjugated knowledges," and his contention that power is dispersed, that "relations of power are always interwoven with other kinds of relations (production, kinship, family, sexuality)."[4] These insights, although rarely applied by Foucault to the study of women, have allowed feminist theorists to challenge the content of the historical narrative while suggesting the masculinist bias in its construction—that is, to call into question how we know what we know and what counts as knowledge. In a pathbreaking critique of E. P. Thompson's classic study, *The Making of the English Working Class,* Joan Scott analyzed the largely unconscious rhetorical strategies that led Thompson to describe class formation in terms that emphatically gendered the emerging working class as male.[5] By representing what he saw as the more "expressive," "feminine" modes of action as domestic and *not* political, Thompson defined working-class politics in terms of its rationalist manifestations in the hands of working men. In this instance, Scott alleges, Thompson in effect recapitulated the desired gender hierarchy of the late eighteenth century and provided us with a clear example of the embedded politics of historical work. Scott's article was a forerunner in what has become an extensive reexamination by feminist theorists of the discipline of history and the politics of knowledge. This line of investigation highlights the ways that the historical record preserves particular developments while suppressing others, foregrounding the operation of assumptions about gender as a primary mechanism of selection.

Bonnie G. Smith's essay on "narrating" Michelet, on what she describes as the enormous project of the postwar French academy to produce the great historian, takes up these themes. In a layered exposition that juxtaposes nineteenth-century historical practice against its twentieth-century counterpart, and sets twentieth-century gender anxieties *and* politics within the same frame, Smith simultaneously undercuts the assumptions of "scientific" professional history and links the production of knowledge to a context informed by both psychic and political needs. The goal of historians to create a discipline free of "the distortions of desire and advocacy"[6] emerges here as an endeavor both illusory and insidious. Collingwood's claim that he studied history "to learn what it is to be a man" was, Smith shows, literally enacted in the interpretive practices of French historians that produced, finally, "a genderless genius," illuminated especially by contrast with his distinctly ungenius-like wife. In making Michelet a figure capable of securing the national patrimony and useful to the profession—the unique and singular author that has come to inhabit "the fantasy life of the scientific historian"—French historians rewrote his life as "sexual inversion and misrule" by invoking the discourse of separate spheres and polarized gender identities, obscuring the more complex erotic and intellectual partnership that Michelet shared with his much-disparaged wife, Athénaïs, who stood, menacingly, at the boundaries of scientific history.

Smith's analysis raises the question of the use and usefulness of the concept of separate spheres that has informed so much social historical work. Feminist historians have begun to take apart a concept that, they argue, directly reproduces in the study and writing of history the very phenomena that need to be analyzed, a concept that is "too much the anxious repetition of nineteenth century society's deepest ideological hope to be entirely satisfactory as a category of historical inquiry."[7] By dividing the history of men and women into separate histories of public and private life, the stories that emerge are, inevitably, inflected throughout by the desires and expectations of the period under investigation. In Linda Kerber's words, "historians found that notions of women's sphere permeated the language [of historical discourse]; they in turn used the metaphor in their own descriptions. Thus the relation between the name—sphere—and the perception of what it named was reciprocal."[8] Because it was/is both a trope and a means to depict and control aspects of lived experience—operating at once descriptively, prescriptively, and instrumentally—the concept of separate spheres is particularly slippery. And, as Carolyn Steedman argues in her essay in this volume, and Leonore Davidoff and Catherine Hall have demonstrated in great detail in *Family Fortunes,* by leaving the concept of separate spheres so long unchallenged, historians have obscured the class formations that produced it and were sustained by it. It has become necessary, then, to distinguish among the possible meanings and effects of "separate spheres" as used in the past—the way in which it invented a past— and to clarify the distinctions between past usages and the language of current historical analysis.

The project of deconstructing this public/private dichotomy has generated an extensive literature concentrating especially on the lives of middle-class Western women. Some of this work has provided a type of intellectual history that demonstrates the origins of the ideology of separate spheres and the persistent gatekeeping efforts on the part of bourgeois men to prescribe codes of behaviors that were continuously breached in actual practice. Above all, this research has made it clear that "permeability" and "overlap" describe more accurately than does "separation" the complex and ambiguous relations between the world prescribed for men and the designated realm of women. Within this looser framework, feminist scholars have explored such themes as the connections between middle-class domestic ideology and the development of industrial capitalism, women's hidden contributions to the family economy, and the ways in which women manipulated the attributes of domesticity to gain a foothold in more public arenas, that is, women as historical actors, making their own history albeit not in circumstances of their choosing.

It has also become clear that by keeping "the private" from a political analysis, the public/private dichotomy has forestalled an analysis of relations between men and women. "From ancient times," Carole Pateman argues, "theorists have struggled over the question of how the rule of some people over others could be justified, but in all the long controversy over rule by slave-masters, by kings, by lords, by elites, by representatives, by the ruling class, by the vanguard party, sexual domination has remained virtually unquestioned."[9] In her essay about periodization in women's history, Judith M. Bennett seeks to respond to this omission by urging historians of women to examine "the mechanisms and operations of patriarchy," to analyze "the (varied and changing) patriarchal contexts of women's lives. We need to understand," she insists, "how patriarchy has worked in certain times and places, how it has been challenged, accepted, and changed by women and men, and how it has adapted and adjusted to changing times." She argues, more specifically, that historians, including feminist historians, have too readily accepted the paradigmatic terms of a master narrative that posits a great divide between medieval and early modern history — have been too willing to preserve the belief that things were better for women in the Middle Ages and worsened in the early-modern centuries. It is this assumption of "a kinder and gentler" earlier period that has, Bennett claims, deflected attention from more significant continuities in the typically low status of women — continuities that feminists must be able to explain. By refusing conventional periodization, and in broader terms, by examining the operations of patriarchy, she argues, feminist historians will be better able to analyze one of the central problems of history: "the nature, sustenance, and endurance of structures of power."[10]

In "*La Théorie qui n'en est pas une*," Carolyn Steedman continues Bennett's critique of the enterprise of doing women's history. Shifting from the problem of periodization to the issue of genre, she illustrates the reductionist effects produced by preserving, unexamined, the established conventions imposed by historical biography. Steedman points to the essential ahistoricity of the figure of "domestic woman," codified in the nineteenth-century domestic novel and preserved by historians and literary critics. Influenced by a tradition that endowed women's life stories with special spiritual significance, and by modern psychologizing that placed domestic struggle at the center of women's development, biographers of women have, she argues, typically "elevated the affective and personal above the political and social context." In her work on Margaret McMillan, Steedman has sought "to steer an individual life story towards collectivity," to place McMillan within the "public space of cultural change," lifting the heavy weight of interiority carried by the genre of women's biography—to write, in effect, history and not female biography. In so doing, she calls into question the boundary between "inside" and "outside" and the patterns of storytelling that inadvertently recapitulate a public/ private divide that is always reductive and typically made along the fault line of sex.

Regina Morantz-Sanchez pursues in quite different terms the critique of separate spheres and of history-writing-as-genre opened by Smith and Steedman. Her account of the place of the physician Elizabeth Blackwell in the transformation of medical practice at the end of the nineteenth century—from a more patient-centered art to a laboratory science concerned primarily with physiological processes—is part of a larger project that seeks to understand the social forces that structure scientific activity. But more specifically, she is interested in the effects of the marginalization of conceptions and behaviors that were encoded as feminine as medical science became a male gendered enterprise. Like Steedman and Smith, she is concerned simultaneously with the developments of the past and with ways of understanding and writing about these developments. But in contrast to these authors, Morantz-Sanchez explores more directly the value of the suppressed "feminine." She argues that, as notions of the good practitioner were regendered, a medical tradition which earlier competed with the victorious tradition of "scientific" medicine disappeared, with unfortunate consequences for both the practice of medicine and the definition of science. Along with numerous feminist critics of mainstream science, she reintroduces what has been labeled as more feminine (maternal, empathic) modes of apprehending reality, pointing ultimately toward an expanded theory of knowledge.[11]

While resisting essentialist assumptions, Morantz-Sanchez seeks to counter the devaluing of knowledge that appears nonscientific in the conventional sense of the term, urging a redefinition of notions of subjectivity and objectivity. Her rereading of Blackwell seems particularly intriguing when placed against, for example, the recent writings of Anatole Broyard, former literary critic and editor of the *New York Times Book Review,* composed in the midst of a terminal illness. Broyard queried his friends/critics for whom "information is a religion" in order to find a doctor who was part physician, part metaphysician, able to treat body and soul. Broyard's ideal doctor would be more than a talented practitioner; he would be someone willing to show "the music of his humanity," who would enter the patient's condition, able to read the poetry of his sickness. Searching for someone with "a spacious flaring grasp of his situation," someone capable of "empathic witnessing," Broyard suggests that the modern hospital must become less like a laboratory and more like a theater, while modern doctors must exchange something of their authority for their humanity.[12] Elizabeth Blackwell would have been pleased. Broyard does not, in fact, identify the empathic and relational qualities that he is looking for as feminine. And Morantz-Sanchez is careful to point to the dangers involved in affirming Blackwell's recoding of certain medical practices as specifically maternal, that is, to the dangers of preserving, in the end, reductionist dualisms. It is this dilemma—identified by Morantz-Sanchez as the tension between "sameness" and "difference"—that remains a central tension within feminism.

Feminist theorists have been preoccupied with a seemingly inevitable oscillation between the felt need to reclaim the identity of "woman" and to give it political meaning, and the equally obvious perils of settling within an identity which has, in Ann Snitow's terms, "an all too solid history."[13] On the one hand, some scholars have found, in exploring the conventional gender division, a women's culture worth examining on its own terms. Rather than emphasizing the problems of subordination and exclusion, this scholarship looks instead at the creation of a distinct women's culture inflected by values generated in women's relationships with each other or through their traditional female roles and activities.[14] But feminist criticism has more and more come to insist on the need to dismantle altogether the category of woman. Linda Gordon cautions that an emphasis on difference encourages the ghettoization of knowledge about women, producing new subfields rather than a critique that challenges the structure of the disciplines.[15] An entire collection of essays edited by French historian Michelle Perrot asks, *Une Histoire des femmes est-elle possible?* (Is a history of women possible?)[16] And, in a much cited study of the category of "women" in history, "*Am I That Name?*," Denise Riley wonders, similarly, "Does a Sex Have a History?" In perhaps her most challenging formulation of this pointedly paradoxical query, Riley poses the theoretical dilemma of feminism in the following terms:

> Could it be argued that the only way of avoiding these constant historical loops which depart or return from the conviction of women's natural dispositions, to pacifism for example, would be to make a grander gesture—to stand back and announce that there *aren't any* "women"?[17]

Riley responds to her own question by modifying Foucault's claim that "the purpose of history . . . is not to discover the roots of our identity but to commit itself to its dissipation." "Whatever does feminism want," she asks, "with dissipated identities?" Instead, while acknowledging the particular needs of concrete women, Riley steers a path between essentialist identity and the "airy indeterminacy" of dissipation by insisting on the historicity of sexed identities—on the fact that " 'women' is historically, discursively constructed, and always relatively to other categories which themselves change; 'women' is a volatile collectivity in which female persons can be very differently positioned."[18] The oscillation, then, between "a concentration on and a refusal of the identity of 'women' " suggests a problematic in the history of women in which feminist scholars are themselves differently positioned.[19]

Feminists' discomfort with the idea of "woman" has raised intriguing questions about the historian's sources for a history of women—about what constitutes evidence and about how information is "obtained, verified, categorized and transmitted."[20] In particular, historians are beginning to examine the ways that the male bias of primary sources has been preserved in secondary accounts. In nineteenth-century history, for example, Alain Corbin has discussed literary and scientific writings about women as evidence, above all, of intense male sexual anxiety, of a preoccupation with the possibility of male sexual inferiority.[21] Cautioning historians to be wary of inadvertently codifying these anxieties, Corbin insists that the documentary proofs offered by nineteenth-century men must be seen as self-interested briefs in a struggle about male authority and female (sexual) autonomy. From a different perspective, but with a similar critique of documentary evidence, Joan Scott has examined statistical reports to demonstrate their immersion in a larger political, gendered discourse that conveys, above all, a specific vision of social reality.[22] In sum, feminist work has promoted an epistemological and contextual interrogation of traditional historical sources.

Such problems about evidence become especially visible in studies of the ancient world where data about women is proportionately more limited and where scholars have long relied primarily on literary sources. Marilyn A. Katz's essay, "Ideology and 'the Status of Women' in Ancient Greece," suggests the kinds of interpretative stalemates that have followed from the persistence of opposing sets of stereotypes in an historiographical argument focused on confirming either women's elevated or debased status. Katz asserts that scholars of the ancient world are not so much "coming up with the wrong answers as . . . asking the wrong questions." Instead, rejecting the validity of "woman" constructed in traditional historiography, she argues for a new history of the history of women. Reconceptualizing the problem so as to focus on the coming into being of gendered categories, Katz moves beyond an examination of the roots of classical scholarship in the nineteenth century and situates the history of "the woman question" in the ancient world in eighteenth-century debates over the form and nature of civil society. She argues that eighteenth-century social theorists like Rousseau used women's exclusion in ancient Athens to construct their model of civil society, while later writers incorporated these ideas on women's nature into their investigation of ancient Greece. In refusing this tautology, in refusing a certain kind of history of women, Katz is able to unfold the possibility of, not only a different historical narrative, but of an alternative historiography.

As the category of "woman" has been deconstructed by historians, feminist scholars have become increasingly wary of yet again preserving "man" as an ostensibly ungendered subject—the implied universal that defines the female as a particular case. For example, the seemingly gender-neutral designations of "individual," "worker," "prostitute" have come under scrutiny as historians have attempted to identify moments in which meanings change and in which specific categories become particularly meaning-full. When do natural rights mean only rights for men? And how is this selectivity justified and maintained? If women are not "Women" to the same degree in every moment of their lives, by what criteria, and in whose terms, are these different possibilities identified? What does it mean, in cultural and symbolic terms, that as a category "working-class women" were "in no way merely the female section of their class," but rather, were conjured as beings whose "femininity filled a distinctive space," overflooding class?[23]

Dislodging from center stage the ungendered male subject of history, feminist scholarship has begun to pose the construction of masculinity as a problem. In focusing more directly on the ways that gender interacts with other axes of power, labor historians in particular have begun to explore the connections between sexual politics and class politics, recasting the history of work and the economy so as to take account of the struggles and solidarities that were constructed and fractured along lines of gender as well as class. In her essay "On Looking at Men," Ava Baron seeks to rectify the tendencies within labor history to study men while assuming that their gender is both invisible and irrelevant. She emphasizes, instead, the contingent and historically specific meanings of manliness that emerged out of particular social conditions and institutional practices. Responding similarly to the self-imposed constraints of more traditional labor history, William Sewell has argued that "we need . . . to hypothesize a world in which work is simultaneously 'ideal' and 'material' and in which everything workers do must be understood as simultaneously structured by discourse, by choice under conditions of scarcity, and by power relations."[24] Baron engages these issues directly, contending that it is by studying the construction and deployment of different historical versions of masculinity that historians can reveal most precisely the complex operations of power in the labor process.

Sylvia Schafer's essay on the French state's child welfare policies addresses this theme of gendered identities and their public effects as she focuses on "the field of meaning" which underwrote the state's administrative decisions. Schafer seeks to move beyond facile assumptions about the state's will, "*la raison d'état*," in order to consider what she terms "*l'imaginaire d'état*" (the government's imagination). In shifting categories in this way, she underscores the cultural embeddedness of the state's identity and its social policies, emphasizing above all the way that gender works as "a primary means of figuring the relationship between government and the governed." Schafer is arguing specifically that the significance of the gendered administrative language that she is investigating is substantive—that rhetoric constrains policy and that the history of the state and its institutions must include a consideration of gender.[25] Yet while Joan Scott has claimed, in a now classic essay, that political history has been enacted on a field of gender,[26] and we are surrounded daily by reminders of the ways that stereotypes of masculinity and femininity are mapped onto contemporary political life,[27] mainstream histories have often been reluctant to see gender as woven into the whole fabric of social relations and institutional practices. In effect, feminist historians are attempting to rewrite the historical record so as to demonstrate that "gender is present even when women are not."[28]

Even as white feminists were succeeding in opening up and problematizing the traditional categories of historical discourse, however, feminists of color pointed to a glaring failure to sufficiently take account of race and ethnicity—a lapse all the more notable in light of feminist preoccupations with the meanings of difference and with strategies of domination.[29] In a synthetic overview of themes and problems in African-American women's history, for example, Evelyn Brooks Higginbotham describes "race" as a metalanguage that covers over, stands in for, and constructs other social and power relations, including relations of gender and class, definitions of sexuality, and the expression of economic and political interests.[30] Because it *is* a metalanguage, Higginbotham argues, race is neither natural, visible, nor transhistorical;[31] rather, it signifies different kinds of difference in diverse social and historical contexts. In effect, it is a principle of organization that positions various groups vis-à-vis one another.[32] It is apparent, then, that just as the story of women could not simply be added to the story of men, the historical implications of race and ethnicity could not simply be tacked on to a history sensitive to issues shaped by class and gender. In particular, women of color have called upon

historians to recognize that gender and class identities are constructed *and* fragmented by race and to explore the ways that
racialized, and often also sexualized, identities preserve and protect
systems of authority.[33]

Nell Painter uses the theme of interracial, interclass sexuality
in the slave South to draw a picture of southern families in which
race and class cut across gender solidarities and conflicts. Confirming feminist arguments that a meaningful women's history cannot
be written without developing methods for reading absences and
silences in extant evidence,[34] Painter searches out the "veiled text"
of a white woman's diary via what she sees as "leakage" and
"deception clues" that reveal the hidden stories of miscegenation
and its effects. On the basis of historical and literary sources, she
speculates that the pervasiveness of polygynous marriages—marriages shared between official wives and unofficial "slave wives"—
made victims and competitors of *both* the sexually exploited black
women and the otherwise privileged white women who saw themselves as "losers in the southern sexual sweepstakes." Painter seeks
to remove race as "an opaque barrier to feminist investigation" by
drawing comparisons between the American South and other
hierarchical societies, especially those with households that included servants, (for example, Freud's Vienna). She argues, in
conclusion, that race must not be understood as an airtight category that flattens out the complexities of human relations, but
rather one that opens doors to more thorny visions of power and
powerlessness.

These are, in fact, the issues that Vron Ware takes up in her essay
"Moments of Danger: Race, Gender, and Memories of Empire."
While women's history has been silent on race, Ware notes, British
imperial history has largely ignored gender. She begins, then, to
outline a set of themes that open the way to explain more adequately the articulation of race, class, and gender. Beginning with
the premise that "blackness" and "whiteness" construct each other—
that whiteness is a racialized identity—Ware examines the instru-
mentalities of white women in different forms of racism and "the
relationship between gender prescriptions and racial boundaries,"
focusing especially on "the interface of sexuality and the wider
political order."[35] Her concern is to deconstruct the blanket term
"racism" so as to reveal the different investments and contradictory

positions that are buried in its generality. In looking at both English and colonial contexts, Ware is seeking to expose the mechanisms whereby systems of domination reproduce themselves, underlining the ways that gender and race are implicated in these processes.

In the final section of Ware's essay—a study of two recent well-publicized stories of women in postcolonial societies—she seeks to demonstrate how historical memories shape contemporary understanding and behavior.[36] Both Steedman's and Ware's essays are responsive to questions about historical memory. Both argue forcefully that "history" does not just proceed, packaged, out of the academy, but is profoundly shaped by outside forces—in Steedman's argument, the public school system, in Ware's, cinema, television, and literature; and both underline the ways that collective and individual historical memory is complicated by the play of desire and imagination. While it is apparent that "history" becomes, in these arguments, something ultimately beyond the control of professional historians, Steedman indirectly, and Ware more explicitly, raise the question of the relationship of academic feminism to "the outside." Ware's academic project is to push feminist theory toward ways of making sense of cultural and racial difference that are at once more subtle and more comprehensive. At bottom, her concern is to equip feminists to "intervene in debates about contemporary politics with a historically informed and 'anti-racist' perspective."

It is clear, then, that feminist theory is not just important for history, but that history must reciprocally inform feminist theory. The point is especially noteworthy in Ware's argument because we are currently in a moment when the issue of politics in the academy has itself become intensely politicized. Nonacademic critics (especially political conservatives) have recently been extremely disparaging of the academic enterprise, while sensitivities around "political correctness" are rife within the university. It is perhaps a comment on the anxieties produced among American feminists by charges of undue partisanship that the two essays that address most directly the politics of feminist work are those by British scholars whose work emerged in the context of a dialogue between feminists on the one hand and activists and scholars in the labor movement on the other. With these issues we are returned, once again, to the problem of objectivity and the politics of knowledge production raised by Smith and Morantz-Sanchez, this time with an emphasis not on epistemology, but on feminism's engagement with contemporary cultural conflicts and political debates. The essays in this volume make it clear that feminist scholars reject, in general, the dichotomy between professionalism and politics as they negotiate the intersections of academic work, historical memory, and life outside the academy.[37]

We have seen that feminist theory has been the means of challenging disciplinary and epistemological premises and a method for generating new categories of analysis. We need to return, however, to Carolyn Steedman's opening challenge to feminist theory itself—to "the theory that is not one." In the first meaning of this title, Steedman alludes to the multiplicity of feminist theories. Work on the meanings of gender is necessarily multi-disciplinary, and academic feminism shares its critique of the politics of knowledge with other scholars who are also reflecting on the nature of their separate disciplines. There is obviously no single feminist theory. And neither is there an easy way to incorporate the necessary attentiveness to difference which feminism espouses—differences of ethnicity, sexuality, and nationality as well as of gender, race, and class.[38] Lata Mani has, for example, written of the need for "a rigorous politics of translation," in order to capture the specificities and particularities of different national experiences.[39] In her discussion of lesbian autobiography, Biddy Martin points to similar complexities around the question of identity. She argues that to put the word "lesbian" before autobiography tends to suggest that sexual identity defines a life, "providing it with predictable content and an identity possessing continuity and universality," thereby formalizing reductionist understandings of subjectivity. Rejecting sexuality as a totalizing identity, she insists, rather, on the "contradictory, multiple construction of subjectivity at the intersections but also in the interstices of ideologies of gender, race and sexuality."[40]

Both of these examples speak to feminist concerns to articulate a conception of the human subject as "neither unified nor singly divided between positions of masculinity and femininity but multiply organized across positions on several axes of difference"—a perspective, explicitly offering a feminist critique of feminism, that has emerged especially in the writings of lesbians and women of color.[41] The essays by Mrinalini Sinha and Jennifer Terry develop these insights in quite different, but also complementary, historical investigations. Sinha's discussion of the controversy surrounding the publication in 1927 of an exposé of Indian society by an American woman provides her with the opportunity to explore the emergence of the alleged "authentic voice of the Indian woman" by tracing its implication in the politics of colonialism, nationalism, and middle-class feminism. By delineating the various subject positions created in the collision of imperial and nationalist struggles, and by juxtaposing the symbolic resonances of "woman" against the class and gender politics of the moment, Sinha begins to tease out the specific identities, or subjectivities, available in a particular historical context, and to suggest the ways that Indian women were both objects and subjects as they sought a position from which to respond to the voices from the West. Her demonstration of the way that voices of Indian women emerged through and within the politics and discourses of their immediate environment speaks above all to the inadequacy of accounts that depend upon ahistorical and essentialized versions of identity.

In telling the stories of the production of "the voice of the Indian woman," Sinha has raised a larger problem that emerges for historians who call into question the coherence, stability, or originary status of identity: How, she asks, can we think about women as historical subjects once we have enumerated the conditions that construct and constrain the possibilities of female identity and behavior? Are these (constructed) "women" thereby deprived of the authenticity of their experience or of agency in their own lives? In "Theorizing Deviant Historiography," Jennifer Terry responds directly to these questions. Like Sinha, her goal is to "lay bare the operations by which 'women,' 'people of color,' and creatures identified as 'lesbians' and 'gay men' are discursively produced, as opposed to taking them as given objects or essential, embodied perspectives from which to tell or 'experience' history." She argues that "experience" cannot be understood as "merely *lived* by its subjects and *discovered* by historians,"[42] and demonstrates, rather, the way that the subjectivities of lesbians and gay men have been forged in collaboration and in conflict with medico-scientific discourses that pathologize homosexuality. Using de Lauretis's model of female subjects who are both inside and outside of an ideology of gender, Terry is reaching toward an analysis of difference, or deviance, that reveals homosexual subjects who are both constrained by, and resistant to, the ideology and history of heterosexuality.

In their critique of ahistorical and essentialized identities—their attentiveness to partiality and multiplicity—feminists are, then, acknowledging "the theory that is not one." But Steedman is pointing to more than complex subjectivities or theoretical conundrums in her provocative echoing of Irigaray's title. Even as she borrows from *l'écriture féminine,* Steedman is raising, at the same time, a question about the costs of such academic poaching. Underlining the fact that much of the theory that feminist historians use has been developed within literary-critical practice, she is asking, in effect, about the consequences of moving theory across disciplinary boundaries. To paraphrase Lata Mani's question, posed from the interdisciplinary perspective of cultural studies, "When does a tool kit degenerate into a grab bag?"[43] Much of the debate about theory within feminism has been stimulated by the focus on language and representation, the turn to poststructuralism represented especially in the work of Joan Scott and Denise Riley. The controversies of this debate involve differences about the way in which challenges to an unmediated "real" can be incorporated into historical writing, and worries about the effects on history writing of a theory that takes causality, agency, and experience—all significant components of traditional historical explanation—to be problems requiring analysis rather than starting points of analysis.[44]

As historians have struggled to resolve these theoretical conflicts, they have begun to focus on how poststructuralist theory can be profitably transformed in historical practice. Judith Newton asks: "What bearing did public written representation with its complex dream work and contradictions have on the way that ordinary men and women conceptualized themselves and lived their lives? How was meaning transmitted from one layer of culture to another? And what force did public written discourse ultimately have?"[45] To respond to these kinds of questions, historians have paid close attention to the ways that systems of meaning interact with material conditions, to the struggle over meaning among willful agents in specific social and political circumstances, to the relationship between prescription and practice, and to the suggestive silences and omissions of the evidence. In *City of Dreadful Delight,* for example, Judith Walkowitz addresses these conceptual and methodological issues. She notes that in order to convey "the dynamics of metropolitan life [in late Victorian London] as a series of multiple and simultaneous cultural contests," she has both observed the conventions of writing social history *and* abandoned elements of a traditional historical narrative. This has meant resisting narrative closure, rejecting fixed polarities based in gender and class, and refusing reductive conceptual oppositions—representation and reality, elite and popular culture, creation/reception and production/consumption of cultural texts—in order to account adequately for the complex interactions of cultural worlds.[46]

In a recent keynote address to a conference of historians of women, Alice Kessler-Harris observed that historical scholarship no longer seemed the leading edge of feminist work, providing neither the source of energy nor the catalyst for change. The lead, she implied, had passed to literary studies with their focus on representations and discursive effects.[47] But because, as Steedman suggests, history is both a form of cognition and a form of writing, historians cannot afford to absent themselves from these debates. The authors in this volume are, then, responding to the challenge to produce theory informed by history and to write history infused by feminist insights and concerns.

Having talked back to the Beadle in this overview of feminists who have, after all, gained access to the library, I want to return, in conclusion, to Virginia Woolf. At the end of her lengthy meditation on the constraints that have inhibited women's intellectual endeavors, she addresses her audience directly to ask: What does it matter?

> Still, you may object, why do you attach so much importance to this writing of books by women when, according to you, it requires so much effort, leads perhaps to the murder of one's aunts, will make one almost certainly late for luncheon, and may bring one into very grave disputes with certain very good fellows?[48]

The question remains, even as more than a half-century later we know that it is not only women who produce feminist work and we are, perhaps, more accustomed to the "very grave disputes with certain very good fellows." What does it matter?

As the articles in this collection demonstrate, feminist historians have succeeded in writing historical narratives that expose the reductionism of the public/private dichotomy, reaching toward a more integrated historical narrative. They have offered trenchant critiques of history writing and revealed the processes that determine what constitutes knowledge and what is relegated to the periphery; and they have told different stories, at once producing a neglected history of women and demonstrating its limitations. By profitably opening up the categories of historical analysis, by questioning the self-evidence of the evidence itself, feminists have pushed historical explanations to account for intersecting axes of power—particularly those of ethnicity, race, class, gender, and sexuality—as strategic constructions that maintain patterns of dominance and subordination. In the end, difference will not disappear nor will the power relations and cultural practices that it enables and sustains. We will continue to need better ways to theorize the importance of difference in the past, to write its history, and to find its meanings in our lives. It is for these projects that feminist theory matters.

NOTES

1. Carole Pateman, "Introduction: The Theoretical Subversiveness of Feminism," in *Feminist Challenges: Social and Political Theory*, ed. Carole Pateman and Elizabeth Gross (Boston, 1986); Catherine Hall, "Feminism and Feminist History," in *White, Male and Middle-Class* (New York, 1992).

2. Joan W. Scott, *Gender and the Politics of History* (New York, 1988); Judith Allen, "Evidence and Silence: Feminism and the Limits of History," in *Feminist Challenges*.

3. Teresa de Lauretis, "Upping the Anti in Feminist Theory," in *Conflicts in Feminism*, ed. Marianne Hirsch and Evelyn Fox Keller (New York, 1990), 255–256.

4. See especially "Two Lectures" and "Power Strategies," in Michel Foucault, *Power/Knowledge* (New York, 1977).

5. Scott, "Women in *The Making of the English Working Class*," in *Gender and the Politics of History*.

6. The phrase is Regina Morantz-Sanchez's. See her chapter, "Feminist Theory and Historical Practice."

7. Carolyn Steedman, see her chapter, "La Théorie qui n'en est pas une."

8. Linda K. Kerber, "Separate Spheres, Female Worlds, Woman's Place: The Rhetoric of Women's History," *The Journal of American History* 75 (June 1988):

10–11. See also, Dorothy O. Helly and Susan M. Reverby, eds. *Gendered Domains: Rethinking Public and Private in Women's History* (Ithaca, 1992).

9. Pateman, "Introduction," p. 5.

10. Judith Bennett, "Feminism and History," *Gender and History* 1 (Autumn 1989), 266.

11. See Morantz-Sanchez's comprehensive footnotes for an extended bibliography of the field of gender and science.

12. Anatole Broyard, "Doctor Talk to Me," *New York Times Magazine*, 26 August 1990.

13. Ann Snitow, "A Gender Diary," in *Conflicts in Feminism*.

14. Carroll Smith-Rosenberg, "The Female World of Love and Ritual," *Signs* 1 no. 1 (Autumn 1975): 1–19 and *Disorderly Conduct: Visions of Gender in Victorian America* (New York, 1985); Nancy Cott, *The Bonds of Womanhood* (New Haven, 1977); Bonnie Smith, *Ladies of the Leisure Class* (Princeton, 1981).

15. Linda Gordon, "What's New in Women's History?" in *Feminist Studies/ Critical Studies*, ed. Teresa de Lauretis (Bloomington, 1986).

16. Michelle Perrot, ed., *Une Histoire des femmes est-elle possible?* (Paris, 1984).

17. Denise Riley, *"Am I That Name?": Feminism and the Category of 'Women' in History* (Minneapolis, 1988).

18. *Ibid.*, 2, 5.

19. This is a tension which occurs not only for academic theorists but for feminist activists who need to determine, strategically, when a woman is a "woman" in seeking political and economic justice.

20. Judith Allen, "Evidence and Silence: Feminism and the Limits of History," in *Feminist Challenges*; Marilyn Skinner, "Classical Studies vs. Women's Studies," *Helios* 12 (Fall 1985): 7.

21. Alain Corbin, "Le 'sexe en deuil' et l'histoire des femmes au XIXe siècle," in *Une Histoire des femmes*, 144. Taking this argument further, Robert Nye has theorized that bourgeois male identity in the nineteenth century was rooted in reproductive capacity, centering around the ability of the bourgeois man to establish a vigorous lineage. Hence, fears of impotence and sexual exhaustion, exacerbated in the fin-de-siècle by greater public acknowledgment of women's right to sexual satisfaction, became a leitmotif in medical discussions in which "the dyad female orgasm/male impotence [was] always a latent feature." Robert Nye, "Honor, Impotence, and Male Sexuality in Nineteenth-Century French Medicine," *French Historical Studies* 16 (Spring 1989): 64.

22. Joan W. Scott, "A Statistical Representation of Work," in *Gender and the Politics of History*.

23. Riley, *"Am I That Name?,"* 57.

24. William H. Sewell, Jr., "Rethinking Labor History: Toward a Post-Materialist Rhetoric," Comparative Study of Social Transformations, University of Michigan, Working Paper 44, May 1990.

25. Additional studies that raise the centrality of gender in explanations of state welfare policies include, Nancy Fraser, "Struggle Over Needs," in *Unruly Practices: Power, Discourse and Gender in Contemporary Social Theory* (Minneapolis, 1989); Denise Riley, *War in the Nursery* (London, 1983).

26. Joan W. Scott, "Gender: A Useful Category of Historical Analysis," in

Gender and the Politics of History. See also, Judith R. Walkowitz, *Prostitution and Victorian Society* (Cambridge, 1980); Claudia Koonz, *Mothers in the Fatherland* (New York, 1987); Lynn Hunt, *The Family Romance of the French Revolution* (Berkeley, 1992).

27.   The theme of family values has saturated the United States presidential campaign of 1992, for example, and the candidates have positioned themselves against each other and in relation to their wives in terms of heavily gendered identities.

28.   Ava Baron, "On Looking at Men," in this volume.

29.   For example, Sara Evans has pointed out that "twice in the history of the United States, the struggle for racial equality has been midwife to a feminist movement," noting that in both the 1830s–1840s and the 1960s, white women gained experience in collective organizing and a language and strategy to challenge oppression from their participation in struggles for black civil rights. Sara Evans, *Personal Politics: The Roots of Women's Liberation in the Civil Rights Movement and the New Left* (New York, 1979), 24.

30.   Evelyn Brooks Higginbotham, "African-American Women's History and the Metalanguage of Race," *Signs* 17 (Winter 1992).

31.   Higginbotham, "The Metalanguage of Race," 253; Barbara Fields, "Ideology and Race in American History," in *Region, Race, and Reconstruction: Essays in Honor of C. Vann Woodward*, ed. J. Morgan Kousser and James M. McPherson (New York, 1982).

32.   Higginbotham, "The Metalanguage of Race," 253.

33.   Higginbotham points out, for example, that the emergence of the figure of the "lady" in nineteenth-century American society represents both a racial and a class-differentiated status within the category of "women." Ladies were women of the middle and upper classes; but "no black woman, regardless of income, education, refinement, or character, enjoyed the status of lady."

34.   See Allen, "Evidence and Silence," 176.

35.   The phrases are Ann Stoler's, "Carnal Knowledge and Imperial Power," in *Gender at the Crossroads of Knowledge: Feminist Anthropology in the Postmodern Era*, ed. Micaela de Leonardo (Berkeley, 1991).

36.   Lata Mani has made a similar point in her discussion of the reception by British, American, and Indian feminists of her work on *sati* in colonial India. Mani argues that "the audiences in these places seized on entirely different aspects of my work as politically significant." The very different responses that her work evoked demonstrated "how moving between different 'configurations of meaning and power' can prompt different 'modes of knowing.'" Lata Mani, "Multiple Mediations: Feminist Scholarship in the Age of Multinational Reception," *Feminist Review* 35 (Summer 1990): 26–27.

37.   See Joan W. Scott's discussion of this issue in *New Perspectives on Historical Writing*, ed. Peter Burke (Pennsylvania, 1992), and Hall, "Feminism and Feminist History."

38.   For a discussion of women's history in an international context, see Karen Offen, Ruth Roach Pierson, and Jane Rendall, eds., *Writing Women's History* (Bloomington, 1991).

39.   Lata Mani, "Cultural Theory, Colonial Texts," in *Cultural Studies*, ed. Lawrence Grossberg, Gary Nelson, and Paula Treichler (New York, 1992). Donald

Meyer, in *Love and Democracy* (Middletown, 1987), was among the first to point to the importance of national differences in explaining the rise of feminist movements. See also, Kumkum Sangari and Sudesh Vaid, eds., *Recasting Women: Essays in Indian Colonial History* (New Brunswick, N. J., 1990) for a discussion of the historiographical problems of recasting the history of women in postcolonial societies.

40.   Biddy Martin, "Lesbian Identity and Autobiographical Difference[s]," in *Life/Lines: Theorizing Women's Autobiography*, ed. Bella Brodski and Celeste Schenck (Ithaca, N.Y., 1988), 78, 82.

41.   Teresa de Lauretis, "Eccentric Subjects: Feminist Theory and Historical Consciousness," *Feminist Studies* 16, no.1 (Spring 1990): 131, 133. De Lauretis argues further that the different axes along which difference is organized (class, ethnicity, color, race, sexuality, gender) must be understood not as parallel "layers of oppression," but as constantly intersecting and mutually implicated, each affecting the others.

42.   Terry, citing Joan W. Scott, "Experience," in *Feminists Theorize the Political*, ed. Judith Butler and Joan Scott (New York, 1992).

43.   Mani, "Cultural Theory, Colonial Texts," 394.

44.   For a recent discussion of the value of theories of language for feminism, see Nancy Fraser, "The Uses and Abuses of French Discourse Theories for Feminist Politics," in *Revaluing French Feminism: Critical Essays on Difference, Agency and Culture*, ed. Nancy Fraser and Sandra Lee Bartky (Bloomington, 1992).

45.   Judith Newton, "*Family Fortunes*: 'New History' and 'New Historicism,'" *Radical History Review* 43 (Winter 1989): 19.

46.   Judith R. Walkowitz, *City of Dreadful Delight: Narratives of Sexual Danger in Late-Victorian London* (Chicago, 1992), 8, 10.

47.   Alice Kessler-Harris, "The Just Price, the Free Market, and the Value of Women," in *Gendered Domains*, 263.

48.   Virginia Woolf, *A Room of One's Own*, (New York, 1929), 189.

Historiography, Objectivity, and the Case of the Abusive Widow

BONNIE G. SMITH

"What is an author?" the philosopher Michel Foucault asked some two decades ago, and although this question has fascinated literary theorists, it has barely interested historians, who are more absorbed by such disciplinary issues as objectivity.[1] Since the nineteenth century the profession of history has taken pride in its ability to purge itself of biases arising from class, gender, race, and politics; and these claims continue to be made and disputed. With each generation the discourse of objectivity is revitalized, most recently and notably at the hands of Peter Novick, who has woven the story of this "noble dream" into a popular saga of origins, testing and challenge, and ultimately rescue by a heroic historian. In his and other accounts the founding myth of objectivity is constantly reworked, refurbished, and thus reborn through challenges from those with political, gendered, racial, or other concerns.

The story of objectivity, as Novick and others tell it, is one in which individual historians, though perhaps acting collectively, subject the founding dream to abuse or rescue it from its challengers. Thus, the virtue of objectivity is unquestioningly attributed to great historians, technically expert and visionary geniuses who soar beyond the passions and interests of ordinary people in ways that allow them to produce compelling if not always perfect history. Studies of one or two great historians per generation often serve to make up historiography, but while we examine "objectivity," we rarely consider the shape of historiography itself and what it has meant to the profession to have its achievements exemplified in the biographies of a handful of great authors. What is the use to which

I thank Donald R. Kelley, Susan Kingsley Kent, and Ann-Louise Shapiro for their contributions to this article, and the ACLS and the National Humanities Center for supporting the early stages of this research.

these biographies are put and, how have these lives of great historians served to fortify the founding myth of objectivity? Why has
the story of the scholar who wrestles with the political, sexual, and
social conditions of everyday life to free his genius been so much
more central an ingredient of professionalization than even objectivity and so much less explored? In this connection "What is an
author?" would indeed be a useful question for historians to ask.

The status of the great historian first became pertinent to my
own work in historiography when I stumbled on an insistent
French fixation—the puzzling case of Michelet's widow, outlined
in an appendix to Arthur Mitzman's *Michelet, Historian.*[2] Mitzman
presented a long history of excoriation of Athénaïs Michelet,
captured in the phrase "abusive widow." In 1936 Anatole de Monzie,
a lawyer and author who had successively been minister of public
works, of finance, and of education, coined this term, oddly
enough, not for outrageously famous consorts like Catherine de
Medici, who could be said to exemplify female "misrule," but for
spouses of intellectuals. He accused these women of criminally
meddling in the literary or artistic legacies of men like Claude
Bernard, Lev Tolstoy, and Jules Michelet. Each of them either
managed a dead husband's reputation, edited his work, or claimed
an independent intellectual status for herself; but of all the offend-
ers Monzie took Athénaïs Mialaret-Michelet as "the model for
these excessive, inopportune, and abusive widows."[3] A little more
investigation showed a consistent pattern of diatribes: Gabriel
Monod and Daniel Halévy opened the attack early in the century
just a year or so after her death in 1899, while some fifty years later
Roland Barthes's *Michelet lui-même* maintained that she "falsified
Michelet's manuscripts, stupidly falsifying the themes, i.e. Michelet
himself."[4] Chosen by Lucien Febvre to edit Michelet's collected
works after World War II, Paul Viallaneix, Claude Digeon, and
associated editors since the mid-1950s have spent hundreds of pages
across multiple volumes repetitiously discrediting Mme Michelet's
role in her husband's life and works, finally damning her as not a
collaborator, but a mere researcher and copyist. This fixation
invites us not only to consider why Athénaïs Michelet has been so
crucial to historiography and the status of its great practitioners but
to ponder the role that gender may actually play in establishing the
centrality of objective authorship.

Literary scholars are more accustomed than historians to these extended fits of pique against wives and widows. *The Ordeal of Mark Twain*, according to Van Wyck Brooks, was that "his wife not only edited his works but edited him."⁵ The widow of T. S. Eliot allegedly denied access to his papers, while Orwell's widow has also been accused of abusively tending his memory. But the historiography business is far from immune to seeing sober and wise men take exquisite pains to blacken a widow's reputation or make her look ridiculous. Harriet Grote, who wrote several books including the biography of her husband, the Greek historian George Grote, "seldom underrated her husband, and never herself," quipped Arnaldo Momigliano in a typically witty dismissal of a historian's bluestocking widow.⁶ Was Michelet's or Quinet's wife responsible for the break between the two inseparable historians, and who was worse when it came to producing posthumous accounts of her husband's life? Such questions and such scorn are an important part of historiography and of the lives of great historians, as we will surely recognize, but what part is it?

Athénaïs Michelet was among the many wives of historians who wrote books themselves or who assiduously worked on their husbands' projects. Indeed, during the course of nineteenth-century professionalization and even into the late twentieth century much historical writing and research was familial. Family members were researchers, copyists, collaborators, editors, proofreaders, and ghostwriters, and much writing took place at home. Sister combinations such as the Stricklands were almost as common as female dynasties such as that of Sarah Taylor Austin, her daughter (Lucie Duff Gordon), and granddaughter (Janet Ross), or Julia Cartwright and Cecilia Ady. François Guizot and his daughters, Pauline Guizot de Witt and Henriette Guizot de Witt, were another commonplace author team of history; but equally pervasive were husband-wife collaborations such as those of Alice Stopford Green and J. R. Green, Barbara and J. H. Hammond, Mary Ritter Beard and Charles Beard. Despite the modern ethos of separate spheres for men and women, historical writing was implicated in domesticity, the family, and sexuality—all of which were rich in possibilities for authorial confusion and unprofessional influences.

History thus had author teams that worked in household workshops in an age of professionalization, but conventions generally assumed authorship to be singular and male. For instance, in reviews of a work by a husband and wife, custom dictated attributing collaborative works to the men alone. This could be done in reviews by talking, say, about Charles Beard's *Rise of American Civilization* series or by noting "the assistance of his wife" and then proceeding as if Charles Beard were the sole author. A compliment to the tender muse who inspired this man of genius was a wink to a knowing readership that the wife's contribution had been negligible. These conventions, veiling the complex authorship of many works, produced ambiguity because historical authorship was so conflicted anyway by the demands of scientific history.[7]

Beginning in the nineteenth century the shift from literary to scientific history ostensibly dealt the historical author a nasty blow by casting suspicion on the authorial presence. Ideally, professional history became a scientific enterprise in which a historical text containing verified facts was constructed into a narrative of the past. Originating in the assiduous research of a well-trained and self-abnegating historian, the best historical accounts contained their own positive truth because the author had put aside politics, class, gender, and other passions and interests, as well as concerns for literary drama, in order to achieve an autonomous, universally valid text. This autonomous text displayed its own verification in an ever increasing proportion of footnotes (*Anmerkungswissenschaft*) to support its assertions, and attained its universal status by purporting to describe the "Past" purified of the contingencies of the present. "Gentlemen, it is not I who speak," as the historian Fustel de Coulanges so famously put it, "but History that speaks through me." Nothing so clearly sets forth not only the pure voice of history but also the subordinate or questionable status of the author.

These claims to scientific impersonality, however, were made during the course of history's professionalization into a discipline that not only abided by a set of standards but that existed in the richly human institutions of the university, archives and libraries, and professional journals and associations. Professional life further comprised such diverse ingredients as offices at home and work, research assistants, copyrights and royalties, translations, editions, editors, and readers, and always the academic hierarchy of flesh and blood human beings which reinforced professorial authority. While

professional standards invoked impersonality, professionalism developed as an arena charged with human affect and fantasy. When
Leopold von Ranke imagined a new set of archival documents, he
fancied them "so many fairy princesses living under a curse and
waiting to be free."[8] The scientifically-minded French scholar
Gabriel Monod confessed that a review of Gregorovius's *Lucrecia
Borgia* had "made my mouth water" for a "more intimate acquaintance with this 'loose, amiable'" woman.[9] Though critical of Michelet's historical methods, Monod could "not escape the contagion of
his enthusiasm, his hopes, and his youthful heart."[10] Seminars
taught lessons in paleography, epigraphy, and other techniques for
the scientific scrutiny of documents—"principles," in the words of
another reformer, "that are transmitted from the fathers to the
sons."[11] Scientific historians variously referred to the reformed
academic community as a fraternity, an army, a monastery, a
workshop, where the most important quality was "deference toward their masters."[12] And history, as the metaphors of princesses,
loose women, masters, and fraternities show, was not unrelated to
masculine identity: "I study history," R. G. Collingwood wrote,
"to learn what it is to be a man." In other words, alongside claims
to impersonality, the professionalization of history provoked the
expression of human sentiments, the development of close relationships, the unfolding of fantasies, and the investment of emotions across the enterprise.[13]

Few historians expressed so many wide-ranging passions and so
complex an authorial experience as Jules Michelet, especially in his
relationship to Athénaïs Mialaret, whom he married in 1849.
Michelet's first wife, Pauline Rousseau, died in 1839, having given
birth to two children and having lived much ignored during her
husband's prodigious efforts to have an important career. Unlike
the comparatively clean separation with Pauline, Jules's marriage to
Athénaïs Mialaret was a complicated, literary experience. For one
thing, Mialaret was already a studious woman, who at the time of
her first contact with Michelet in 1848 tutored the children of the
Princess Cantacuzène in Vienna. Their relationship began with her
letter asking his moral advice because her reading of his *Du prêtre,
de la femme, et de la famille* had left her in need of guidance. Each
soon fell to writing the other about the revolutionary politics of
1848, which she reported from Vienna and he from Paris. When

Athénaïs first visited his apartment in the fall of 1848, their interview took place in his study, and he reciprocated by delivering a copy of *Histoire de la révolution* to her hotel. Their relationship thus began and progressed as a literary one, and it remained so throughout twenty-six years of marriage. According to both their accounts Athénaïs Michelet did research and reported on it, wrote sections of his books, discussed projects and recorded details of their daily conversations on topics for books, and offered her judgments on the work that was published under Jules's name. She wrote books of her own, one of them a story of her childhood, and he drafted an unpublished manuscript ("Mémoires d'une jeune fille honnête") of her young adulthood, while she published selections from his journal and a story of his youth after his death as well as a posthumous edition of their love letters. Meanwhile, Michelet recorded many incidents in their work life and descriptions of her personal feelings in his journal.

Athénaïs was twenty-two at the time of their meeting and Jules, at fifty, was passionately attracted to her. But the marriage, despite his extreme sexual arousal, was consummated only with difficulty and then after Jules had taken his young wife to consult with several physicians. These matters too were literary, for he recorded the course of the consultations in his letters and journal, noted her menstrual periods for more than two decades, and wrote about both their thwarted and successful sexual relations. Literary events constructed and even permitted Michelet's final conquest of his wife. Before their marriage he noted his growing desire, which was crushed on their wedding night: "all was refused me. By her? No, her good little heart burned to make me happy."[14] On 20 March 1849, eight days after their marriage, Jules noted that the couple had worked together for the first time, but "physically, it's impossible to be less married."[15] This pattern continued for some time, with work during the day followed by "insoluble difficulties" at night.[16] Michelet alternated reports of his increasing sexual despair with moments of "very tender abandon," "of certain sweet and kindly signs that . . . her poor young body, so suffering and charming, is nonetheless not insensitive to the breath of May," all of them concentrating desire on Athénaïs and building an extraordinary, almost gothic literary drama of pursuit and escape.[17] "My sweetheart, very sweetly, received me for a moment in her bed."[18]

Finally, on 8 November 1849, "in the morning, before my work," the couple had sex: "I penetrated her fully . . . very hard as my doctor indicated."[19]

Michelet fashioned his journal into a sexual saga, and after this consummation his account of the marriage continued to charge domestic study and writing with sexual negotiation. Looking back over eight years of marriage at his remembrances of their best sex, he picked a date in 1850, "near the end of the fourth volume of the *Révolution (Death of Danton's Wife)*, a vivid, nervous emotion. She was moved also. . . and calmed this storm in an act of tender humility."[20] This was written in 1857, a year of particularly intense intellectual discussion surrounding composition of the book *The Insect* and a year in which Michelet filled his journal with sexual detail. "After menstruation, extreme passion. I long to plunge myself into this fountain of life. . . . She herself is burning, delectable, tasty."[21] These heady descriptions did not indicate inter-course, according to Jules's account, at more than a ten-day inter-val, but it often happened after reading and writing. While Athénaïs cut flowers to study for their work, he read from the draft of *The Insect;* later, "she came to me like a little lamb and was very good."[22] Two days later, he describes her reading another section, "and in an isolated alleyway, the second behind the grand canal, she showed me a great deal of friendship."[23] By this time, Michelet had written more than once of their intertwined endeavors—sexual and intellectual—and of their intertwined personalities. The ideal marriage, and one he often claimed to have, displayed constant impregnation with the other partner, a transformation and move-ment, in which "she, imbibing of him, is him while remaining herself."[24] He found himself absorbed in her, but he tried to prevent that absorption from being complete. Writing gave him some sense of individuation, but he also struggled "to maintain a point apart from her where I can be strong."[25]

Michelet further complicated his interpretation of their mar-riage by constantly referring to it as an incestuous one in which he consciously played the role of father to her role of daughter. With Athénaïs virtually the same age as his own daughter Adèle, Michelet wrote of her as "my child" even before they were married and continued to refer to her in that way thereafter. "*The most permitted of incest.* Marriages of people unequal in age have a sweetness when the older resembles the father or mother of the younger and can thus be loved as such."[26] Even while noting his wife's orgasms, he referred to her as a little girl, her innocence: "All [her] pleasure. . . is true tenderness, affection, simultaneously conjugal and filial, and even more." And a few days later: "God forgive me for having been and for being so in love with a woman . . . and yet with a child. I was greedier and greedier for her sweet and wise words and for her virginal body; and the more I entered it, the more I left full of desire."[27] For her part Athénaïs reportedly frolicked like a young colt, making saucy faces for Jules's paternal observation. Two layers of family relationships—father/daughter and husband/wife—enveloped these literary lives.

Thus the collaboration of Jules and Athénaïs Michelet on such works of "natural" history as *The Bird* (1856), *The Insect* (1857), *The Sea, The Mountain,* and other writing was fraught with the ambiguities of domestic literary production.[28] Although published under Michelet's name, he himself opened the question of authorship, first by dedicating *The Bird* to her as the product of "the foyer, of our sweet nightly conversations."[29] The work, Michelet explained, issued from domestic "hours of leisure, afternoon conversations, winter reading, summertime chats," and other joint efforts.[30] A reviewer in the *Moniteur* was not alone in acknowledging the hint of collaboration by citing the work as having "the style of a superior man softened by the grace and delicate sensitivity of a woman,"[31] and Michelet wrote to journalists suggesting its familial origins and asking them "to take this into account" in their reviews. The next year Michelet reported the authorship of *The Insect* somewhat differently to an Italian journalist as "in reality the work of my wife, but composed and edited by me."[32] Victor Hugo offered his praise for the complimentary copy of *The Insect:* "Your wife is in it, and I've sensed her pass in these subterranean corridors like a fairy, like your *luciole* guiding your genius with her ardent light. . . ."[33] In his two testaments of 1865 and 1872 Michelet accorded Athénaïs literary rights to his books and papers, not only because she had served as secretary, researcher, and proofreader, but because she had "written considerable sections of these books."[34]

When Michelet died in 1874, his widow put aside some of the projects on which she had been working with special interest. She sorted out the papers remaining from those he himself had destroyed and used them as the basis for several books, including a summary of his youth, an abridged version of his journal, a history, a travel book, and a biography. Jules's son-in-law—a literary figure of some influence and reputation—and grandchildren contested his legacy to Athénaïs in court, but she won, ultimately taking as her patron in these publishing endeavors Gabriel Monod, one of the founders of the *Revue historique,* a pioneer in making historical writing more scientific in France, and a friend of the family. Monod introduced selections from Michelet's work, wrote an appreciation of him in *Renan, Taine, Michelet* (which also paid tribute to Mme Michelet's devotion to her husband's memory and to her continuation of his work), wrote a biography, and gave a course on Michelet's historical writing at the Collège de France. At her death, Athénaïs Michelet gave Monod control over the disposition of many of Michelet's papers. With that her real troubles began.

From Monod to Lucien Febvre and beyond, attention to Jules Michelet swelled among the most prominent French intellectuals, but it has invariably involved extraordinary invective toward Athénaïs, growing ever more pronounced over the course of the twentieth century. Monod, who during Athénaïs's lifetime acknowledged her contribution to Jules's work ("faithful trustee of his ideas"),[35] and particularly the publication of many posthumous papers, deftly changed course. Practitioner of a different, more scientific history, Monod attributed his choice of career to Michelet, but "the feelings I have for him are not those of a disciple for a master whose doctrine one adopts."[36] Michelet embodied a French historical spirit, "a sympathy for the untolled dead, who were our ancestors"[37] and as such served as the model historian of French nationalism, so deeply important to Monod's generation of scientific historians.[38] In fact many scientifically oriented historians in this era of professionalization, although disavowing political interests and aiming to purge it from their work, were unabashedly nationalistic, had friends in politics, or engaged in politics themselves, especially (but not only) during the Dreyfus Affair. As with the case of Monod, a love of the nation-state was constitutive of the historical mind in this era,[39] but these scientific historians projected that patriotism back onto an earlier generation, conserving nationalism for history while divorcing it from scientific practice through frank discussions of patriotism and objective portraits of biased, dead historians.

Monod's first work on Michelet thus avoided a full discussion of Michelet's method but touted the connection between patriotic sentiment and history. In 1905 Monod wrote *Jules Michelet. Etudes sur sa vie et ses oeuvres,* which began sketching the outlines of the "historical Michelet"—one useful to the scientific aspirations of the profession. Invoking the study of history based on the scientific evaluation of documents, Monod published a few of Michelet's papers that had so recently fallen into his hands. The book opened by posing the question of authorship in Michelet's work, citing rumors that not he but his wife had actually written much appearing under his name. Monod used the introduction to start defining what was written by Jules, what by Athénaïs in the work written during their marriage and in Jules's posthumously published writings. He pointed to the liberties Athénaïs had taken in certain posthumous works and he affirmed Jules's genius in the strongest possible terms, but in general his judgment was positive about her contribution. The book additionally published intimate parts of their journals to show the complexities of their relationship and of Michelet's relationship with other members of his family. For all its measure, Monod's work was crucial to analyzing Michelet's authorship in "scientific terms," singling him out as the representative figure of romantic historiography, and clearly delineating the contours of an autonomous Michelet, the great historian. Chapters on two of Michelet's children and material on his first wife enlarged public knowledge of his family circle, diminishing the place of his second wife to one among these many supporting actors. During these years Monod also gave a course on Michelet at the Collège de France, and these further filled in the profile of Michelet scholarship by exhaustively examining the origins of his historical writing and establishing an interpretative precedent that his most important work had been done during his first marriage and before the Revolution of 1848.[40]

Monod had begun to separate Jules from his wife, but never definitively did so. He had neither ruptured the bond celebrated in Michelet's journal nor completely discredited the sense of fusion Athénaïs had additionally promoted in handling posthumous publications. Other authors were bolder. In 1902 Daniel Halévy published a widely-read article in the *Revue de Paris* on "Michelet's Marriage" that followed the line of asserting Michelet's utter failure after his dismissal from all his positions by Napoleon III (and by implication after his marriage).[41] But he also attributed this failure to Athénaïs, who, he maintained, "suffered from spiritual frigidity" that contrasted sharply with Jules's "feverish mysticism and enthusiasm."[42] Distinct but also disturbed, she aimed for total and unnatural domination of her husband: "from the bedroom, because that was an essential step, to the worktable. It was the table she aspired to and Michelet at first defended it, while she controlled the bed. For several months, the marriage was chaste. Finally Michelet got the bed and soon after Athénaïs the worktable."[43] Halévy thus painted a chaotic, disordered domestic scene, from which he as historian could constantly rescue Jules's character, traced in bold, clear lines that further distinguished him from the surrounding cast of characters: not only were he and Athénaïs opposites, her rule separated him from family and isolated him from friends, making him "the most miserable of modern men."[44] Whereas Michelet professed to have profited from the blurred authorship of domestic collaboration, subsequent biographers and editors rewrote the scenario as sexual inversion and misrule. The drastic overhaul of Michelet's scripting of a tender, erotic, and collaborative domestic life was underway, maintaining the whiff of sexual secrets that motivated research while clarifying authorship.

Thus dragged onto the historiographical stage, the widow served an important literary function by helping set the boundaries around the historical author and by acting as double with whom the hero struggles in a classical *agon* of self-definition. Instead of being the dutiful daughter to a dominant father, Athénaïs became "one of those women who avariciously dispenses her sex," with Jules locked in battle to get more of it.[45] Monzie converted their fraught sexualities (as reported in both their journals) into an evil repression by the wife, the result of which was to turn what he believed to be Jules's innate puritanism into an obsession with women that ruined his historical sense. Monzie made the observation of George Sand (Michelet was "incapable of alluding to women without lifting their petticoats over their heads"[46]) into the fault of his wife's parsimonious control of the conjugal bed. Any weaknesses in his writing resulted from her authority over sex, but also from her interference in writing. A quote in Athénaïs's travel diary, in which she described exactly the food she apportioned to Jules, Monzie took as typical of her *"vue comptable."* Widowed, however, and freed from his sanguine influence, she showed her true colors, when gathering quotes from his journals and letters, she "mixes this hash with passages from the *Hundred Years' War,* stirs the whole thing, seasons it with oil and vinegar like a salad, then serves the dish to guests at the republican table with this tasty title: *Sur les chemins de l'Europe.*" This account contrasted Michelet's intellectual stature with the domestic "hash" the "widow-cook," as Monzie called her, served up as history.[47] Monzie's tactic in his pairings of intellectuals and their abusive consorts contrasted, for instance, Rousseau's partner Thérèse Levasseur's tendency to interrupt his learned discourses with questions about "the soup or the laundry" with his regal response. "He would have ennobled a piece of cheese had he spoken of it."[48] Sexuality and domestic detail were part of the wife's character, and detachment and ennoblement part of the authorial husband's, as the distinctions between the two grew greater when the discourse of separate spheres was put into service.

Monzie's and Halévy's characterizations seem rough, crude even, but they were no more so than the portrait of the "abusive widow" solidified by the legendary intellectuals who next took up the project of confirming Michelet's stature and who further rescripted his life. Monzie, minister of education in the 1920s, was a friend and mentor of Lucien Febvre, student of Gabriel Monod, co-founder of the *Annales,* and Monzie's choice to edit the massive *Encyclopédie française*—a work designed to compete with Soviet and British encyclopedias by substituting a conceptual organization for the conventional alphabetical one. In 1946 Febvre published a sampling of Michelet's historical writing, a sampling whose introduction was lengthier than the material it presented. Febvre's *Michelet* served to announce the postwar era of freedom in the series "The Classics of Liberty." "Why Michelet," Febvre asked rhetorically, "his history full of errors. . . . a superpatriot, a liberal: a crybaby domesticated by a shrew?"[49] Having endured immense deprivation in a family that struggled each day not for such luxuries as liberty but for daily bread, Michelet was the perfect symbol of all the French had endured during the war. But he also

represented "the France of twenty-five centuries . . . eternal
France."[50] For Michelet embodied "history" or what Febvre saw
(following Michelet) as the "successive victory of human liberty
over the fatality of nature."[51] Under the Napoleonic Empire and
the Restoration, censorship and political repression had prevented
France from having any history at all. Then came the Revolution of
1830, when, according to Febvre, Michelet suddenly used the new
freedom to start writing the first history in modern times. The
deprived Parisian struggling to teach his students thus became the
"Father of History."[52] In making Michelet relevant for "those who
today have experienced Munich, the disasters of 1940, of 1942, of
1944,"[53] Febvre had willfully to discount the careful scholarship of
his mentor, Monod, whose detailed work on Michelet's texts had
shown his *Universal History* of 1830 to be the work of the preceding
six years and its introduction to have been written on the whole in
the months preceding the "Trois Glorieuses,"[54] that is, before the
so-called era of freedom had begun. Constructing a usable author
took precedence over scholarly accuracy, and Febvre would constantly refer to Michelet in his work, ultimately writing an article
"How Michelet Invented the Renaissance."

Taking command of the postwar project of publishing a scholarly edition of Michelet's papers and works, Febvre chose Paul
Viallaneix and Claude Digeon as the editors, himself oversaw the
project, and continued his great interest in Michelet. The volumes
that have thus far appeared contain (among others) Michelet's
journal, his youthful writings, and the collaborative works with his
wife, all of them featuring conspicuous attacks on any claims that
Athénaïs had a substantive or even minor role in their authorship.
Proving this point has taken several forms, all of them accepted as
part of the "scientific" method. First, manuscripts of *The Birds* and
other of the natural history writings were scrutinized for their
handwriting. Anything in Jules's handwriting indicated to the
editors his authorship, Athénaïs's script led to an opposite conclusion: that she was a "simple copyist." The editors allowed that she
had done much of the preparatory work of research and drafting
the outlines of the book, but they undercut that single, generous
attribution by citing notes to indicate the "importance of [Jules's]
personal work at documentation." Finally, the editors juxtaposed
her copious first drafts with the final version of the book and

judged that in contrast to her "verbosity," the final version was so "definitively" stamped with Michelet's "originality" that his wife's ideas and thus any claims to authorship were completely eradicated. Thus, "'the collaboration' of Mme. Michelet. . . ceases to be a problem. . . ."[55] Professing to be scientific, the editors saw Michelet's "creative spirit" firmly stamped on the work. "Her contribution to *The Birds* was effectively limited to the preparation . . . ." Transformed by his "vast design," her "childish book became an epic."[56] The editors constructed authorship out of handwriting and even then applied gendered standards to what that indicated. In no instance could they admit to substantive collaboration between husband and wife, but rather they cast the book as the product of a struggle between male and female in which male genius triumphed, giving the world another masterpiece.

Retelling Michelet's story, the editors dropped Monod's progressive but qualified disapproval of Athénaïs's authorship and instead constructed an utterly negative account of her "false" literary productions. Published after Michelet's death, these included the editions of Michelet's youthful writings, excerpts from his journal, travel writings, and his love letters to Athénaïs. The scholarly edition (1959) of Michelet's *Ecrits de jeunesse* opens with a description of the inspiration taken from an early version of this work both by young innocents, who receive the book from their schoolmasters, and by more sophisticated youth, who see in Michelet's friendships the noble relationships they have drawn from their study of the classics. But going to the Michelet archives, both groups of readers would find that despite helpful lessons in the book, they had been betrayed and were the "blissful dupes of a fraud."[57] What is the nature of this fraud? Instead of revealing it and its perpetrator immediately, the editors hold the readers in suspense by switching to the inspiring story of Michelet's life, which they represent as passed in a "mental fever" of preparing his various histories. Toward the end of his life, "considering his *Ecrits de jeunesse* as a relic," Michelet began destroying many of his other papers. Although Jules describes the destruction in the first person singular as his own doing, the editors add Athénaïs to the scene of destruction and provocatively ask: "To what extent did his young wife, gripped by a kind of retrospective jealousy, herself censor these vestiges of a passionate life in which she had not been queen?"[58] Besides suggesting that she, not he, had burned the papers, thus rewriting Michelet's own journal, the authors scorned her publication of selections from the various early writings in a lone book, *Ma jeunesse,* as a travesty. Yet the editors themselves proceeded by gathering up what they admit are random notes, mixed reading lists and observations, drafts, notes, and sketchy essays and by making them into an integrated volume for which they devised a similar title—*Ecrits de jeunesse.* Moreover, Michelet had expressly written that one section of his early writings "should never be published, but may be excerpted," a condition to which Athénaïs adhered far more faithfully than the twentieth century editors,[59] who prided themselves on publishing everything.

Another edition of Michelet's writing entitled *Journal* by the same editors contains, according to their own admission, dispersed papers of different sorts, an intimate journal, various travel journals, and random notes from his course outlines assembled in chronological order. Holding Athénaïs in contempt for omitting vivid sexual detail, the edition of Viallaneix sees to it that from Michelet's jottings, notebooks, and other scraps of writing paragraphs are made, spelling and punctuation corrected, and other "problems eliminated"—"We didn't think that accuracy demanded us to respect those."[60] Thus the men who accused Athénaïs of eliminating those phrases that failed to coincide with her values explain away their own changes where Michelet fails to meet their own, different criteria. The editors have in fact created from fragments and assorted writings a "unique and complete" account, an integrated and whole Michelet separated from his perfidious wife. This Michelet was nonetheless, over the multiple volumes of these *Complete Works,* their own production.[61]

Arthur Mitzman's recent study of Michelet has generously tried to absolve Athénaïs Michelet of many of these charges by explaining that she had no training as a scholar.[62] Moreover, as Mitzman points out and as his own work shows, this "abusive widow," even though she may have suppressed some sexually explicit material, still left so much that Michelet's obsessions are more than amply documented. He also notes that the modern editors' version of Jules's love letters (a "sacred relic," the editors claim, sacralizing Jules) omit Athénaïs's, which she had used in the original edition, often making his letters unintelligible. Mitzman continues to refer to the "false Michelet" created by his widow, but he acknowledges the interactive nature at least of the posthumous publications.

Feminist scholarship would seem to support Mitzman's sympathetic treatment of a woman author, endorse an appreciation for her work, and strive to achieve at least a historically accurate contextualization of her accomplishments. However, this scholarship also runs the risk of replicating the historiographical problem of authorship, if, for instance, one argued that Athénaïs was an equal genius to her husband or tried to carve her out as a distinct author. Devising some way of treating Athénaïs as historian or author is not the intent of this paper. Rather, I intend to broach the subject of her authorship in order to suggest (along with Mitzman) its dialogic and collaborative qualities, to indicate the way in which she edited passages in the travel journals to describe women instead of men, and to note that a major part of the much condemned editing of Jules's love letters involved omitting those letters in which he discussed her sexual and physiological state and the doctors' opinions of it.

The attacks on Athénaïs Michelet's authorship are interesting in themselves because in using gender to create a historical author they help define the historical field: in another example Michelet's editors ask whether she "reconciled her literary pretensions and her wifely love without asking herself if literary genius wasn't profoundly individual, if the most faithful writer doesn't find himself alone with his conscience and his talent when he writes and if the first duty of fidelity toward his memory isn't to respect to the letter the work he has left behind."[63] Such statements remind us that the language of scholarship combines passages listing archival citations and professions of "respect to the letter" with emotionally-packed or sexually loaded phrases. Despite Hayden White's insight about the "middle-brow" and "genial" rhetorical style of scientific history, in fact it has simultaneously been highly charged, contentious, loaded with gendered fantasy, passion, and outrage. The case of Michelet's widow shows all of these being deployed to establish the scientific confines of history at whose bounds she menacingly stood.[64]

Second, the great author, created in so gendered a way, has served the authorial dilemmas of other historians. For example,

Lucien Febvre's direction of the project to publish a new edition of Jules's work and his postwar devotion to and creation of the cult of Michelet covered ambiguities in his own authorship of the *Annales* and other works during the 1930s and World War II. Febvre cofounded the *Annales* with Marc Bloch, and their collaboration was never easy, as many historians point out. From the mid-1930s funding for the *Encyclopédie française* paid for Febvre to have an assistant, Lucie Varga, a young Austrian historian and regular contributor to the *Annales*. Febvre, who was also married to the scholar Suzanne Dognon Febvre, relied on Varga for research, and her detailed summaries and observations on books allowed him rapidly to produce book reviews. By the late 1930s Varga had lost her job because Febvre's growing romantic attachment to her threatened his marriage and career.[65] A second dilemma emerged under the occupation, as Natalie Davis has pointed out, when Febvre and Bloch were embattled over whether the journal should appear without Bloch's Jewish name on the cover. To Bloch's insistence that they resist Nazi policies for ridding the scholarly world of Judaism, Febvre responded "One name only on the cover, so what? It's the enterprise that counts."[66] Davis illuminates the difficulties of authorship during the Occupation, citing the many alternatives, compromises, and resistances possible. Febvre chose neither to collaborate openly nor to resist openly but rather took a middle way that would allow him to continue to appear an important historical author. Michelet's authorship firmly established in the gendered historiographical discourse of the preceding decades, Febvre consolidated his own by incanting the ritualized attacks on the abusive widow and by overseeing a project one of whose major outcomes would be a definitive destruction of her claims to authorship.

Establishing the bounds of history and the authorial identity of generations of subsequent historians, the saga of Jules and Athénaïs Michelet may even have opened onto questions of French identity and the shape of its history. Twentieth-century France was particularly tried by issues of nationalism, gender, and history. While Monod and Halévy were outlining a story of female misrule in the Michelet household, the falling birthrate, the feminist movement, and the new woman had already raised questions of gender and provoked fears of the declining virility of French men. Since 1870 the French had faced a world turned upside-down by defeat, reparation, and annexation after the Franco-Prussian War. Only after 1920, however, did the discourse of the "abusive widow" take full and effective shape as France struggled with its hundreds of thousands of war widows and with a gender order troubled by the effects of war and economic depression. Those men who returned from the war were often deeply disturbed; others found that their wives had abandoned them, and a confident feminist movement demanded rights equal to those of men. Misrule—the "decline of the Third Republic," most historians of France would have it—led to the defeat in 1940 and to lingering malaise after World War II. The "abusive widow" offered a timely explanation wherein her stupidity, inferiority, and frigidity symbolized an inversion of all that French intellectuals took as their defining characteristics.[67]

If, as Hayden White suggests, factual storytelling or narrativity "moralizes reality," then Michelet scholarship had a direct relationship to the political reality of French history. Michelet's biography as a historian recapitulated the story of postrevolutionary France, using gender as its trope. Before 1848 Michelet engaged in heroic struggles for greatness as a historian, muting other attachments, but that revolutionary year was a watershed for him as it was for France, entrancing him, even enslaving him to an illegitimate ruler. Michelet continued to be productive, even opening new avenues of research, but his enslavement was continually wearing. Michelet died in 1874, and with the advent of republicanism born of military defeat came French decline as well as the abuse of his writings, an erosion of his genius. But the interwar period launched his rebirth as well as that of history and of France, culminating in the triumph of scientism, planning, technocracy, and the professions that would rehabilitate France as they rehabilitated Michelet's reputation. Narrating Michelet, an enormous project of the postwar French academy, moralized the story of France, using gender to mark out where science ended and error began. If France were destitute economically and defeated militarily, its tradition of individual genius would help it survive.

These conclusions about Michelet and the history of modern France are truly speculative and secondary to my real concerns about the relationship between gender and historiography, between authorship and objectivity. Recently Lionel Gossman has proposed a "middle ground" between claims that history corresponds to reality (or objectivity) and claims that history may be relative or arbitrary ("decisionism").[68] Instead of saying that history is commensurable with reality, Gossman suggests that good historical accounts have some degree of commensurability among themselves, while in place of arbitrariness, decisionism, or relativity, he invokes "the ability to change one's mind for good reason."[69] In trying these hypotheses on the case of Michelet's widow, I find myself in agreement with the objective conclusions about her scholarly inadequacy—that is, in all good faith I could also write a commensurable account about her inadequacy as a historical writer. In addition the changing evaluations of Michelet as author make perfectly good sense, allowing both commensurability and relativity their day. But Gossman's criteria still fail to account for the repetitious attention to someone so insignificant as Athénaïs Michelet; only exploring the ways in which gender may be constitutive of history can do that.

Michelet has been useful to individual careers not so much for the way he provides a nationalist refuge to those like Febvre, who may have unconsciously worried about their own decisions during the unbelievably difficult time of war and holocaust, but for the way he has helped construct the individual fantasy life of the scientific historian entranced by achievements of "great" predecessors. Wrapped in the mantle of science and impartiality, the saga of Michelet mutilated by his widow and rescued by heroic researchers is a melodrama whose psychological dimensions we should begin attending to, if only to understand the world of history better. Like most professionals, the surviving co-founder of the *Annales*—so deeply indebted to Michelet's work on mountains and seas, to the sense of the local in the Michelet travel journals, and to the complicated relationship between historical actors and their environments on which Michelet pondered—fantasized unique and singular authors as the forefathers of and contributors to his new school of history, and he worked to script it that way as had many before him. The category "author," as Foucault proposed, has helped organize the discipline around the classification of historical writing and the development of other critical procedures that the invocation of a single author facilitates, allowing for such genealogies of influence and parentage to arise. What is a historian?

we ask, altering Foucault's query. Until now a historian has been the embodiment of universal truth, who, constructed from bits of psychological detail and having passed through the purifying trials dealt by the contingencies of daily life, human passion, and devouring women, emerges a genderless genius with a name that radiates extraordinary power in the profession and in the mind of the individual practitioner. It is time to begin thinking about the ways in which this authorial presence has in fact been gendered as masculine and how it comes into being through repetitive pairings of a male "original" with a female "copy(ist)" or "falsifier" or "fake." Such a consistent pairing suggests that historical science with its aspirations to objectivity is grounded in the rhetorical tradition of classical misogyny.[70]

NOTES

1. Michel Foucault, "Qu'es-ce que c'est l'auteur," *Bulletin de la société française de philosophie* 64 (1969): 73–104.

2. Arthur Mitzman, *Michelet, Historian: Rebirth and Romanticism in Nineteenth-Century France* (New Haven, 1990), 284–285, "Appendix A: Michelet's Second Wife."

3. Anatole de Monzie, *Les veuves abusives*, 6th ed. (Paris, 1936), 126.

4. Roland Barthes, *Michelet lui-même*, trans. Richard Howard (1954, reprinted New York, 1987), 206.

5. Van Wyck Brooks, *The Ordeal of Mark Twain* (1920, reprinted New York, 1970), 138.

6. Arnaldo Momigliano, *George Grote and the Study of Greek History* (London, 1952), 7.

7. Jack Stillinger, *Multiple Authorship and the Myth of Solitary Genius* (New York, 1990) calls for a more complex view of authorship that would acknowledge the work of editors, but his book tends to reinforce the view that men were geniuses whose editors and wives made no "substantive" contributions. For instance, although John Stuart Mill calls the "whole mode of thinking" in *On Liberty* his wife's, Stillinger says that scholars should really focus on Harriet's editorial role (66) and stop worrying about whether she had ideas—she didn't, he implies. Ultimately, he describes her role as "the middle-aged Mill being spruced up by his wife for attractive autobiographical presentation" (182). Although appreciative of Stillinger's concern that some term be born to cover editorial contributions, I take a different view of the matter of historical authorship.
Another fascinating recognition of authorial complexity comes in Lionel Gossman's *Toward a Rational Historiography,* Transactions of the American Philosophical Society (Philadelphia, 1989) which sympathetically describes the community of criticism absorbed into scholarly publications. Yet Gossman, except for the first mention, comes to cite a work with three authors exclusively as that of Steven Toulmin even referring to it as "Toulmin's" thought, argument, thesis, and so on.

8. Leopold von Ranke, *Briefwerke*, quoted in Leonard Krieger, *Ranke: The Meaning of History* (Chicago, 1977), 104–105.

9. Letter to Gaston de Paris, 6 August 1874, in Bibliothèque nationale, Manuscrit Nouvelle acquisition française 24450, Fonds Gaston de Paris, ff. 131–132.

10. Gabriel Monod, *Renan, Taine, Michelet*, 5th ed. (Paris: n.d.), 178.

11. Victor Duruy, quoted in William R. Keylor, *Academy and Community: The Foundation of the French Historical Profession* (Cambridge, Mass., 1975), 70.

12. Ernest Lavisse quoted in *ibid.*, 70–71.

13. See Bonnie Smith "Gender and the Rise of Scientific History," in *Objectivity and Its Other*, ed. Wolfgang Natter (Lexington, Ky., forthcoming).

14. Jules Michelet, *Journal*, ed. Paul Viallaneix (Paris, 1962), 2:32.

15. *Ibid.*, 34.

16. *Ibid.*, 35.

17. *Ibid.*, 37, 47.

18. *Ibid.*, 73.

19. *Ibid.*, 75. Athénaïs Michelet's prolonged virginity has been attributed to vaginismus by Jeanne Calo, to willful frigidity by Halévy, Monzie, and Michelet's editors (among others), and to various ailments and physical fragility by Michelet. See Jeanne Calo, *La création de la femme chez Michelet* (Paris, 1975).

20. *Ibid.*, 326.

21. *Ibid.*, 329.

22. *Ibid.*, 330.

23. *Ibid.*, 331.

24. *Ibid.*

25. *Ibid.*, 127.

26. *Ibid.*, 323.

27. *Ibid.*, 343, 345.

28. On these works and their very important connection to Michelet's evolving conceptualization of historical issues see Linda Orr, *Jules Michelet: Nature, History, and Language* (Ithaca, N.Y., 1976).

29. Jules Michelet, *Oeuvres complètes*, ed. Paul Viallaneix (Paris, 1986), 17:45.

30. *Ibid.*

31. *Ibid.*, 41.

32. *Ibid.*, 17:279.

33. *Ibid.*, 17:280.

34. Testament of 1872 quoted in *ibid.*, 188.

35. Monod, *Renan, Taine, Michelet*, 289.

36. *Ibid.*, 179.

37. *Ibid.*, 178.

38. Keylor, *Academy and Community*, 43–44 and *passim*.

39. See "Gender, Objectivity, and the Professionalization of History," in *Objectivity and Its Other*.

40. Gabriel Monod, *La Vie et la pensée de Jules Michelet 1798–1852: Cours professé au Collège de France*, 2 vols. (Paris, 1923). This posthumous publication clearly influenced Arthur Mitzman's engaging psychological interpretation, which ends in 1854 even though Michelet lived two more decades, wrote abundantly, and produced works of natural history that would influence Febvre and other historians of the *Annales* school.

41. Daniel Halévy, "Le Mariage de Michelet," *Revue de Paris* 15, no. 9 (1 August 1902), 557–579.

42. *Ibid.*, 577.

43. Daniel Halévy, *Jules Michelet* (Paris, 1928), 133.

44. Halévy, "Le Mariage de Michelet," 579.

45. Monzie, *Les veuves abusives*, 105.

46. *Ibid.*, 111.

47. *Ibid.*, 114, 118.

48. *Ibid.*, 35.

49. *Michelet*, ed. Lucien Febvre (Geneva and Paris, 1946), 11.

50. *Ibid.*, 82–83.

51. *Ibid.*, 58.

52. *Ibid.*

53. *Ibid.*, 30.

54. Monod, *Vie et pensée*, 1:185–187. Febvre surely knew Monod's careful scholarship on Michelet's work that showed the *Introduction to Universal History* not to have been "écrits sur les pavés brulants. . . d'un incroyable élan, d'un vol rapide," as Michelet would claim forty years later.

55. Michelet, *Oeuvres complètes*, 17:187.

56. The quotes refer specifically to the editors' discussion of *The Birds*: Michelet, *Oeuvres complètes*, 17:187–206.

57. Jules Michelet, *Ecrits de jeunesse*, ed. Paul Viallaneix, 5th ed. (Paris, 1959), 10.

58. *Ibid.*, 17.

59. *Ibid.*, 10.

60. Michelet, *Journal*, 1:31.

61. Those with further interest in the editors' relationship to Michelet might consult the introductions to his "journal" and other work. Many of them rely on purple writing; the introduction to volume 2, for instance, is a dramatic imagining of Michelet's life with Athénaïs, written in the second person plural: "You leave without your companion. She is out of sorts today, 'a sick person, a wounded one' like all women. You pass your friend Quinet's door without knocking. You haven't the heart to expound on the future of democracy. The sky is too pure, the light too warm. This September evening is given to you freely. It requires meditation." *Ibid.*, 2:XI.

62. Mitzman, *Michelet, Historian*. Mitzman's two appendices excusing Athénaïs provided the inspiration for this article.

63. Michelet, *Journal*, 1:25.

64. In this regard readers can consult the way in which Novick uses such words as "sexy," "hot," and "fashionable" to discredit certain groups of historians. In this case we see the language of bad history as the language of women, while in others employed by Novick ("Clio is going to be just a gal around town on whom anyone with two bits of inclination can lay claim") metaphors of prostitution are used to nail down a point about the impending end of historical standards. See also Hayden White, *The Content of the Form: Narrative Discourse and Historical Representation* (Baltimore, 1987), 71.

65. See Peter Schöttler, *Lucie Varga: Les autorités invisible* (Paris, 1991). Schöttler has done an extraordinary job discovering the details of Varga's obscure

life and reprinting her essays and articles. He outlines Bloch's misogynous attitude toward women intellectuals, but more important Bloch's distress at finding Febvre's and his collaboration still further complicated by Varga's work. Schöttler was loathe to reveal the extent of Varga's and Febvre's personal relationship: "La vie scientifique et l'amour . . . are not considered pertinent in accounts of the life of a scholar." Nonetheless, Schöttler considered it necessary to reveal the romance because "its consequences were sufficiently determining that one could not keep it quiet without falsifying history" (57, n.142). This ambiguous statement may refer to Varga's exile from the profession, forcing her into subsequent employment selling vacuum cleaners, working in a factory, and then in an advertising agency after which under Vichy her utter destitution kept her from getting the necessary medicine to treat her diabetes. She died at the age of 36 in 1941.

Natalie Zemon Davis, "Women and the World of the *Annales*," *History Workshop Journal* 33 (1992): 121–137, describes the contributions of Suzanne Dognon Febvre to Lucien Febvre's work as well as considers the important part played by Paule Braudel in Fernand Braudel's work. I thank Professor Davis for communicating this article to me before publication.

66.   Lucien Febvre to Marc Bloch, 1941, quoted in Natalie Davis, "Rabelais among the Censors," *Representations* 32 (Fall 1990): 5.

67.   This part of my argument relies on Mary Louise Roberts's important thesis, "The Great War, Cultural Crisis, and the Debate on Women in France, 1919–1924" (unpublished Ph.D. diss., Brown University, 1991).

68.   Lionel Gossman, *Towards a Rational Historiography*, (Philadelphia, 1989) 61–62.

69.   *Ibid.*, 62 and *passim*.

70.   On this point see R. Howard Bloch, "Medieval Misogyny," *Representations* 20 (Fall 1987): 1–24.

Medieval Women, Modern Women
Across the Great Divide

JUDITH M. BENNETT

In our dominant vision of the past, a great chasm separates the medieval world from the world of early modern Europe. This chasm partly reflects the genuine historical transitions of the fourteenth through seventeenth centuries—the development of humanism and reformed Christianity, the advance of capitalism and urbanization, the rise of nationalism and national monarchies, the "discovery" and exploration of "New World" territories. Yet this breach in historical continuity has been deepened far beyond its natural contours by scholarly depictions of the great divide. As Lee Patterson has most recently argued, all of us collaborate in a master narrative that, in identifying our contemporary world with the changes of the early modern era, perceives the middle ages as a sort of socio-cultural palindrome of modern life; medievalism functions in this narrative as an inversion of modernity, as a premodern society and culture utterly foreign to the modern world that succeeded it.[1] This master narrative offers advantages to both early modernists (for whom it privileges their period) and medievalists (to whom it offers segregated protection). It waxes strong in both literary and historical studies.

This account of a great divide between medieval and early modern life has never fully drowned out competing stories, but in recent years its preeminence as *the* interpretation of European history between the fourteenth and seventeenth centuries has been coming under particularly strong assault. Literary scholars have

For a fellowship held during 1990, I am grateful to the John Simon Guggenheim Foundation, and for their criticisms of an early draft, I would like to thank Cynthia Herrup, Maryanne Kowaleski, and Lyndal Roper. This essay is an abridged version of an essay that originally appeared in David Aers, ed., *Culture and History 1350–1600: Essays on English Communities, Identities and Writing* (London and Detroit: 1992), 147–175. By permission of Harvester Wheatsheaf and Wayne State University Press. I have not incorporated into this version any work published since the original essay was completed in September 1990.

been questioning some of the most basic assumptions of cultural difference between the two eras. David Aers, for example, has attacked the customary contrast between a medieval world of organic social harmony (in which the self was absorbed into the community) and an early modern world of competitive individualism. As Aers has demonstrated, many late medieval texts show a strong sense of selfhood, a strong individualism. He has concluded that "it is thus time to put a self-denying ordinance on claims about the new 'construction of the subject'" in the sixteenth century.[2]

Historians also have been vigorously questioning some of our basic assumptions about social and economic differences between the world of the middle ages and the world of early modern Europe. The most vigorous questioner has been Alan Macfarlane, whose wide-ranging and polemical work has defined (and perhaps set back) recent discussions of continuities across the late medieval and early modern centuries.[3] Macfarlane's argument that England in 1300 was already a capitalist, market economy governed by a rampant individualism has been rigorously and justly criticized from many quarters, but his basic premise—that English society c. 1300 was quite similar to English society c. 1700—has found solid support in other quarters. For example, medievalists have successfully attacked the model that posits, based largely on the arguments of Philippe Ariès and Lawrence Stone, an early modern emergence of affective family relations. Studies by Barbara Hanawalt, Lorraine Attreed, and others have demonstrated not only that medieval people recognized the special nature of childhood but also that medieval family relations could be quite warm, intimate, and affectionate.[4]

In this essay, I would like to extend these challenges to the master narrative into a new realm—the study of women. The assumption of a dramatic change in women's lives between 1300 and 1700 (and of a consequent definitive distinction between "medieval women" and "early modern women") remains exceptionally strong. Both medievalists and early modernists tend to agree—without trespassing much into each other's periods—not only that women's lives changed over these centuries but also about the nature of the change: things were better for women in the middle ages, and they worsened during the early modern centuries. Social historians, such as Martha Howell and Merry Wiesner, argue that the early modern economy severely limited and disad-

vantaged women workers.[5] Intellectual historians, such as Joan
Kelly and Margaret King, argue that humanist ideas denigrated and
marginalized women in new and nefarious ways.[6] Literary scholars,
such as Linda Woodbridge, Catherine Belsey, Katharina Wilson,
and Elizabeth Makowski, trace in literary texts a new reduction of
women's options and status.[7] And even modern-day philosophers,
such as Ivan Illich, have built major theoretical models around the
notion of a massive change for women between the medieval and
early modern centuries.[8]

This idea of a great transition in the history of women has been
accepted for many reasons: because it rests on authoritative works
in the field of women's history (especially Alice Clark's study in
1919 of seventeenth-century Englishwomen's work and Joan Kelly's
critical reassessment in 1977 of women in the Renaissance);[9] because it suits our presumptions about the problems and evils of our
own society and our longings for another (in this case, premodern)
world of a kinder and gentler variety; because it fits within the
dominant historical tradition, neatly inverting Burckhardt's history
in a feminist rereading of the past (yes, there was a Renaissance, but
it was no Renaissance for women); because it accords well with
Marxist historiography; and because women's history, revolutionary in its subject matter and marginal in its institutional status,
simply cannot afford to question the master narrative.

Although this assumption of a dramatic and negative transition
for women has not been entirely unchallenged, it nevertheless
wields a strong and paradigmatic force over the field of women's
history.[10] Based on authoritative solutions, this model of a great
divide between medieval and early modern women fits within an
accepted master narrative (what Kuhn would call a "disciplinary
matrix") and provides a useful guide for problem-solving research.
Most importantly, it functions like a paradigm in its ability to shape
what Kuhn has called our "ways of seeing," even our ways of seeing
things far beyond our own research interests. Thus, Caroline Barron
has concluded in her recent article on women in medieval London
that "In some senses women lost ground in the sixteenth century
in the City of London which has still to be recovered."[11] Thus,
P.J.P. Goldberg has asserted in his recent dissertation that women in
early fifteenth-century York "enjoyed a fuller economic role than
at any subsequent period before the latter part of this present
century."[12] Barron and Goldberg, careful researchers and judicious

historians, are driven to make these statements (which are entirely unwarranted according to their own standards of historical argumentation) by the force of the paradigm. Neither has compared medieval women to twentieth-century women (or indeed, to sixteenth-century women), but both work within a paradigm that causes them to see a clear contrast across the centuries. And we—their readers—accept these statements (when we would normally demand rigorous comparisons) because we also work within the paradigm; Barron and Goldberg (and others) are merely telling us what we expect to hear.

It is time, however, to abandon this compelling model of dramatic change and to seek new interpretative schemes to guide our research into the history of women between 1300 and 1700. For the notion of a great and negative transition for women over these centuries is now faced with too many anomalies to be sustained. Its main authoritative works—the studies of Clark and Kelly—are valued today for their breadth of vision and theory, but generally acknowledged to be flawed in matters of detail and analysis.[13] And its usefulness is eroding under the onslaught of substantial evidence of continuity in women's experiences across the late medieval and early modern centuries, continuity that belies the paradigmatic assumption of a great transition. Let me illustrate these anomalies by examining in detail one specific aspect of women's history, the history of women's work in England between 1300 and 1700.

I have chosen women's work to illustrate the inaccuracies that plague the paradigm of great transition not only because of my own interest in the field but also because it provides exceptionally clear examples of both the paradigm and its anomalies. In examining women's work I shall focus (as have most historians) on women's productive work, setting to one side women's extensive labors in biological and social reproduction. The notion of a dramatic downturn in women's productive work, articulated authoritatively early in this century by Alice Clark, remains widely accepted among both medievalists and early modernists. In the early part of this century, medievalists such as Annie Abram, Marian Dale, and Eileen Power emphasized women's extensive role in the medieval economy, arguing, as Eileen Power put it, that medieval women

enjoyed a "rough and ready equality" with men.[14] Today, medievalists such as Caroline Barron, Peter Franklin, P.J.P. Goldberg, Barbara Hanawalt, Simon Penn, and Kay Lacey have repeated and
redrawn this positive assessment of the medieval economy, which
they are even willing, at times, to label as a "golden age" for
working women.[15] Early modernists like Susan Cahn, Roberta
Hamilton, Bridget Hill, Keith Snell, Michael Roberts, W. Thwaites,
and Margaret George agree that women's options as workers declined after 1500, although some would date the decline later than
others.[16] Objections to this paradigm have been raised, to be sure,
but most historians of Englishwomen's work during these centuries
generally agree with some version of what Susan Cahn has called
"woman's descent from paradise."[17]

Yet the history of women's work provides exceptionally clear
(and sometimes quantifiable) evidence not only of the low status of
women's work in the middle ages (belying the notion of a lost
golden age) but also of continuity between 1300 and 1700 (belying
the notion of a medieval/early modern great divide). Anomalies
that plague the paradigm are particularly clear in four crucial
aspects of women's work in late medieval and early modern England: the work of women within the family economy; the types of
work undertaken by women; the involvement of women in guilds;
and the wages paid to female workers.

In almost all histories of women's work, the "family economy"—
in which household and workplace were merged and in which
family members worked interdependently in order to meet the
needs of their household—is assumed to have provided women
with a relatively egalitarian working relationship with men. To
Alice Clark, until the seventeenth century most people labored
within such family-based work units in which all family members
shared from the profits of their collective labor and in which, Clark
believed, women's work was especially valued and respected because women's work was essential to family survival. When work
moved outside the household and became more individualized (a
change Clark located in late seventeenth-century England), women's
work declined in extent and value. In the time since Clark's book
was published, her rosy view of the family economy has been
repeated and elaborated by numerous scholars. Eileen Power has
echoed Clark's views in her evocation of a "rough and ready

equality" in medieval households; Barbara Hanawalt has written
about the economic "partnership" of medieval husbands and wives;
Louise Tilly and Joan Scott have argued that women's ability to
work was "strongly correlated" with the family economy; and
Susan Cahn has attributed supposed changes in the family economy
to the transformation of women's work in early modern England.[18]

But how much of a true partnership was the family economy?
If we look hard, we will find that it never really offered women
anything close to equality with men. First, on the basis of theory
alone, we should treat the family economy with much more
caution. We know that households are not natural phenomena, we
know that families are not natural organic units free from individual variance and conflict, and we know that women's work in
social reproduction is not naturally ordained, but we nevertheless
tend to treat the family economy as the best *natural* venue for
women's work.[19] It might have often been the best accommodation
that women could reach in their working lives, but it is not a
natural accommodation. Instead, it was required by (among other
social forces) marriage patterns, household structures, guild regu-
lations, childrearing customs, and the sexual division of labor. The
family economy was a social phenomenon, and as such, it reflected
the patriarchal authority of men in medieval society.

Second, it is quite clear that women were firmly subordinated
to men in the productive functions of the medieval family economy.
We should beware of assuming, as some historians have done, that
evidence of women's extensive and essential work within the
family economy suggests appreciation of women; instead, we have
considerable evidence (much of which will be reviewed below)
that women's work—although extensive and essential—was less
highly valued than men's work. Work within the medieval family
economy was divided according to sex (as well as age and status),
and women's work was generally less specialized, less skilled, and
less valued than men's work. Men often worked at a single main
task, recognized as a husbandman, artisan, or merchant. Their wives
worked at many tasks—their skill was the skill of juggling many
responsibilities and many demands. The late medieval "Ballad of a
Tyrannical Husband," for example, depicted a squabble between a
husband and wife over who worked harder. The husband spent his
day plowing. The wife spent her day brewing, baking, caring for

poultry and dairy animals, making butter and cheese, working wool and flax into cloth, as well as performing basic reproductive work by watching children, cleaning house, and preparing meals.[20] The multiple tasks of women received legislative sanction in 1363 when a statute restricted male artisans to only one trade, but permitted women to follow several.[21] We should not misinterpret this occupational eclecticism. As shown in almost any occupational listing of preindustrial populations, the labor of the husband was the recognized and defining occupation of the family; women were, in the words of L. F. Salzman, "eternal amateurs."[22]

Third, the distribution of resources within the family economy was just as inequitable as its division of labor. We should beware of assuming that women controlled the value produced by their labor, for women clearly did not enjoy equal access to the collective resources of their family economies. Sons generally took more from their family economies than daughters. In most English medieval villages, inheritance laws favored sons over daughters, and parental *inter vivos* gifts to children (which might have overridden the sexual bias inherent in *post mortem* distributions) similarly favored sons. In towns inheritance customs often dispersed goods equally to sons and daughters (at least in theory; no one has yet studied actual practice), but sons alone usually enjoyed the privileges of following their fathers' trades, gaining admittance to their fathers' guilds, and acquiring the freedom of their municipalities via patrimony. The effects of these legal and customary prescriptions were very real. In my studies of the rural community of Brigstock in the early fourteenth century, for example, I found that daughters were considerably less involved in landholding than were sons—roughly one daughter traded or received land for every four sons that did so.[23]

Once married, a woman experienced even more sharply the economic inequality of women in the family economy. In both law and custom, a husband enjoyed extensive authority over all familial resources (including properties brought to the marriage by his wife or given explicitly by others to her). The condition of the married women, the *femme couverte* in common law, was a condition of virtual nonexistence (especially in economic matters). As Glanvill succinctly put it, "since legally a woman is completely in the power of her husband, . . . her dower and all her other property are

clearly deemed to be at his disposal."[24] A woman brought resources
to the family economy created by her marriage and she worked
hard to support it, but *control* of the family economy rested firmly
in the hands of her husband. Any wife could find, as did Quena ad
Crucem of Brigstock in 1315, that she could not sell land without
her husband's involvement because, as the court put it, "a wife's
sale is nothing in the absence of her husband."[25]

Even in death and dissolution, the distribution of resources
within the family economy was inequitable. Widowers usually
retained full control of all household resources, for the death of a
wife did not precipitate dissolution of the family economy. Widows, however, faced a much more difficult situation, for the death
of a husband effectively dissolved the family economy (whose
resources were then dispersed, at least in part, to the next generation). Some widows could claim full control of household resources, but many others were able to claim only one-half or
one-third of family property. Although rules varied widely, many
widows faced not only bereavement but also impoverishment.[26]

We might like to think that these laws and customs were
mitigated in actual practice, but we should posit such mitigation
with extreme caution. As John Stuart Mill advised in another
context over a century ago, we must judge the family economy not
by the behavior of good men (who often ease the force of patriarchal institutions), but rather by the behavior of bad men (who
often exploit such institutions to their fullest extent).[27] Hence, we
cannot ignore the fact that English laws and customs in the middle
ages permitted husbands to deny their wives control over both
their capital resources and their labor. With a good husband and a
happy marriage, a woman could achieve a satisfying working life.
But such voluntary egalitarianism—if it existed—was shadowed by
inequality. Even in sharing, the greater material resources of the
husband bespoke inequality. And even in sharing, the husband's
power remained merely suspended, not fully yielded. With an
indifferent husband or an abusive marriage, a woman could find
herself a sort of servant to her husband or even cast aside altogether. We can rarely catch glimpses of such miseries in medieval
sources, but ecclesiastical courts—a recourse only for women of
some wealth or power—offer a few. In such courts, women, like
Matilda Trippes of the Canterbury diocese in 1373, had to seek

court orders to force their husbands to provide them with the basic necessities of life.[28] The experiences of women such as these underscore the relative economic powerlessness of women within their family economies.

One escape hatch existed: the urban custom of *femme sole*.[29] In some towns, married women were permitted, if formally registered as *femmes soles,* to trade independently of their husbands. Although this custom potentially mitigated the economic subservience of women within the family economy, it did not alter the family economy *per se;* it offered women not equal control of the resources of the family economy, but rather the opportunity to work outside the family economy altogether. A wife who traded as a *femme sole,* therefore, had some independence, but very little support; she probably often found it difficult to compete effectively with either married men (who were supported by the labor of wives and children) or single women (who were relatively more free of family responsibilities). Moreover, the actual effects of this custom are hard to assess. It was confined only to urban areas and indeed, only to some urban areas; towns such as Shrewsbury and Salisbury apparently offered no such reprieve to married women.[30] It has been observed more as a rule than as an actual practice. In London, for example, we know about the theory of the *femme sole,* but we have very few records demonstrating its actual use, and some of these records show wives, designated as *femmes soles,* nevertheless acting in concert with their husbands (acting, in other words, as *femmes couvertes*).[31] And finally, it possibly evolved not as a means of liberating women from the legal coverage of marriage, but instead as a means of freeing husbands from the debts and obligations of their wives; the custom, in other words, benefited men.

The family economy, then, was never a haven of rough and ready equality for women; instead, it was shot through with sexual inequality—from its basis as a social construction of a patriarchal society, to its sexual division of household labor, and to its distribution of control over material resources. Hence, although the medieval family economy has been repeatedly described by historians as a "partnership" of husband and wife, this description masks practical inequality beneath an ideal of mutuality. The family economy might be idealized by historians as a mutual partnership, but this ideal was rarely approached in actual practice. Daughters worked as hard as sons, but they took much less than their brothers from their family economies; wives worked as hard as their husbands, but their tasks were ancillary and their control over family wealth was strictly abrogated; widows also worked hard, but they often faced massive insecurity, as the resources of their family economies—deemed dissolved by the deaths of their husbands—were dispersed in part to the next generation. The medieval family economy was a very weak foundation for a working woman's "golden age"; women worked within it, but its resources usually belonged in the final resort to men.

Our second important index of women's work—the types of work undertaken by women (whether within a family economy or not)—demonstrates that women's work retained certain crucial characteristics across the late medieval and early modern centuries. In many respects, the actual occupations of women remained remarkably unchanged. Comparisons of women's occupations across the centuries are difficult to draw: extant sources vary widely (and are often incomparable), occupational designations shifted over time, and of course, economic contexts also changed. I have attempted, however, a rough comparison based on occupations of unmarried women noted in the Southwark poll tax of 1381 and Peter Earle's tabulation of women's occupation in London (including the Southwark suburb) in c. 1700. As shown in table 1, I have matched as closely as possible the occupations of late fourteenth-century women to the broad categories used by Earle for the seventeenth and eighteenth centuries.

A comparison of this nature is fraught with difficulty. Are fourteenth-century servants fully comparable to domestic servants c. 1700? Can a fourteenth-century suburb (and a poor suburb, at that) be fairly compared to a seventeenth-century metropolis? Should glovers and girdlers be regrouped with manufacturers? Yet if we pass over these conundrums and look at *general patterns,* some striking similarities emerge. First, note the basic stability in the occupational structure. Some occupations attracted remarkably similar proportions of single female workers—especially domestic service, but also laundering, making clothes, and victualing. Others varied, but in ways that suggest either changing economic structures in the London area (e.g., the decline in textile manufacture) or problems of categorization (e.g., shopkeeping vs. hawking

Table 1

Unmarried Women's Work in London and Vicinity 1381 vs. c. 1700

EARLE'S OCCUPATIONAL CATEGORIES	SOUTHWARK WOMEN 1381	LONDON WOMEN 1695–1725	CATEGORIZATION OF 1381 OCCUPATIONS
Domestic Service	38.0%	39.8%	Servants (62)
Making/Mending clothes	12.3%	17.9%	Dressmakers (11) Tailors (4) Cappers (2) Girdler (1) Lacemaker (1) Glover (1)
Nursing/Medicine	1.2%	8.4%	Midwife (1) Barber (1)
Charring/Laundry	3.7%	7.0%	Washerwomen (6)
Shopkeeping	1.8%	7.8%	Upholdsters (3)
Catering/Victualing	8.0%	5.9%	Brewers (3) Cooks (2) Ostilers (2) Tapsters (2) Baker (1) Garlicmonger (1) Fisherman (1)
Hawking/Carrying	13.5%	4.5%	Fruitier (1) Hucksters (21) Fishbearer(1)
Textile manufacture	17.2%	3.6%	Spinsters (24) Kempsters (2) Dyer (1) Fuller (1)
Misc. Services	.6%	2.8%	Gardener (1)
Misc. manufacture	3.7%	1.7%	Skinner (3) Shoemaker (1) Saddler (1) Carpenter (1)
Hard labor/day work	0.0%	.6%	

SOURCE: Data for London 1695–1725 extracted from table 10 of Peter Earle, "The Female Labor Market in London in the Late Seventeenth and Early Eighteenth Centuries," *Economic History Review*, 2nd ser., 42 (1989): 328–353. Earle breaks his data down by marital status; since the 1381 poll tax reports occupations only for unmarried women, I have used only Earle's data for spinsters and widows. Data for Southwark in 1381 from P.R.O. E179 184/30. I have excluded from my figures unmarried women whose occupations were unstated.

and carrying). Second, consider that most unmarried women—in 1381 as well as 1700—worked in either service or the textile and clothing trades. In both 1381 and 1700, two of every five single women found employment in service and another two found employment in textile or clothing manufacturing. Third, note the absence in both the fourteenth century and the seventeenth century of certain high status and high income occupations. In neither 1381 nor 1700 were single women able to find employment in long-distance trade, in professional occupations, in civil service.[32] It is quite misleading to state, as one medieval historian has recently done, that women's occupations constituted the "medieval equivalent of the Yellow Pages."[33] Single women found work in very discrete sectors of the economy and were conspicuously absent from a large number of high status occupations.

These continuities in the occupations of single women are highly suggestive. Yet more important than occupations per se are continuities in the *defining characteristics* of women's work, no matter what their actual employment. Women's work throughout these centuries tended to be low skilled; it usually yielded low remuneration in terms of either wages or profits; it was regarded with low esteem; it was work that combined easily with a wide variety of other remunerative tasks or schemes. These characteristics are repeated in an almost numbing echo throughout studies of women's work in medieval and early modern England: in my study of early fourteenth-century Brigstock; in Maryanne Kowaleski's study of late fourteenth-century Exeter; in Diane Hutton's study of Shrewsbury in the same century; in P.J.P. Goldberg's study of fifteenth-century York; in Sue Wright's study of early modern Salisbury; in Mary Prior's study of early modern Oxford; in Carole Shammas's study of seventeenth-century Lancashire; in Peter Earle's study of London c. 1700.[34] No matter what the actual occupations of women, they tended to work in low skilled, low status, low paid jobs, and they also tended to be intermittent workers, jumping from job to job or juggling several tasks at once. This was true in 1300, and it remained true in 1700.

These basic characteristics are, to my mind, much more important in the history of women's work than any shifts in actual occupations pursued by women (and as we have seen, there were relatively few such shifts). Brewing provides a good example.[35] As

Alice Clark noted in her study, brewing was once a female trade that had, by the seventeenth century, come under the increasing control of men. The shift from a feminized industry to a masculinized one occurred much earlier and less completely than Clark suggested, but it did occur. In 1300 many villages boasted numerous female brewers who supplemented their households' income by selling ale to friends and neighbors; in 1700, those same villages often hosted only a handful of male brewers.

The history of brewing, then, seems to fit the paradigm of a dramatic and negative transformation in women's work. Women ceased to brew commercially as frequently as they had done in the past, suggesting a substantial change for the worse in the history of women's work. Two perspectives, however, belie this interpretation. First, the change was not cataclysmic. Women were not, after all, forced out of a trade that had once offered them high profits and high status; when women brewed, brewing yielded low profits and low esteem. Second, the substantial change occurred in brewing itself, not in women's work. In 1300 brewing was a localized, small-scale industry that required little capital investment and yielded small profits; it was, therefore, a classic sector of women's work characterized by low status, low skill, and low remuneration, and suitable for intermittent work patterns. By 1700 brewers often served regional, national, or even international markets, and the successful pursuit of the trade required considerable capital investment and considerable technical skill.[36] Therefore, women, whose work continued to be concentrated in low skilled, low status, low paid sectors, were no longer able to compete in brewing. They continued to brew in regions unaffected by the transformation of the trade, and they continued to find employment in less profitable sectors of brewing (for example, as petty retailers of ale and beer). In general, however, the brewing industry had developed beyond the realm of women's work. Although women ceased to brew for profit as frequently as in the past, their work didn't really change, it was simply relocated—as brewing grew in prestige and profits—into other sectors of the economy that better suited women's low status as workers. In brewing, then, the real change was in the industry itself, not in women's work per se.

A third measure of women's work—women's access to guilds and guild-supervised work—has been a keystone of many arguments for a great transition. Two sources have suggested a decline in women's place within English guilds: apprenticeship records and guild ordinances. Both provide very ambivalent evidence of a real decline in the relationship between women and guilds. Although some scholars cite apparent declines in female apprenticeships in the sixteenth century, hard evidence for such a trend has yet to be adduced.[37] Consider London. For the later middle ages, Lacey and Barron have uncovered miscellaneous contracts and cases involving female apprentices. These can provide us with examples and anecdotes, but little more. For the late sixteenth century, we have exactly the same thing—several dozen agreements involving female apprentices.[38] Guild ordinances provide equally weak evidence of a decline. It is tempting to cite guild restrictions on female work—such as the 1461 order of Bristol weavers that guild members were not to employ their wives, daughters or female servants in weaving—as indicating a progressive decline in female guild participation.[39] But such restrictions are very hard to interpret: they can be found in every century between 1300 and 1700; they probably reflect more prescription than actual practice; they especially proliferate in later centuries simply because more guild records are extant for later periods; and they often suggest short-term responses to economic crisis, not long-term declines in female work.[40] In short, our evidence does not (as yet) show any clear transition in guild treatment of women workers over the late medieval and early modern centuries.

Our evidence does, however, demonstrate one fact very clearly: women were never—even in the high middle ages—full members of guilds in England. Unlike some towns on the continent, no English towns boasted exclusively female guilds, and even the silkworkers of London failed to organize themselves into a guild until significant numbers of men had joined the trade.[41] As a result English women, insofar as they participated in guilds at all, participated in guilds controlled by men; in these guilds, women's roles varied by town, by trade, and by marital status, but women never participated as fully as men.[42] The history of women's relationship with guilds needs further examination, but our evidence at hand suggests neither a great transition nor a medieval "golden age."

The same conclusion is suggested by our final index of women's work—the history of women's wages between 1300 and 1700. Not all women worked for wages to be sure, but sums paid to wage-earning women provide crucial measures of not only the perceived value of women's work but also the earning power of women. Our very earliest records show clearly that women's work was poorly valued. In the twelfth and thirteenth centuries, the *famuli* employed on an annual basis by manorial estates were mostly males. Tasks designated for females were very few, quite unskilled, and relatively poorly paid. These patterns continued into the fourteenth century and beyond.[43]

Women's work performed on a day basis was also poorly remunerated. Before the plague the day tasks most clearly designated for female workers were planting beans and collecting stubble—both were generally paid at the rate of 1d. per day (occasionally ¾d.). Men hired for such tasks as digging were usually paid at least 1½d. and as much as 2½d.[44] Indeed, the wage differential between "women's work" and "men's work" seems to have been remarkably stable, with women paid about two-thirds to one-half the wages of men: this was true of female laborers in the early fourteenth century; of female reapers and other workers in the seventeenth century; of female agricultural workers in the nineteenth century; and of women working in the modern wage market.[45] Medieval employers were apparently as well aware as modern employers of the possibilities of exploiting the sexual division of labor in order to cut costs. In the thirteenth century the author of a treatise on estate management advised hiring a woman for certain tasks because she could be relied on to work "for much less money than a man would take."[46]

Why, then, do some historians claim that, as William Beveridge put it in 1955, the "principle of equal pay as between men and women for the same work was . . . accepted and put into practice more than 600 years [ago]"?[47] The answer is a straightforward one: on occasions when women found employment in tasks also undertaken by men, they were *sometimes* paid equally with men. Historians have made much of evidence—such as that for reapers at Pocklington in 1363—that shows female workers doing the same jobs as men receiving the same wages. Equal pay for equal work was not—it must be emphasized—an invariable rule, and many examples can be proffered of women paid less than men for equal work. At Pocklington itself, only nine women were paid the same rate as men; the other twenty-one women received only 3d. while the men were paid 4d.[48] Or, for another example, unskilled female laborers at Alton Barnes in 1404 were paid 2d. per day, while unskilled males received 4d.[49] Hence, we must treat evidence of equal pay for equal work with considerable caution. Since we know that equal work by women and men was often not remuner-ated with equal pay, we must ask: How common was it to pay men and women equally for equal tasks? Since we know that wages often distinguished persons by age as well as sex, we must ask: Were the "men" paid equally with women at places like Pocklington actually "boys"? And since we know that most women continued to work in low-paid "women's work," we must ask: How many women were able to benefit from working alongside men?[50] Until we can answer questions such as these, we simply cannot assess the importance of evidence showing women as paid equally with men for the performance of equal tasks, nor can we assess how this changed over time. We must, on balance, remain very skeptical of claims about the earning potential of female wage-workers during the middle ages.

In the history of women's work between 1300 and 1700, then, these four measures—women's place within the family economy, the types of work pursued by women, women's roles within guilds, and the wages paid to women—suggest that there was no great divide between a medieval "golden age" and an early modern age of growing inactivity and exploitation. Changes occurred to be sure—the family economy lost its effectiveness in some economic sectors, women left some trades (such as brewing), guilds became generally more exclusive, female wage-earners competed more or less effectively for better wages. Yet, we must view these changes (and others) with a strong skepticism. First, many of the changes that occurred were of quite short duration. For example, it seems possible—from both our extant evidence and economic theory— that the labor shortages of the decades that followed the Black Death improved the wage-earning potential of women. During the late fourteenth and early fifteenth centuries, wage differentials between unskilled and skilled laborers narrowed considerably, and since "women's work" was generally unskilled work, its wages— together with wages for unskilled male labor—gained ground on skilled wages. At the same time, women might have been able to bargain more effectively not only for better pay but also for equal work paid at equal wages; most of our examples of equal pay for equal work come from these labor-short decades.[51] But these changes were a short-term phenomenon, confined to the peculiar circumstances of a population ravaged by disease. For another example, many guild ordinances against women's work seem to have been prompted by adverse economic conditions and seem to have only applied (if they ever had real effect at all) to years of hard times. Hence, such ordinances were very common in London during the difficult years of the 1540s; they are rare before and rare after.[52] Changes such as these are very telling, for they indicate both the vulnerability of female workers and the economic usefulness of their occupational adaptability. We need to study these changes (and others) in more detail, but we also need to remember that they proved to be ephemeral. They were small and temporary shifts, not transformations.

Second, even the most positive shifts affected only a tiny minority of women. Most of our evidence for an improvement in the working opportunities of women after the plague, for example, involves wage-earning women or women in urban locales. Yet only a very small proportion of women would have been able to take advantage of these short-term changes. Relatively few people (and even fewer women than men) worked for wages in the later middle ages and relatively few people lived in towns.[53] Moreover, even in the best of times and places, most women were unable to take advantage of new opportunities that were potentially theirs; most wage-earning women still worked in lower paid female jobs, as did most urban women. For example, more women gained the freedom of York in the early fifteenth century than in earlier or later periods, but only fifty-two women were able to take advantage of this opportunity (compared to literally thousands of men who entered the freedom at this time).[54] Even genuine shifts, then, had quite limited effect.

Third, these changes—as ephemeral and as limited as they were—must also be placed within a context of enduring continuities in the circumstances, status, and experiences of women workers. As I have demonstrated from four perspectives, most women—in 1300 as in 1700—sought to support themselves (and their families) through a variety of low skilled, low status, low paid occupations.

In the world of preindustrial England, all people—men as well as women—worked hard, long, and in difficult circumstances, but the working status of women—compared to that of men—was consistently lower: they received less training, they worked at less desirable tasks, they enjoyed less occupational stability and a weaker work identity, they received lower wages. This was as true in the best of times (as perhaps in some locales after the plague) as in the worst of times. We need to collect much more information about how women's work and women's wages shifted and altered within this framework of economic subordination, but the framework remained: there was no transformation.

In one sense, my argument with those who posit a great transition in women's work is a perceptual one. Scholars like Caroline Barron and Susan Cahn look at the "glass" of women's economic activity in fifteenth-century England and see it as half full; I see the same "glass" but I see it as half empty. My disagreement is, however, more substantial than merely a matter of perspective. For scholars who work within the paradigm of great transformation see women's work within an entirely different framework, a framework that best accommodates not small and temporary shifts but instead transformative and dramatic change. This framework suits well a liberal historiographic tradition, for it implies that a "golden age" for women—part of the relatively recent past of the West—can be easily recovered in the future without major structural changes.[55] Within this framework, the medieval period becomes a "golden age," a "paradise" which early modern women lost.

Women's work is, of course, just one aspect of the paradigmatic assumption of a great transition in women's history coinciding with the end of the middle ages and the emergence of modern Europe. Yet it illustrates well both how strongly the paradigm operates within a specific research area and how many anomalous findings now undercut the paradigm's efficacy. Women's work certainly changed over these centuries, but it was not transformed. If we look critically at other aspects of women's history across these centuries—family relations, patterns of marriage and fertility, political participation, religious life, and so on—we will discern similar continuities across the centuries. The paradigm of a great divide, quite simply, does not hold.

The shattering of this paradigm requires that we rethink the history of women between 1300 and 1700. Instead of searching for a great transition and its effects on women, we should develop a "way of seeing" women's history that better recognizes continuity and that, indeed, takes continuity as its chief problematic. In the study of women's work, to continue with the central example of this essay, we should take as our central question not transformation (whether, when, and why it occurred) but instead continuity. We should ask: Why has women's work retained such dismal characteristics over so many centuries? We should ask: Why did women leave brewing as it became profitable and capitalized? We should ask: Why have wages for "women's work" remained consistently lower than wages paid for work associated with men? We should ask, in short: Why has women's work stood still in the midst of considerable economic change?

The shattering of this paradigm also requires that we rethink the history of women in general. For the issues raised in this essay pertain to *all* of women's history, not just women's history across the medieval/early modern divide. To medievalists and early modernists, this essay speaks directly about how we conceptualize our research, writing, and teaching about European women between the thirteenth and seventeenth centuries. But to all historians of women (medievalists and early modernists, to be sure, but also those working in modern European history, African history, Asian history, United States history, or whatever), this essay raises critical questions about how we approach the very subject of women's history: about how we conceptualize the periodization of women's history, and about how we integrate the study of patriarchy into the history of women.

Historians of women have long questioned the relevance of traditional periodizations. In her classic article on "The Social Relation of the Sexes" published in 1976, Joan Kelly counted periodization as one of the three ways in which women's history had then "shaken the conceptual foundations of historical study." Accepting the notion that "significant turning points in history" applied to women as well as men, Kelly did not question traditional periodization per se; she argued instead that our assessment of those turning points must consider how they often led to "the advance of one sex and oppression of the other." In other words, while accepting that a "Renaissance" had occurred, Kelly advocated a feminist re-evaluation of what that Renaissance had really meant for both sexes.[56]

My essay suggests a very different sort of challenge to traditional periodization; it suggests that our traditional "turning points" simply do not work for the history of women. The thirteenth through seventeenth centuries might well have encompassed a great turning point in economic history—an Age of Emerging Capitalism—but if so, it had no fundamental effects on women's work. Must we not then look critically at other turning points? Did the Renaissance or the Industrial Era, or the Age of Democratic Revolutions really affect the status of women in any significant ways? In other words, where Kelly once saw "change for the worse" for women in the Renaissance, I now think we might see startling continuities and no real "turning point" at all.

In reassessing the traditional periodization of history, feminist historians need to keep two important perspectives in mind. First, we need to distinguish between the *experiences* of women and the *status* of women. In women's work between 1200 and 1700, for example, many things changed in the experiences of women (what work they did, where, and under what terms), but little changed in the overall status of their work (which remained poorly remunerated, and low in both status and skill). Second, we need to think harder about the pace of change in women's history, for although change has occurred, it might have moved at a much slower pace than historians commonly expect. In women's history, many events (such as the accession of Henry VII on Bosworth field) were not transformative, many medium-term changes (such as the Protestant idealization of motherhood) had ambiguous effects on women, and certain continuities (such as women's low status as workers) run across many centuries. In writing women's history, therefore, we need to talk about change very carefully, balancing our evaluations of experience and status, expecting slow movements, and recognizing that some apparent changes occurred within a context of long-term continuities.

Kelly herself was unwilling to reperiodize history from a feminist viewpoint because she feared that it might cause "a potential isolation of women's history from . . . the mainstream."[57] Yet as my evocation of *annaliste* ideas about short-term, medium-term, and long-term changes suggests, a re-periodization of women's history will contribute to a larger project of historical reperiodization, not an isolation of women's history from the rest of the discipline. Consider, for just one example, how my specific re-evaluation of women's work in this essay contributes to a broader historical reassessment of the medieval/early modern divide.

Others might object to this project because its emphasis on continuity evokes the hoary argument that women have no history because women's lives have never changed. Yet in taking continuity as a central issue in women's history, we are certainly not denying change. As the research of recent years has shown again and again, women's lives have been very diverse and women's lives have changed constantly over time. This essay suggests that—*despite* these diversities and *despite* these changing experiences—the *overall* status of women has changed much more slowly. To my mind, this stickiness in women's status must be taken as a central problem for women's history.

As I have argued elsewhere, this emphasis on continuity demands an attention to the mechanisms and operations of patriarchy in the history of women.[58] In other words, I think that we need to pursue our historical study of women with a greater attention to the (varied and changing) patriarchal contexts of women's lives. We need to understand how patriarchy has worked in certain times and places, how it has been challenged, accepted, and changed by women and men, and how it has adapted and adjusted to changing times. As used by feminist historians, the project of historicizing patriarchy assumes that the subordination of women is neither preordained nor natural but is instead a complex historical phenomenon. This project offers a framework within which to pursue questions about continuity and change in women's history, without dictating what the answers must be. And it simply fits our historical evidence much better than a paradigm that forces us to see "turning points" or "great transitions." As illustrated here by the history of women's work in preindustrial England, assessing the balance of continuity over change in women's history requires an approach that can better accommodate a history of small shifts, short-term changes, and enduring continuities. We can find such an approach in the historical study of patriarchy.

Notes

1. Lee Patterson, "On the Margin: Postmodernism, Ironic History, and Medieval Studies," *Speculum* 65 (1990): 87–108.

2. David Aers, *Community, Gender, and Individual Identity: English Writing 1360–1430* (London, 1988), 17.

3. Alan Macfarlane, *The Origins of English Individualism: The Family, Property, and Social Transition* (Oxford, 1978). For one critique, see Stephen White and Richard Vann, "The Invention of English Individualism: Alan Macfarlane and the Modernization of Pre-Modern England," *Social History* 8 (1983): 345–363.

4. The main authorities for the dominant model are: Philippe Ariès, *Centuries of Childhood: A Social History of Family Life*, trans. Robert Baldick (New York, 1962); and Lawrence Stone, *The Family, Sex and Marriage in England 1500–1800* (New York, 1977). For critiques by medievalists, see Lorraine Attreed, "From Pearl Maiden to Tower Princes: Towards a New History of Medieval Childhood," *Journal of Medieval History* 9 (1983): 43–58, and Barbara Hanawalt, "Childrearing among the Lower Classes of Late Medieval England," *Journal of Interdisciplinary History* 8 (1977): 1–22.

5. Martha C. Howell, *Women, Production and Patriarchy in Late Medieval Cities* (Chicago, 1986). Merry E. Wiesner, *Working Women in Renaissance Germany* (New Brunswick, N.J., 1986).

6. Joan Kelly, "Did Women Have a Renaissance?" 1977 essay reprinted in her *Women, History and Theory* (Chicago, 1984), 19–51; Margaret King, "Book-Lined Cells: Women and Humanism in the Early Italian Renaissance," in *Beyond Their Sex: Learned Women of the European Past*, ed. Patricia H. Labalme (New York, 1984), 66–90; and Margaret King with Albert Rabil, Jr., eds., *Her Immaculate Hand* (Binghampton, 1983).

7. Linda Woodbridge, *Women and the English Renaissance* (Urbana, 1984); Catherine Belsey, *The Subject of Tragedy* (London, 1985); Katharina M. Wilson and Elizabeth M. Makowski, *Wykked Wyves and the Woes of Marriage* (Albany, 1990).

8. Ivan Illich, *Gender* (New York, 1982).

9. Alice Clark, *Working Life of Women in the Seventeenth Century* (1919; reprinted London, 1982); Kelly, "Did Women Have a Renaissance?".

10. For recent challenges, see Chris Middleton, "Women's Labor and the Transition to Pre-Industrial Capitalism," in *Women and Work in Pre-Industrial England*, ed. Lindsey Charles and Lorna Duffin (London, 1985), 181–206; Chris Middleton, "The Familiar Fate of the *Famulae*: Gender Divisions in the History of Wage Labor," in *On Work*, ed R. E. Pahl (Oxford, 1988), 21–47; Judith M. Bennett, "'History That Stands Still': Women's Work in the European Past," *Feminist Studies* 14 (1988): 269–283.

11. Caroline Barron, "The 'Golden Age' of Women in Medieval London," in *Medieval Women in Southern England*, Reading Medieval Studies 15 (1989): 49.

12. P.J.P. Goldberg, "Female Labor, Status, and Marriage in Late Medieval York and Other English Towns," (Ph.D. diss., Cambridge University, 1987), quote from abstract.

13. For Clark, see criticisms of Miranda Chaytor and Jane Lewis in their introduction to the reissue of her book *Working Life of Women* in 1982. For Kelly, see the criticisms of Judith Brown, "A Woman's Place Was in the Home: Women's Work in Renaissance Tuscany," in *Rewriting the Renaissance*, ed. Margaret Ferguson, et al.

(Chicago, 1986), 206–224; see also David Herlihy, "Did Women Have a Renaissance? A Reconsideration," *Medievalia et Humanistica*, n.s. 13 (1985): 1–22.

14.   Annie Abram, "Women Traders in Medieval London," *Economic Journal* 26 (1916): 276–285; Marian K. Dale, "The London Silkwomen of the Fifteenth Century," *Economic History Review* 4 (1933): 324–335; Eileen Power, *Medieval Women* (Cambridge, 1975), quote from 34 esp. 57–75.

15.   Barron, "Golden Age"; Peter Franklin, "Peasant Widows' 'Liberation' and Remarriage before the Black Death," *Economic History Review*, 2nd ser., no. 39 (1986): 186–204; Goldberg, "Female Labor, Status," and articles extending the conclusions of this dissertation, such as "Female Labor, Service and Marriage in the Late Medieval Urban North," *Northern History* 22 (1986): 18–38, and "Women in Fifteenth-Century Town Life," in *Towns and Townspeople in the Fifteenth Century*, ed. John A. F. Thomson (Gloucester, 1988), 107–127; Barbara A. Hanawalt, "Peasant Women's Contribution to the Home Economy in Late Medieval England," in *Women and Work in Preindustrial Europe*, ed. B. A. Hanawalt, (Bloomington, 1986), 3–19; Simon A. C. Penn, "Female Wage-Earners in Late Fourteenth-Century England," *Agricultural History Review* 37 (1987): 1–14; Kay E. Lacey, "Women and Work in Fourteenth and Fifteenth Century London," in *Women and Work*, ed. Charles and Duffin, 24–82; Rodney Hilton has argued not for a medieval golden age, but for the relatively higher status of working women in the middle ages vis-à-vis women of other classes. See R. H. Hilton, "Women in the Village," in *The English Peasantry in the Later Middle Ages* (Oxford, 1975), 95–110, and "Women Traders in Medieval England," *Women's Studies* 11 (1984): 139–155. In a recent study, David Herlihy has posited a similarly dramatic and negative transition, but has dated it much earlier (in the high middle ages); see David Herlihy, *Opera Muliebria: Women and Work in Medieval Europe* (New York, 1990).

16.   Susan Cahn, *Industry of Devotion: The Transformation of Women's Work in England, 1500–1660* (New York, 1987); Roberta Hamilton, *The Liberation of Women: A Study of Patriarchy and Capitalism* (London, 1978); Bridget Hill, *Women, Work, and Sexual Politics in Eighteenth-Century England* (Oxford, 1989); Keith Snell, *Annals of the Laboring Poor* (Cambridge, Eng. 1985), 270–319; Michael Roberts, "Sickles and Scythes: Women's Work and Men's Work at Harvest Time," *History Workshop Journal* 7 (1979): 3–29; W. Thwaites, "Women in the Market Place: Oxfordshire c. 1690–1800," *Midland History* 9 (1984): 23–42; Margaret George, "From 'Goodwife' to 'Mistress': The Transformation of the Female in Bourgeois Culture," *Science and Society* 37 (1973): 152–177. I shall not deal in this essay with women's work outside England, but the idea of a great transition also dominates continental work; see particularly the studies of Howell and Wiesner.

17.   For explicit queries of the paradigm, see Middleton, "Women's labor" and "Familiar Fate," and Bennett, "History That Stands Still." For examples of findings contrary to the paradigm, see Maryanne Kowaleski, "Women's Work in a Market Town: Exeter in the Late Fourteenth Century," in *Woman and Work in Preindustrial Europe*, 145–164; and Diane Hutton, "Women in Fourteenth Century Shrewsbury," in *Women and Work in Pre-Industrial England*, 83–99. For quote see, Cahn, *Industry of Devotion*, 9.

18.   Power, *Medieval Women,* 34; Hanawalt, "Peasant Women's Contribution"; Louise Tilly and Joan Scott, *Women, Work and Family* (New York, 1978), 230; Cahn, *Industry of Devotion.*

19.   Olivia Harris, "Households as Natural Units," in *Of Marriage and the*

Market, ed. Kate Young et al. 2nd ed. (London, 1984), 136–155; Rayna Rapp, et al., "Examining Family History," *Feminist Studies* 5 (1979): 174–200.

20.   "Ballad of a Tyrannical Husband," in *Reliquiae Antiquae*, vol 2, ed. Thomas Wright and James O. Halliwell (London, 1845), 196–199.

21.   *Statutes of the Realm*, vol. 1 (London, 1810), 379–380.

22.   L. F. Salzman, *English Industries of the Middle Ages* (Oxford, 1923), 328–329.

23.   Judith M. Bennett, *Women in the Medieval English Countryside* (New York, 1987), 78–84.

24.   *The Treatise on the Laws and Customs of the Realm of England Commonly Called Glanvill*, ed. G.D.G. Hall (London, 1965), Book 6, no. 3, 60.

25.   Northamptonshire Record Office, Montagu Collection, Box x364B, court for 20 March 1315. The jurors stated "*vendicio illa nulla est de uxore in absentia mariti sui.*"

26.   For a fuller discussion of the circumstances faced by rural widows, see chapter 6 of Bennett, *Women*.

27.   John Stuart Mill, *The Subjection of Women* (1869), esp. chapter 2.

28.   R. H. Helmholz, *Marriage Litigation in Medieval England* (Cambridge, Eng., 1974), 102.

29.   Mary Bateson, ed., *Borough Customs*, 2 vols., Selden Society 18 (London, 1904): esp. 222–228; and 21 (London, 1906): C–CXV, 102–129.

30.   Diane Hutton, "Women in Fourteenth-Century Shrewsbury," in *Women and Work in Pre-Industrial England*, 86; Sue Wright, "'Churmaids, Huswyfes and Hucksters': the Employment of Women in Tudor and Stuart Salisbury," in *Women and Work in Pre-Industrial England*, 107.

31.   For discussion of *femmes soles* in London, see Lacey, "Women and Work," esp. 41–45; and Barron, "Golden Age," esp. 39–40.

32.   In the Southwark poll tax, for example, numerous skilled occupations were identified with men alone, including: spicer, vintner, goldsmith, marshall, armiger, weaver, cooper, and smith. See also the occupations of males and females listed in Penn, "Female Wage-Earners," 5 (table 1).

33.   Goldberg, "Female labor, Service," 30.

34.   Bennett, *Women*; Kowaleski, "Women's Work"; Hutton, "Women"; Goldberg, "Female Labor, Service"; Sue Wright, "Churmaids"; Mary Prior, "Women and the Urban Economy: Oxford 1500–1800," in *Women in English Society 1500–1800*, ed. Mary Prior (London, 1985), 93–117; Carole Shammas, "The World Women Knew: Women Workers in the North of England during the Late Seventeenth Century," in *The World of William Penn*, ed. R. Dunn (Philadelphia, 1986), 99–115; Earle, "Female Labor Market."

35.   What follows is a summary of my on-going work on women in the brewing industry over these centuries. Some of the material is presented in greater detail in my "The Village Ale-Wife: Women and Brewing in Fourteenth-Century England," in *Women and Work in Preindustrial Europe*, 20–38; and in "Misogyny, Popular Culture, and Women's Work," *History Workshop Journal* 31 (1991): 166–188.

36.   Peter Mathias, *The Brewing Industry in England 1700–1830* (Cambridge, Eng., 1959).

37.   Barron, "Golden Age," 48.

38.   Nancy Adamson found 73 agreements for female apprentices in late sixteenth-century London; see her dissertation, "Urban Families: the Social Con-

text of the London Elite, 1500–1603," (Ph.D. diss, University of Toronto, 1983), 245–250. Barron in "Golden Age," 48 cites V. B. Elliott's finding of no agreements involving female apprentices between 1570 and 1640; I can only assume that Adamson's work covered companies not examined by Elliott.

39. Francis B. Bickley, ed., *The Little Red Book of Bristol*, vol. 2 (Bristol, 1900), 127–128.

40. For an example of a fourteenth-century restriction, see Adamson, "Urban Families," 238 (Girdlers of London in 1344). For the short-term purposes of such ordinances, see Wright, "Churmaids," 106; and Steve Rappaport, *Worlds within Worlds: Structures of Life in Sixteenth-Century London* (Cambridge, Eng., 1989), 38–39.

41. For the silkworkers of London, see Dale, "The London Silkwomen"; and Walter B. Stern, "The Trade, Art or Mistery of Silk Throwers of the City of London in the Seventeenth Century," *The Guildhall Miscellany* 1, no. 6 (1956): 25–30.

42. For a fuller discussion of the low status of women in guilds, see Maryanne Kowaleski and Judith M. Bennett, "Crafts, Gilds, and Women in the Middle Ages: Fifty Years after Marian K. Dale," *Signs* 14 (1989): 474–488.

43. M. M. Postan, "The Famulus: the Estate Laborer in the xiith and xiiith Centuries," *Economic History Review*, supplement 2 (1954); Middleton, "Familiar Fate."

44. I extracted wages paid *specifically* to males or females from the data listed in James E. Thorold Rogers, *A History of Agriculture and Prices in England*, vol. 2, *1259–1400* (Oxford, 1866), 273–334. Between 1262 and 1350, women received ¾d to 1d. per day (usually for planting or gathering); men received 1½d to 2½d per day (usually for digging). Between 1350 and 1400, women received 1d. to 2d.; men received 2d. to 3d. On the continent women were also paid roughly two-thirds of men's wages before the plague, and roughly three-fourths in the decades immediately after. See the work of G. d'Avenal as cited in Shulamith Shahar, *The Fourth Estate* (London, 1983), 198–199.

45. For the seventeenth century, see Roberts, "Sickles," 19; and Shammas, "The World Women Knew," 110–111. For the nineteenth century, see comment of Thorold Rogers in *A History of Agriculture and Prices in England*, vol. 1, (Oxford, 1866), 274 that wages paid female agricultural workers before the plague were "relatively as good" as those paid nineteenth-century female farm workers.

46. Dorothea Oschinsky, ed., *Walter of Henley and Other Treatises on Estate Management and Accounting* (Oxford, 1971), 427.

47. Lord Beveridge, "Westminster Wages in the Manorial Era," *Economic History Review*, 2nd series, 8 (1955): 34. See also Hilton, "Women in the Village," 102–103; Hanawalt, "Peasant Women's Contribution," 11; Penn, "Female Wage-Earners."

48. Penn, "Female Wage-Earners," 9.

49. J. E. Thorold Rogers, *A History of Agriculture and Prices in England*, vol. 3, *1401–1582* (Oxford, 1882), 585.

50. Even Beveridge notes ("Westminster Wages," 34) that "for the most part women were used for special kinds of work" (i.e. that most women worked at tasks designated specifically as "women's work" that were paid at different wage rates).

51. Penn, "Female Wage-Earners."

52. Rappaport, *Worlds within Worlds*, 38–39. Wright, "Churmaids," 106.

53. Perhaps as much as one-third of the populace worked for wages at least occasionally, but only a minority of these wage-workers would have been women; perhaps 1 in every 4 wage-earners (or less). See Simon A. C. Penn and Christopher Dyer, "Wages and Earnings in Late Medieval England: Evidence from the Enforcement of the Labor Laws," *Economic History Review*, 2nd series, 43 (1990): 356–376. Similarly, perhaps as many as 1 in 6 persons lived in towns. See Christopher Dyer, "The Past, the Present and the Future in Medieval Rural History," *Rural History* 1 (1990): 47.

54. Goldberg, "Female Labor, Service," 35.

55. Two curiosities about the liberal feminism behind this interpretive framework are worth noting. First, the role of Marxist historiography in supporting the paradigm of a great transition is largely indirect. It motivated some early authoritative work in the field (especially the work of Clark and Kelly), but it does not lie behind the arguments of Barron, Goldberg, Hanawalt, et al. Second, although the political impact of this framework within women's history supports a liberal feminist perspective, it is, of course, part of a master narrative whose politics are much more conservative. See Patterson, "On the Margin." My own framework, which focuses on continuities than run across major economic shifts, suggests that women's condition can only be improved through major structural changes, indeed through changes of a revolutionary nature.

56. Joan Kelly, "The Social Relation of the Sexes: Methodological Implications of Women's History," 1977 essay reprinted in her *Women, History and Theory*, 1–18, quotes from 1–4. See also Kelly, "Did Women Have a Renaissance?"

57. Kelly, "Social Relations of the Sexes," 4.

58. Judith M. Bennett, "Feminism and History," *Gender and History* 1 (1989): 251–272.

La Théorie qui n'en est pas une; or, Why Clio Doesn't Care

CAROLYN STEEDMAN

The first problem inherent in considering a relationship between the history of women and contemporary feminist theory, is—perhaps—*la théorie qui n'en est pas une*, at least, isn't one in relation to recent British historical writing about women. To suggest that feminist criticism has not constituted a theory within feminist historiography over the last twenty years is not to deny that feminist theory exists, for it evidently does. In Britain it was elaborated for the main part within a literary-critical practice that borrowed heavily from *l'écriture féminine* and that now largely defines itself within the discourses of postmodernism. But a recent account of the role of history in the development of British feminist thought points to the conclusion that feminism among historians constitutes a *politics* rather than a theory: that the history of women produced by British feminism has resulted from a survey of the past, an observation of women's absence from conventional accounts, and a reconstitutive putting of women "into the frame."[1] Through Terry Lovell's selection of historical writing in her compilation of *British Feminist Thought,* we are invited by implication to see women's history as part of a larger project of the postwar years, of recovering "lost" histories—of "the people," of the working class; and we are also invited to observe that the focus of recent historical writing by feminists has been on the previously lost history of nineteenth-century bourgeois women.[2] It is clear as well that for a crucial period in the 1970s, women's history was used in and outside the academy for the purposes of consciousness-raising—used in fact as a pedagogy of the emotions and of individual experience in much the same way as was the oral history and the

An earlier version of this essay was published as part three of *Childhood, Culture and Class in Britain: Margaret McMillan, 1860-1931* (London and New Brunswick, N.J., 1990).

working-class writing movement with which it was so closely connected in origins.[3]

Feminist thought has been most elaborated as *theory* within radical feminism, and has produced its most detailed expression in a literary criticism that has recourse to theories of patriarchal oppression as explanatory of women's subordination—in what Rita Felski has outlined as a modern feminist aesthetic, largely constructed out of the study of the experimental literary text.[4] Felski has suggested that this aesthetic is framed by an assumption that modernist texts constitute the only subversive, radical, feminist texts capable of resisting or undermining patriarchal ideology. This suggests the allure of postmodernism for many feminists, in its proffered visions of indeterminacy, dizzying choice of identities, death of centers, and its eschewal of any form of authority, including masculine authority. But the historian must pause for thought about the material constraints that the practice of history offers to a structure of thought developed in a different discipline and out of very different textual sources. Feminist theory can be put to work on the literary text, and an indeterminate, fractured, and split feminine subject found and celebrated. But even should a feminist historian turn her attention to the past out of a desire to find myriad competing identities for women, or, propelled by the imperatives of radical feminism, set out to find an oppression of women by men that is transhistorical, "primary, fundamental, and irreducible,"[5] nevertheless, the work of *writing* that history will finally be constitutive rather than fragmentary: it will serve to *add* women to the past, to alter accounts we already have by placing them "within the frame." The written history of women, prompted by no matter what feminist theory, cannot do the work that the feminist aesthetic attempts in literary studies: of writing polyvalency and fragmentation as resistance and critique of an existing patriarchal order.

In the following pages—and after I have discussed yet another problem in the relationship between women's history and feminist theory—I want to suggest, by way of one example of women's history (an example that I actually wrote), that perhaps Clio simply doesn't care—cares no more about the women's story told under the impulses of feminism than she does about anything else. No matter what feminist theory accompanies the historian, the tale she tells in the end will always be about something else, something other, of which women are only a part, and only (like men, like children) a category that changes in different historical circumstances: in the circumstances that are being described. Clio (as in Auden's poem of homage to her) turns her blank face to all her followers: whoever is there, it is still the same old story.[6] It is not that changing the story cannot be attempted, for the account is rewritten on a daily basis: women, children, new categories of working people, enter her train constantly; but she simply does not care. . . .

If the first problem in the relationship between feminist theory and women's history (in the making of a theory that isn't one) is the obdurate material fact that "the past" is a very different matter— very different *stuff*—from the literary text, then the second problem is the meeting place of the two. In fact, the relationship itself has happened elsewhere, has *not* been effected in the history seminar room nor in the pages of historical monographs and journals. Rather, the meeting place of women's history and feminist theory has been for the main part in the academic *literary* imaginary. "Imaginary" here makes no reference to Jacques Lacan, but indicates rather that necessary—though vastly under-investigated— cognitive workshop where literary critics (including feminist literary critics) have perforce to imagine—to figure—the writers and the readers of the texts from the past on which they work. This practice of the imagination must exist for all disciplines, and the notion of personification is probably central to its process. A helpful discussion like Stephen Knapp's in his *Personification and the Sublime* not only alerts us to the importance of eighteenth-century critical arguments about the religious and moral propriety of transforming abstract ideas into animated beings, but also and incidentally reminds us of the paucity of discussion of this literary trope (and our consequent unfamiliarity with it as an analytic tool) under the antihumanist sway of structuralism and poststructuralism.[7] Personification, whether in the restricted literary-critical sense or as descriptive of an act of cognition, whereby thought is embodied in varieties of shapes and figures, has been difficult to discuss in recent years because it so clearly involves the giving of a *human* shape to abstract ideas and entities.

It is my speculation that some form of personification is at work when historical material (in the case in point, women's history) is used within the field of literary studies. But other factors too, besides the imaginative transmutation of historical research to support feminist literary criticism, must also be taken into account. First for consideration must be the shaping of a common historical imagination by national educational systems and the consequent political understandings that are constructed by people—children for the main part, but with the adult use dependent on the childish one—out of the historical knowledge imparted in schools. I have attempted elsewhere to describe the particular import of history teaching in British schools for the structuring of the adult historical imagination (an imagination that exists in professional historians and professional literary theorists just as much as it does in everyone else growing up in the society). I have suggested that the point of the historical story, from the child's point of view, is the *truth-burden* (not truth: a quite different proposition) that it carries. This is to say that while all other narratives concerning people living in the past delivered to children in classrooms carry the label "not true," or "story," or "fiction," children are told that history is true, that *it really did happen.* The items of information that the child is invited to order, manipulate, analyze (draw, copy, enact, write about) all have the *it-really-did-happen* embedded in them. Their truth claim, and the truth claim of the discipline of history itself, is not an assessment or a judgment bestowed from outside, but rather that which constructs, composes, and constitutes the items of information themselves. This is the manner in which historical information *is*—the way in which it exists as information—for both children and adults, in their different ways. It is this truth-burden which gives the historical narrative a distinct function in the child's (and the adult's) imaginative life.

The child uses the figures from her books, the drawings of ladies in farthingales and crinolines, to construct her own fantasy. The argument here is about the allure of the grand figures when those figures are illustrated and made accessible to the visual imagination; it has much to do with the gorgeousness of clothes and appurtenances, and the child's desire for them, and the relative pleasures involved in tracing round the clothes of a Princess and those of a poor hand-loom weaver. The child appropriates to the imagination the grand figures, makes them operate in her own family romance, as she might use the figures of the fairy-tales, so that by writing and drawing and making a project folder full of Kings and Queens and abandoned Princesses, she can manipulate in fantasy her own familial and emotional drama, and make it work to her greater satisfaction.[8]

I summarize these arguments here by way of suggesting that any scholarly use of historical material takes place not only within the academy, but also in the commonplace, everyday world of which the academy is a part, and that, in the construction of arguments, literary theorists (and indeed, historians themselves) are most profoundly affected by this prosaic and everyday structuring of the past within any given society.

From the history of women in eighteenth- and nineteenth-century Western society, powerful imaginative constructs have been taken of a hegemonic "domestic ideology," of a legal organization of society that rendered married women propertyless, of generations and generations of women who were "mastered for life," who "kissed the rod," who "learned not to be first," who were "private persons" not "public someones," who constituted a "silent sisterhood," who—above all—mark out the boundaries of an absolutely determining split between the public and private realms. I have attempted to trace the origins of this last and most powerful of modern historiographical orthodoxies,[9] and to have done so is not to have denied its power. The idea of "the public and the private" allows the historian of women to act effectively upon texts and documents, and allows her (or him) to produce an account that is evidently much desired by a number of audiences. In all modern curricula, from those of the secondary school to the higher degree program, that employ the category of public and private, the divide is made along the fracture of sex: it concerns women who are private people, domestically confined, and men who are public persons. It has, in the course of its dissemination, become divorced from the questions of class formation that evolved it,[10] and as a concept has been very closely linked—too closely linked—to the circumstances it seeks to describe, too much the anxious repetition of nineteenth-century society's deepest ideological hope to be entirely satisfactory as a category of historical inquiry. Many of us, for instance, first will have encountered Elizabeth Gaskell's Mrs. Carson outside the pages of *Mary Barton*—

shut upstairs in her stuffy dressing room, "indulging in the luxury of a headache," or out in her carriage, encased in shawls and cloaks and bonnet and ignorance—used to illustrate the social forms of conspicuous idleness, domestic privacy and inaction, and impractical dress in women which conferred status on the bourgeois husband. What we may not understand from her several appearances as women's history, is that Mrs. Carson (like the other ladies who have lain on sofas fictional and real from the 1780s onwards, like Jane Austen's Lady Bertram, like Mary Wollstonecraft's Lady Kingsborough) was created for her author's own ironic purposes and in celebration of a certain kind of very hard-working middle-class womanhood that Elizabeth Gaskell herself represented.[11] In an otherwise excellent recent account of the way in which the family culture of ten Victorian women active in social welfare both promoted and hindered their progress to the public world, Julia Parker, in her use of Mrs. Carson as a historical type, incidentally reveals how this historical category of analysis, "the public and the private," has sometimes been unproblematically evidenced out of the beliefs, dreams, desires, and satires of a society—expressed in all its forms of writing, but particularly in the domestic novel of the period 1840–1870.[12]

To make this point is not—for the moment—to question the assumptions of twenty years of women's history, nor indeed to question the veridicality of the classic British accounts referred to above. It is, rather, to make a prosaic observation that is always a matter of great irritation to scholars, that their work *will* get used, outside the epistemological and disciplinary field that produced it, to shape thought and structure the imagination. Because Nancy Armstrong and Mary Poovey so honestly reveal their own work of personifying historical argument for the purposes of literary analysis, the figures "Domestic Woman" and "Proper Lady" show the process at work with a particular clarity, so that in the latter case, we can actually witness the coming-into-being of the demure figure with downcast eye, her lips pressed firmly in a faint smile, who will allow her author the exploration of ideology (the historical category of "domestic ideology") as style, in the work of Mary Wollstonecraft, Mary Shelley, and Jane Austen.[13] Poovey's and Armstrong's work also shows the historical woman personified and used by literary criticism to be an isolated figure, trapped in silence and privacy, cut off from the social world, untrammeled by its hierarchies and degrees of status, outside any of its ranks. She—the Proper Lady, Domestic Woman, Silent Sister—has been so firmly written out of prescription (out of the eighteenth- and early nineteenth-century conduct book in particular) that she is necessarily rendered innocent of all questions of class relation and class antagonism, and one would never guess, for instance, what Mary Wollstonecraft told us so firmly in 1787, that far from being cut off from the world of social and class relations, that world *occupied* her, entered the door, walked the corridor, climbed the stair (cleaned the stair) of the private place: one would never guess that "the management of servants is the great part of the employment of a woman's life, and her own temper depends very much on her behaviour to them."[14]

The tendency of feminist literary theory to use an isolated and individual female figure as a historical type has also been encouraged by the large quantity of women's history that has been produced—in Britain at least—in the form of biography. Biographical accounts of women rescued from historical obscurity rest—of course—on the existence of documentation, and so, for the main part, have rescued middle- and upper-class women; and they impart historical information according to the chronology of a human life. Indeed, these observations and questions and the ones that follow were raised by my own writing of what is, in effect, a historical biography of Margaret McMillan (1860–1931), who was an important figure in British socialism, particularly within her own party, the Independent Labor party, but whose several earlier biographers had canonized as a kind of apolitical saint and savior of working-class children. Dense thickets of hagiography and sentimentality surrounding McMillan's story would not have yielded to the analytic conventions of women's history; and the determining and enclosing notion of "the public and the private" offered me only newer constraints to the writing of her life.

Innovative attempts to reform child welfare were indeed an important aspect of McMillan's work, but my direct concern was to restore her political purposes and intentions and to make sense of her work and writing within a known social and political history of the period 1880–1930 in Britain. At the same time, I wanted to reflect on the extremely strong cultural tendency, which was given such dramatic shape in her work and its reception, to return all questions of children and childhood to a prelapsarian and apolitical Eden.[15] That universal tendency to the sentimentalization of childhood—what Viviana Zelizer has called the sacralization of child life—was not only the conceptual undergrowth of existing accounts of McMillan's work, but was also a cultural tendency that McMillan had played a significant role in developing in Britain between 1895 and 1930.[16]

The shade of an autobiography—a story of the self presented as a biography of another—moved through the pages of *Childhood, Culture and Class* and that shade was a major source for its writing. In her *Life of Rachel McMillan* of 1927, McMillan purported to write the biography of her sister and in fact wrote her own.[17] This elision of forms, of biography and autobiography, is a further item in what I argued for as McMillan's particular importance, that is, her manipulation and use of genres (particularly in her fiction writing) and rhetorical forms (in her political journalism and platform speeches). What is more, literary usage constitutes a specifically historical form of evidence, of the ways in which ideas get used, manipulated, and transmuted in historical contexts, so to discuss literary form and literary usage—the form and use of biography and autobiography—was to come to some conclusions about the historical developments and changes that McMillan was agent of and actor within.

Modern literary studies separate autobiography from biography in a very clear way, with autobiography having the more detailed and sophisticated attention paid to it. While biography is generally understood to be both popular and theoretically dull, autobiography is conventionally analyzed as a complex and problematic form.[18] This is largely because of a modern intellectual interest in the fragmented human subject, an interest which forces a series of compelling questions about the act of splitting oneself off from oneself in order to write a life story. Yet there are historical cases like that of Margaret McMillan, who blurred the distinction between the two and who must make us reconsider the source of the division between the two forms as it has been established in the literary theory of the last century and a half. Indeed, there may be a longer and more general history that suggests a certain indivisibility of the forms for both writers and readers.[19]

Literary forms are both permissive and preventative. On the last score, they prevent writers and readers from doing things— from thinking in particular ways, making particular causal links, performing particular acts of interpretation. What follows is partly a discussion of such constraints and permissions: those that the biographical form presented to a historian of the 1980s, discussing a historical figure who was a woman (among all the other things she was), and the constraints that the form of autobiography offered to McMillan, writing her own—very odd—life story in 1927. The restrictions that the form enforced as far as *Childhood, Culture and Class* was concerned had to do with the current state of feminist biography (and the history of biographical form that it carries around its neck), with the legacy of a certain kind of women's history, and finally, and as it was in the beginning, with the subject—with McMillan—herself and the ease with which various retellings of her story had been given hagiographical shape.[20] That McMillan's life has permitted, well into the 1980s, such extensive hagiography is partly due to a Protestant tradition of life-writing, to a hermeneutic form that has drawn writers' and readers' attention to the meaning of recounted lives (rather than to their narration, their unfolding story), from the mid-seventeenth century onwards.[21]

Autobiographical writing in early modern Protestant societies situated a life within the context of God's purpose, and reckoned up its *meaning,* through the act of placing it, in written language, in the time and space of a particular spirituality. For the development of the secular form, the important point is that time and space were specified in some detail: religious and social milieux were often itemized, and it was such detailing of the material world that was important for the development of autobiographical forms. The standard histories of autobiography which we possess describe a development over the last four hundred years of a specifically historical consciousness, that is, an understanding of the self as formed by a historicized world, by an environment or setting that exists and changes independently of the human actors who find themselves within it.[22]

The spiritual biography, a parallel development to the spiritual autobiography, was exemplary in form, its purpose being not just to give an account of a life, but also to make a demonstration of the possible purposes, meanings, and uses that might be made of that life story by others. We now possess many accounts of the way in which women came to bear the greater weight of affect in the secular world of the nineteenth and twentieth centuries, and biographies of this period often employ the structures of an earlier spiritual form in order to demonstrate to readers the meaning and usefulness of the heroine's progress. In 1932 McMillan's life was offered by her first posthumous biographer, Albert Mansbridge, as an exemplar:

> So, in reality Margaret the conqueror is an inspiration to all women, hindered in their normal expression, to conquer by love and by loving serve, though the day be dark and the night looms ahead; to love as much as possible, before the chance goes. In the strength of her inspiration, life will radiate love, fulfilling itself and moving perfectly in the rhythm of the glorious purposes of God.[23]

Three centuries of readers have wanted something from the biographical form—from the purposeful tale—and still get it, if modern best-seller lists may be produced as evidence. The biography of women, produced out of publishers' women's studies lists over the last ten years, has shared a more general success, and owes much to what makes the form generally popular, which is the confirmation it offers that life stories *can* be told, that the inchoate experience of living and feeling can be marshalled into a chronology, that central and unified subjects reach the conclusion of a life, and come into possession of their own story.[24] In *The Private Lives of Victorian Women,* Valerie Sanders notes in passing the resemblance that much Victorian autobiography written by women bears to the older form, the way in which, for many women writing their own life, "the discovery of a career is preceded by a period of dullness and dissatisfaction, roughly corresponding to the mood of hopelessness associated, in spiritual autobiography, with a first conviction of sin."[25] We, the modern audiences for women's history, evidently want narratives that will explain and give meaning to so many lost lives, to what we understand to have been so much silence and repression, and we want them quite as badly as the women who actually lived the lives, and showed their desire through their particular choice of narrative form.

As a result of these developments, made by readers and writers of the form, modern biography also partakes of a kind of historical romance, or romance of history. The historical romance can be defined as a *hope* that readers hold (their particular expectation of any particular text being a reflection of a much wider one), that that which is gone, that which is irretrievably lost, which is past time, can be brought back and conjured before the eyes "as it really was," and that it might be possessed. Biography takes us much closer to its subject matter than does other historical writing, and within the romance of getting closer, women must and do figure with greater depth and delight than men, for as all schoolchildren know when they are set to copy figures from the history books, the Queen is a more interesting figure to trace around than the King, possessing a plethora of lace collars, and farthingales, and ropes of hair.[26] It is by the satisfactory *detail* they offer—which can be sartorial, emotional, domestic—that women are the visible heroines of the historical romance, and the biography usually offers a very clear telling of it.

It may be satisfying, but it is also very dull, for there is a less sexy and more practical point to make here about the popularity of biography as a form, and that is that its seeming innocence also outlines its *boringness*. Biography does not have the theoretical glamour of the problematized popular forms, such as detective fiction or the gothic. It can present itself as respectable and worthy, particularly when it operates under the banner of history, but it is not the intellectual firecracker that autobiography has become, there is "something inescapably second-rate that seems to cling to biography and its practitioners."[27] It may be hailed, as Robert M. Young has recently hailed it, as the "basic discipline for human science," but to do this is to claim no more than that all of us find abstract ideas or the theoretical structure of unfamiliar disciplines easier to understand and appropriate if they are presented in their evolution through the life story of philosophers and scientists and other theoreticians.[28]

The popularity of biography as a form also allows an observation about a legacy of women's history, produced over the last twenty years, that might be described as an altered sense of the historical meaning and importance of female *insignificance*. The absence of women from conventional historical accounts, discussion of this absence, and discussion of the real archival difficulties that lie in the way of presenting their lives in a historical context, are at the same time a massive assertion of the littleness of what lies hidden.[29] A sense of that which is lost, never to be recovered completely, is one of the most powerful organizing devices of modern women's history. The sadness of its effect is also to be found in much working-class history, where indeed, a greater number of lives lie lost. But a comparison between the two forms—people's history and women's history— demonstrates that in the latter case, loss and absence remain exactly that, in a way that is not the case in the writing of working-class history. Until very recently the organizing principles of working-class history—the annals of labor, class struggle, the battles (particularly the good fights of trade union history) that could be seen to foreshadow a greater and final revolutionary struggle—all allowed the lack of detail about working lives a greater *prefigurative* force than women's history can allow the women whose absence it notes from the written and recorded past. Oppression and repression have a *meaning* within the narrative structure of people's history and labor history in a way that is not the case in women's history.

We could say then that women's absence from conventional historical accounts is "meaningless" in this particular way. At the same time, it is important to distinguish "meaninglessness" from the literary delineation of "uneventfulness," which has been a structuring idea within the biography of women for longer than the last twenty years. Lives of heroines have been written as the eruption from uneventfulness into public life, and that early life has been presented through a domestic detail that asserts how little really happened in it. The nineteenth-century heroine of modern biography remains perforce an exceptional and unusual figure whose life story explains only itself. The exceptional female figure is produced out of the biographer's use of a personal, or individual, frame of time. Early uneventfulness, in which nothing much happens to the heroine, is seen to produce and structure what happens later within a public arena. In this way, the public life is presented as a reverse image of the old, private, and uneventful life, rather than as a product of the interaction between the subject and the political and social circumstances in which she finds herself. So, as Valerie Sanders noted, just as in the tradition of exemplary religious biography from an earlier period, spirituality (that which is created in adversity, in isolation, in a life in which "nothing happened") is understood to shape and form later conduct.

A theoretical and historical understanding of the insignificance of women's lives in the past did indeed place the biographer of a woman who lived a public life in a political space in some conceptual and organizational difficulty. The problem was this: in the political culture in which Margaret McMillan operated, women were not an absence by simple virtue of their disenfranchisement, nor by the social and legal barriers to their action; rather, their absence and obscurity were organized by a wide variety of political thought, and by various theories of femininity. These actually allowed women to operate politically across a wide arena, and it was one of the purposes of my book to outline the historical setting that provided that sphere of action.

A further difficulty was presented by the way in which old assumptions about an individuality formed in struggle and isolation are reinforced by a modern psychology of women, in which particular domestic struggles are universalized, and calls are made for the structure of biography to follow a delineated female life-cycle.[30] A struggle with a father is then seen to mirror and foreshadow a social struggle against the assumptions of a patriarchal society. Women's dependency and failure to break from it is understood as a transhistorical factor, and allows a life story to be constructed in terms of relationships with others and the vicissitudes of those relationships. That a particular pleasure lies in such personal accounts, and that readers search after such personal and domestic detail in male biography and wish that there were more of it, should not blind us to the fact that a biographer has made a choice of narrative construction, and decided to elevate the affective and the personal above political and social context.

But Margaret McMillan left no collection of papers, no journal with which to peel away the layers of public form in order to reveal the "true" woman. There could be no attempt to unveil her for the delectation of an audience, for there were no secrets to tell about her. Within the form, such secrets are usually sexual, and McMillan appears never to have had a sexual relationship with anyone. In *Childhood, Culture and Class* her relationship to children, to her own childhood and that of the working-class children whose cause she espoused, and in particular, her passionate and sensual depictions of various children, both real and fictional, may be seen to function as that kind of central "secret," the relationship that explains the trajectory of a life. But in fact, what was important about McMillan was precisely that these were not solely individual and personal relationships; rather, her public and political significance lay in the fact that she gave expression to a large-scale cultural shift in understanding of the self that had to do with ideas and theories of development and growth in the human subject and a new relationship to time. "The child" (that is, real children and child-figures) embodied this understanding that was conceptualized across a wide variety of public forms at the turn of the century. As a politician, an orator, and a journalist, McMillan's own reconceptualization had particular and far-reaching historical *effects*, but it was not hers alone.

She seemed then to be a woman who demanded a public life; in some way, she prevented the delineation of an inside that is "personal" and "real" and that lies beneath the public persona; she appeared to ask for a biographical telling that took as its central device the arresting rhetorical moment of the woman on the public platform, or even more appropriately, the woman in the public square, in the Market Place, Nottingham, during the miners' strike of 1893, when an obscure young draper's assistant leaving his counter and going outside to be uplifted by her words was "touched by something vaguely, unattainably fine."[31]

It was Mikhail Bakhtin who, in discussing Greek rhetorical autobiography and biography, showed us the public square, the place and form of the ancient state, and the civic funeral orations and memorial speeches delivered there, in which spoken and valedictory biographies "there was not, nor could there be, anything intimate or private, secret or personal . . . [where] the individual is open on all sides, he is all surface."[32] To have actually found Margaret McMillan in a public square was a moment to gladden the heart of the historian. But though that moment may be used, as I tried to use it, to draw the reader's attention to the dead weight of interiority that hangs about the neck of women and their depiction, it is not of course possible now in the late twentieth century to dissolve the boundary between inside and outside. However, the moment can be used as a trope that might alert us to a *historical* argument about McMillan's significance. Her "insideness," her meaning, which was her remaking and reassertion of childhood, actually spells out the public space of cultural change. What is more, McMillan's own writing and her odd evasion of autobiography might lead us to the speculation that in the recent historical past—and against the grain of modern theories of subjectivity—there is to be found at least one person who in the act of figuring herself did not create a split and fragmented self, but a most powerfully integrated self, so that in this particular case, the woman might stand there and speak in the public square.

The speaker tells stories about herself. McMillan told many, particularly writing and rewriting various narratives of childhood that had their origins in her own. To consider a life story in fictional terms is not to suggest that its subject told lies about herself, or practiced more genteel or general concealments. It is rather to propose that as well as all the other things that they do with a life, people imagine themselves and make public presentations of themselves by using a society's fictional forms. What is available to people depends on their socialization and their education as well as on their class circumstances, and the forms of popular romance, myth, or melodrama are only the most obviously chosen. In McMillan's case it was useful to speculate about the stage training that she received, and the means of manipulating and refining the popular form of the public lecture with which it probably provided her. Such performance, in person and in writing, allowed her to negotiate the difficulties of being a single woman from an uncertain class background and difficult childhood, allowed her a way of circumnavigating the awkwardness that she felt about herself. At first, it was McMillan's audiences—others—who labeled her a female magus, the possessor of great wisdom and almost mystic powers and knowledge. But after her sister Rachel's death in 1917, it is possible to see her own mythic appropriation and use of her childhood, an appropriation she effected by eliding her own story with that of Rachel, and by telling it in the guise of her sister's. The constant movement between herself and the dead Rachel in *Life of Rachel McMillan,* the handing over of herself and her past to the image of Rachel, meant that in making her sister a saint, she made herself one too.

To have found herself and a mission in life through work with children was not an unusual solution to the problem of a woman's

life in this period. What I tried to present as particular and interesting about McMillan's writing of childhood, and the connection
of her own selfhood with working-class childhood, was that it
formed part of a *socialist* vision. The political particularity was
useful: having begun to outline the ideological framework to
McMillan's claims for children, we may be in a better position to
uncover and specify other theories of childhood, in this and other
historical periods.

McMillan's theoretical understanding of childhood was as a
phenomenon that could act as a form of agency, a means of
bringing about great social change. Quite particularly, after McMillan
had healed children in her clinic and camp-school, had washed and
fed them, straightened their limbs by remedial gymnastics and
removed their diseased tonsils, working-class parents were to see in
their restored and beautiful children the exact measure of what
they had been deprived. They would then cast their lot with the
political wing of the labor movement, vote for one of its political
parties, and bring about even greater social change.

This political project has to be understood by considering the
subjects upon which and with whom McMillan performed her
life's work—not women, not working-class women—but children.
In general, it can be said that during the nineteenth century the
state of childhood came to be understood as an extension of the
self: an extension in time, into the future, and an extension of
depth and space, of individual interiority—a way of describing the
place lying deep within the individual soul; always a lost place, but
at the same time, *always there.* We, as late-twentieth-century inheri-
tors of this Romantic and post-Romantic configuration, are probably most familiar with it in the form of psychoanalytic description
of depth and interiority mapped out in childhood and carried
unconsciously through life. McMillan used and worked with some
of these ideas; but at the same time—her biography makes this
clear—the means of symbolizing the self through the image of
childhood was available from many other sources at the end of the
last century. McMillan's work and writing reveals such heterogeneous sources as, for example, the mainstream of nineteenth-
century realist fiction and neurological science. The particularly
interesting use made by McMillan of a wide variety of literary
reconstructions of childhood, in particular her effacement of her-

self in the chapters of *Life of Rachel McMillan* that contain her sister's *Jugenderinnerungen* have already been mentioned. Through working on McMillan's use of these literary forms, I gained some insight into the way in which the literary and cultural construct of "childhood," in which children appear as serious representatives of the human condition, is one that is bound to be in conflict with itself, for it has to operate by denying in some way that childhood is merely a stage in human development and that children grow up and go away.

I came to understand through a growing acquaintance with McMillan's writing and thought how very little distinction we make (are able to make) between real children and our fantasy children, that we want something from them, desire them, want the thing we can't have, which is the past: our own lost childhood. Now, with an account of McMillan's life and work completed, a question becomes clear that was not clear before. What are the implications of the kind of symbolizing of childhood that McMillan tried to put on a political agenda? What is the import of our various theories of childhood, implicitly or overtly held? There is much work to be done here, though we do have sketch-maps held towards an answer, mainly drawn up by the literary theorists on whose work I relied so heavily. It seems to me that this is how we must start, in literary and representational terms, by recognizing that children are the first metaphor for all people, whether they have children or not, whether they are literate and in the business of constructing literary metaphors or not: a mapping of analogy and meaning for the self, always in shape and form *like us*, the visual connection plain to see. As they are produced materially out of women's bodies, and as in all known societies women, whether actual mothers or not, have played the greater role in their care, we should expect variation in the uses of childhood made by men and women; but not that much variation, as it is in the power of children to represent the loss of the self and the extension of the self into the future that the theoretical purchase lies. The history of women—certainly this now completed history of one woman—will always take us somewhere else, in this case to a history of socialist thought in Britain, to a history of the idea of childhood in European thought.

Told in this way, McMillan's life story allows a spectacle of the determined accretion of stories around other stories, autobiographies around other tellings of a life. When the task of actually doing it (writing it) is over, there are the modest pleasures that consciousness of literary form and rhetorical organization actually bring: the way in which it could be argued, for instance, that my biographical study carried with it its own engine of internal deconstruction, and foregrounded its major source, which was McMillan's own *Life of Rachel McMillan*, and showed how the living Margaret canonized the dead Rachel, so that this *doppelganger* bore the whole narrative of McMillan's life. The biography that McMillan wrote (and mine, of her) both could then serve as an exploration of a romantic variant of the form, in which the biographer seeks a shade of herself in the subject she delineates in the pages of her book. However, at the prosaic and technical level of organization and writing, the solution to my intense anxiety *not to write a biography*, my determination to subject the genre of historical biography to scrutiny and to steer an individual life story towards collectivity, was to present McMillan's life as briefly as possible, and then to take up a series of themes raised by its telling—"socialism," "childhood," "women,"—there were twelve of them in all—and deal with them in a series of linked essays.

I do not think now that my attempt to hack away the constraints of the biographical form—to write history, not biography—were entirely successful, for the historical narrative, whatever form it takes, is in some kind of conflict with the written life story, in both its biographical and autobiographical mode. This conflict can be seen most clearly if we consider history, biography, and autobiography as forms of narrative, and history as a narrative form that has its own—highly convincing—rhetoric of persuasion.

The account I gave of McMillan was presented as a form of history, and that presentation must be seen as its own rhetorical device, allowing the writer to present a plot that seemingly *had* to be shaped in a particular way, according to what the documents used for its composition authorized, or what they forbade. The writer of any kind of historical narrative can always present herself as the invisible servant of archive material, as merely uncovering what already lies there, waiting to be told.[33] The historian is always able in this way to appropriate to him or herself the most massive authority as a storyteller. And even if the historian does not do this, even if she tells the story in a more speculative way, allowing that things might have happened in a different manner, or that there are different interpretations available, then still there are the decencies of the craft to measure: the huge weight of footnotes at the end of the volume of history, the list of archives consulted, that appear to say, here, look: you may write down the accession number, take the train to the distant city, call for the papers, untie the bundle and see then that it is the truth that is being told here, or at least see that the interpretation made of what lies in those papers is both possible and reasonable. And again, the authority of the historian as narrator is confirmed.

If stories are only truly narrativized when they take on the same meaning for the listener as they have for the teller, then they come to an end when there is no more to be said, when teller and audience both understand that the point that has been reached, this end-place, this conclusion, was implicit in the beginning, was there all along.[34] In spoken and written autobiography, there is in operation a simple variant of this narrative rule. The man or woman, leaning up against the bar or writing a book, is the embodiment of something completed. That end, the finished place, is the human being, a body in time and space, telling a story, a story that brings the listener or the reader to the here and now, or to this finished character in the pages of the book. And this argument holds good no matter how much we may learn of the fragmented nature of the form, of the endless rewriting of the eighteenth-century life story, of the hundreds of hack hands that Defoe's Moll passed through, for instance, to feed the chap-book market.[35] Written autobiography still ends in the figure of the writer, and the narrative closure of biography is the figure that has been created through the pages of the book.

In narrative terms like this, these forms of writing—biography and autobiography—must always remain in conflict with the writing of history, which does indeed come to conclusions and reach ends, but which actually moves forward through the implicit understanding that *things are not over*, that the story isn't finished, can't ever be completed, for some new item of information may alter the account as it has been given. In this way the writing of history represents a distinct cognitive process precisely because it is constructed around the understanding that things are not over, that the story isn't finished: that there is no end. In fact, in their day-to-day practice, historians do know and acknowledge this. Closures have to be made in order to finish arguments and get manuscripts to publishers, but the story can't be finished because there is always the possibility that some new piece of evidence will alter the argument and the account. Historians have as their stated objective exhaustiveness (finding out again and again, more and more about some thing, event, or person), and they proceed upon the path of refutation by pointing to exceptions and to the possibility of exception. The practice of historical inquiry and historical writing is a recognition of temporariness and impermanence, and in this way is a quite different literary form from that of the life story in both its modes, which presents momentarily a completeness, a completeness which lies in the figure of the writer or the teller, in the here and now, saying: that's how it was; or, that's how I believe it to have been. At the center of the written history, on the other hand, lies some kind of recognition of temporariness and impermanence.

I t is because the historical story is contingent in this way that Clio doesn't care. To imagine Clio in this way, as the blank-faced girl with nothing to say, is to recognize history as a form of cognition and a form of writing, to understand that for historians as well as all the other people who use history in their various ways, history cannot work as either cognition or written narrative without the assumption on the part of the writer and the reader that there is somewhere the great story that contains everything there is and ever has been—"visits home, heartbeats, a first kiss, the jump of an electron from one orbital position to another," as well as the desolate battlefield, the ruined village—from which the smaller story, the one before your eyes now—in this case, a woman's story—has simply been extracted.[36] What the meeting of women's history with Clio's vacant, encompassing gaze might effect—at last—is an abandonment of the *artisanat* tendencies of historians in general, that historians of women share: their collective contentment to let others do their historiography for them. That meeting might force some consideration by historians of what kind of act the *writing* of history is, what the form they are using permits, what it prevents: what kind of tale they're telling.

NOTES

1. Terry Lovell, *British Feminist Thought* (Oxford, 1990), 21–67.

2. *Ibid.*, 51–67.

3. Sally Humphries, "What Is Women's History," in *What Is History Today?*, ed. Juliet Gardiner (London, 1988), 87. Dave Morley and Ken Worpole, eds., *The Republic of Letters: Working Class Writing and Local Publishing* (London, 1982).

4. Rita Felski, *Beyond Feminist Aesthetics: Feminist Literature and Social Change* (London, 1989), 19–50.

5. Lovell, *British Feminist Thought*, 23.

6. "You had nothing to say and did not, one could see/Observe where you were, Muse of the unique /Historical fact." W. H. Auden, "Homage to Clio," *Collected Shorter Poems, 1927–1957* (London, 1966), 309.

7. Steven Knapp, *Personification and the Sublime: Milton to Coleridge* (Cambridge, Mass., 1985).

8. Carolyn Steedman, "True Romances," in *Patriotism: The Making and Unmaking of British National Identity*, ed. Raphael Samuel (London, 1989), 26–35; Steedman, "Living Historically Now?" *Arena* 97 (Summer 1991): 48–64.

9. Carolyn Steedman, "'Public' and 'Private' in Women's Lives," *Journal of Historical Sociology* 3 (September 1990): 294–304.

10. For the evolution of the notion, see Catherine Hall, "The Early Formation of Victorian Domestic Ideology," in *Fit Work for Women*, ed. Sandra Burman (London, 1979). Catherine Hall, "Private Persons versus Public Someones: Class, Gender and Politics in England, 1780–1850," in Carolyn Steedman, Cathy Urwin, and Valerie Walkerdine, *Language, Gender and Childhood* (London, 1985), 10–33. Leonore Davidoff and Catherine Hall, *Family Fortunes: Men and Women of the English Middle Class, 1780–1950* (London, 1987).

11. Winifred Gerin, *Elizabeth Gaskell: A Biography* (Oxford, 1976), 72; Jane Austen, *Mansfield Park* (1814, reprinted Harmondsworth, Eng., 1988); Ralph M. Wardle, *Collected Letters of Mary Wollstonecraft* (Ithaca, N.Y., 1979), 120–133; for Mrs. Carson, Elizabeth Gaskell, *Mary Barton* (1848, reprinted Harmondsworth, Eng., 1970), 254–266.

12. Julia Parker, *Women and Welfare: Ten Victorian Women and Social Service* (London, 1989), 12–13.

13. Mary Poovey, *The Proper Lady and the Woman Writer: Ideology as Style in the Works of Mary Wollstonecraft, Mary Shelley and Jane Austen* (Chicago and London, 1984), 3–47; Nancy Armstrong, *Desire and Domestic Fiction: A Political History of the Novel* (New York, 1987).

14. Janet Todd and Marilyn Butler, eds., *The Works of Mary Wollstonecraft*, vol. 4, *Thoughts on the Education of Daughters: With Reflections on Female Conduct in the More Important Duties of Life* (1787, reprinted London, 1989), 38–39.

15. Steedman, *Childhood, Culture and Class in Britain* (London and New Brunswick, N.J., 1990).

16. Viviana A. Zelizer, *Pricing the Priceless Child: The Changing Social Value of Children* (New York, 1985).

17. Margaret McMillan, *Life of Rachel McMillan* (London, 1927).

18. For an account of the excitements of autobiography, see Laura Marcus, "'Enough about You, Let's Talk about Me': Recent Autobiographical Writing," *New Formations* 1 (Spring 1987): 77–94. For the theoretical dullness of biography, in a book that belies its title, see Eric Homberger and John Charmley, eds., *The Troubled*

Face of Biography (London, 1988). For a mission statement about theorizing and glamorizing biography, see William H. Epstein, *Recognizing Biography* (Philadelphia, 1987), 1–12.

19.   On this point, see Felicity Nussbaum, *The Autobiographical Subject: Gender and Ideology in Eighteenth-Century England* (Baltimore and London, 1989), 1–29.

20.   Elizabeth Bradburn, *Margaret McMillan, Framework and Expansion of Nursery Education* (Redhill, Eng., 1976); Bradburn, *Margaret McMillan: Portrait of a Pioneer* (London, 1989); D'Arcy Cresswell, *Margaret McMillan: A Memoir* (London, 1948); Albert Mansbridge, *Margaret McMillan, Prophet and Pioneer: Her Life and Work* (London, 1932).

21.   Linda H. Peterson, *Victorian Autobiography* (New Haven, 1986), 7–22.

22.   Roy Pascal, *Design and Truth in Autobiography* (London, 1960); John Morris, *Versions of the Self: Studies in English Biography from John Bunyan to John Stuart Mill* (New York, 1966); David Vincent, *Bread, Knowledge and Freedom: A Study of Nineteenth-Century Working Class Autobiography* (London, 1981).

23.   Mansbridge, *Margaret McMillan, Prophet and Pioneer*, 167.

24.   In Homberger and Charmley, eds., *The Troubled Face of Biography*, the editors make what I think is essentially the same point in the following way: "The broad appeal of biography is reassuring. It suggests that in our interest in the lives of others there is at least the possibility, the hint of a surviving common culture." Homberger and Charmley, "Introduction." See Felski, *Beyond Feminist Aesthetics*, *15–16, 86–121*, on the popularity of women's confessional writing in the realist mode.

25.   Valerie Sanders, *The Private Lives of Victorian Women: Autobiography in Nineteenth-Century England* (Brighton, Eng., 1989), 81.

26.   For a development of this argument, see Steedman, "True Romances," 26–35.

27.   Robert Skidelsky, "Only Connect: Biography and Truth," in Homberger and Charmley, eds., *The Troubled Face of Biography*, 1.

28.   Robert M. Young, "Biography: The Basic Discipline for Human Science," *Free Associations* 11 (1988): 108–130.

29.   A point indicated by Elizabeth Fox-Genovese, "Placing Women's History in History," *New Left Review* 133 (1982), but not argued through there. A particularly effective example of the sadness of this absence is to be found in Davidoff and Hall, *Family Fortunes*, "Prologue" and "Epilogue."

30.   Ruth Oldenziel, "Gender, Self and the Writing of Biography," paper presented to the International Conference on Women's History, 1986; Estelle C. Jellinek, ed., *Women's Autobiography: Essays in Criticism*, (Bloomington, 1980). For a brief comment on claims like these, see Natalie Zemon Davis, "What Is Women's History?," in Gardiner, ed., *What Is History Today?*, 85–87.

31.   Percy Redfern, *Journey to Understanding* (London, 1946), 18–19.

32.   Mikhail Bakhtin, *The Dialogic Imagination: Four Essays*, ed. Michael Holquist (Austin, 1981), 130–146.

33.   On this point, see Carolyn Steedman, "Prisonhouses," *Feminist Review* 20 (Summer 1985): 7–21.

34.   Louis O. Mink, "Everyman His or Her Own Annalist," *Critical Inquiry* 7 (1981): 777–783.

35.   Nussbaum, *The Autobiographical Subject*, 17–19.

36.   Paul A. Roth, "Narrative Explanations: The Case of History," *History and Theory* 27 (1988): 1–13.

Feminist Theory and Historical Practice
Rereading Elizabeth Blackwell

REGINA MORANTZ-SANCHEZ

In the last thirty years, ever since Thomas Kuhn demonstrated that culture has historically influenced the pursuit of science and helped shape which scientific paradigms eventually prevail, the image of scientific knowledge as neutral, value-free, and privileged has become slightly tarnished. Indeed, post-Kuhnian debates within a variety of disciplines have only added to suspicions that the structures of knowledge that have informed and dominated Western culture since the Enlightenment are less authoritative than they originally seemed. Busy philosophers from many different perspectives are rejecting the foundationalism that has guided the post-Enlightenment search for "truth," itself premised on the belief that thoughtful and reasonable people can, indeed, explain the world as it actually exists. Instead, they prefer versions of William James's argument that "What we say about reality . . . depends on the perspective in which we throw it."[1]

Meanwhile, historians and sociologists have looked into the social production of science, asking questions about how power struggles among various groups, institutional rivalries, competing research programs, cultural worlds, and social processes unique to a particular, historically specific collective order structured the pursuit, indeed the very definition, of scientific activity. Finally, assorted poststructuralists and thinkers interested in the archeology and sociology of knowledge have focused on the relationship among language, the creation of individual consciousness, social organization, and power, offering alternative epistemological ap-

The author wishes to thank George Sanchez, Ann Lombard, Mario Biagoli, Emily Abel, Anita Clair Fellman, Margaret Finnegan, Barbara Bair, Gerald Grob, and especially Louise Newman, who rendered helpful critical readings of this essay.

proaches, not only to what we can know, but how what we think we know came to be.

While such thinking has raised fundamental questions about the nature of truth, objectivity, rationality, empiricism, observation, and experience, all of which lead inevitably toward a social constructivist view of science, feminist theorists have been diligently making their own contribution to this collective critical endeavor. First, they have turned their attention to separating gender from biological sex as a category of analysis, arguing that "woman" and "man" are historically produced social classifications fashioned, as is science itself, through culture. Second, as historians, sociologists, and philosophers, they have taken to heart Virginia Woolf's observation in *Three Guineas* that "Science . . . is not sexless; she is a man," and have demonstrated how the identification of objectivity, reason, and mind as male and subjectivity, feeling, and nature as female developed over time.[2]

The results have been especially exciting for historians interested in the biological sciences and medicine, because we have been given leave to look at science in a new, more critical light. Scholars such as Londa Schiebinger, Thomas Laqueur, Cynthia Russett, Ludmilla Jordanova, Ornella Moscucci, Joan Brumberg, and others, have written especially intriguing accounts of how various medical scientists, all the while viewing themselves as investigators free of the distortions of desire and advocacy, constructed medicine and the natural sciences in a manner that reinforced the subordination, exclusion, and marginalization of women. We learn, for example, that the elimination of women from science was neither inadvertent nor inevitable, but came about because of the confluence of a specific set of historical developments. Moreover, politics, male anxiety about shifts in power relations between the sexes, social and political upheaval, professional concerns, and changes in the family all had an impact on the production of knowledge regarding the female body, including the "discovery," definition, and treatment of a wide range of female ailments, from anorexia nervosa to fibroid tumors.[3]

In what follows, I, too, plan to use the insights of contemporary feminist and critical theory, both as a tool for demonstrating how past medical science became a gendered enterprise and as a means for retrieving submerged and marginalized alternatives to dominant modes of scientific discourse. I wish to offer a critical rereading of the writings of a particularly significant nineteenth-century woman physician, Elizabeth Blackwell. I will demonstrate that Blackwell, faced with rapidly changing definitions of science in medicine at the end of the nineteenth century, remained critical of "objectivity" as the "best" form of knowing and suspicious of the laboratory medicine that promoted it so enthusiastically. Her response makes her a fascinating, if problematic, intellectual antecedent to contemporary critiques of radical objectivity and scientific reductionism. I shall argue that Blackwell deserves a place in a tradition that includes, not just present-day poststructuralist theorists, but feminist philosophers and thinkers such as Sara Ruddick, Evelyn Fox Keller, Sandra Harding, Ruth Bleier, Iris Murdoch, Nancy Hartstock, and others.

I have written about Elizabeth Blackwell before. In an essay conceived almost a decade and a half ago, I compared her ideas regarding women in medicine with another accomplished nineteenth- century woman physician, Mary Putnam Jacobi. At the time my primary concern was to raise objections to some prevailing notions about pioneer women physicians that represented them as a unified, coherent voice unalterably critical of male-dominated medical practice. I argued that women doctors—as citizens, as professionals, as clinicians, as framers of cultural and medical discourse—demonstrated a considerable range of views and behaviors. Among these pioneers, I selected two individuals who held divergent ideas about the role and capabilities of women in medicine and speculated that their differences were linked to starkly contrasting assessments of developments in medical science.

On the eve of the bacteriological revolution, which at the time I took rather uncritically to be the dawn of modern "scientific" medical practice, I found Jacobi receptive to and excited about the promise of the laboratory, while Blackwell, troubled by the new developments, brooded about the dangers of "medical materialism," a term she used to accuse laboratory physicians of likening the body to a machine and turning real patients into objects. I tried to understand what kept Blackwell so hesitant, especially because I was impressed with her ability to predict from the vantage point of the end of the century how ambiguous would be the legacy of the new science. She guessed correctly, for example, that one possible outcome of making medicine an applied science would be a less humane and holistic approach to patient care.

To borrow from the language of contemporary feminism—language not readily available thirteen years ago—Blackwell spoke like a "difference feminist." She focused primarily on women's difference from men and occasionally, though not consistently, she essentialized those differences. In other words, she sometimes referred to certain "female" attributes as dictated by God, Nature, and common sense, rather than seeing them as effects of a historically and culturally specific gender system. Though I was deeply sympathetic to her privileging of the qualities of nurturing and caring which our culture identifies with women, I found Jacobi's hardheaded concern to integrate women doctors into the profession as quickly and as quietly as possible and her willingness to play down sex differences more congenial to my own personal struggles as a professional historian.[4]

Part of the problem was that women's historians had hardly begun to use gender as a category of analysis. We wrote primarily about the varied and complex landscape of women's *experience*. We were only just beginning to define gender as a *system of representation* that gave meaning to biology and structured social relationships in society at large.[5] Moreover, feminist thinkers had not yet produced the theoretical work that would have helped me view more critically both Jacobi's fierce commitment to scientific objectivity, as well as my own determination to write "objective" history. Consequently, I lacked the theoretical tools that could have facilitated a different assessment of Blackwell's significance to the fields of intellectual history, medicine, and gender studies. I believed along with Jacobi that women were *not* different from men in any *essential* way. Blackwell's special pleading on behalf of them made me profoundly uneasy, and I remained ambivalent about her contention that women who entered medicine would occupy "positions men cannot fully occupy," and exercise "an influence which men cannot wield at all."[6]

Since that time, an entirely new field of gender and science studies has appeared.[7] In addition, historians of medicine have begun to look more carefully at the relationships among epistemology, knowledge, and practice and have identified competing notions of science and professionalism at the end of the nineteenth century. Their findings have changed my understanding of Blackwell's struggles with bacteriology and have enabled me to locate her ideas within a larger professional community. Finally, feminist thinkers have been hard at work exposing the critical tensions in feminist theory itself, especially regarding what many have called "sameness" and "difference" feminism. In the process of trying to recover women's various voices out from under hegemonic male discourse, we have become more sympathetic to the feminine. We have also been made aware of how simple assertions of equality can hurt women by ignoring a number of socially constructed disadvantages—in education, work, and family life, for example—that remain very much a part of most women's daily lives.[8]

These new refinements in theory and historical practice have driven me back to some of the questions that remained unresolved in my earlier examination of Elizabeth Blackwell. Why was I both attracted and repelled by her ideas? Why did she seem prescient and backward-looking at once? In the pages that follow I will try to answer some of these questions. I will begin by returning briefly to her theories and to her medical world. I will then sketch out some of the feminist critiques of science that resonate most deeply with her ideas. In conclusion, I will reassess her contribution as an eyewitness to medicine's late-nineteenth-century scientific revolution.

Best remembered as America's first woman doctor, Elizabeth Blackwell (1821–1910) was, in fact, more than just a professional pioneer. She was also a self-conscious reformer who saw the practice of medicine as an opportunity for women to bring about fundamental social change. As a founder of the woman's medical movement in the United States and in England, she spent much of her life formulating and disseminating these ideas.

A member of a prominent, reform-minded family, her interest in moral reform antedated her attraction to medicine. Forced to study privately for several years while she searched for a school that would train her, Blackwell was finally accepted at Geneva Medical College in upstate New York. She gained the degree in 1849, after which she sought more training in Paris and London. In 1856, she, her sister Emily, also a doctor, and another recent medical graduate, Dr. Marie Zakrezewska, founded the New York Infirmary for

Women and Children, a showcase hospital and women's medical school run and staffed by women that lasted until the end of the century. In 1869, Blackwell settled permanently in England, where she continued to be a prominent spokesperson on behalf of female physicians until her death in 1910.

Blackwell completed her medical training at mid-century, when the role of the physician was shaped by a traditional system of belief and behavior that still explained sickness, not as the specific affliction of a particular part of the body, but as a condition affecting the entire organism. Therapy was consequently designed to treat the whole patient; the science of medicine lay with the doctor's ability to select the proper drug in the proper dose to bring about the proper physiological effect. To be sure, this task required a thorough knowledge of the therapeutic armamentarium, but it demanded "art" as well: the good practitioner was familiar with the patient's unique personal history and familial influences, all of which were assessed. Physicians treated patients in their own homes, a social context that emphasized the sacredness of personal ties with clients and the relevance of family history to clinical judgments. Professional identity itself was embedded in these ritualized interactions between doctors and patients; individualized treatment gave testimony to the character, moral sensitivity, and therapeutic acumen of the practitioner.[9]

In 1849 Blackwell found herself in Paris at the tail end of a thirty-year period in which its medical institutions, reorganized and revitalized after the French Revolution, became vibrant centers of clinical learning, attracting hoards of students from England and the United States. At the core of Parisian medicine was "the birth of the clinic"—the gathering together of vast patient populations in a government sponsored hospital system that provided clinicians and their students free access to patients' bodies for physical examination, observation, the gathering of statistics, autopsy. Here, Blackwell, like many other American physicians who came to Paris between 1820 and 1860, learned to mistrust the highly rationalistic systems that had dominated American medicine in the first half of the century. While older physicians still believed in certain laws of disease that tended to simplify and routinize practice, Blackwell and others put their faith in clinical empiricism. Observation, experience, painstaking differential diagnosis, individualized treatment—these are the lessons she learned in Paris.[10]

Advocates considered this empirical framework wholly scientific, but Blackwell and her contemporaries understood the word "science" differently than we do today. For example, few physicians in the nineteenth century would have ignored the importance of intuitive or subjective factors in successful diagnosis and treatment. "The model of the body, health and disease," Charles Rosenberg has written, "was all inclusive, antireductionist, capable of incorporating every aspect of man's life in explaining his physical condition. Just as man's body interacted continuously with his environment, so did his mind with his body, his morals with his health. The realm of causation in medicine was not distinguishable from the realm of meaning in society generally."[11] Blackwell's colleague at the Woman's Medical College of Pennsylvania, Professor Henry Hartshorne, who held a professorship of hygiene similar to the one Blackwell had created for herself at the Woman's Medical College of the New York Infirmary, could have been speaking for her when he observed in an 1872 commencement address:

> It is not always the most logical, but often the most discerning physician who succeeds best at the bedside. Medicine is indeed, a science, but its practice is an art. Those who bring the quick eye, the receptive ear, and delicate touch, intensified, all of them, by a warm sympathetic temperament . . . may use the learning of laborious accumulators, often, better than they themselves could do.[12]

Taking Hartshorne's admonitions to heart, Blackwell developed an approach to her profession which was as much shaped by her moral and religious beliefs as it was by her scientific training. Her early influences were Christian evangelism, New England Transcendentalism, Swedenborgianism, and Kantian philosophy. She adhered to an idealist metaphysics and epistemology which she combined with Christian socialism. Thus, her enthusiasm for French empiricism did not include embracing its tendency to separate the body from the soul. Like many American and English visitors to Paris, she was highly critical of how French clinicians treated their patients. She shared a widespread belief that the French preferred the impersonal aspects of scientific investigation over the art of healing and cared more about gathering data than curing disease. Forty years later, she still remembered vividly a visit with the great experimental physiologist Claude Bernard in 1850, who, though not a clinician himself, represented for her the moral failings of Parisian medical practice. When she asked him how his investigations "could be applied to the benefit of man," Bernard replied that "the time had not come for the deductions I sought; experimenters were simply accumulating facts." Medical schools, she argued, "whilst sharpening the intellectual faculties of their students," must take care not to neglect "the moral sense" which was, she believed, "indispensable to the physician in his relations with patients."[13]

Advances in Parisian physiology ultimately discredited the traditional heavy dosing characteristic of the prevailing medical systems. By mid-century, many clinicians emphasized French *médecine expectante*, citing the self-limiting quality of most disease. Increasingly skeptical of the utility of traditional drug therapy, many sought merely to minimize pain and suffering and "wait on nature." Practitioners like Blackwell responded by elevating the "art" of medicine to even greater importance.

In addition, Blackwell was a "sanitarian" in her conviction that there was a social, political, and moral component to sickness. The professional community with which she had the most contact, especially after her move to England, consisted of physicians and social reformers who believed that the health of the body and the health of the body politic were inevitably linked. Sanitary science, which arose as a response to the poverty and disease generated by industrial development, advocated social change guided by scientific knowledge and humanitarian concern.[14] Indeed, many physicians saw hygienic management as the best means of furthering clinical medicine, and some advocated public prevention as a way out of the excessive skepticism and therapeutic gloom generated by Paris medicine's denigration of traditional dosing.[15]

When a series of dramatic bacteriological discoveries were announced in the last two decades of the nineteenth century, they came as a welcome relief to some of Blackwell's contemporaries. But especially for a new generation of practitioners younger than Blackwell, the germ theory offered the paradigm of experimental science as a way out of the doldrums of therapeutic stagnation.

Researchers had not only begun to isolate pathogenic bacteria for numerous epidemic diseases. They fashioned as well a new ideology of science in medicine consisting of an acceptance of the germ theory, the identification of specific diseases, increasing specialization within medical practice, and a growing willingness to resort to evidence produced in the laboratory. While older practitioners trained before mid-century continued to emphasize the importance of clinical observation and the inevitability of individual differences in treatment, those enthralled with experimental science argued that the chemical and physiological principles derived from laboratory work must inform therapeutics. Patient idiosyncrasies and environmental differences were gradually stripped of their significance, while reductionist and universalistic criteria for treatment took their place. Inevitably, the experimental therapeutist focused less on the patient and more on the physiological process under investigation. The result was a competing definition of what constituted science in medicine and "a thoroughgoing rearrangement of the relationships among therapeutic practice, knowledge, and professional identity."[16]

Blackwell did not share in the high hopes accompanying the new discoveries in the laboratory and remained suspicious of their usefulness. Like many of her colleagues, she was reluctant to de-emphasize the importance of physician-patient interaction at the bedside. Hence she was not alone in rejecting the new medical materialism or the increasingly reductionist approaches to patient care. Indeed, several historians have demonstrated how and in what ways laboratory medicine threatened the epistemological categories that had grown out of the rejection of rationalistic systems and the mid-century embrace of empiricism.[17] But what is especially intriguing about Blackwell's critique, in contrast to that of her male colleagues, is that her arguments are cast in the language of "domesticity." Moreover, her thinking about medicine was deeply influenced by her conceptions of gender. Indeed, her writings about the good practitioner frame an alternative discourse that privileged empathic expertise over the new science of the laboratory and associated the one with women and the other with men.

At the core of the nineteenth-century ideology of domesticity was the concept of the moral mother. The female qualities of nurturing, empathy, and moral superiority were depicted as naturally flowing from the experience of maternity. As the family was romanticized, women were depicted increasingly at its moral and spiritual center and assigned a pivotal role in the preservation of values intended to inform, not only family life, but the social institutions for society at large. Women's elevated moral status, however, was integrally connected to their alleged disinterestedness—not just in terms of selflessness, but also because they stood "outside" of politics. "Only by giving up all self-interest and 'living for others,'" Joan Williams has observed, "could women achieve the purity that allowed them to establish moral reference points for their families and for society at large." Suddenly women's role was invested with cosmic moral significance.[18]

Blackwell believed that motherhood, much like the practice of medicine itself, was a "remarkable specialty" because of the "spiritual principles" that underlay the ordinary tasks most mothers performed daily. These principles she labelled collectively "the spiritual power of maternity," and they informed not only her notions of moral responsibility, but her formulations of what constituted good science. Indeed, for Blackwell this power had much in common with the psychologist Erik Erikson's idea of generativity, a concern for insuring the healthy moral and physical growth of the next generation. Not only physicians, but all mankind, she argued, must learn to harness it.

And what were the lessons spiritual maternity had to teach? "The subordination of self to the welfare of others; the recognition of the claim which helplessness and ignorance make upon the stronger and more intelligent; the joy of creation and bestowal of life; the pity and sympathy which tend to make every woman the born foe of cruelty and injustice; and hope—which foresees the adult in the infant, the future in the present." These, Blackwell insisted, were great "moral tendencies;" they were insights derived from the social practice of mothering, and they could not be measured or reproduced in the laboratory.[19]

The microbe hunters posed three fundamental dangers to medicine as Blackwell understood it. First, their conception of disease etiology was reductionistic and materialistic. Laboratory researchers believed in studying nature "objectively" and assumed that they could keep themselves separate and independent from the object of study. They sought knowledge free of specific context and reducible to universal laws, generalizations, or rules. The careful investigator made an effort to strip away differences and find common elements which bound successive examples together. As John Harley Warner has observed regarding experiments on physiological processes, "it made relatively little difference whether the process was going on in an Irish immigrant or a laboratory dog."[20]

Blackwell deplored such assumptions, and not just because the laboratory physician's search for universal laws smacked too much of the old rationalistic systems her experience in Paris had led her to mistrust.[21] Though medicine deserved to be called scientific, the definition of science must not be forced within the narrow confines of bacteriology's deterministic model. "Science is not . . . " she insisted,

> an accumulation of isolated facts, or of facts torn from their natural relations. . . . Science . . . demands the exercise of our various faculties as well as of our senses. . . . Scientific method requires that all the factors which concern the subject of research shall be duly considered. . . . [For example] the facts of affection, companionship, sympathy, justice . . . exercise a powerful influence over the physical organization of all living creatures.

The "true" physician had two obligations to the patient: to cure disease and to relieve suffering through empathy, or what she and most Victorians called "sympathy."[22]

Blackwell's second objection was to the practice of vivisection, an experimental tool essential to laboratory physiology. It was not so much the plight of animals that concerned her, but the process of detachment from the object of research that experiments on live animals inevitably encouraged. She believed such laboratory experiences would harden medical students and inure them to "that intelligent sympathy with suffering, which is a fundamental quality in the good physician." Soon, she predicted, they would be regarding the sick poor simply as "clinical material." Objectivity in the clinician would lead to the objectification of the patient. "The attitude of the student and doctor to the sick poor," she wrote, "is a real test of the true physician."[23]

These two fundamental objections to bacteriology inevitably led Blackwell to her third: the fear that a preoccupation with the laboratory would turn the profession away from an emphasis on clinical practice and severely threaten the doctor-patient relationship. Though research was indispensable to the physician's task, it must be focused on the patient, not on abstract physiological laws, and certainly not on the physiology of animals. Like other colleagues similarly contending with changes in medicine, Blackwell emphasized behavior over biomedical knowledge as the basis for professional identity. More important than long hours in the laboratory was a physician's skills in clinical observation and ability to maintain "character" at the bedside. "It is not a brilliant theorizer that the sick person requires," she reminded her students, "but the experience gained by careful observation and sound common-sense, united to the kindly feeling and cheerfulness which make the very sight of the doctor a cordial to the sick."[24]

Blackwell's notion of the empathic physician was essential to her conception of professionalism. By modeling the doctor-patient relationship on the interaction between mother and child, Blackwell was clearly gendering such behavior, though she was careful to assert that it was something men could learn. She went even further in her elaboration of gender dualisms, however, when she gendered the new experimental science as "male." Indeed, she blamed bacteriology on the "male intellect," and warned her students against the tyranny of male authority in medicine. "It is not blind imitation of men, nor thoughtless acceptance of whatever may be taught by them that is required," she wrote. Women students, she regretted, were as yet too "accustomed to accept the government and instruction of men as final, and it hardly occurs to them to question it."[25]

Blackwell's invocation of culturally available gender symbols to criticize bacteriology represented a contestation of changing power relationships in medicine. Her association of empathic *expertise* with femininity was something relatively new in medical discourse.[26] When we recall the comments of Henry Hartshorne cited at the beginning of this essay, we are reminded of the older concept of professionalism, advocated by and potentially accessible to both sexes, which maintained a place for intuition and sympathy and stressed the therapeutic powers of moral and social concerns. Indeed, Blackwell was joined in her opposition to the new science by highly respected clinicians like Austin Flint and Alfred Stille, both past presidents of the American Medical Association, who also viewed the shift of focus to the laboratory as a conspiracy to ignore the particular needs of individual patients. "There is an art of medicine," Stille opined, "[that] completely eludes, or flatly contradicts science, by means of empirical facts, and gives the palm to sagacity and common sense over laws formulated by experiment." "Clinical experience," he noted, "is the only true safe test of the virtues of medicines."[27] But, whereas Stille and Flint struggled to preserve a particular style of behavior for all clinicians, Blackwell re-gendered it as a female characteristic, one that arose, not out of woman's "nature," but from the social practice of mothering.

Thus, drawing on aspects of an older tradition, Blackwell reformulated it, valorized it, and connected it with women. Implicit as well was her rendering of objectivity and professional disengagement—qualities intensely identified with the new version of scientific medicine—as male. Ironically, though her goal was to call attention to and condemn recent changes in medicine, defining certain forms of behavior as female not only validated the position of her adversaries but worked at cross purposes with her intended effect, because it linked empathy with a subordinate social group and reinforced other cultural genderings of scientific activity which worked to exclude women from scientific practice.[28] Nurses, for example, who struggled to professionalize during this period, could never identify themselves successfully with science, and, as practitioners in an occupation comprised almost solely of women, were easily designated auxiliary to physicians, as care was gradually split off from cure.[29]

Indeed, it seems Blackwell was losing her audience. Bacteriology had already forced public health advocates to rethink their work. Formally, the field was broad-based, encompassing, especially in the United States, the interests of a variety of professionals, including engineers, lawyers, female reformers, political economists and other social scientists. But by the 1890s public health was increasingly dominated by physician-scientists, who abandoned the costly and politically sensitive program of environmental reform for the more dramatic and immediate rewards of the laboratory. Indeed, the psychological impact of bacteriology proved striking. "Before 1880 we knew nothing," explained William T. Sedgwick, a leader in the United States public health movement and himself a laboratory scientist. "After 1890 we knew it all; it was a glorious ten years."[30]

The new epidemiology concentrated on the scientific control of specific diseases. As Hibbert Winslow Hill explained in his book *The New Public Health*, managing tuberculosis no longer required providing healthful living conditions to the impoverished, only preventing the two-hundred thousand infected individuals from contaminating others. "Need any more be said," he commented of this solution, "to indicate the superiority of the new principles, as practical business propositions, over the old?"[31]

Indeed, even the language of science was changing. Gendering certain forms of scientific thinking as male was already well underway. Londa Schiebinger charts not only the decline at the end of the eighteenth century of the feminine icon of Scientia, the mythical muse of philosophers, but also of the literary style such iconography represented. Scientists increasingly rejected the poetic flourishes and metaphorical grace of Renaissance tracts, writing increasingly viewed as feminine, for more vigorous, flat-footed "masculine" prose.[32]

At the end of the nineteenth century scientific language became further refined. The social sciences, for example, struggled hard to reconcile tensions over reform advocacy with the need to create an authoritative body of knowledge based on objective, dispassionate investigation that could provide disinterested guidance for society as a whole. Professional standards of academic science narrowed the agenda of the American Social Science Association, and do-gooders were increasingly characterized as amateurs, partisan and unscientific, and female. Moreover, while the language of reform was becoming rapidly less acceptable in science, the scientific text itself became a more standardized cultural genre, replacing what Nancy Stepan and Sander Gilman have described as a "more open, varied, metaphorically porous" literary form. They find that, by the early decades of the twentieth century, "the metaphors of scientific language" have become "more tightly controlled." "The modern scientific text had replaced the expansive scientific book, and the possibilities of multivalent meanings being created out of scientific language were thereby curtailed." Such a change had the effect of marginalizing and delegitimating a range of critical writing—especially writing like Blackwell's, which continually used moral and political argument—because it did not fit the more modern, impersonal scientific style.[33]

It is no wonder that Blackwell's faultfinding with the new ideology of science reached a relatively small and circumscribed group of male practitioners, most of whom were losing ground in the face of rapid changes in the organization and practice of medical care. And, although women physicians still welcomed her ideas about the unique qualities they had to offer the profession, in part because the argument proved a powerful justification for their occupational aspirations, more and more of them found her tirades against the new science irrelevant to their training, philosophy, and practice of medicine.[34]

In calling for the restoration of "the spiritual power of maternity" to medical practice, Blackwell was making a case both for the importance of subjective forms of knowing in the clinical encounter and for the broad social responsibility of the profession. Outside of the domestic life itself, she wrote in 1891, there is "no line of practical work . . . so eminently suited to . . . noble aspirations as the . . . study and practice of medicine." But that study required the preservation in the physician of the qualities of "tenderness, sympathy, guardianship," qualities which she identified with mothering. When these were combined with the more objective methods of scientific inquiry, she argued, they formed the essence of "true" scientific medicine.[35]

Though perhaps somewhat camouflaged in baroque Victorian prose, Blackwell's ideas regarding spiritual maternity are deeply resonant with an approach to science and to human relationships shared by a group of feminist scholars currently wrestling with many of the same problems that she confronted. Of course, Blackwell lived in a moral and intellectual world where categories of analysis were less flexible and less complex, but she clearly identified how and in what ways modern medicine would go wrong. Without necessarily imposing twentieth-century standards upon her, perhaps we can establish her significance as a thinker by identifying strains in contemporary feminist scholarship that help us better appreciate her contribution.

While historians of science have concentrated on questions having primarily to do with the legitimation of modern scientific knowledge, feminist scholars have focused on the processes by which various forms of knowledge became gendered.[36] The scientific revolution not only validated a specific kind of inquiry—controlled laboratory experiments, counting and measuring results, the establishment of protocols of publication and replication—it relegated more subjective and informal modes of knowing to the marginal and the feminine. Francis Bacon, a favorite example, filled his writings with metaphors of mind as masculine and nature as feminine, picturing the latter as something that had to be subdued and controlled. Feminist philosophers have exposed the fallacious dualisms produced by this revolution in thought—dualisms that have consistently separated reason and intuition, active and passive, public and private, male and female. Such thinking, they have argued, has not only subordinated and marginalized women in the past, but is a flawed intellectual legacy for the profitable pursuit of science itself. They have sought to develop alternative epistemologies that can free women from their enthrallment to biology, while still cherishing the life-preserving qualities and character traits that have been persistently identified with them. To this end, some thinkers have scrutinized the relationships between the tasks most women perform in our society and intuitive, more subjective ways of knowing. Their findings offer a deeper understanding of Blackwell's concept of "the spiritual power of maternity."

In an important article entitled "Maternal Thinking," the philosopher Sara Ruddick proposed to revise common sense notions about mothering which tend to contrast abstract and formal thought—usually identified with men—with the more informal modes of knowing involved in childrearing—generally identified with women. Her purpose is to critique the opposition of "reason" and "intuition" by challenging the assumption that because mothering takes place in a private, less structured, and allegedly a more "natural" sphere, a mother's knowledge is not as legitimate as formal learning. On the contrary, Ruddick contends, mothers engage in a "discipline" just as systematic as the pursuit of medicine or law. Moreover, reason is an essential component of a mother's knowledge and "maternal thinking" deserves to have its forms acknowledged. Indeed, she writes, the task of analyzing and describing this thinking—a way of knowing shaped by maternal practice—can lead toward the creation of a new public ethic with a greater emphasis on caring.

Women's activities in childrearing, Ruddick explains, require preparation, foresight, experience, training, and the ability to reason. While it is true that most mothers love their children and wish to respond to their needs, that response is neither random nor automatic. Nor are maternal feelings simply instinctive; they are the product of historical, social, and cultural mores, thought, knowledge, and experience. In the process of living with children, mothers, Ruddick argues, "acquire a conceptual scheme—a vocabulary and logic of connections through which they order and express the facts and values of their practice." This knowledge and experience, though comparable to that acquired by a mathematician or a theoretical physicist, more readily emphasizes the particular and the individual than the scientist's attempt to construct "universal" generalizations. Indeed, because much of mothering entails the fostering of emotional and intellectual growth, a task that requires responding to a being (or object) who is continually growing, changing, and intentionally moving away, a mother's work involves a willingness to gradually alter her relationship with her child. "The idea of 'objective reality' itself," Ruddick observes, paraphrasing philosopher and novelist Iris Murdoch, "undergoes important modification when it is to be understood, not in relation to 'the world described by science,' but in relation to the progressing life of a person." It is just this "unity of reflection, judgment and emotion" that Ruddick labels "maternal thinking."[37]

Part of Ruddick's purpose is to show that the devaluation of "women's" intuition derives from a more general cultural suspicion of all forms of knowledge that are nonscientific in the conventional sense. And, indeed, scholars in many disciplines are questioning the adequacy of using the scientific model as an absolute measure of what counts as knowledge. Thus feminist theorists are not alone in this work, but their contribution to the endeavor has been remarkable. In seeking a redefinition of notions of subjectivity and objectivity, they have attempted to modify the radical separation between subject and object that has become characteristic of scientific thinking in the last three hundred years and of medical practice in the last century. Moreover, they have sought to incorporate into scientific discourse a different form of knowing, one that makes effective use of subjective experience.

For example, the physicist, Evelyn Fox Keller, argues that objectivity as it has been previously understood is too "static." The assumption that one can sever oneself completely from the object of study, hence regarding one's investigations as unbiased and absolute, is untenable. She proposes instead an expanded, "dynamic objectivity," whose aim is to "grant to the world around us its independent integrity," but to do so "in a way that remains cognizant of, and indeed relies on, our connectivity with that world." In short, Keller seeks a special kind of empathy, "a form of knowledge of other persons that draws explicitly on the commonality of feelings and experience in order to enrich one's understanding of another in his or her own right."[38]

Thoughtful women physicians have drawn strength from recent feminist critiques of science, and have begun to complain about the ways the traditional scientific method can interfere with humane approaches to patient care. They have especially criticized the limitations of a theory of knowing that does not take into account the intersubjectivity between doctor and patient. When the trained physician expects to find objective reality conforming to a specific set of medical theories, when reductionist signs arrived at by mechanical or chemical tests become the sole basis on which practitioners are taught to reach a diagnosis, patients are rendered unimportant reporters about their own bodies. This is especially true when their subjective experience does not easily conform to the doctor's "educated" perception of that reality. When pushed, many doctors would likely admit to using another form of knowing in diagnosis when necessary—one that readmits the patient's subjectivity, and perhaps even the doctor's own, as significant to the healing process. But, as one feminist in family practice has recently claimed, few would do so publicly. "We have up to the present failed to acknowledge the legitimacy" of this approach, she asserts, "and instead have attempted in our research and our writings to employ what is more accepted as the 'scientific' way of knowing."[39]

Unlike Elizabeth Blackwell, who lived in an intellectual climate dominated by powerful gender dualisms which she tried to recast but could not overturn, few contemporary thinkers identify such a form of knowing *solely* with women. They argue only that women in our society are generally taught maternal thinking, while men are not. In fact, Marxist scholars, who believe thought arises out of social practice, have recently studied forms of work that are most likely to utilize such thinking. Feminist theorists generally tend to attribute women's greater reliance on subjective forms of knowing to our culture's gender-differentiated socialization experiences, especially those of mothering and of being mothered. Others have related such epistemologies to class differences and the experience of subordination.[40]

But whatever its origins, the aim is to temporarily abstract such thinking from its social context and measure its potentialities against more traditional methods of scientific inquiry. Feminists offer an alternative paradigm which stresses intuition and the interaction between the knower and the known, arguing that traditional definitions of objectivity actually constrain the future development of science itself. The goal is an expanded and more effective theory of knowledge—one which can better accommodate not only the pursuit of science, but the development of a more holistic and life affirming culture.

Blackwell would probably have felt comfortable with modern feminist refinements of maternal thinking and critiques of "objectivity." Unlike modern feminists, of course, her notion of the social construction of gender was vague; she was never clear about whether the nurturing she identified with women was socialized or innate. Though I believe she ultimately came down on the side of environmentalism over biology, she did blame bacteriology on the "male intellect," and warned her students against accepting male authority without thinking for themselves. She wanted women to learn to question. Yet she also insisted that men could be taught to nurture. "Methods and conclusions formed by one-half the race only," she often pointed out, "must necessarily require revision as the other half of humanity rises into conscious responsibility."[41] Bacteriology constricted conscious responsibility by reducing the patient "to the limits of the senses" and ignoring the fact that each human being was a "soul as well as body." In addition, it obscured "the importance of unsanitary conditions," by playing down "the multiple causes of disease." The effects were already visible:

"intellectual ability" was being diverted from "the true path of sanitation by an exaggerated search for bacilli." Worst of all, the profession was losing its social conscience.[42]

It should be clear by now that recent feminist theoretical work can aid the historian in opening up new avenues of research in the history of medicine. If nothing else, we have learned to look for gender in scientific language originally assumed to be neutral and value-free. But the task of applying new theoretical approaches to the history of medicine has only just begun. What historical conditions prevailed at the end of the nineteenth century to determine why certain definitions of medical science became privileged over others? John Harley Warner has recently shown how the clash between conflicting ideals of science had far-reaching implications, not just for the scientific and technological content of medical practice, but for the development of a new professional and moral identity.[43] In focusing attention on Elizabeth Blackwell, I have tried to suggest that re-gendering notions of the good practitioner were also part of this important transformation. But both the positive and negative effects of this re-gendering need further examination.

Rereading Blackwell with contemporary feminist theory in mind has helped me better appreciate the elements of her thinking that attempted to revitalize the significance of the feminine in a changing medical world that rapidly pushed caring aside in favor of hard-headed, technological, "objective" treatment. It is not that the doctor denied completely the importance of caring in managing the sick. Indeed, nurses were expected to perform such services. Physicians argued only that handholding was unnecessary to produce results, just as public health advocates turned away from the extensive social reform program of the sanitarians in favor of research and inoculation.

By the beginning of the twentieth century, the very language of caring came to be suspect to the scientist, whose authority depended, at least in part, on ethical neutrality.[44] Blackwell well understood the moral and social dangers inherent in such ethical neutrality, and she deplored vivisection for fostering an inferior professional morality. She encouraged a healthy skepticism in her students, cautioning that "medicine is necessarily an uncertain science" and that "all human judgment is fallible." She warned them against accepting "the imperfect or erroneous statement of what is often presented as truth."[45]

Modern critiques of radical scientific objectivity and feminist theoretical examinations of the components of caring have resurrected some of her deepest concerns about the direction of medical practice. Some have used the insights of literary textual criticism to echo Blackwell's suspicions of scientific neutrality. For example, the late feminist neurophysiologist Ruth Bleier reminds us that scientific dogmatism can no longer exempt the scientific text from the kind of scrutiny being given other written products of our culture. "Scientists believe," she has written, that

> the language they use is simply a vehicle for the transmission of information about the objects of their research, another part of the scientist's toolbox, separate from the scientist's subjectivity, values and beliefs. They do not recognize or acknowledge the degree to which their scientific writing itself participates in producing the reality they wish to present nor would scientists acknowledge the multiplicity of meaning of their text. . . . As literary criticism has "debunked the myth of linguistic neutrality" in the literary text, it is time to debunk the myth of neutrality of the scientific text.[46]

Regrettably, Blackwell's attempts to do so could not be heard over the din of public enthusiasm for the new science.

In the final analysis, how do we assess Blackwell's contribution? Surely, her redefining, recoding, and re-gendering of certain medical practices as "feminine" has been an ambiguous legacy. My uneasiness with her essentializing language when I first began to examine her work fifteen years ago came out of an understanding of the ways in which positing "difference" could hold women and people of color back from full participation in the body politic. Moreover, recent feminist theory has understandably taught us to mistrust the dualisms upon which her theories inevitably drew. Indeed, Blackwell herself was a prisoner of those dualisms. They kept her from fully appreciating the emancipatory role experimental science has played in the conquest of epidemic disease. Moreover, we see clearly as she did not that for male colleagues unfriendly to her cause, the feminization of empathic expertise provided an excuse to discredit an older professional value system and relegate the work of caring in medicine to nurses and other ancillary personnel. In our century, the medical hero has not been the family practitioner or the public health professional, but the lone researcher, working for humankind in the abstract, not the particular.

And yet, poised at the beginning of a new century, Blackwell understood the dangers of reducing medical practice to an applied science. Much of what she feared would develop has come to pass. How appropriate a time, then, for historians to give her ideas a second hearing, and for feminists to take us beyond her critical analysis to tackle the more formidable task of reinventing science.

NOTES

1. James is quoted in Joan Williams, "Rorty, Radicalism, Romanticism: The Politics of the Gaze," *Wisconsin Law Review* (1992): 131.

2. Virginia Woolf, *Three Guineas* (New York, 1938), 139.

3. See Londa Schiebinger, *The Mind Has No Sex? Women in the Origins of Modern Science* (Cambridge, Mass., 1989); Thomas Laqueur, *Making Sex* (Cambridge, Mass., 1990); Cynthia Russett, *Sexual Science* (Cambridge, Mass., 1989); Ludmilla Jordanova, *Sexual Visions: Images of Gender in Science and Medicine between the Eighteenth and Twentieth Centuries* (Madison, 1989); Ornella Moscucci, *The Science of Woman: Gynecology and Gender in England, 1800–1929* (Cambridge, Eng., 1990); Joan Jacobs Brumberg, *Fasting Girls: The Emergence of Anorexia Nervosa as a Modern Disease* (Cambridge, Mass., 1988).

4. See Regina Morantz, "Feminism, Professionalism and Germs: The Thought of Mary Putnam Jacobi and Elizabeth Blackwell," *American Quarterly* 34 (Winter 1982): 461–478.

5. For a comparison of women's history and gender history see Louise Newman, "Critical Theory and the History of Women: What's at Stake in Deconstructing Women's History," *Journal of Women's History* 2 (Winter 1991): 58–69. See also the already classic essays in Joan Scott, *Gender and the Politics of History* (New York, 1988).

6. Elizabeth Blackwell, "On the Education of Women Physicians," 1860. Blackwell Papers, Library of Congress.

7. See Nancy Stepan, "Women and Natural Knowledge: The Role of Gender in the Making of Modern Science," in *Gender and History* 2 (Autumn 1990): 337–342.

8. See Carol Gilligan, *In a Different Voice* (Cambridge, Mass., 1982). For the clearest explication I have read to date of the political and social implications of the two positions see Joan C. Williams, "Sameness Feminism and the Work/Family Conflict," *New York Law School Law Review* 35 (1990): 347–360, and "Domesticity as the Dangerous Supplement of Liberalism," *Journal of Women's History* 2 (Winter 1991): 69–88. See also Chris Weedon, *Feminist Practice and Poststructural Theory* (London, 1987), chaps. 1 and 2.

9. Charles Rosenberg, "The Therapeutic Revolution: Medicine, Meaning

and Social Change in Nineteenth-Century America," in *The Therapeutic Revolution: Essays on the Social History of American Medicine*, ed. C. Rosenberg and Morris Vogel (Philadelphia, 1979), 10–11; John Harley Warner, *The Therapeutic Perspective: Medical Practice, Knowledge, and Identity in America, 1820–1885* (Cambridge, Mass., 1986).

10.   See John Harley Warner, "Remembering Paris: Memory and the American Disciples of French Medicine in the 19th Century," *Bulletin of the History of Medicine* 65 (Fall 1991): 301–325, for a fascinating analysis of the collective meaning of the Paris experience for a select generation of American medical practitioners. Other interpretations of the Parisian medical system are Michel Foucault, *The Birth of the Clinic*, trans. A. M. Sheridan Smith (New York, 1973) and Erwin Ackerknecht, *Medicine at the Paris Hospital, 1794–1848* (Baltimore, 1967).

11.   Rosenberg, "The Therapeutic Revolution," 10–11.

12.   Henry Hartshorne, *Valedictory Address* (Philadelphia, 1872), 6–7.

13.   Sandra Holton, "'Christian Physiology': Science, Religion and Morality in the Medicine of Elizabeth Blackwell" (paper delivered at the Pacific Coast Branch of the AHA Convention, Kona, Hawaii, August, 1991); Elizabeth Blackwell, "Erroneous Method in Medical Education," *Essays in Medical Sociology* (1902, reprinted New York, 1972), 38, and "Scientific Method in Biology," *ibid.*, 96. For the American and British response to the moral failings of Parisian practice, see Warner, *The Therapeutic Perspective*, 185–196.

14.   See Elizabeth Fee and Dorothy Porter, "Public Health, Preventive Medicine and Professionalization: Britain and the United States in the 19th Century," in *A History of Education in Public Health*, ed. Elizabeth Fee and Roy Acheson (New York, 1991), 15–43.

15.   Warner, *The Therapeutic Perspective*, 235–243.

16.   *Ibid.*, 258; Russell Maulitz, "'Physician versus Bacteriologist': The Ideology of Science in Clinical Medicine," in *The Therapeutic Revolution*, 91–107.

17.   In addition to Warner and Maulitz cited above, see Warner's two articles, "Remembering Paris," and "Ideals of Science and Their Discontents in Late-Nineteenth-Century American Medicine," *Isis* 82 (1991): 454–478.

18.   Williams, "Domesticity as the Dangerous Supplement of Liberalism," 71. For a fascinating and innovative study of what being outside of politics meant for various female activists, see Louise Michele Newman, "Laying Claim to Difference: Ideologies of Race and Gender in the U.S. Woman's Movement, 1870–1920," (Ph.D. diss., Brown University, 1992).

19.   Erik Erikson, *Childhood and Society* (New York, 1950), 267; Elizabeth Blackwell, "The Influence of Women in the Profession of Medicine," in *Essays in Medical Sociology*, 9–10.

20.   Warner, *The Therapeutic Perspective*, 249.

21.   Warner has skillfully examined the ramifications of these fears, which Blackwell shared, in "Ideals of Science and Their Discontents."

22.   Blackwell, "Scientific Method in Biology," 126–130.

23.   Blackwell, "The Influence of Women in the Profession of Medicine," 13; "Erroneous Method in Medical Education," in, *Essays in Medical Sociology*, 10–12.

24.   Blackwell strongly supported clinical casework, postmortem and gross pathology, pathological chemistry, microscopic anatomy, and other types of patient-centered investigations. See "Scientific Method in Biology," in *Essays in Medical Sociology*, 105. Sandra Holton has explored not only Blackwell's thought in this

regard, but that of other British physicians as well. See Sandra Holton, "'Christian Physiology'"; and Sandra Holton, "State Pandering, Medical Policing and Prostitution: The Controversy with the Medical Profession concerning the Contagious Diseases Legislation, 1864–1886," *Research in Law, Deviance and Social Control* 9 (1988): 149–170.

25.   "Why Hygienic Congresses Fail," 57, 74–75; "Influence of Women in the Profession of Medicine," 12, 19–20, 27–29, in *Essays in Medical Sociology.*

26.   I am not arguing that gender dualisms were new in scientific thinking, but that the quality of sympathy in medical practice was a professional value for all physicians earlier in the century.

27.   Quoted in Warner, "Ideals of Science and Their Discontents," 463.

28.   Louise Newman has argued cogently that when female thinkers spoke of "women" in this period, they invariably meant white, middle-class women. This was true of Blackwell as well. One response among women's movement activists in the years between 1870 and 1910 to justify their attention to the public sphere was to revalue feminine sexual traits like emotionalism, intuition, moral sensitivity, altruism in order to claim that "woman" was, in crucial ways, the superior of "man." See Louise Michele Newman, "Laying Claim to Differences," 117.

29.   See Susan Reverby, *Ordered to Care: The Dilemma of American Nursing, 1850–1945* (Cambridge, Eng., 1987); Barbara Melosh, *"The Physician's Hand": Work, Culture and Conflict in American Nursing* (Philadelphia, 1982).

30.   Cited in Fee and Acheson, *A History of Education in Public Health,* 160.

31.   Hibbert Winslow Hill, *The New Public Health* (New York, 1916) 19–20, cited in *ibid.,* 35.

32.   Schiebinger, *The Mind Has No Sex?,* 150–159.

33.   On American social science see Mary O. Furner, *Advocacy and Objectivity: A Crisis in the Professionalization of American Social Science, 1865–1905* (Lexington, 1975). See also Stepan and Gilman, "Appropriating the Idioms of Science: The Rejection of Scientific Racism," in *The Bounds of Race,* ed. Dominick LaCapra (Ithaca, N.Y., 1991), 79.

34.   See Regina Morantz-Sanchez, "How Women Physicians Became More Empathic than Men," in *The Empathic Practitioner: Empathy, Gender, and the Therapeutic Relationship,* ed. Ellen More and Maureen Milligan, (New Brunswick, N.J., forthcoming); and *Sympathy and Science: Women Physicians in American Medicine* (New York, 1985), chap. 7.

35.   Blackwell, "Influence of Women in the Profession of Medicine," 12.

36.   See, for example, Caroline Merchant, *The Death of Nature* (New York, 1980); Ruth Hubbard and Marion Lowe, eds., *Woman's Nature, Rationalizations of Inequality,* ed. (New York, 1983); Evelyn Fox Keller, *Reflections on Gender and Science* (New Haven, 1985); Ruth Bleier, *Science and Gender* (New York, 1984); Ruth Bleier, ed., *Feminist Approaches to Science* (New York, 1986); Carol MacCormack and Marilyn Strathern, eds., *Nature, Culture and Gender* (Cambridge, Eng., 1980); Sandra Harding, *The Science Question in Feminism* (Ithaca, N.Y., 1986) and *Whose Science? Whose Knowledge? Thinking from Women's Lives* (Ithaca, N.Y., 1991); Ann Fausto-Sterling, *Myths of Gender* (New York, 1985); Nancy Hartsock, "The Feminist Standpoint: Developing the Ground for a Specifically Feminist Historical Materialism," in *Discovering Reality,* ed., Sandra Harding and M. D. Hintikka (Dordrecht, Holland, 1986).

37. Sara Ruddick, "Maternal Thinking," *Feminist Studies* 6 (Summer 1980): 342–367.

38. Keller, *Reflections*, 116–117. See also Gilligan, *In a Different Voice*; M. F. Field, B. Clinchy, N. R. Goldberger, and J. M. Tarule, *Women's Ways of Knowing* (New York, 1986). See also Robert J. Lifton, "Woman as Knower: Some Psychohistorical Perspectives," in *The Woman in America*, ed. Lifton (Boston, 1967), 27–51. Another important proponent of a reconstructed epistemology is Hilary Rose. See her "Hand, Brain and Heart: A Feminist Epistemology for the Natural Sciences," *Signs* 9 (Autumn 1983): 73–90, and "Beyond Masculinist Realities: A Feminist Epistemology for the Sciences," in *Feminist Approaches to Science*, 57–76.

39. Lucy Candib, "Ways of Knowing in Family Medicine: Contributions from a Feminist Perspective," *Family Medicine* 20 (April 1988): 133–136.

40. Rosenberg, "The Therapeutic Revolution," 10–11.

41. This passage sounds like Blackwell was groping toward some concept of androgyny, some higher union of masculine and feminine. Sandra Harding reminds us that androgyny can't really solve the dilemma of recreating science because masculinity and femininity are both partial subject positions, distorted and constrained by culture. Merely putting them together will not magically turn two halves into a coherent whole. Harding, *The Science Question in Feminism*.

42. Rosenberg, "The Therapeutic Revolution," 10–11; Warner, *The Therapeutic Perspective*.

43. Warner, "Ideals of Science and Their Discontents."

44. For a discussion of the way Sinclair Lewis's novel *Arrowsmith* represents this changing ideology see Morantz-Sanchez, *Sympathy and Science*, 309–311.

45. Blackwell, "The Influence of Women in the Profession of Medicine," 19, 21.

46. Ruth Bleier, "Sex Differences in Research: Science or Belief?" in *Feminist Approaches to Science*, 159–161.

Ideology and "the Status of Women" in Ancient Greece

MARILYN A. KATZ

Is a "History of Women" possible? Does Woman exist? The first of these provocative questions was the title of a 1984 collection of essays by French feminists;[1] the second was addressed recently by the British feminist, Denise Riley.[2] With some exceptions, such challenges to the category of research have not disrupted the smooth surface of the study of women in antiquity, which, as Marilyn Skinner observed in 1986,[3] was incorporated readily into the field of classics and defined according to existing parameters of scholarly investigation.[4]

The dominant research question in the field, centered around the "status" of women in ancient Athens, has, in fact, only recently been redefined fully, but without developing an adequate historiographic basis. That is to say, we now know that the status question is the wrong one, but we have not made clear why this is so, nor do we have a clear understanding of why the study of women in Greek antiquity was originally formulated around this issue. The object of this essay is to provide this missing historiography, to identify the ideological parameters that informed the constitution of the original research question, and to suggest that the new reformulation, centered around women in Greek society, must itself be modified in order to incorporate an analysis of female sexuality in ancient Greece.

I first investigate the constitution of the dominant research question in the field, under the heading of "Patriarchy and Misogyny." I trace the origins of this question back to the late eighteenth century, and I take note of the continuing force of this paradigm. Under "Women in Civil Society," I examine the ideological basis of this hegemonic discourse, arguing that it derives from the eighteenth-century debate over women's place in civil

This essay is drawn from a manuscript in progress, *Women and Ideology in Ancient Greece: An Historiographic Essay.*

society, where the example of the women of ancient Athens served a legitimating function within a wider political framework. I conclude with a section discussing "Recent Challenges" to the traditional interpretive paradigm for the study of women in ancient Greece and the "Future Directions" of current research in the field.

PATRIARCHY AND MISOGYNY

The hallmark of the approach I shall examine is its focus on "woman" as a category and its preoccupation with the question of status. I have classified it under the heading of "Patriarchy and Misogyny" in order to highlight the concern with dominance and subordination which informs it throughout, but which is often hidden from view.

In a famous 1925 polemic the historian A. W. Gomme[5] described the then prevailing orthodoxy as the view that the status of women in ancient Athens in the classical period was an "ignoble" one by comparison with their position in the Dorian states of the same period, and with that in the earlier, archaic period (89). Most contemporary discussion of the question has taken its start from this essay and from the similar chapter on "Life and Character" in Kitto's The Greeks.[6]

A more complete account of the common opinion of the time, however, may be gleaned from the sections on "Die Frauen" in the second edition of Beloch's 1893 Griechische Geschichte.[7] The Ionians, according to Beloch, under the influence of the neighboring peoples of Asia Minor, inaugurated the exclusion of women from the public sphere and their confinement to the home and to the company of female friends. The Athenians adopted the practice from their fellow Ionians, but among non-Ionian Greeks women retained the freedom they had enjoyed in Homeric times. Prostitution—inspired by the example of the Lydians—sprang up among the Ionians as the inevitable corollary to the seclusion of well-born women, and the practice of homosexuality developed along with it (1.1, 406–408).

The Ionian practice of seclusion became more widespread in Athens during the fifth century, at just the time when democratic ideals of liberty were institutionalized: "it was as if the women had wanted to devise a counterweight to their husbands' boundless strivings for freedom" (2.1, 159). Athenian men now turned to the company of hetairas ("female companions") for the female intellectual stimulation which they had "sought at home in vain."[8] These "emancipated" women flourished especially among the Ionians, their aspirations toward freedom nourished by the Ionian exaltation of learning and instigated by the cloistered lives of ordinary free women (*ibid.*, 160).

By the fourth century, under the influence of their fathers and husbands, a few women rejected traditional roles and turned to the study of philosophy; the notion of marriage for the sake of children began to yield to an ideal of companionate union for mutual fulfillment. This development was resisted vigorously, and it gave rise to expressions of misogyny, but mostly from "crybabies [whose] wives were too good for them." Hetairas continued to play an important role, and functioned as companions for almost all of the important men of this period (3.1, 434).

In the Hellenistic period the lives of ordinary women remained restricted, and hetairas retained a prominence in Athens which was later transferred to Alexandria. But the hetaira in her role as symbol of female emancipation was eclipsed by a new type of woman—the Hellenistic queen of the Macedonian and Alexandrian realms (4.1, 416–420).[9] The example of her life of complete freedom within the court influenced the Greek world at large, leading to such developments as the extension of citizenship rights (proxeny), the institutionalization of education for women, the possibility of unaccompanied travel abroad, and the refinement of manners in social intercourse between the sexes.

This was, then, the "orthodoxy" on the status of women in ancient Athens which prevailed in the early twentieth century and which Gomme was concerned to challenge. But how did it come into being, and on the basis of what evidence? In my search for an answer this question, I came across a long essay by a classical scholar who was prominent in his time, but who has been remembered since primarily as the editor of various Hellenistic Greek texts.

This man was Friedrich Jacobs who, in a long essay on "The History of the Female Sex" published in 1830, challenged, in terms similar to those of Gomme, what he regarded as the prevailing orthodoxy on the matter of women's status among the ancient Greeks.[10] Jacobs remarked that in his own time this question was a debated issue: "Some have regarded women's position in Greece as demeaned, in the manner characteristic of barbarians; others have disputed this interpretation; and a third group thinks that the housewife was little esteemed and loved, but that hetairas by contrast, because of their education, enjoyed love and respect" (161). Jacobs divides his own treatment of the issue into an introductory section on marriage, followed by a discussion of "The Greek Woman," and concludes with a lengthy section on "The Hetairas."

In disputing the claim that ancient Greek, and especially Athenian, women were regarded with contempt, secluded, uneducated (with the exception of the hetairas), and unfree and unequal until the advent of Christianity (228), Jacobs cites evidence of "Christian" sentiments among the pagans, and expressions of misogyny by the Church fathers. Thus, he argues, the disparagement of women was no more characteristic of pagan thinking than was their high regard inherent in Christianity. Jacobs goes on to discuss Homer and Hesiod, characterizing the *Odyssey* as "a love song to Penelope" (234), and arguing in general that the archaic picture gives us representations of both good and bad women. If the latter predominate in Hesiod, this has to do both with the poet's view of life, in which evil predominates over good, and with "the nature of things," rather than with "a contempt for the gender predominating in his time" (241). It is in "the nature of things," Jacobs argues, that as long as there are two sexes there will be two kinds of women, but praise of the good woman will be remarked less frequently than blame of the bad (229, 242).

Concerning the claim that women in ancient Greece were secluded and uneducated, Jacobs argues that restriction to home life was a matter of custom rather than law (254, 273), and that similar practices have been the rule all over western Europe up to the present time. Furthermore, if seclusion originated in the Orient, it was nonetheless consistent with Christian belief and practice, albeit in a milder form (255). The housebound life of the Athenian matron, and the tradition, attested to in Thucydides, of silence about even her virtues, means that we have little evidence about women's education. But girls' training was in all likelihood entrusted to their mothers who instructed them in the domestic arts and "womanly wisdom"; and their education was completed by their husbands, as Hesiod and, above all, Xenophon make clear (248ff.).

Overall, Jacobs insists, the Greek woman's intelligence and moral sensibility was sufficiently developed so that she was not an object of her husband's contempt (251), and he cites Xenophon's *Oeconomicus* in defense of his claim that the Athenian wife was regarded with respect (205–206). While recognizing the existence of a misogynistic and antimarriage tradition,[11] he nevertheless concludes that the ancient Greeks, in Athens and elsewhere, recognized the moral worth of wives and marriage and honored the "sanctity" of this union (314).

The interpretive framework which guides Jacobs's judgments on ancient Greek women is set forth in his first chapter, "A General View of Marriage," in which he defends the general proposition that marriage is ideally a social institution representing "a union and interpenetration of the physical and moral strivings of human nature" which find their fullest and most complete realization in society at large, but whose first elements are represented by the marital union (165–166). To the man belongs the right of rule, derived from the fact of his physical and intellectual superiority, and to the woman, on account of her sense for order and beauty, as well as her capacity for detail, belongs both "the authority and duty to execute the laws set down by the man" (167–168). And he concludes: "it is a general rule that it is proper for the woman to obey the man" (187).

If one compares the premises and conclusions of Jacobs's essay with those of Gomme and Kitto, the similarities are striking. All agree that, as Gomme puts it, "Athenian society was, in the main, of the normal European type."[12] Jacobs would not have disputed Gomme's contention that "there is no reason to suppose that in the matter of the social consequence and freedom of women Athens was different from other Greek cities, or the classical from the Homeric age" (114). Like Gomme, Jacobs subscribed to the view that "Greek theory and practice [did not] differ fundamentally from the average . . . prevailing in mediaeval and modern Europe" (115). Gomme claims, "when Theognis said, 'I hate a woman who gads about and neglects her home,' I think he expressed a sentiment common to most people of all ages" (115). This is similar to Jacobs's comments on a fragment of Menander in which a husband admonishes his gadabout wife that the courtyard door is the customary limit of a freeborn woman's realm: "in Berlin and Vienna, in Paris and London a husband in such a situation would say to his wife:

'within the limits of your house your tongue may have free reign; beyond the door your realm ends.'"[13]

Kitto remarks, "[t]he Athenian had his faults, but preeminent among his better qualities were lively intelligence, sociability, humanity, curiosity. To say that he habitually treated one-half of his own race with indifference, even contempt, does not, to my mind, make sense."[14] Jacobs found the view that ancient Greek women were tolerated only as a necessary evil, and that romantic love was directed only toward the educated hetaira, similarly incredible: "such is the harshness then, with which, it is claimed, the stronger sex exercised its mastery; such is the ignominy that the weaker sex tolerated in a land which we have been accustomed from childhood to revere as the cradle of culture, among a people whom we have learned to regard as the patrons of all that is beautiful, great and masterful."[15]

The so-called "orthodoxy" on the question of women's status among the ancient Greeks, then, was already dominant in the early nineteenth century, when Jacobs argued against it. And there is a striking continuity in both the tone and the terms in which the argument against the orthodoxy of women's seclusion in ancient Athens was formulated over the course of the century that lies between Jacobs and Gomme. I shall suggest below that this continuum is even longer, stretching across the two hundred years from 1796 to 1971 and beyond. But we must first still attempt to answer the question I posed above: how did the orthodoxy itself come into being, and on the basis of what evidence?

Jacobs in 1830 was concerned, at the most general level, to refute the contention of Christoph Meiners that "Homer makes it incontestably clear that women in the earlier period were as little regarded as in the later, and no less secluded [then] than later," a notion which Meiners explained on the basis of a postulated kinship between Greeks and Slavs.[16] Jacobs regarded as similarly misguided Thöluck's idea that "the female sex, whose status among the pagans was low, was first through Christendom accorded a human dignity similar to that of men" (224). And he objected as well to de Pauw's claim "that the hetairas, who were accustomed to attend the schools of the philosophers, were infinitely better educated than the women of standing, who perhaps never spoke [their] language correctly" (246), and to Böttiger's contention "that Athenian men kept their wives secluded; that this was a dominant

custom; that Athenian women sighed under 'oriental harem-slavery'"
(224).

Karl August Böttiger, who served as director of the Museum of
Antiques in Dresden in the early nineteenth century, was also one
of the first classical scholars of the modern period. In one of his
earliest contributions to the genre of classical scholarship, "Were
Athenian Women Spectators at Dramatic Festivals?,"[17] Böttiger
took the opportunity to address the question of women's status in
ancient Greece overall, and to do so with reference to what he
called "das neumodische right of Women [sic]," citing Mary
Wollstonecraft. He argued that the question of women's attendance
at dramatic performances should be addressed from within the
framework of the Greeks' general practice of secluding their women
and confining them "to oriental harem-slavery."[18]. Böttiger thus
became the first classical scholar to articulate the "negative" view
which achieved canonical status in the nineteenth century—namely,
that ancient Greek women were in general less well off than their
modern counterparts.

Böttiger's views on women in Greece and Rome were subsequently popularized in a historical novel, *Sabina, or Morning Scenes
in the Dressing-Room of a Wealthy Roman Lady* (Leipzig, 1806),
through which he became the founder of the genre of "antique
domestic literature."[19] His novel was adapted to the Greek situation
in 1840 by Wilhelm Adolf Becker, who in *Charicles* recounts the
adventures of an Athenian youth of the same name who, in the
waning years of the fourth century B.C.E., having been ensnared as
an adolescent by a hetaira in Corinth, goes on as a young adult to
marry the young and beautiful heiress, Cleobule.

Becker appended to *Charicles* an excursus on "The Women," in
which he acknowledged that

> a variety of views have been entertained on the social position of the
> Greek women, and their estimation in the eyes of the men. The
> majority of scholars have described them as despicable in the opin-
> ion of the other sex, their life as a species of slavery, and the
> gynaeconitis [women's quarters] as a place of durance little differing
> from the Oriental harem; while a few writers have stoutly con-
> tended for the historic emancipation of the fair sex among the
> Greeks (462).

While arguing overall that "the truth lies between the contending parties," Becker goes on to defend, on the basis of an extensive consideration of the evidence from the poets, orators, and philosophers, and from vase-paintings as well, the view that the women of the classical period "were less respected and more restrained [than in the heroic era], and that the marriage relationship was less tender and endearing" (462).

Becker's picture, although tempered in many cases by qualifications, may be summarized as follows: in the classical period

> the women were regarded as a lower order of beings, neglected by nature in comparison with man, both in point of intellect and heart; incapable of taking part in public life, naturally prone to evil, and fitted only for propagating the species and gratifying the sensual appetites of the men (463).

> The only *arete* [virtue] of which woman was thought capable . . . differed but little from that of a faithful slave (464).

> [Women's] education from early childhood corresponded to the rest of their treatment . . . their whole instruction was left to the mother and the nurses, through whose means they obtained, perhaps, a smattering *en grammasi* [of letters], and were taught to spin and weave, and similar female avocations. . . . Hence there were no scientific or even learned ladies, with the exception of the hetaerae (465)

> The gynaeconitis, though not exactly a prison, nor yet an ever-locked harem, was still the confined abode allotted, for life, to the female portion of the household (465).

> Marriage, in reference to the procreation of children, was considered by the Greeks as a necessity enforced by their duties to the gods, to the state, and to their ancestors. . . . Until a very late period, at least, no higher considerations attached to matrimony, nor was strong attachment a frequent cause of marriage. . . . Sensuality was the soil from which . . . passion sprung, and none other than a sensual love was acknowledged between man and wife (473).

As to the wife's household duties: "the province of the wife was the management of the entire household, and the nurture of the children; of the boys until they were placed under a master, of the girls till marriage" (490). At another point, he notes: "still it is an unquestionable fact that in many cases the wife was in reality the ruling power in the house, whether from her mental superiority, domineering disposition, or amount of dower" (493). Becker concludes with a consideration of the "double standard": "the law imposed the duty of continence in a very unequal manner" (494), noting that "infidelity in the wife was judged most sharply," and that the law required an adulterous wife to be divorced (494).

This is, then, the nineteenth-century orthodoxy on the status of women in ancient Greece, formulated on the basis of an extensive consideration of the evidence. The matter was, of course, far from settled. In the second half of the nineteenth century and in the first half of the twentieth, articles, dissertations, and monographs on the subject of women's status proliferated, and a complete bibliography on the topic for this century would run to more than fifty items.

I shall argue that beneath both the question of women's emancipation in ancient Greece and that of their purported seclusion we can detect the operation of a specific politico-philosophical framework. The lineaments of this ideological perspective, however, particularly in the years after 1850, have most often lain hidden from view. This, I suggest, is because, once the orthodoxy gained widespread currency, its origins in a specific philosophical discourse were ignored, and the scholarly dispute was conducted on the basis of its particulars. Before proceeding to a discussion of this framework, however, I want to turn my attention to some works by the current generation of scholars in the field of women's studies in Greek antiquity.

Pomeroy's 1975 *Goddesses, Whores, Wives and Slaves* was the first full-length study of this generation to take the question of women in antiquity seriously as a scholarly issue. In the decades immediately preceding, in the anglophone world at any rate, the discussion had degenerated into a succession of articles repeating Gomme's arguments of 1925 and upholding his views, always with the same reassurances that "the attitude toward women among the Athenians was much the same as among ourselves,"[20] and sometimes with patronizing references to "a healthy strain of misogyny and misogamy running through Greek literature" or "a quite normal measure of husbandly jealousy" on the part of Athenian men, defended as reasonable on the basis of ancient Greek women's supposed sexual licentiousness.[21] Otherwise, research on women had become confined to the dissection of the minutiae of quotidian reality, in a manner reminiscent of Plato's remarks about women's familiarity with "weaving and watching over rising cakes and boiling pots" (*Republic* 5.455c), or of Böttiger's study on the use of pocket-handkerchiefs by Greek ladies.[22]

Pomeroy divided her treatment of women in ancient Greece into a discussion of the female divinities of the Olympian pantheon, followed by chapters on women in the Homeric period, in the Archaic Age (800–500 B.C.E.), and a section on women in ancient Athens, divided into chapters on women in Greek law, private life, and images of women in literature. As the chapter headings indicate, Pomeroy did not call into question the historiographic validity of the category "woman," nor did other scholars in the field who took up research on this subject. In the discipline of history, by contrast, Natalie Zemon Davis had suggested already in 1976 that "we should be interested in the history of both women and men, [and] we should not be working only on the subjected sex any more than a historian of class can focus exclusively on peasants."[23] But in the field of classics, surveys conceptualized similarly to that of Pomeroy have continued to appear and now exist in the major European languages.[24]

Pomeroy did, however, raise a number of important questions about how to conceptualize the study of women, and some of these have continued to dominate discussions of theory and methodology in classics. First, she noted the presence of male bias or of the masculine point of view in many of the sources, both primary and secondary. This indisputable fact about ancient sources—of material authored by women we have only the fragments of a few women poets—has even led recently to the recommendation that the study of women in antiquity be refocused away from literature to culture more generally, on the grounds that "the study of women in ancient literature is the study of men's views of women and cannot become anything else."[25]

The notion that texts authored by men represent a "male" point of view is widely shared.[26] This idea, however, not only introduces an artificial distinction between text and culture, but also implicitly relegates women to an entirely passive role in patriarchal society—a view which could hardly be substantiated with reference to our own culture, and which is furthermore easily discredited through the comparative study of women in contemporary traditional, patriarchal societies.[27]

Second, Pomeroy took note of the tendency in the scholarly literature to "treat women as an undifferentiated mass," without introducing distinctions having to do with "different economic and social classes" and with "categories of [citizenship]" (that is, full citizens, resident aliens, and slaves).[28] This was often, but by no means always the case. Radermacher, for example, had specifically remarked that his conclusions applied only to citizen women, and that women of the lower classes lived a very different kind of life.[29] And the debate overall, as we have seen, was generally constructed with reference to a status difference between hetairai (noncitizens) and legitimate wives. In addition, almost no information survives on women of other classes, and it is this that accounts for the absence of studies discussing them in the scholarly literature. But in any case, the historiographical difficulties in writing the history of women are not met simply by accounting for the factor of class or status, as the following discussion will show.

Finally, when addressing herself to the question of "the dispute over status," Pomeroy argued that "the wide divergence of scholarly opinion" resulted from "the genre of the evidence consulted" (1975, 60). The same argument informed an essay by Just published in the same year, who remarked that "the real basis of the divergence of opinion is, however, an evidential one," and was subsequently taken up by Gould in 1980 who, despite his recognition that "the explanation . . . is largely a matter of methodology," goes on to discuss women in classical Athens under the traditional rubrics, law and custom/myth.[30]

I argued against this view in 1976, suggesting instead that "the shifting currents of opinion" should be attributed to the influence of ideology, namely that "behind the debate on women's status in Athens there can be detected an apologia both for the patriarchal bias of modern society and for the liberal pretensions of the ancient and modern democratic ideal."[31] As the present study makes clear, I continue to subscribe to that view, believing now, however, that a less simplistic understanding of ideology and its functions must be applied to the question. In addition, it is even clearer now, as I also argued in 1976, that radically different assessments of the same material abound in the literature and indeed continue to proliferate.

To cite just two examples from current literature: Eva Keuls, in *The Reign of the Phallus*, assembles a formidable array of evidence to demonstrate that: "In the case of a society dominated by men who sequester their wives and daughters, denigrate the female role in reproduction, erect monuments to male genitalia, have sex with the sons of their peers, sponsor public whorehouses, create a mythology of rape, and engage in rampant saber-rattling, it is not inappropriate to refer to a reign of the phallus. Classical Athens was such a society."[32] Mary Lefkowitz, by contrast, finds that "[Greek] myth portrays marriage and motherhood, with all the difficulties they involve, as the best conditions most women desire, and in which women can be best respected by society and happiest in themselves," and goes on to suggest that "Greek men may not have been so concerned with repressing women as protecting them."[33]

The question of women's status in ancient Athens, then, as well as the character and interpretation of their "seclusion," continues to be debated in the scholarly literature,[34] and surveys on women in ancient Greece continue to appear, as noted above. But the question of the historiographic adequacy of the category "woman" has not been addressed by classicists in the anglophone world. I raised it myself tentatively, in 1982,[35] concluding that "the problem . . . is not so much that we are coming up with the wrong answers as that we are asking the wrong questions."[36]

But it was Pauline Schmitt-Pantel who first posed the question in a trenchant and challenging manner, in her contribution to the 1984 volume edited by Perrot, *Une Histoire des femmes est-elle possible?* In her essay, Schmitt-Pantel contended: "an assessment of the last ten years' great profusion of studies demonstrates, in my view, that any treatment of Greek women as an isolated category leads to a methodological impasse."[37] I shall return to Schmitt-Pantel's discussion of the *sortie* from this impasse. But now I want to turn to the historiographic issue which she raised, and which has only recently been theorized adequately for the field of Greek antiquity.

Josine Blok in 1987[38] and Beate Wagner-Hasel in 1988 and 1989[39] both argued that, in Blok's words, "the 19th century provided the paradigm that was to define inquiry on women in antiquity until far into the 20th century" (2). Blok's analysis is important; it deserves further discussion and debate from the perspective of the historiography of woman as a category in history. But her interpretation is insufficiently particularized to the specifics of the history of women in Greek antiquity to make it useful in the present context.

In this respect Wagner-Hasel's recent interventions—based on her 1980 Berlin dissertation[40]—are more compelling, in that they are organized around a specific critique of the nineteenth-century opposition between the public and private spheres and its applicability to the ancient Greek social order. I want to draw attention here in particular to a remark that Wagner-Hasel makes in passing and on which, with one important exception to be discussed below, she does not expand: the debate over the status of women in ancient Greece, she says, "is not only an attempt to reconstruct a bygone way of life, it is also a discourse over woman's place in modern bourgeois society which had its beginnings in the Enlightenment and has continued up until the present time."[41]

WOMEN IN CIVIL SOCIETY

In recent years, feminist political scientists like Carole Pateman[42] and Susan Moller Okin[43] have argued that the theory of the liberal democratic state, the study of which has flourished recently in mainstream political science, has remained unaffected by feminist theory. This is not to say that "women's issues" have not been addressed. But, as Pateman notes, "the underlying assumption is that questions which have been taken up as 'women's issues' can be embraced and incorporated into mainstream theory" (1989, 2). She goes on to argue that feminist theory introduces a new and challenging perspective into this discourse. For "feminism does not, as is often supposed, merely add something to existing theories and modes of argument" (1989, 14). Rather, feminist theory demonstrates that "a repressed problem lies at the heart of modern political theory—the problem of patriarchal power[44] or the government of women by men" (1989, 2).

To be more specific: classical social contract theory, on which the contemporary theory of civil society is based, is founded on the

Lockean premise of freedom and equality as a birthright. This birthright constitutes men as individuals possessing a natural political right, and "as 'individuals' all men are owners, in that they all own the property in their persons and capacities over which they alone have right of jurisdiction."[45] These free and equal individuals form a political association through a social contract which establishes obligations and to whose authority its members accede by means of their consent to be governed.

Women, by contrast, are understood to agree to subordinate themselves to their husbands, a subjection which has "a Foundation in Nature,"[46] and though husband and wife "have but one common Concern; . . . it being necessary that the last Determination, *i.e.* the Rule, should be placed somewhere, it naturally falls to the Man's share as the abler and stronger."[47] As Pateman observes: "the contradiction between the premise of individual freedom and equality, with its corollary of the conventional basis of authority, and the assumption that women (wives) are naturally subject has . . . gone unnoticed. . . . [Yet] if women are naturally subordinate . . . then talk of their consent or agreement to this status is redundant."[48]

Locke did not specifically theorize women's subordination, but Rousseau's theory of the social contract, based on the premise that man, in passing from the state of nature to civil society, loses his natural liberty but gains both civil liberty and moral freedom,[49] did explicitly justify it. Rousseau, who like other Enlightenment thinkers, as Wagner-Hasel says, "developed the theoretical foundations for the interrelationship between ancient and modern democracy, and regarded as their models Attic generals like Pericles or Roman Senators of Cicero's kind,"[50] modeled his "people's assembly" on the *comitia tributa* ("tribal" or popular assembly) of the ancient Romans, drawing certain additional features from the constitution of the Spartans.

Rousseau generally regarded ancient Sparta as "the example that we ought to follow."[51] But in *Emile*, published, along with *The Social Contract*, in 1762, it was classical Athens that provided the paradigm for the incorporation of women into the ideal state. There, Rousseau expanded upon arguments that he had first advanced in the 1758 "Letter to M. d'Alembert on the Theatre," where he remarked that "the ancients had, in general, a very great respect for women."[52] And he explained in more detail:

Among all the ancient civilized peoples [women] led very retired lives; they did not have the best places at the theatre; they did not put themselves on display; they were not even always permitted to go; and it is well known that there was a death penalty for those who dared to show themselves at the Olympic games. In the home, they had a private apartment where the men never entered. When their husbands entertained for dinner, they rarely presented themselves at the table; the decent women went out before the end of the meal, and the others never appeared at the beginning. There was no common place of assembly for the two sexes; they did not pass the day together. This effort not to become sated with one another made their meetings more pleasant. It is certain that domestic peace was, in general, better established and that greater harmony prevailed between man and wife than is the case today.[53]

Among others, Mary Wollstonecraft, in *A Vindication of the Rights of Woman* (1792), argued against Rousseau's views. There she insisted that the confinement of women's instruction to such frivolities as Rousseau had envisioned, would produce "weak beings . . . only fit for a seraglio!"[54]

The question of women's status in ancient Greece, and of the extent and meaning of their "seclusion," then, did not originate in the nineteenth century, nor was it raised first by scholars of classical antiquity. Rather, as the above citations indicate, it formed part of the intellectual currency of the eighteenth century, and played an important role in the general debate over the form and nature of civil society. (Böttiger, as we saw above, cited Wollstonecraft less than admiringly when he first turned his attention to the question of women's status in ancient Greece.) Furthermore, some of the specific terms of this discourse were set in the eighteenth century. Rousseau, for example, had remarked in 1758 that women in the ancient world were "respected" and that this was connected with their having led "very retired lives." What is more, the formulation of the question itself relied on a certain circular logic: Rousseau in 1758 cited the example of women in ancient Athens to substantiate his views on women's nature; Jacobs in 1830 relied on the eighteenth-century view of women's nature to authenticate his interpretation of the ancient evidence.

RECENT CHALLENGES AND FUTURE DIRECTIONS

It is only in the last ten years or so that the "status" model has been challenged as a research paradigm, and this has been achieved principally by introducing a discontinuity between the ancient conception of the relationship between *polis* (city-state) and *oikos* (household) and the analogous modern distinction between "public" and "private." The landmark 1979 study on the question, Sally Humphreys's "*Oikos* and *Polis*," treats the opposition in Athenian society and culture overall, showing that such modern distinctions as that between the political and economic spheres are misleading when applied to ancient Athens. Humphreys forgoes discussion of women's status as such, but treats aspects of women's incorporation in and exclusion from the functioning of the sociocultural totality. In addition, she makes the important observation that "the separation of men and women in social life meant that in a sense the public world of the city reached into the house."[55]

Others have followed Humphreys's lead. Beate Wagner-Hasel, in an equally important 1982 full-scale study of women in early Greek society, proceeds from the premise that "the first question of determining the status of the particular members of a society must always be [constituted] first as the question of the character of this society itself—its social, political, and economic structure."[56] Both Humphreys and Wagner-Hasel emphasize the importance of applying ethnographic and anthropological models to the study of ancient Greece, and in 1981 and 1982, I used analogies drawn from the anthropology of contemporary traditional Mediterranean societies to redraw the conceptualization of women in ancient Greece under the heading of "a divided world."[57]

Helene Foley in 1981 drew attention to the inadequacy of interpreting ancient Greek tragedy in accordance with a concept of *oikos* and *polis* as equivalent either to nature and culture or private and public, and proposed a reading overall in which *oikos* and *polis* "are mutually defining institutions; order in one sphere is inextricably related to order in the other."[58] Froma Zeitlin, in a important 1985 study, extended the analysis of Greek drama to embrace the generation itself of the categories "masculine" and "feminine."[59] And Giulia Sissa recently has carried out an investigation of the construction of sexual difference in the philosophical works of Plato and Aristotle.[60]

The study of women in antiquity, then, has evolved over the last ten years or so from "the history of women" to the "history of 'gender,'" as Schmitt-Pantel has observed recently, adding that the concepts "sexual asymmetry, social relations between the sexes, and gender" now serve as the "basis for further progress."[61] But there are other dimensions to this history which are not adequately comprehended through the reorientation around the newer categories. I am referring in particular to questions regarding the constitution of the self, or more specifically, the constitution of the gendered or sexual self.

These questions in the field of classics have been addressed recently by scholars working within two separate subfields, those of ancient Greek medicine and ancient Greek sexuality.[62] Ancient Greek and Roman medical writers discussed the matter of female physiology at great length, and in a series of gynecological treatises developed an extensive discourse on the subject of the female body. Some aspects of their theories—for example, Galen's notion that the female reproductive structure was equivalent to that of the male turned outside in—survived into the Renaissance and served as the basis for theories of human physiology which remained unchallenged until the late eighteenth century.[63]

The Greco-Roman medical writers, however, concerned themselves almost exclusively with the reproductive aspects of female physiology. As Ann Hanson observes, even when they acknowledge the existence of female orgasm, the medical writers' concern is with its relation to the woman's capacity to conceive: "the Hippokratic gynecologies center attention not on woman's desire or pleasure, but on whether or not she has taken up the seed."[64]

Recent discussions of ancient Greek sexuality have centered their attention on male sexuality, and in particular on questions having to do with the character of male homosexuality in ancient Greece.[65] This work has given rise to a lively debate on whether there exists a discontinuity between "the Greeks and us" in the conceptualization of sexuality, and on whether Greek culture, like our own, constructed a distinction between "homosexuals" and "heterosexuals."[66]

The issue is itself a historiographic one, formulated principally around Halperin's contention that the category "homosexual" was itself a product of the late-nineteenth-century discourse on sexual pathology. But the matter of woman's sexual desire and the question of female erotics have, by and large, received little attention, in this or other literature.[67]

What is, in fact, the nature of women's eros? And what was the character of female sexuality in Greek antiquity? The answers to these questions remain an unfinished project for the study of women in ancient Greece.[68] To undertake it would require both a historiography of the question and a consideration of ancient Greek laws on adultery and of ancient conceptualizations of such phenomena as prostitution, rape, and pornography. Some important new research in these areas has appeared, for example Cohen's chapters on adultery,[69] Zeitlin's and Scafuro's essays on rape in Greek myth,[70] and a new volume on pornography edited by Richlin.[71] But a full discussion that takes into account distinctions between our own notions and those of the Greeks awaits formulation.

It has been the overall point of this section to argue that our own understanding of sexuality and of the difference between the sexes has been critically mediated by the nineteenth- and twentieth-century discourses on this same subject. Thus, however much the ancients may appear to resemble or anticipate us, in this as in other areas, such as their notions of "woman's place," they were also working within a radically different cultural framework which has been illegitimately assimilated to our own. And it is, therefore, no less important to the project of understanding our own values than to that of comprehending theirs that we reconstruct the divide which separates the "Greeks" *from* "us."

Such a project would require also that we reconstruct the point at which the history of the construction of sex and sexuality intersected with that of the construction of race. From the perspective of the history of women in ancient Greece, that point is marked by Meiners's coinage of the term "oriental seclusion" to characterize the condition of the women of ancient Greece. Meiners, in his *History of the Female Sex*,[72] published from 1788–1800, found that the ancient Greeks, who "in certain respects so nearly resembled the most spirited and magnanimous nations of our division of the globe" seem more like Slavons or Orientals: "in other points, and especially in its general conduct to the sex, and its laws

concerning women, [the Greeks] appeared much more closely
allied to the Orientals and to the Slavonic nations of Europe"
(1.260).

The metaphor of the seraglio or harem originated in the
seventeenth century, developed a widespread currency in the eighteenth century, and forms part of the general history of what
Edward Said has called *Orientalism*.[73] Thus, when Mary Wollstonecraft,
in her discussion in 1792 of women's education, referred to the
"seraglio," she was drawing on an idea that was current in the
popular culture of the time. Its application to the condition of the
women of ancient Greece continues to be debated,[74] but it is now
generally discussed under the heading of "seclusion."

The very term "oriental seclusion," however, should have
warned us against attempting to interpret it outside the ideological
context in which it arose—a context which cannot be eliminated
simply by dropping the adjective and referring to "seclusion"
instead, as we have all been inclined to do, in recognition of the
now embarrassing overtones of the phrase. But adjustments in
usage, while salutary from a political point of view, also constitute
evasions from the historiographic perspective.

Thus, an adequate historiography of the history of women in
ancient Greece would require that we discuss the formulation of
the question of women's seclusion in ancient Athens in the light of
the history of Orientalism generally, taking note of such issues as its
origin in the linguistic theories of the time, and its subsequent
evolution, in the late eighteenth and nineteenth centuries, into a
generalized theory of racial difference. Such an investigation would
also reveal an important further historical point of intersection—
between the theories of racial and sexual difference—on the basis
of which the theory of sexual pathology was constructed in the late
nineteenth century.[75]

Recent challenges to the "status" model, then, have served to
redefine and reorient a research paradigm which, as I have attempted to demonstrate, is now almost two hundred years old. The
new directions in research that have been marked out offer the
promise of adding important new dimensions to our understanding
of the ancient Greeks' cultural particularity. But much remains to
be done in order to integrate this new history with the old, and to
redefine and reformulate the character of the continuities and
discontinuities which both connect and separate them.

SUMMARY AND CONCLUSIONS

The burden of this essay has been, first, to show that the
question of women's status in ancient Greece has continued to be
addressed in contemporary scholarship in much the same terms as
it was formulated in the nineteenth century. Scholars generally,
even when they have acknowledged this history in long and pon-
derous footnotes, have generally stopped at this point, availing
themselves of what I shall call the "European seclusion theory"—
the notion that their nineteenth-century predecessors developed
the foundations of classical scholarship alone in their studies with
their books. (One need only think here of the frontispieces frequently prefaced to biographies, depicting the scholar poring over
his voluminous tomes in solitary concentration.) In the second
section, I have attempted to demonstrate that the formulation of
the question of women's status in ancient Greece has a far more
complex history, and that its terms were intimately bound up with
the eighteenth-century discourse on freedom, the individual, and
civil society.

This history is well known, but within the field of classics it is
generally relegated to the subdiscipline known as the history of the
classical tradition or the classical heritage.[76] Within this framework,
not only are the ideological specifics of the tradition widely
overlooked,[77] as Martin Bernal lately has made clear,[78] but the
discussion of women and their history is largely left out of account,
except where it touches on themes having to do with Greek
mythology and religion.

What I have tried to show, with reference to the study of
women in antiquity, is that its history and historiography are in fact
constituted through a complex intersection between classical scholarship and the classical tradition, and that this interpenetration was
itself significantly conditioned by the contemporary discussions on
language, nationalism, and race. To evaluate this history properly,
we must take into account, therefore, not only Rousseau's reading
of antiquity, but such further considerations as his contribution to
the formation of political theory, and the contemporary rereading
and critique of his influence.[79] Furthermore, the exemption of
women from civil society in political theory should be understood,
not only in terms of the perseverance of patriarchy and a motivated
nostalgia for the ancient Greek past, but within the context of
eighteenth-century medical inquiry, its rereading of the ancient

theory of biology, and its eventual intersection in the nineteenth century with the discourse on language, race, and nationality.

It should be clear that what has interested me here is not the history of ideas, although I do regard it as important to know that a certain continuity can be found among the ideas of, for example, Rousseau, Jacobs, and A. W. Gomme, and that this continuity is based on a shared notion, inherited from the eighteenth century, of women's proper sphere and its correlation with their "nature." Rather, I have been concerned to make clear how the terms of the discussion themselves came into being, and to identify their ideological valences.

Thus, from the historiographic point of view, there is not a "history of women" as such. But there is a history of women in society, as Wagner-Hasel and others have shown, and there is also a history of the gendered individual, as recent studies on sexuality in ancient Greece have demonstrated. In this essay, I have concentrated on the history of the history of women, which, as I have argued, still awaits reconstruction in its fullest particulars. This can only be achieved, not by dismissing as outdated what has gone before, but by exposing the ideological foundations of a hegemonic discourse that has dominated the discussion of ancient women and that continues to make its powerful influence felt in the discussion of women generally as part of civil society at the present moment in history.

NOTES

1. Michelle Perrot, ed., *Une Histoire des femmes est-elle possible?* (Paris, 1984).

2. Denise Riley, *"Am I That Name?" Feminism and the Category of "Women" in History* (Minneapolis, 1988).

3. Marilyn Skinner, "Classical Studies, Patriarchy and Feminism: The View from 1986," *Women's Studies International Forum* 10 (1987): 181–186.

4. I have not attempted to be comprehensive in this essay: some books or articles are discussed in detail; many other important items are omitted altogether. My discussion is restricted to works that I consider representative of the principal analytic approaches and that are useful for demonstrating the theoretical and ideological premises of the various interpretive methods.

5. A. W. Gomme, "The Position of Women in Athens in the Fifth and Fourth Centuries B.C.," here cited from the reprint in Gomme, *Essays in Greek History and Literature* (Oxford, 1937), 89–115.

6. H.D.F. Kitto, *The Greeks* (Harmondsworth, Eng., 1951).

7. Karl Julius Beloch, *Griechische Geschichte*, 2nd ed. Here cited from the

second edition as follows: 1.1 (Strassburg, 1912); 2.1 (Strassburg, 1914); 3.1 (Berlin, 1922); 4.1 (Berlin, 1925).

8. The term is the feminine of *hetairos* meaning "companion"; the Greek plural is *hetairai*, sometimes Latinized to *hetaerae*. Gomme suggests the translation *"demi-mondaine"* (*Essays in Greek History*, 105); and Beloch renders *hetairai* as "Damen der Halbwelt" (3.1:434).

9. For the most recent discussion of these women, see S. B. Pomeroy, *Women in Hellenistic Egypt: From Alexander the Great to Cleopatra* (New York, 1984).

10. Friedrich Jacobs, *Beiträge zur Geschichte des weiblichen Geschlechtes*, in *Abhandlungen über Gegenstände des Alterthums*, Vermischte Schriften vol. 4; Leben und Kunst der Alten vol. 3 (Leipzig, 1830), 157–554.

11. See especially his discussion of Meiners, 206–210.

12. Gomme, "The Position of Women in Athens," 99, n.2.

13. Jacobs, *Beiträge*, 264. Compare Gomme's statements about this same fragment, in "The Position of Women in Athens," 99.

14. Kitto, *The Greeks*, 222.

15. Jacobs, *Beiträge*, 243–244.

16. *Ibid.*, 224. I discuss briefly the "racial" aspects of Meiners's formulations later in this article.

17. Originally published in 1796, and reprinted in Böttiger's *Kleine Schriften*, ed. Sillig, vol. 1 (Leipzig, 1837), pages 295–307.

18. *Ibid.*, 295. On the concept of "oriental harem-slavery," see below.

19. According to Frederick Metcalfe, in the "Translator's Preface" to Wilhelm Adolf Becker, *Charicles or Illustrations of the Private Life of the Greeks* (London, 1866), vii. All subsequent citations of *Charicles* are from this translation.

20. M. Hadas, "Observations on Athenian Women," *Classical Weekly* 29 (3 February 1936): 97–100, citation 100; cf. L. R. Shero, "Xenophon's Portrait of a Young Wife," *Classical Weekly* 26 (17 October 1932): 17–21; C. Seltman, "The Status of Women in Athens," *Greece and Rome* ser. 2 (1955): 119–124; D. C. Richter, "The Position of Women in Classical Athens," *Classical Journal* 67 (1971): 1–8.

21. Richter, "The Position of Women in Classical Athens," 5, 7. Cf. Richter's view that "the young wives [of ancient Athens] were as undisciplined a bevy of nymphs as Hellas ever reared," *ibid.*, 7.

22. An exception to this general rule was the study of women's status in ancient law, which the nature of the subdiscipline obliged scholars to discuss in a wider sociocultural context.

23. Natalie Zemon Davis, "Women's History in Transition: The European Case," *Feminist Studies* 3 (1976): 83–103, citation 90.

24. C. Mossé, *La femme dans la Grèce antique* (Paris, 1983); E. Cantarella, *Pandora's Daughters: The Role and Status of Women in Greek and Roman Antiquity*, trans. M. B. Fant. (Baltimore, 1987); W. Schuller, *Frauen in der griechischen Geschichte* (Konstanz, 1985); G. Clark, *Women in the Ancient World*, Greece and Rome: New Surveys in the Classics 21 (Oxford, 1989); Roger Just, *Women in Athenian Law and Life* (New York, 1991).

25. Phyllis Culham, "Ten Years after Pomeroy: Studies of the Image and Reality of Women in Antiquity," *Helios* n.s. 13 (1986): citation 15.

26. For example, Roger Just, "Conceptions of Women in Classical Athens," *Journal of the Anthropological Society of Oxford* 6 (1975): 153–170, esp. 154, and Just, *Women in Athenian Law*, 4; John Gould, "Law, Custom and Myth: Aspects of the

Social Position of Women in Classical Athens," *Journal of Hellenic Studies* 100 (1980): 38–59, esp. 38.

27. Cf. Nicole-Claude Matthieu's critique of the anthropologist Edwin Ardener's notion of women as a "muted group" (E. Ardener, "Belief and the Problem of Women," in *The Interpretation of Ritual*, ed. J. S. LaFontaine [London, 1972], 135–158), and of the biological essentialism implied by the concept: "there is no 'autonomous female way of seeing'; there is no woman's way of seeing on the one hand and man's way of seeing on the other; there is only that of the society as a whole": Matthieu, "Homme-Culture et Femme-Nature?," *L'Homme* 13 (1973): 101–113, citation 112. Both Just and Gould draw freely on Ardener in constructing their own analytic paradigms.

28. Sarah B. Pomeroy, *Goddesses, Whores, Wives, and Slaves: Women in Classical Antiquity* (New York, 1975), 60.

29. Ludwig Radermacher, "Die Stellung der Frau innerhalb der griechische Kultur," *Mitteilungen des Vereins der Freunde des Humanistischen Gymnasiums* 27 (1928): 16.

30. Roger Just, "Conceptions of Women," 154; cf. 157; John Gould, "Law, Custom and Myth," 38–59, citation 39.

31. M. B. Arthur (= M. A. Katz), "Review Essay: Classics," *Signs* 2 (1976): 382–403, citation 383.

32. Eva Keuls, *The Reign of the Phallus: Sexual Politics in Ancient Greece* (New York, 1985), 1.

33. Mary Lefkowitz, "Epilogue," in *Women and Greek Myth* (Baltimore, 1986), 133–136, citations 133, 134. Cf. also the same author's *Heroines and Hysterics* (Baltimore, 1981), *passim*.

34. For example, David Cohen, "Seclusion, Separation, and the Status of Women in Classical Athens," *Greece and Rome* 36 (1989): 3–15. See also Cohen, *Law, Sexuality, and Society: The Enforcement of Morals in Classical Athens* (Cambridge, Eng., 1991), 171–202.

35. M. B. Arthur (= M. A. Katz), "Women and the Family in Ancient Greece," *Yale Review* 71 (1982): 532–547.

36. *Ibid.*, 535.

37. Pauline Schmitt-Pantel, "La différence des sexes: histoire, anthropologie et cité grecque," in *Une histoire des femmes? est-elle possible?*, ed. M. Perrot, (Paris, 1984), 98–119, 105.

38. Josine Blok, "Sexual Asymmetry: A Historiographical Essay," in *Sexual Asymmetry: Studies in Ancient Society*, ed. Josine Blok and Peter Mason (Amsterdam, 1987), 1–57; first published in Dutch in 1984.

39. Beate Wagner-Hasel, "Das Private wird politisch," in *Weiblichkeit in geschichtlicher Perspektive*, ed. Ursula A. J. Becher and Jörn Rüsen (Frankfurt, 1988); "Frauenleben in orientalischer Abgeschlossenheit? Zur Geschichte und Nutzanwendung eines Topos," *Der Altsprachliche Unterricht* 2 (1989), 18–29.

40. Published in a revised and expanded form as *Zwischen Mythos und Realität: Die Frau in der frühgriechischen Gesellschaft* (Frankfurt am Main, 1982).

41. Wagner-Hasel, "Frauenleben," 19.

42. Carole Pateman, *The Disorder of Women* (Stanford, 1989). For a recent discussion of Pateman's work overall in the context of political theory, see Anne Phillips, "Universal Pretensions in Political Thought," in *Destabilizing Theory:*

Contemporary Feminist Debates, ed. M. Barrett and A. Phillips (Stanford, 1992), 10–30.

43. Susan Moller Okin, *Women in Western Political Thought* (Princeton, 1979).

44. I shall not embark here upon a definition of the term "patriarchy," an understanding of which, despite its widespread popular currency, requires a thoroughgoing historiographic and political analysis. For some preliminary remarks on a contrast between "paternal" and "fraternal" patriarchy, see Pateman, *Disorder of Women*, 35–36.

45. *Ibid.*, 10.

46. John Locke, *Two Treatises of Government*, ed. Peter Laslett, 2nd ed. (Cambridge, Eng., 1967), 191–192 (I.47–48).

47. *Ibid.*, 339 (2.82).

48. Pateman, *Disorder of Women*, 213. Cf. also her chapters, "Women and Consent" and "Feminism and Democracy," in *Disorder of Women*, 71–89; 210–225. For a theoretical critique of John Stuart Mill's theory of sexual egalitarianism, see Susan Moller Okin, "John Stuart Mill, Liberal Feminist," in *Women in Western Political Thought*, 197–223.

49. Jean-Jacques Rousseau, *The Social Contract*, trans. M. Cranston (Baltimore, 1978), 64–65 (1.8).

50. Wagner-Hasel, "Das Private wird politisch," 26.

51. Rousseau, "Letter to M. D'Alembert on the Theatre," in *Politics and the Arts*, trans. Allan Bloom (Glencoe, Ill., 1960), 133.

52. *Ibid.*, 48.

53. *Ibid.*, 88–89.

54. Mary Wollstonecraft, *A Vindication of the Rights of Woman: An Authoritative Text, Backgrounds, The Wollstonecraft Debate, Criticism*, ed. Carol H. Poston, 2nd ed. (New York, 1988), 10; cf. 29. On the metaphor of the seraglio or harem, see below.

55. S. C. Humphreys, "*Oikos* and *Polis*," in *The Family, Women and Death: Comparative Studies* (London, 1983), 1–21, citation 16. See also, "Public and Private in Classical Athens," in D. Cohen, *Law, Sexuality, and Society*, 70–97.

56. Wagner-Hasel, *Zwischen Mythos und Realität*, 5. See also her extensive discussion of public and private spheres, their relationship to the social and economic structure of the polis overall, and women's roles, in *ibid.*, section B, 67–272.

57. In a talk presented on 3 April 1981 at Wesleyan University to the Department of History Faculty Seminar, "Marx and History," under the title, "Ideology and the 'Status' of Women in Ancient Greece," one section of which was published as Arthur, "Women and the Family." For a fuller discussion, see Cohen, *Law, Sexuality, and Society*, esp. 14–69.

58. Helene Foley, "The Conception of Women in Athenian Drama," in *Reflections of Women in Antiquity*, ed. Foley (New York, 1981), 127–168, citation 156.

59. Froma Zeitlin, "Playing the Other: Theater, Theatricality, and the Feminine in Greek Drama," *Representations* 11 (1985): 63–94. On the opposition between masculine and feminine in Greek culture, see also Schmitt-Pantel, "La différence des sexes," 101 and *passim*.

60. Giulia Sissa, "The Sexual Philosophies of Plato and Aristotle," in *From Ancient Goddesses to Christian Saints*, ed. P. Schmitt-Pantel, trans. A. Goldhammer, vol. 1 of *A History of Women in the West* (Cambridge, Mass., 1992), 46–81.

61. P. Schmitt-Pantel, "Women and Ancient History Today," in Schmitt-Pantel, ed., *A History of Women*, 464, 466.

62. For a review of recent work in these subfields, see Marilyn Katz, "Sexuality and the Body in Ancient Greece," *Métis. Revue d'anthropologie du monde grec ancien* 4 (1989): 155–179 (= *Trends in History* 4 [1990]: 97–125).

63. For discussion, see Thomas Laqueur, "Orgasm, Generation, and the Politics of Reproductive Biology," *Representations* 14 (1986): 1–41, and Laqueur, *Making Sex: Body and Gender from the Greeks to Freud* (Cambridge, Mass., 1990).

64. Ann Hanson, "The Medical Writers' Woman," in *Before Sexuality: The Construction of Erotic Experience in the Ancient World*, ed. D. M. Halperin, J. J. Winkler, and F. I. Zeitlin (Princeton, 1990), 309–337, citation 315. For further discussion of this topic, see also G.E.R. Lloyd, "The Female Sex: Medical Treatment and Biological Theories in the Fifth and Fourth Centuries B.C.," in *Science, Folklore and Ideology: Studies in the Life Sciences in Ancient Greece* (Cambridge, Eng., 1983), 86–94; and Helen King, "The Daughter of Leonides: Reading the Hippocratic Corpus," in *History as Text*, ed. A. Cameron (Chapel Hill, 1989), 11–32.

65. On which see especially, in addition to the essays in Halperin, Winkler, and Zeitlin, eds., *Before Sexuality*; David Halperin, *One Hundred Years of Homosexuality and Other Essays on Greek Love* (New York, 1992); and John J. Winkler, *Constraints of Desire: The Anthropology of Sex and Gender in Ancient Greece* (New York, 1990).

66. For some recent contributions to this debate, see David Cohen, "Debate [with Clifford Hindley]: Law, Society and Homosexuality in Classical Athens," *Past and Present* 133 (1991): 167–194, and "Law, Social Control, and Homosexuality," in *Law, Sexuality, and Society* (Cambridge, Eng., 1991), 171–202; John Thorp, "Review Article: The Social Construction of Homosexuality," *Phoenix* 46 (1992): 54–61; John Boswell, "Concepts, Experience, and Sexuality," *differences* 2, no. 1 (1990), special issue on "Sexuality in Greek and Roman Society," 67–87.

67. For some exceptions to this general pattern, see Anne Carson, "Putting Her in Her Place: Woman, Dirt, and Desire," in *Before Sexuality*, 135–169; Giulia Sissa, *Greek Virginity*, trans. A. Goldhammer (Cambridge, Mass., 1990); and Aline Rouselle, *Porneia: On Desire and the Body in Antiquity*, trans. F. Pheasant (New York, 1988).

68. It is worth noting in this connection that, as my student Audrey Prins Patt pointed out to me recently, Scarborough's *Medical Terminologices: Classical Origins* (Norman, Okla., 1992) omits the term clitoris (which is Greek, and which is discussed by the ancient medical writers and lexicographers) from his discussion of "Sexual Anatomy: The 'Parts' (female)."

69. Cohen, "The Law of Adultery," and "Adultery, Women, and Social Control," in *Law, Sexuality, and Society*, 98–132 and 133–170, respectively.

70. Zeitlin, "Configurations of Rape in Greek Myth," in *Rape*, ed. S. Tomaselli and R. Porter (Oxford, 1986), 122–161; Scafuro, "Discourses of Sexual Violation in Mythic Accounts and Dramatic Versions of 'The Girl's Tragedy,'" *differences* 2, no. 1 (1990), special issue on "Sexuality in Greek and Roman Society," 126–159.

71. Amy Richlin, ed., *Pornography and Representation in Greece and Rome* (New York, 1992).

72.   Christoph Meiners, *History of the Female Sex* (Hannover, 1788–1800); hereafter cited in the English translation by F. Shoberl (London, 1808), by volume and page number.

73.   Edward Said, *Orientalism* (New York, 1978), whose study is limited to "the Anglo-French-American experience of the Arabs and Islam, which for almost a thousand years together stood for the Orient" (17).

74.   E.g., Cohen, "Seclusion, Separation, and the Status of Women."

75.   For some preliminary discussion of these issues, see my remarks in the longer version of the present essay, Marilyn Katz in "Ideology and 'The Status' of Women in Ancient Greece," *History and Theory* Beiheft 31, *History and Feminist Theory* (Middletown, 1992): 86–92, and the references cited therein.

76.   For example, Frank M. Turner, *The Greek Heritage in Victorian Britain* (New Haven, 1981).

77.   Or relegated to footnotes: see, for example, the remarks on the part played by "contemporary racial thinking" in Matthew Arnold's work, in Turner, *The Greek Heritage*, 20–21, n.4.

78.   Martin Bernal, *The Fabrication of Ancient Greece*, vol. 1 of *Black Athena: The Afroasiatic Roots of Classical Civilization* (London, 1987). I shall not comment on the extensive dispute to which this book has given rise, other than to say that I regard the general burden of the historiographic account as largely correct, notwithstanding the fact that Bernal has sometimes been careless with the evidence.

79.   See, for example, the recent discussion by A. Koppelman, "Sex Equality and/or the Family: From Bloom vs. Okin to Rousseau vs. Hegel," *Yale Journal of Law and Humanities*, 4 (1992): 399–432, which contrasts Susan Okin's and Allan Bloom's views on the implications of Rousseau's theory of the family to contemporary feminist debate on the place of women in the social order.

On Looking at Men
Masculinity and the Making of a Gendered Working-Class History

AVA BARON

For the labor historian interested in issues of gender and class today may be both the best of times and the worst of times. Research on women workers has demonstrated the centrality of gender to women's work experiences and to our understanding of labor markets and labor organizing. In the process of making women visible by restoring women to history, women's historians wrote a comparable "herstory."[1] But women's historians learned that dealing with women's marginality in history entailed more than adding women to the conventional narratives. It required rewriting the core narratives of history itself. Feminist historians have challenged existing categories of analysis and several important tenets of the field that have operated to marginalize women, including periodization and the dichotomizing of public and private spheres.[2] In the past few years research demonstrating the diversity of working-class experience along lines such as race, ethnicity, and gender, as historian Jane Caplan put it, have "burrowed deeply under the wall of Marxist class analysis."[3] As a result, class has begun to weaken as the privileged category of analysis.[4]

But while the concept of class has been called into question, it has not been displaced, nor have work, the workplace, and class formation been removed from center stage.[5] One of the major

An earlier version of this essay was presented at the Conference on "Reworking American Labor History: Race, Gender and Class," cosponsored by the State Historical Society of Wisconsin and the History Department, University of Wisconsin-Madison, Madison, Wisconsin, 9-11 April 1992. I am deeply grateful to Leora Auslander, Susan Porter Benson, Mary Blewett, Richard Butsch, Patricia Cooper, Alan Dawley, Nancy Hewitt, Sonya Rose, Philip Scranton, and especially Joan Scott, for their comments, (sometimes sharp) criticism and support in revising this essay. I appreciate Ann-Louise Shapiro's patience and insightful editorial advice.

concerns of American labor historians continues to be explaining the rise and/or fall of a working class.[6] Since the primary issue has been class solidarity, women and nonwhite people appear in labor history primarily as "problems" for the true "cause" of class.

At the same time that the walls holding up class have begun to crumble, new walls of resistance to incorporating gender into working-class history have begun to be built. Few historians today would deny that women worked and participated in class struggles. The question now being raised by some historians who are resistant to gender analysis is: so what? Does adding gender really make a difference to our understanding of what happened? For these historians, knowing that women were "there" in the riots and revolutions, workplaces and strikes, has not changed the grand narrative of capitalist development and social change.[7]

While some now claim that women's history can be said to "have arrived," it is clear that in certain respects it remains ghettoized and marginalized in history.[8] Labor history typically refers to the history of workingmen and their work, while women's labor history is cast as the particular, that which is different.[9] Labor history and women's history have been characterized as "separate tribes" each with their own journals, conferences, and networks of communication. Some men's labor historians see this separatism as unfortunate, but inevitable, resulting from the differences in the organizing concepts used in the two fields: labor historians write about class and relations of production, concepts, they see as inherently materialist; women's historians are largely concerned about gender, a notion that leads them to study ideology, and that is conceived as residing in the household and the "private sphere."[10]

Given this characterization of the two areas of study, it is not surprising that some men's labor historians fear that incorporating gender into labor history means either abandoning class analysis altogether, or winding up with nothing but a jigsaw puzzle of disparate experiences.[11] These labor historians equate gender with women. They believe that attending to gender will shift the field's focus away from questions of class and economic transformations, away from formal and public centers of power, and away from work and the workplace.[12]

In this essay I want to examine whether a more constructive and meaningful relationship can be formed between labor history and women's history. Are there points of convergence between the dual goals of understanding class inequality, on the one hand, and maintaining a commitment to uncovering the dynamics of women's subordination, on the other? Can women's historians continue to ask what some consider to be the "hard feminist questions" in such a convergence?[13]

I propose that a key ingredient in the making of a gendered working-class history is exploring how meanings of masculinity as well as femininity are constructed and naturalized and then structured into the fabric of social relations and institutions, including those predominantly or even exclusively male. As long as labor historians focused on the workplace, treated men as typical workers, and equated gender analysis with the study of women, gender was considered subsidiary to the "really important" questions in labor history, and the marginalization of women's history seemed inevitable, though perhaps unfortunate. The absence of women has often been used as a justification for bracketing gender when dealing with male-dominated unions and workplaces or when addressing issues such as class formation or the transformation of industrial capitalism. Ira Katznelson, for example, justifies the exclusion of gender from an otherwise broad analysis of class formation by claiming that the focus of the research presented is on production at a particular point in history and, therefore, "principally about men in the working class."[14] Women and gender are relegated to the private sphere of family and community. The author's claim to recognize gender differences in the impact and experience of industrialization, and his regret at having left women out of the study, in no way obviates the problem. As has often been the case, issues of gender have been sidestepped on the grounds that they are not relevant to the world of men's work.

But gender is present even when women are not, just as race is significant for studying whites as well as blacks.[15] There has been little attention given to how male workers are constituted by gender and to how work and the workplace have been structured around masculinity. Rarely have labor historians explicitly examined masculinity even when dealing with quintessentially masculine work.[16] Despite the fact that labor history primarily has been about men and their institutions, their gender has been treated as "natural" and, therefore, has been invisible in our research. We have not seen masculinity because we have learned to ignore gender when studying men. By accepting as unproblematic the gender and race assumptions of their subjects of investigation (male workers, labor leaders, and political economists) historians have been central actors in the construction of "the worker" as white and male.[17]

My earlier research is a good example of how it was possible to study men while ignoring their gender. I had studied the transformation of printing for years, focusing on women printers and the threat to men's class positions by the feminization of the work.[18] When I first realized that I had been examining the making of men's work I was amazed at how much men spoke about gender. Suddenly the light bulb went on and I saw so much that had been hidden in the dark. And like the excitement that comes from engaging in other forbidden endeavors, I experienced a certain pleasure from looking at what had been taboo.

The silences in labor history have spoken most articulately of its gender biases. For some time feminist historians have argued that the invisibility of women in labor history reflected deep prejudices that could not easily be rectified by simply adding more women into the narrative.[19] Women continue to be marginalized because the task of rewriting history could not be complete without decentering the "his" in history. The gendering of labor history entails dislodging "man" as the universal historical subject, and this requires recognizing that men are gendered.[20]

New lines of research have exposed the male-centeredness of some of the organizing concepts in labor history—such as production and the wage. The notion of "the worker" dramatically represents women's marginality in labor history. While presented as ostensibly gender neutral, the term is instead sexually particular, referring to men. The male worker is the universal, the measure or standard from which others are gauged; the woman worker is the particular, that which is different.[21] The male worker and masculine symbols have been used to represent unionism despite women's labor activism and union participation. Women were made invisible even when they were present.[22]

Some women's historians resistant to examining masculinity rather than focusing on women have argued that such a shift decenters women from women's history. But by defining only "woman" as a historical topic for investigation, "man" remains the

universal subject against which women are defined in their particularity. "To the extent that feminist discourse defines its problematic
as 'woman,'" Jane Flax explains, "it, too, ironically privileges the
man as unproblematic."[23] Studying masculinity transforms the question
of sexual difference from asking how women are different from
men, to investigating how man is constituted by gender. By posing
the problem in this way we begin to problematize rather than take
for granted the male prototype as the subject of history.[24]

One step in dislodging man as the universal subject is to
understand men in terms of their particularity—making "man"
historically specific. This requires studies of the formation of
masculine gender identity in various contexts, exploring the ways
social institutions and practices have been shaped by different
notions of manliness.[25] Some scholars have begun to examine the
ways masculinity has shifted in content, demonstrating the contingent nature of meanings of manhood; such work establishes that
masculinity is neither fixed nor unitary; it has a history.[26] Only very
recently have a few studies gone beyond documenting changes in
gender meanings to examine the social and political contests that
gave rise to them.[27] We need further historical investigation into
the ways sexual difference has been conceived and naturalized and
how some notions of masculinity and femininity became hegemonic and others silenced.

Masculinity is not just a "feminist" issue, it is also crucial to the
study of labor history. The invisibility of masculinity in labor
history has kept men's activities from critical scrutiny and been a
roadblock to understanding the dynamics of social change.[28] Women's
historians already have transformed our understanding of what
happened by including women in the historical narrative. But we
can further expand our reply to the question: what difference does
gender make? by exploring the way the study of men and masculinity revises our analysis of *how* history happened. New labor
historians, disillusioned by their inability to explain social transformation, can benefit by studying masculinity as well as femininity,
not as static concepts, but as processes, embedded in social, political, and economic relationships, institutions, and practices.

Questions of gender figured prominently in the discourses of
nineteenth-century workingmen and their employers. One of these
gender problematics was the "woman question"—the respectabil-

ity of paid work for females. Historians' adoption of the terms used in nineteenth-century debates about "the woman worker" was one of the ways the "white male" was created as the universal subject in labor history. Like their typically white male subjects, contemporary labor historians have problematized the woman worker—she has been the "question" to be answered, the "riddle" to be solved.[29] By treating the woman worker as a problem, equating her with social disorder, and viewing her presence in production as a violation of nature, man's relation to work was further naturalized. In many of the discourses of the American past as well as in today's labor history, the world of work has been conceived of as belonging to men. Women's entry into a trade rather than their absence has been the starting point for investigation.

Popular histories of work treated women workers as if they were a new phenomenon. The woman question was posed in ways that denied any continuity with the past: the woman worker was defined as a problem "recently created" and in need of "urgent resolution."[30] Debates about the woman worker were framed in terms of "new" crises that arose from the recent separation of home and work.[31] But as feminist historians already have shown, the hegemony of capitalist discourse lay, at least in part, in its ability to label public and private spheres as if they were distinct and independent realms of activity.[32] As a result, women's on-going participation in waged labor was erased from public memory.

Among printers, for example, there probably was no topic that was more frequently or hotly contested than the "woman question." But the historian is hard pressed to reconcile the voices of male printers speaking about the "recent influx" of women in the trade in the 1850s and 1860s, which they dubbed the "petticoat invasion," with the long and continuing participation of women as printers in the United States, as family members and as respected printers in their own right. Forgotten were women like Katherine Goddard, printer of the Declaration of Independence, and Lydia Bailey, official printer for the city of Philadelphia from 1830 to 1850. In constructing a history of women workers, nineteenth-century printers experienced collective amnesia.[33]

Popular histories of work formed the lens through which workers, male and female, understood their relation to each other, to their work, and to their employers. The "past" legitimated women's marginality from production and justified male workers' exclusionary strategies. By rewriting the history of the woman worker in light of the present, male workers created the terms for collective action.[34] We need to be sensitive to "the process of invented pasts," the ways workers used tradition and custom in innovative and adaptive ways to legitimate existing practices, the ways contemporaries constructed the past to conform to perceptions of the present.[35]

Exploring the discourses on the "woman question" turns our attention to how and why particular gender meanings were created and how collective memory about the woman worker was justified. Research on women workers is still important, but it is not sufficient for the making of a gendered labor history. Answers to questions about women workers, their work, their lives, and their relations with men provide necessary background. What comes to the foreground are questions about how the history of the woman worker was constructed in popular conceptions of work and how that popular history was used to legitimate particular gendered practices.

The nature of the questions posed about the woman worker and the types of answers given reveal much about the construction of the woman worker; but they also tell us a great deal about male identities and anxieties, and of the ways various institutions and practices became male-coded. The discourse on the woman question was saturated with workingmen's expressions of anxieties about their masculinity and its implications for class relations: they frequently spoke of their fears of being "unmanned," "unsexed," and "made impotent" in their warfare with their employers. By decoding the woman question we transpose the problem: it is not only women's presence or absence that requires explanation but men's as well. Both the masculinization of work as well as its feminization become topics for analysis.

An examination of masculinity is a necessary ingredient to analyzing the workings of power, the social practices through which power has been exercised—issues that have been problematic in the new labor history. The primary task of the historian, Eric Hobsbawm wrote, "is to pursue the central issue of how power, in *all* its dimensions, is constructed, maintained and exercised."[36] Examining masculinity can reveal a great deal about how power operates, not only in relations between men and women, but in other relations of inequality, including those between workers and employers and among different groups of workers.[37] For these reasons questions about the workings of male power need to be placed firmly on the agenda of labor historians.

Recent work on masculinity in the rapidly developing area of men's studies has been valuable because it has brought attention to men as gendered subjects. This research has yielded fruitful insights into the issues that men confront at different stages in their life cycle and the variations in men's experiences as men in relation to race, ethnicity, class, and sexual preference. But the primary emphases in men's studies have been to understand men's experience of masculinity, to explore the ways patriarchy has victimized men as well as women, and to liberate men from the confines of the male role. Often research explores men's experience of manhood in isolation from their relation to others in the social hierarchy. Questions about how male power has operated has not been central to its agenda.[38]

Despite feminists' concerns with women's subordination and their efforts to uncover the motive force for male domination, an adequate theory is still lacking. Debate continues as to whether women's subordination is central to capitalist production, a vestige of precapitalist patriarchal ideology, a consequence of men's efforts to benefit from women's labor power in the home, or a result of men's desire to control women's reproduction and/or sexuality.[39] The operation of and basis for men's power as men remain somewhat mysterious. Causes for men's antagonism toward women workers have been sought in some set of "natural" gender interests to which men sometimes have sacrificed class benefits. This formulation sidesteps exploration of how collective masculine identities are constructed and treats as unproblematic how men come to identify themselves as a group with a particular set of interests. Once male domination has been naturalized in the historical narrative of gender relations its existence seemingly requires no further explanation.[40]

The concept of patriarchy already has been criticized for implying a universal and ahistorical form of male oppression and for its lack of clarity.[41] Theorizing a separate sex/gender system that interacts with capitalism has also been unsatisfactory since it leaves intact the gender biases of theories of capitalism.[42] A gendered labor history requires a more sophisticated account of masculinity than is possible by conceiving gender and class as independent systems of oppression. Rather than seeing gender as analytically separate from other systems of domination, some recent studies have begun to document the ways gender is embedded in the organization of production and the social relations of the workplace.[43]

Many women's labor historians have ceased using the term patriarchy, or capitalist-patriarchy, finding the concept of gender more open to historical variability. Critics of this trend have charged that the displacement of the concept of patriarchy is politically regressive since it shifts attention away from women's oppression and the fact that it is men who are the oppressors.[44] On the surface, a focus on masculinity appears to lack the "critical-political sharpness" of patriarchy and to deflect attention from women's oppression.[45] But studying masculinity in ways that problematize men's power can be enormously valuable for feminist analysis. The more the mechanism of men's power is examined, the more its foundation can be understood and effectively challenged.

By exploring the dependence of the masculine subject on the female "other" the foundation for men's power may become exposed, resulting in what Judith Butler refers to as a "dialectical reversal of power." Nineteenth-century debates on the woman question, for example, reveal the dependency of masculinity on "woman." As Simone de Beauvoir put it, women are "the lack against which masculine identity differentiates itself."[46] In fact, whatever women have been thought to lack in relation to men have been the defining features of the male worker.[47]

The view that men shape work to protect their gender interests assumes that gender identity is monolithic rather than multidimensional and internally inconsistent. It assumes that men are omniscient and omnipotent—that they know what their gender interests are and that they have the power to construct the world the way they want. But these very questions require historically documented answers. Research needs to question male power rather than to assume its existence and to examine its limitations and its variations among different groups.

Some men have had more power than others. Not all men have

been similarly situated in ways to universalize themselves. One can easily imagine some men posing a question comparable to Sojourner Truth's, saying "Ar'n't I a Man?"[48] But the notion of a separate sex/gender system analytically segregates men's oppression of women from other forms of exploitation, such as that based on class and race. And it artificially homogenizes the varying relationships of different groups of men to male power and the different social relations that stem from these relationships.

Historians of women workers have demonstrated the significance of gender for the formation of female bonds, friendships, and networks, within and outside the workplace. Women's shared experience of male domination has often been invoked as the basis for sisterhood. But women's historians have pointed to the diversity of women's experiences and thereby challenged the notions of a common gender identity and shared gender interests.[49] They have also uncovered a more complex history of relations among women: between plantation mistresses and slaves, between social reformers and working women, between married and single women, to name just a few. We now see the diversity of women's experiences and the complex ways gender has served both to create sisterhood as well as to divide women.[50]

If the voices of black women are just beginning to emerge in labor historiography, those of black men are still relatively silent. But feminist research on black women suggests that understanding black masculinity cannot simply be derived from white masculinity in any formulaic way. If black women's experiences cannot be understood by the simple addition of the "burdens" of race and sex oppression, then black men's cannot be surmised by subtracting gender as a factor in race and class power.

Insights into the operation of gender solidarity and divisions among women can be helpful in studying gender relations among men. Labor historians, of course, have explored divisions among workers along lines of race, ethnicity, and skill, but they have not specifically examined how differences in masculinity figure into working-class identities and the making of the working class. How, when, and in what ways did notions of manliness not only divide women from men, but also create bonds or sever them among men? How did differences in masculine identities among black and white, native and immigrant, skilled and unskilled, workers and employers, shape relations in the coal mines, the fields, the facto-ries, and the unions?[51] Did the different versions of manliness clash or blend among workers of the North and South and West, of the urban and rural regions, and among the many ethnic groups widely discussed in the new labor history? Understanding the formation of class solidarities and divisions requires studying these relations among men.

Women's historians' recent attention to gender relations has broadened the study of gender by recognizing the interconnectedness of men's and women's lives; however, it also narrowed the field of vision by limiting the study of gender to relations between men and women.[52] Workingmen also defined their manliness in relation to their employers and to other workers, of different ages, races, classes, ethnicities, religions, occupations, and sexual orientations. By exploring the ways workingmen posed gender concerns in relation to others besides women we broaden our understanding of the operations of gender beyond simple dichotomies.

Age, for example, is an important, although much neglected, component in the construction of masculinity.[53] Workingmen have exhibited great antagonism toward boy laborers, apprentices, and helpers. Adult male workers contrasted themselves to boys as a measure of their manliness; boys were what workingmen had once been and what they feared resembling. A male worker became a man through initiation into a trade.[54] A boy learned to be a man in class terms and to be a worker in gender terms. Since the corre-spondence between man and masculinity is not transparent, exam-ining man-boy relations at work can help us understand how masculinity is acquired. In so doing we move away from a conceptualization of gender as rooted in the private sphere which, somehow mysteriously, is imported into the workplace, to a view that treats gender as created and recreated at work as well.

Skill is another dimension of gender relations at work. Femi-nists have pointed to the significance of gender in defining work as skilled and its impact on relations between men and women work-ers.[55] Exploring the politically contested nature of skill and its relationship to masculine respectability can also illuminate rela-tions among men who are differently situated in the skill hierarchy. Male workers' beliefs that skill was linked to particular versions of manhood influenced the form and content of labor politics. Skill placed nineteenth-century craftsmen in a contradictory bind. They adopted some of the trappings of bourgeois manhood and respect-ability and sought to distinguish themselves from "rough" and "rowdy" workers associated with the less skilled. As a result skill came to be contrasted with manual labor. In staking out a status claim in the occupational hierarchy craftsmen also became dis-tanced from the "brute strength" of the manual worker. At the same time, however, they also rejected aspects of middle-class definitions of manhood that looked down upon physical labor, adopting a version of masculinity that affirmed the very character-istics that were viewed negatively in bourgeois ideology. To the extent that workingmen continued to value muscular strength as the basis of masculinity, as studies of working-class iconography suggest, skill threatened to strip workers of degrees of manliness.[56] In the late nineteenth and early twentieth centuries, skilled male printers, for example, emphasized the physically demanding as-pects of their work to ensure its definition as "manly work." This formed the basis for their exclusion of women from the new work on the Linotype. But it also may have helped to assuage men's fears that Linotype work was effeminate and might make their own manliness suspect.[57]

Nineteenth-century discourse on the family wage reveals some of male workers' multiple and conflicting loyalties. Attacks on scabs, wage demands, and norms of work sharing were articulated in terms of their impact on either feeding or starving men's families. By emphasizing the interconnections between men's work and family lives and men's relations to women as central to manly respectability, demands for a family wage operated to individualize gender interests. But it conflicted with men's identification as members of a male work fraternity.[58] Manly respectability was also dependent on men's relations with other men; its construction was a collective affair that became part of the "moral economy" of workingmen. Men were dependent upon each other as well as upon women for establishing their manliness.[59]

Tests of manhood on the shop floor influenced relations among workers. A few studies of workers in the current era highlight the ways male workers became preoccupied with proving their manli-ness on the shop floor by competing with each other for status, thereby reinforcing internal class divisions rooted in skill levels, age, and sex.[60]

While labor historians have not directly examined gender

relations among male workers, the relationship of male sexuality and work, or the making of masculine subjectivities, they have created a rich body of material on working-class culture, demonstrating the significance of workers' sense of pride and respectability for class action. Workers' self-respect, argued Eric Hobsbawm, had more significance to workers than purely economic, market considerations.[61] Men's efforts to defend their respectability as workers shaped their work, the strategies they developed, and the ways they pursued them. And, most importantly, these efforts took place on a gendered terrain.

David Montgomery's 1976 study of workers' control in the nineteenth century noted the significance of manliness for craftsmen's ethical code. To be a "manly" worker implied "dignity, respectability, defiant egalitarianism, and patriarchal male supremacy."[62] Thanks to more detailed research on men's work culture, we have begun to understand the importance of gender to male workers' practices and values and the links between manliness and skill, respectability, and independence.[63]

For men work was often used as a measure of self-worth. Manly honor and shame shaped men's goals, strategies, and behavior. Manly pride could be a useful resource in struggles with employers, and union organizers often appealed to manliness as a call to unionism and activism. In some cases male workers used manliness to assert their control over their work and to challenge managerial authority. But in other instances bosses were able to co-opt notions of manliness to enhance workers' competitiveness and drive them to increase productivity.[64] Thus, masculine culture has sometimes operated to undermine workers' class positions. Manliness could be a source of divisiveness between male and female workers and among male workers, operating to separate "real men" from the "boys."

Relations between employers and workers have similarly been based on more than material interests. Workers have employed a "moral discourse," appealing to issues of fairness and justice to legitimize their economic claims and demands.[65] Workers have defended their right to work and to a just wage, as Alice Kessler-Harris has shown, in highly gendered ways.[66]

What were the gender influences on employment relations? Did masculinity serve as a point of convergence or antagonism between male workers and their typically male bosses? Did men agree about masculinity, did it serve to create a brotherhood among men, or did it operate to accentuate class differences? Did it provide a foundation for cooperation at the workplace, or did it undermine management's efforts to secure compliance? The limited research on these questions has provided equivocal answers. Where some have seen manliness as operating to divide workers from their bosses, others have concluded that manliness served as an interclass bonding mechanism. To make matters even more complicated, Patricia Cooper discovered male cigar workers at once at odds with their employers but also seeking to emulate them—wearing neckties at work symbolizing their efforts to lay claims to equality with their bosses.[67]

Gender is typically conceived as relational, masculine to feminine are juxtaposed and linked to sets of dichotomous terms: aggressive/passive, strong/weak, work/home, culture/nature, and so forth. This binary gender framework is employed even in research that has explored the historicity of gender and uncovered the changing meanings of masculinity and femininity. Researchers often have taken for granted the dichotomous character of gender categories even as they have begun to dissect the categories themselves. Yet in American labor politics gender meanings were continually contested. Gender definitions were simultaneously dichotomous and fluid; they were seen as fixed and unchanging but were continually challenged and in flux.[68]

Masculinity not only changed over time, many versions coexisted; any effort simply to juxtapose masculinity to femininity faces inherent difficulties. While masculine and feminine are constructed in relation to each other they do not necessarily exist in any simple binary opposition. Gender meanings do not make up a stable dichotomy; rather these meanings are socially constructed and politically contested.[69]

Masculinity may be dependent on femininity for its meaning, but the on-going debates on the woman question reveal that femininity has been continually in flux. Manliness, therefore, must have been ever in search of its referent.

The historical record reveals, then, a more complex picture of gender than a simple dichotomous framework allows. The representation of sexual difference as a dichotomy, expressed in terms of nature and biology, is itself a question requiring explanation.[70] The lens of the historians can expose the alternative voices, the other possible meanings that have been silenced.

Numerous versions of gender have been put forth by different groups of workers and employers over the course of U.S. industrial development. These various gender discourses have existed in uneasy tension with each other and have competed for the allegiance of individuals. This multiplicity of gender definitions points to the precarious nature of gender identity, a precariousness hidden by conceiving gender in dichotomous terms. Among printers, for example, the very intensity of the debates by male printers on the woman question at national meetings during the nineteenth and twentieth centuries highlights the instability of gender categories. The suppression of alternative gender meanings took place as a result of struggle in particular historical contexts. The work of building and constructing gender has been on-going and has been continually subject to redefinition and renegotiation.

Historians' reliance on a binary gender framework in historical inquiry has enabled masculinity to escape scrutiny. Masculine identity cannot be deduced from the study of femininity. Each is a topic in its own right. A full history of gender at work requires looking into the complex relationship between the categories of both "woman" and "man."

Since the concept of class has become one of the ways that the white man has become the universal subject in both class politics and labor history, we need to turn our attention to the gender and race assumptions that went into the "making of class"—assumptions that not only contributed to the marginalization of women and African Americans as workers, but also shaped the nature of class politics, creating solidarities and defining divisions among workers.

Labor historians have identified "republicanism" as a central theme in deciphering how workers articulated and understood their class interests.[71] But, as women's historians have pointed out, ideas of republicanism "were incontestably male."[72] The idea of citizenship upon which republicanism rested was linked to manhood; and manhood entailed "self-reliance, self-ownership, and autonomy."[73] Control of property was a central tenet of citizenship rights; and all forms of property, whether in labor or in things, were defined as masculine. Workingmen's independence was linked to their "property in labor."[74] They referred to receiving a wage as "earning an independence." This independence held out multiple meanings: among other things, it signified freedom from employers' dictates, and respectability in relation to other workingmen. But these are only suggestive of how masculinity figured into workingmen's goals and demands. They raise rather than settle other questions: how did efforts to maintain manly dignity influence workingmen's critique of capitalism, the alternatives they could envision, and ultimately the nature of their expectations and demands in the employment relation?

Men also contrasted their independence to women's dependence and to blacks' enslavement.[75] Republicanism emphasized the value of autonomy and self-government for white male Americans while casting negative qualities onto African, Mexican, and Native Americans. Republican leaders identified white men with rationality and mind, and women and peoples of color with passion and body. Like subordinated races, women were depicted as threats to the nation. Women represented chaos and disorder; temptresses who would lead republican men away from rational and virtuous behavior.[76] White republicanism emerged together with masculine identity.

Thus, the equality rhetoric of workers' republicanism created boundaries of inclusiveness and exclusiveness. Despite the abundance of well documented historical examples of the ways class was splintered by industry, skill level, religion, geographic region, ethnicity, race, and sex, the workings of class divisions are still somewhat mysterious. Questions abound: how is solidarity created? what makes it possible for groups of workers to identify with each other? Simply positing similar experiences and interests is insufficient, for we still need to know how individuals signify themselves as members of a particular group.[77] This raises the question of how a collective gender identity is constructed: how is the subject "male worker" created?[78]

In sum, arguments about the centrality of gender do not imply that class does not matter. Class matters a great deal, albeit differently than in the classic Marxist formulation.[79] We can build on E. P. Thompson's crucial contribution to the study of the working class—that we need to understand "men [sic] in relationship over time"—how "class" comes into existence, not through one's position in production, but by people actively engaged in constructing their world.[80] In the nineteenth century class became one of the more important ways the social order was symbolically represented. Examining the formation of collective class identity is central to working-class history rather than peripheral to it. In this version of class analysis we turn our attention to how individuals constituted themselves as members of a particular class and how class interests were identified; how was the "worker" constituted as white and male, despite the gender and race diversity of the American laboring population.[81]

A gendered analysis need not mean turning attention away from the workplace and the economy. Quite the contrary, gender was central to both. But the connection between male workers and paid work needs to be problematized rather than assumed to be natural. Feminists already have pointed to how the assumption that men worked in paid production and women did not distorted our analysis of women workers. Less apparent has been the way this assumption has biased our understanding of male workers. Discontinuous employment resulting from cyclical economic fluctuations, technological changes, seasonal work, sickness, and disability, were central features of male workers' experience.[82] If work was so central to workingmen, as labor historians have assumed, what does the discontinuity of employment suggest about the precariousness of workingmen's gender identity? How could a man sustain his "manly independence" when it rested on so shaky a foundation? Without exploring the construction of masculinity we will be unable to understand the implications of such discontinuous and unstable employment patterns for the respectable workingman who situated his wage demands on his right to a family wage.

The emerging work on masculinity has begun to document its variability, showing the ways men's gender identities served to bond or divide workers. We now need to address how and why these versions of manliness developed. We cannot presuppose that masculinity simply emerged from a preexisting male work culture since the "past" itself is constructed, a process of selective and creative collective memory.

The challenge for the next stage in labor and women's history is to explore numerous important, yet unaddressed questions: how has gender shaped social relations of power between workers and employers and among groups of workers; and why has it had the capacity to work in these ways? How and why did workers select particular versions of manhood as a means to bolster their position as workers or to contest the authority of their bosses? How has masculinity operated to limit and direct male workers' critique of capitalism? How have meanings of manhood been incorporated into the structure of men's work, practices, and institutions, and into the bargaining strategies of employers and workers? Thus, I conclude by returning to the original issue of the significance of masculinity for integrating gender into labor history: how and why did the white man come to signify the working class, and what implications has this had for class identity and labor politics during the course of capitalist development? In pursuing answers to these questions the agendas of women's history and labor history merge.

NOTES

1.   For a discussion of the relation of women's history to history generally see Gisela Bock, "Women's History and Gender History: Aspects of an International Debate," *Gender and History* 1, no. 1 (Spring 1989): 7–30.

2.   For a feminist critique of the periodization in American labor history, see, Susan Porter Benson, "Response to David Montgomery's 'Thinking About American Workers in the 1920s,'" *International Labor and Working-Class History* 32 (Fall 1987): 31–38. On how women's history challenges traditional periodization, see, Joan Kelly, "Did Women Have a Renaissance?" in *Becoming Visible: Women in European History*, ed. Renate Bridenthal and Claudia Koonz, (Boston, 1977), 139–164; and Linda Kerber, *Women of the Republic: Intellect and Ideology in Revolutionary America* (Chapel Hill, 1980). On the public/private dichotomy, see, for example, Dorothy O. Helly and Susan Reverby, eds., *Gendered Domains: Rethinking Public and Private in Women's History* (Ithaca, N.Y., 1992).

3.   "The Point Is to Change It," review of Bryan D. Palmer, *Descent into Discourse, The Nation*, 13/20 August 1990, 74.

4.   On the value of gender and race as analytic categories for historical analysis, see, Joan Scott, "Gender: A Useful Category of Historical Analysis," in *Gender and the Politics of History* (New York, 1988), 28–52; Evelyn Brooks Higginbotham, "African-American Women's History and the Metalanguage of Race," *Signs* 17, no. 2 (Winter 1992): 251–274. On these as categories in American labor history, see, Ava Baron, "Gender and Labor History: Learning from the Past, Looking to the Future," in *Work Engendered: Toward a New History of American Labor*, ed. Baron (Ithaca, N.Y., 1991), 1–46; Alice Kessler-Harris, "A New Agenda for American Labor History: A Gendered Analysis and the Question of Class," in *Perspectives on American Labor History: The Problems of Synthesis* ed. J. Carroll Moody and Alice Kessler-Harris, (DeKalb, Ill., 1989), 217–234; David R. Roediger, *The Wages of*

Whiteness: Race and the Making of the American Working Class (New York and London, 1991).

    5.   See, for example, David Montgomery, *Fall of the House of Labor: The Workplace, the State, and American Labor Activism, 1865–1925* (New York, 1987); and Bruce Laurie, *Artisans into Workers, Labor in Nineteenth-Century America* (New York, 1989).

    6.   Jonathan Prude discusses this point in his review of Laurie, *Artisans into Workers*, and Montgomery, *The Fall of the House of Labor*, "Directions in Labor History," *American Quarterly* 42, no. 1 (March 1990): 136. On the gender biases in German labor historiography, see, Kathleen Canning, "Gender and the Politics of Class Formation: Rethinking German Labor History," *American Historical Review* 97, no. 3 (June 1992): 736–768.

    7.   This question has been raised by a male historian about research in women's history at virtually every conference I have attended in the past five years. Louise Tilly argues that we should take seriously historians who ask of women's history: what difference does it make? in "Gender, Women's History, and Social History" *Social Science History* 13, no. 4 (Winter 1989): 439–462.

    8.   For a discussion of whether women's history "has arrived" see Tilly, *ibid.*, and responses by Gay Gullickson and Judith Bennett, in *ibid.*, 463–477.

    9.   On the marginalization of women's labor history, see, Baron, "Gender and Labor History," esp. 1–9; and Kessler-Harris, "A New Agenda for American Labor History."

    10.   For an example of this view, see, Richard Oestreicher, "Separate Tribes?: Working-Class and Women's History," *Reviews in American History* 19 (1991): 228–231.

    11.   Eric Foner, "Labor Historians Seek Useful Past," *In These Times*, 12–16 December 1984, 11. See also, Alan Dawley, "A Preface to Synthesis," *Labor History* 29 (Summer 1988): 363–377.

    12.   According to Leon Fink, most labor historians continue to subordinate gender to class relations because they view work and other "public spaces" as the important sites of contests for power. "Culture's Last Stand: Gender and the Search for Synthesis in American Labor History," Paper presented at North American Labor History Conference, Wayne State University, Detroit, 17 October 1991.

    13.   On the concern that women's history may lose its explicit "feminist" perspective, see, Judith Bennett, "Feminism and History," *Gender and History* 1, no. 3 (Autumn 1989): 251–272.

    14.   Ira Katznelson, "Working-Class Formation: Constructing Cases and Comparisons," in *Working-Class Formation: Nineteenth-Century Patterns in Western Europe and the United States*, ed. Ira Katznelson and Aristede Zolberg (Princeton, 1986), 4, n.2.

    15.   See Roediger, *Wages of Whiteness*; Alexander Saxton, *The Rise and Fall of the White Republic: Class Politics and Mass Culture in Nineteenth-Century America* (New York and London, 1990); Vron Ware, *Beyond the Pale: White Women, Racism and History* (New York and London, 1992); and Paul Taillon, "'That Word White': Racism and Masculinity in the Debate in the International Association of Machinists, 1890–1895," paper presented at the North American Labor History Conference, Wayne State University, Detroit, 20 October 1990.

    16.   Gender analysis has largely been absent from research on sailors, cigar

workers, printers, and shoe workers. Recent studies on these trades by women labor historians have begun to provide some valuable correctives. On cigar workers, see, Patricia Cooper, *Once A Cigar Maker: Men, Women, and Work Culture in American Cigar Factories, 1900–1919* (Urbana, Ill. 1987); Eileen Boris, "'A Man's Dwelling House Is His Castle': Tenement House Cigarmaking and the Judicial Imperative," and Nancy Hewitt, "'The Voice of Virile Labor': Labor Militancy, Community Solidarity, and Gender Identity among Tampa's Latin Workers, 1880–1921," in Baron, *Work Engendered*, 114–141 and 142–167. On shoe workers, see, Mary Blewett, *Men, Women, and Work: Class, Gender, and Protest in the New England Shoe Industry, 1780–1910* (Urbana, Ill., 1988). On printers, see, Ava Baron, "Questions of Gender: Deskilling and Demasculinization in the U.S. Printing Industry, 1830–1915," *Gender and History* 1, no. 2 (Summer 1989): 178–199; Cynthia Cockburn, *Brothers: Male Dominance and Technological Change* (London, 1983). On sailors, see, essays by Margaret S. Creighton and Valerie Burton in Colin Howell and Richard J. Twomey, eds., *Jack Tar in History: Essays in the History of Maritime Life and Labour* (Fredericton, New Brunswick, Can., 1991).

17. On the gender assumptions of nineteenth-century French male workers and political economists, see, Joan Scott, "Work Identities for Men and Women: The Politics of Work and Family in the Parisian Garment Trades in 1848," and "'L'ouvrière! Mot impie, sordide . . .': Women Workers in the Discourse of French Political Economy, 1840–1860," in Scott, *Gender and the Politics of History*, 93–112 and 139–166.

18. For example, see my, "Women and the Making of the American Working Class: A Study of the Proletarianization of Printers," *Review of Radical Political Economics* 14, no. 3 (Fall 1982): 23–42.

19. Judith Allen, "Evidence and Silence: Feminism and the Limits of History," in *Feminist Challenges: Social and Political Theory*, ed. Carole Pateman and Elizabeth Gross (Boston, 1987), 187–188.

20. William Sewell Jr., "Review of Joan Wallach Scott's *Gender and the Politics of History*," *History and Theory* 29, no. 1 (1990): 78. On the resistance of many historians to recognize the gendered particularity of men and its consequences for women's history and women's historians, see, Joan Scott, "American Women Historians, 1884–1984," *Gender and the Politics of History*, 178–198.

21. On the general ways in which man constitutes the universal, see, Carole Pateman, "Introduction: The Theoretical Subversiveness of Feminism," in Pateman and Gross, *Feminist Challenges*, 7.

22. On how masculine symbols came to represent union legacy even in a female dominated union, see, Elizabeth Faue, *Community of Suffering and Struggle: Women, Men, and the Labor Movement in Minneapolis, 1915–1945* (Chapel Hill, 1991), chapter 3. On the meaning of unionism as masculine despite women's participation, see, for example, Hewitt, "'The Voice of Virile Labor'."

23. "Postmodernism and Gender Relations in Feminist Theory," *Signs* 12, no. 4 (Summer 1987): 629. See also, Kaja Silverman, *Male Subjectivity at the Margins* (London and New York, 1992) and Kathy E. Ferguson, *The Man Question: Visions of Subjectivity in Feminist Theory* (Berkeley, 1993).

24. Once the body was abstracted from the individual in liberal theory the male worker could become the universal figure and women became "naturally" invisible. Pateman, "Introduction: The Theoretical Subversiveness of Feminism," 8.

25.   Sewell, Jr., "Review of Joan Scott," 78.

26.   Mark C. Carnes and Clyde Griffen, eds., *Meanings for Manhood: Constructions of Masculinity in Victorian America* (Chicago, 1990); Michael Roper and John Tosh, eds., *Manful Assertions: Masculinities in Britain since 1800* (New York, 1991); Bock, "Women's History and Gender History,"; and Baron, "Gender and Labor History." Calls for the study of masculinity are not entirely new, see, for example, Natalie Davis, "Women's History in Transition: The European Case," *Feminist Studies*, 3 no. 3/4 (Spring/Summer 1976): 83–103. But they are now heard with increased frequency and intensity.

27.   See, for example, essays in Baron, *Work Engendered*.

28.   As a more general problem in research see, Michael Kimmel, "After Fifteen Years: The Impact of the Sociology of Masculinity on the Masculinity of Sociology," in *Men, Masculinities and Social Theory*, ed. Jeff Hearn and David Morgan (London and Boston, 1990).

29.   On this point see, Flax, "Postmodernism and Gender Relations in Feminist Theory," 629; Simone de Beauvoir, *The Second Sex* (New York, 1952).

30.   Joan Scott, "The Woman Worker," in vol. 4 of *A History of Women in the West*, ed. Genevieve Fraisse and Michelle Perrot (Cambridge, Mass., 1993), originally published as vol. 4 of *La Storia della Donne in Occidente*, (Roma-Bari, 1991), 399–426.

31.   On the emergence of the conception of the housewife as engaged in "worthless" unproductive activities, see, Nancy Folbre, "The Unproductive Housewife: Her Evolution in Nineteenth-Century Economic Thought," *Signs* 16, no. 3 (Spring 1991): 463–484; and Jeanne Boydston, *Home and Work: Housework, Wages, and the Ideology of Labor in the Early Republic* (New York, 1990).

32.   Leonore Davidoff, "'Adam Spoke First and Named the Orders of the World': Masculine and Feminine Domains in History and Sociology," in *The Politics of Everyday Life: Continuity and Change in Work, Labour and the Family*, ed. H. Corr and L. Jamieson (London, 1990), 229–255.

33.   On the relationship of collective memory to historical understanding, see, "Memory and American History," special issue of *Journal of American History* 75, no. 4 (March 1989); Patrick Hutton, "The Role of Memory in the Historiography of the French Revolution," *History and Theory* 30, no. 1 (1991): 56–69; Stuart Hall, "Notes on Deconstructing 'the Popular,'" in *People's History and Socialist Theory*, ed. Raphael Samuel (London, 1981), 227–240; Patrick Joyce, "The Sense of the Past," in *Visions of the People: Industrial England and the Question of Class, 1840–1914* (Cambridge, Eng., 1991), 172–192. On the construction of public memory, see, John Bodnar, *Remaking America: Public Memory, Commemoration, and Patriotism in the Twentieth Century* (Princeton, 1992); and Michael Kammen, *Mystic Chords of Memory: The Transformation of Tradition in American Culture* (New York, 1991).

34.   On how gender discourses shaped labor politics, see, Scott, "Work Identities for Men and Women."

35.   Joyce, *Visions of the People*, 20–21; see also essays by Michael Sonenscher and Richard Whipp in *The Historical Meanings of Work*, ed. Patrick Joyce (Cambridge, Eng., 1987). For important discussions and examples of how the historic past has been sometimes invented and inserted into new practices, see, Eric Hobsbawm and Terrence Ranger, eds., *The Invention of Tradition* (Cambridge, Eng., 1983).

36. Quoted in Pat Thane, Geoffrey Crossick, and Roderick Floud, eds. *The Power of the Past: Essays for Eric Hobsbawm* (New York, 1984), 2 (emphasis mine).

37. On this point, see, Scott, "Gender: A Useful Category of Historical Analysis."

38. Jeff Hearn and David Morgan, leading figures in men's studies, described the significance of the study of men and masculinity as appreciating "the positive features of men's lives, and especially the variety of men's lived experiences." *Men, Masculinities and Social Theory*, x. On the goals of men's studies, see, Harry Brod, ed., *The Making of Masculinities: The New Men's Studies* (Boston, 1987). The literature in men's studies is expanding rapidly and evolving in the kinds of questions it seeks to answer. See, Michael Kimmel, ed., *Changing Men: New Directions in Research on Men and Masculinity* (Beverly Hills, 1987); Michael S. Kimmel and Michael A. Messner, eds., *Men's Lives*, 2nd ed. (New York, 1992); Kenneth Clatterbaugh, *Contemporary Perspectives on Masculinity: Men, Women and Politics in Modern Society* (Boulder, Co., 1990). For a discussion of some of the problems with men's studies from the vantage point of women's history, see, Lois Banner's review essay of books in men's studies, *Signs* 14, no. 3 (Spring 1989): 703–708; and Nancy F. Cott, "On Men's History and Women's History," in *Meanings for Manhood: Constructions of Masculinity in Victorian America*, ed. Mark C. Carnes and Clyde Griffen (Chicago, 1990), 205–212.

39. See, for example, Heidi I. Hartmann, "The Family as the Locus of Gender, Class, and Political Struggle: The Example of Housework," *Signs* 6 (Spring 1981): 366–94; Mary O'Brien, *The Politics of Reproduction* (Boston and London, 1981); Catherine MacKinnon, "Feminism, Marxism, Method, and the State: An Agenda for Theory," *Signs* 7 (Spring 1982): 515–544; Michele Barrett, *Women's Oppression Today: Problems in Marxist Feminist Analysis* (London, 1980); Cynthia Cockburn, "The Material of Male Power," *Feminist Review* 9 (October 1981): 42–58.

40. On the tendency to assume that men have a natural and undifferentiated proclivity for domination, see, Roper and Tosh, *Manful Assertions*, 9.

41. The term patriarchy has been used in myriad ways: as a structure of rule by fathers, as a system of social relations in which men oppress and exploit women, as male control over women's sexuality specifically, and as the institutional structure of male domination. For discussions of the problems with the concept of patriarchy, see, Sheila Rowbotham, "The Trouble with 'Patriarchy'," in Samuel, *People's History and Socialist Theory*, 364–369; Barrett, Women's Oppression Today; also, Scott, "Gender: A Useful Category of Historical Analysis, esp. 33–36; Joan Acker, "The Problem with Patriarchy," *Sociology* 23, no. 2 (May 1989): 235–240; Robert W. Connell, "How Should We Theorize Patriarchy?," in *Which Way Is Up?: Essays on Class, Sex and Culture*, ed. Robert W. Connell (Sydney, 1983), 50–62. For a defense of the concept, see, Sylvia Walby, "Theorizing Patriarchy," *Sociology* 23, no. 2 (May 1989): 213–234; Sally Alexander and Barbara Taylor, "In Defence of 'Patriarchy'," in Samuel, *People's History and Socialist Theory*, 370–374; Jeff Hearn, *The Gender of Oppression: Men, Masculinity, and the Critique of Marxism* (New York, 1987), chapter 3.

42. For calls to rethink class analysis more fully to incorporate gender see, Joan Kelly, "The Doubled Vision of Feminist Theory," in *Sex and Class in Women's History*, ed. Judith L. Newton, Mary P. Ryan, and Judith Walkowitz (London and Boston, 1983); Joan Acker, "Class, Gender and the Relations of Distribution,"

Signs 13, no. 3 (Spring 1988): 473–497. For discussions of the dual systems approach, see, Lydia Sargent, ed., *Women and Revolution: A Discussion of the Unhappy Marriage of Marxism and Feminism* (Boston, 1981).

43. See, for example, Sonya Rose, *Limited Livelihoods: Gender and Class in Nineteenth-Century England* (Berkeley, 1992); and essays in Baron, *Work Engendered*.

44. For a discussion of this position, see, Bennett, "Feminism and History."

45. Acker, "The Problem with Patriarchy," 239.

46. Judith Butler, *Gender Trouble: Feminism and the Subversion of Identity*, (London and New York, 1990), ix; de Beauvoir quoted in *ibid.*, 9–10.

47. See, Sally Alexander, "Women, Class, and Sexual Difference," *History Workshop Journal* 17 (Autumn 1984): 125–149.

48. This slogan was apparently created by Truth's publicist as a marketing strategy. Nell Painter, "Selling Truth: Slave Women as Commodity," paper presented at Workshop on Mass Consumption and the Construction of Race, Center for Historical Analysis, Rutgers University, 18 August 1992.

49. Studies of African-American women often have identified race, rather than gender, as the most significant force in shaping women's experiences. Higginbotham, "African-American Women's History and the Metalanguage of Race," 256.

50. For a discussion of how sisterhood has been splintered by race and class, see, Evelyn Brooks Higginbotham, "Beyond the Sound of Silence: Afro-American Women in History," *Gender and History* 1, no. 1 (Spring 1989): 50–67; and Nancy Hewitt, "Beyond the Search for Sisterhood: American Women's History in the 1980s, *Social History* 10 (October 1985): 299–320.

51. On race and ethnic divisions among workers, see, Zolberg and Katznelson, *Working-Class Formation*; Joe W. Trotter, *Coal, Class, and Color: Blacks in Southern West Virginia, 1915–1932* (Urbana, Ill., 1990); Robert Asher and Charles Stephenson, eds, *Labor Divided: Race and Ethnicity in United States Labor Struggles* (Albany, 1990); Eric Arnesen, *Waterfront Workers of New Orleans: Race, Class, and Politics, 1863–1923* (New York, 1991).

52. An excellent example is Blewett, *Men, Women, and Work*.

53. On man/boy relations in the printing industry, see, Ava Baron, "An 'Other' Side of Gender Antagonism at Work: Men, Boys, and the Remasculinization of Printers' Work, 1830–1920," in Baron, *Work Engendered*, 47–69; and Cockburn, *Brothers*, chapter 2.

54. See, Keith McClelland, "Some Thoughts on the 'Representative Artisan' in Britain, 1850–1880," *Gender and History* 1, no. 2 (Summer 1989): 164–177.

55. See, Anne Phillips and Barbara Taylor, "Sex and Skill: Notes toward a Feminist Economics," *Feminist Review* 6 (October 1980): 79–88; Ava Baron, "Contested Terrain Revisited: Technology and Gender Definitions of Work in the Printing Industry, 1850–1920," in *Women, Work, and Technology: Transformations*, ed. Barbara Wright et al. (Ann Arbor, 1987), 58–83; Rose, *Limited Livelihoods*, esp. chapter 6.

56. On twentieth century working-class iconography, see, Faue, *Community of Suffering and Struggle*, chapter 3. On nineteenth-century working-class iconography, see, Eric Hobsbawm, "Man and Woman in Socialist Iconography," *History Workshop Journal* 6 (Autumn 1978): 121–138. For a feminist reply to Hobsbawm, see, Sally Alexander, Anna Davin, and Eve Hostettler, "Labouring Women: A Reply to Eric Hobsbawm," *History Workshop Journal* 8 (Autumn 1979): 174–182.

57.   I am grateful to Leora Auslander for reminding me of the heterosexual assumptions embedded in male workers' notions of manliness. On the ways masculinity has been equated with heterosexuality, see, Blye Frank, "Hegemonic Heterosexual Masculinity," *Studies in Political Economy* 24 (Autumn 1987): 159–170. On male printers' emphasis on the physicality of their work see, Baron, "Contested Terrain Revisited," esp. 71–75.

58.   See, Merry E. Weisner, "Guilds, Male Bonding and Women's Work in Early Modern Germany," *Gender and History* 1, no. 2 (Summer 1989): 125–137.

59.   McClelland, "Masculinity and the 'Representative Artisan.'"

60.   See, David L. Collinson, David Knights, and Margaret Collinson, *Managing to Discriminate* (London and New York, 1990), 192–213. David Collinson shows how shop floor relations were mediated through the double-edged nature of male humor at a truck factory in England (1979–1983). "'Engineering Humor': Masculinity, Joking and Conflict in Shop-floor Relations," *Organization Studies* 9, no. 2 (1988): 181–199. Paul Willis's exploration of working-class boys in contemporary England further highlights the contradictory nature of working-class masculinity. See his *Learning to Labour* (London, 1977). For an example of the contradictions in working-class masculinity and its sometimes self-defeating consequences, see, Baron, "Contested Terrain Revisited."

61.   Eric J. Hobsbawm, "Custom, Wages, and Workload," in *Labouring Men: Studies in the History of Labour* (London, 1964), 351.

62.   David Montgomery, "Workers' Control of Machine Production in the Nineteenth Century," *Labor History* 17 (Fall 1976): 485–509. Similarly, Gregory S. Kealey pointed to the centrality of nineteenth-century Canadian coopers' view of manly pride to their struggle with their employers, "The Honest Workingman and Workers' Control: The Experience of Toronto Skilled Workers, 1860–1892," *Labour/Le Travail* 1 (1976): 32–68; and according to Nick Salvatore, Eugene Debs viewed "personal honor" an essential attribute of manhood. *Eugene V. Debs: Citizen and Socialist* (Urbana, Ill., 1982), 46.

63.   See, for example, Cooper, *Once a Cigar Maker*; Mary Blewett, "Manhood and the Market: The Politics of Gender and Class among the Textile Workers of Fall River, Massachusetts, 1870–1880," in Baron, *Work Engendered*, 92–113; Hewitt, "'The Voice of Virile Labor'"; and Joy Parr, *The Gender of Breadwinners: Women, Men, and Change in Two Industrial Towns, 1880–1950* (Toronto, 1990).

64.   On manliness and unionism, see, Faue, *Community of Suffering*, chapter 3. On the relation of manliness to managerial control, see, Kealey, "The Honest Workingman and Workers' Control,"; Mark Rosenfeld, "'It Was a Hard Life': Class and Gender in the Work and Family Rhythms of a Railway Town, 1920–1950," *Historical Papers* (Windsor, 1988); and Steven Maynard, "Rough Work and Rugged Men: The Social Construction of Masculinity in Working-Class History," *Labor/Le Travail* 23 (Spring 1989): 159–169.

65.   See, Joyce, *Visions of the People*, chapter 4. On workers' moral discourse, see, Keith McClelland, "Time to Work, Time to Live: Some Aspects of Work and the Re-formation of Class in Britain, 1850–1880," in Joyce, *Historical Meanings of Work*, 180–209; and Rose, *Limited Livelihoods*, chapter 6.

66.   Alice Kessler-Harris, *A Woman's Wage: Historical Meanings and Social Consequences* (Lexington, Ky., 1990).

67.   See, Montgomery, "Workers' Control of Machine Production,"; Judith McGaw, *Most Wonderful Machine: Mechanization and Social Change in Berkshire Paper*

Making, 1801–1885 (Princeton, 1987). On McGaw's conception of masculinity, see, Mary Blewett's review, *Journal of Social History* 22 (Winter 1989): 368–369; Mary Ann Clawson, *Constructing Brotherhood* (Princeton, 1989); Cooper, *Once A Cigar Maker.*

68. On the limitations of a dichotomous view of gender, see, Linda Gordon, "On 'Difference'," *Genders* 10 (Spring 1991): 95. Carole Turbin demonstrates the value of employing nondichotomous gender categories for understanding labor activism, in *Working Women of Collar City: Gender, Class, and Community in Troy, New York, 1864–1886* (Urbana, Ill., 1992).

69. On identity as "a locus of multiple and variable positions," see Teresa de Lauretis, "Eccentric Subjects: Feminist Theory and Historical Consciousness," *Feminist Studies* 16, no. 1 (Spring 1990): 115–150; also Jacquelyn Hall, "Partial Truths," *Signs* 14, no. 4 (Summer 1989): 909.

70. For a discussion of the development of the binary model of men's and women's bodies in the late eighteenth century, see, Thomas Laqueur, "Orgasm, Generation, and the Politics of Reproductive Biology," in *The Making of the Modern Body: Sexuality and Society in the Nineteenth Century*, ed. Catherine Gallagher and Thomas Laqueur (Berkeley, 1987), 1–41.

71. An excellent example is Sean Wilentz, *Chants Democratic: New York City and the Rise of the American Working Class, 1788–1850* (New York, 1984).

72. Kessler-Harris, "A New Agenda for American Labor History," 227. On women and republicanism, Kerber, *Women of the Republic*, esp. chapter 9. For examples of various ways gender difference was woven into republican citizenship, see, Linda Kerber, "The Paradox of Women's Citizenship in the Early Republic: The Case of Martin vs. Massachusetts, 1805," *American Historical Review* 97, no. 2 (April 1992): 349–378 and her "The Republican Ideology of the Revolutionary Generation," *American Quarterly* 32 (1985): 474–495; Stephanie McCurry, "The Two Faces of Republicanism: Gender and Proslavery Politics in Antebellum South Carolina," *Journal of American History* 78, no. 4 (March 1992): 1245–1264; Ruth Bloch, "The Gendered Meaning of Virtue in Revolutionary America," *Signs* 13, no. 1 (Autumn 1987): 37–58; Joan Gundersen, "Independence, Citizenship and the American Revolution," *Signs* 13, no. 1 (Autumn 1987): 59–77. On gender and the rights of citizenship in France, see, Joan Scott, "French Feminists and the Rights of 'Man': Olympe de Gouge's Declarations," *History Workshop Journal* 28 (Autumn 1989): 1–20.

73. Gwendolyn Mink, "The Lady and the Tramp: Gender, Race, and the Origins of the American Welfare State," in *Women, the State and Welfare*, ed. Linda Gordon (Madison, 1990), 95.

74. On property in labor, see, McClelland, "Time to Work, Time to Live."

75. Ronald Takaki, *Iron Cages: Race and Culture in Nineteenth Century America* (New York, 1979); Roediger, *Wages of Whiteness.*

76. See, Kerber, *Women of the Republic*; and Takaki, *Iron Cages*, 13, 40–41; Bloch, "The Gendered Meanings of Virtue in Revolutionary America," 37–58.

77. See Joan Scott, "The Evidence of Experience," *Critical Inquiry* 17 (Summer 1991): 773–797.

78. On the construction of gender identity and subjectivity, see, de Lauretis, "Eccentric Subjects"; Catherine Belsey, "Constructing the Subject: Deconstructing the Text," in *Feminisms: An Anthology of Literary Theory and Criticism*, ed. Robyn R. Warhol and Diane Rice Herndl (New Brunswick, N.J., 1991), 593–609.

79.   On the historical emergence of class as a category, see, Harold Benenson, "Victorian Sexual Ideology and Marx's Theory of the Working Class," *International Labor and Working Class History* 25 (1984): 1–23. For various critiques of the concept of class as a social reality with a particular identity and set of interests, see, Scott, "Gender: A Useful Category" and "On Language, Gender, and Working-Class History"; Joyce, *Visions of the People*, esp. chapter 1; William Reddy, *Money and Liberty in Europe: A Critique of Historical Understanding* (Cambridge, Eng., 1987); and Harvey J. Kaye and Keith McClelland, eds., *E. P. Thompson: Critical Perspectives* (Philadelphia, 1990); Gareth Stedman Jones, *Languages of Class: Studies in English Working Class History, 1832–1982* (Cambridge, Eng., 1983).

80.   E. P. Thompson, *The Making of the English Working Class*, (New York, 1966), 11.

81.   On the emergence of the American republican citizen as white, male, and middle class, see, Carroll Smith-Rosenberg, "Dis-Covering the Subject of the 'Great Constitutional Discussion,' 1786–1789," *Journal of American History* 79, no. 3 (December 1992): 841–873.

82.   On this point in Britain, see McClelland, "Some Thoughts on Masculinity and the 'Representative Artisan'."

When the Child Is the Father of the Man

Work, Sexual Difference and the Guardian-State in Third Republic France

SYLVIA SCHAFER

In his 1894 report on one of Paris's agencies for the care of abandoned children, departmental councilor Henri Rousselle reminded his colleagues that the public protection and rearing of vulnerable children was essential to national survival. "Among social questions," he asserted, "the protection of childhood is one of the most serious. To make of the child an honest man, a productive worker, and a brave soldier concerns both the wealth and the strength of the fatherland [*la patrie*]."[1] In this statement, Rousselle gave voice to one of the most important motifs in the discourse on assistance to children as it was developed between 1870 and 1914: the future of both society and nation hung in delicate balance with the fate of each and every French child.

Speaking in particular as an advocate of state action, Rousselle tied the "serious question" of child protection to the necessity of expanding the government's role in the rearing of children whose own parents had abandoned them or had proven—by recently established juridical standards—to be "unfit" or "morally danger-ous."[2] Only through concerted government action in the realm of assistance to children could the wealth and strength of *la patrie* be adequately restored, preserved, and reproduced.

Given the sense of extreme vulnerability that haunted France since its defeat by the Prussians in 1870 and the Paris Commune of 1871, Rousselle's remarks represent far more than a statement of abstract nationalism. They spoke directly to a specific historical moment; they recalled a specific social context. In particular, Rousselle's call to protect both endangered children and national interests drew upon a well-established anxiety about international and internal conflict after the "terrible year" of 1870–1871. It invoked the common fear that France was slipping downward, the nation's spirit eroded by moral degeneracy and its body by a natality rate so low it was several times surpassed by the national death rate in the 1890s.[3] Finally, Rousselle's words recalled and reinforced the contemporary faith that in fostering a solid familial order, the Third Republic could buttress the nation and the nascent republic against international conflict and internal unrest.

Rousselle's declaration is notable in another respect, one intimately related to the anxiety about national decline and social disorder. In defining public assistance to children as a relationship between the "fatherland" and future generations of "honest men," "productive workers," and "brave soldiers," Rousselle laid bare the play of gender and gendered identities that saturated both representations of "the state" and the substance of its social policy in the last decades of the nineteenth century. In the Third Republic's underlying vision of social order, so perfectly embodied in Rousselle's remarks, *la patrie* was father of the child, the child the father of the man, and the state the protector of both *patrie* and child.[4]

The use of child, or *"enfant,"* in this discourse of public assistance requires particular attention. Gendered masculine in a language that does not permit neuter nouns, the word *enfant* can and did properly refer to both girls and boys. Nonetheless, as an abstract category in the French Third Republic's conceptual universe of public welfare, *enfant* invokes a deeply entrenched set of gendered meanings and relationships. What feminist critic Luce Irigaray argues about the use of "man" as a universal place holder was true, albeit in a more subtle fashion, for the use of "child" in the nineteenth-century discourse of state childrearing: "the subject is always inscribed as masculine, even when it would pose itself as universal or neuter: *man*. Yet man—at least in French—is not neuter, but sexed."[5] Within the bureaucratic enclave of the Bureau of Public Assistance, the discussions of how state wards should be protected from their pasts and molded for the future encompassed a similar slip-and-slide between those male-gendered terms presumed neutral in a language where masculine and feminine are the only options in the assignment of gender to nouns, and male-gendered terms fully engaged in the hierarchies of social roles and cultural values that differentiated males from females from the moment of birth.

The clear inflections of gender thus were not simply a matter of rhetorical convenience or lexical imperative. Nor were they the consequence of an interest in limiting state protection to young boys.[6] Instead, the attribution of gendered and familial identities was intrinsic to a process of interpreting collective and individual experience in the context of a broad vision of the state and its historical relationship to the French populace. The masculine essence of these terms was most common in the administration's prescriptive and prognostic flights; gender identity was located in a future state of being. It would appear at some indeterminate future moment when the administration's investment in "the child" would produce an adult defined in terms of the three main poles of publicly affirmed male identity: citizen, worker, and soldier.

The significance of this gendered language far exceeds the boundaries of theoretical or rhetorical abstraction. The neutral/masculine language customarily used to categorize "children" in state care was also the language of administration. The invocation of gender identities and the use of familial metaphors grounded the constitution of new institutions of assistance to children and new administrative practices in the late nineteenth century as fundamentally as they structured parliamentary debates or administrative reports.

It was not, therefore, that this discourse and practice of assistance to children was overtly and intentionally exclusive. Instead, the Third Republic's language of public assistance to children was shaped by the unsuccessful repression of sexual difference; the specters of "honest men" and "brave soldiers" haunted efforts to speak generically of the state and its relationships to future generations. At certain key moments, moreover, feminine specificity broke through the surface of the Third Republic's masculine-neutral language, creating new categories, institutions, and practices in the rearing of state wards.[7] These instances centered in particular on the girl's transition from childhood to the world of adult labor and sexuality. That is, they centered on the very moments where a female child became not an "honest man," but a woman; not a "productive worker," but a woman worker in an unstable relationship to the world of waged labor; not a soldier, but a female adult defined by her "natural" state of moral and physical vulnerability and most of all, social dependency.

In short, the Third Republic's organization of public assistance to children encoded a highly gendered set of social and political relationships under the guise of a neutral and inclusive universalism. The inflections of masculine identity structured the discourse of public child protection, while those of feminine identity—particularly where it came to guiding children across the threshold of adolescence—tended to upset it. To borrow from Irigaray again, the Third Republic's discourse of child protection turned on a logic of "sexual indifference," universalizing masculine values and making the feminine a troubling exception.[8]

This doubled vision of the state and its relationship to children had serious effects on the new regime's efforts to rationalize and expand its programs of assistance to children. It gave rise to awkward disjunctions and troubling contradictions in the cultural work behind the government's strategies for the public protection and cultivation of youth. It undercut the rationale of new institutions devoted to the care and education of the abandoned child. Finally, in establishing the foundation for evaluating and interpreting the objectives of assistance to children, it informed the most banal elements of everyday administration.

The insights of feminist criticism and cultural analysis open the work of the administrative state to questions that tease out the fundamental role of gender in structuring both conceptions of social order and the institutions of social government. By looking at those moments where sexual difference simultaneously shaped and disrupted the structures of public assistance and child protection, we gain access to the highly contingent and culturally constituted foundation of "the state" and its operation in the social world. Such an approach allows the historian to go beyond the common resting points in the critical study of welfare, state, and society: the allegation of bourgeois plots of social control, or the unexplored identification of "paternalism" in state policies of assistance. More often than not, these two conclusions coexist in the same argument.[9]

The exercise of power and the centrality of class in the operation of public assistance should not, of course, be excluded from the historian's analysis of familial paradigms.[10] Rather, focusing on the efforts to bring discordant cultural materials—particularly cultural constructions of sexual difference—into line through the development of "rational" and "progressive" policy allows us to discard the limiting analytical language that reifies the state and attributes to it its own unproblematic free will and intentionality. We might also correct the reductive and overly Machiavellian use of "*la raison d'état*" by scholars investigating the state regulation of childhood. While the exercise of power in the name of national interests was—and continues to be—an essential element of modern politics, it cannot occur in a cultural vacuum. Along with our use of *raison d'état*, therefore, we might explore something that could be termed "*l'imaginaire d'état*" or the imagined universe of government. Locating the boundaries of possible meaning within which "the state" was constructed in the discourse, institutions, and practices of the past, within which agents of "the state" interpreted, spoke, and acted, permits us to move towards a more historical understanding of the politics of family regulation. It gives the state itself—as concept and institution—a history, and thus historicizes questions of public policy more fully. Critical to this venture, I would argue, is the recognition that gender has served historically as one of the primary means of figuring the relationship between government and the governed, most of all in matters related to the definition and fulfillment of familial roles.[11]

As Councilor Rousselle's remarks suggest, the operations of difference were crucial to the organization of state assistance to abandoned children under the French Third Republic. One case in particular is worthy of extended consideration: the problem of training female wards of the state to be skilled independent workers. This issue, of great concern to politicians and administrators on a national and local level beginning in the 1880s, provides a revealing example of precisely how the cultural understanding of feminine particularity, deeply inflected by class identity, disturbed the dominant models of state child-rearing. In attempting to create highly trained and properly moral women workers, prepared for the urban marketplace, the authors of the republic's policies of state assistance to children had to negotiate what would prove to be an unbridgeable conceptual and practical gap between the female ward-of-state and the honest man, productive worker, and brave soldier of the future.

It was in the department of the Seine, the administrative region surrounding and including Paris, that the most revealing experiment in transforming female wards into skilled workers took shape.

In all matters related to the protection and education of abandoned children, the Seine stood as the national vanguard, especially under the Third Republic. High government officials watched the Parisian administration with great interest, at times using its administrative innovations as prototypes for national policy. Conversely, the departmental council appears to have served as a springboard from local to national politics, particularly for those members concerned with questions of public assistance. Thus Paul Strauss's career took him from General Council, to the National Assembly, and eventually to the position of Minister of Hygiene. In absolute numbers, moreover, the department led the rest of the country in the population of children in public care.[12]

During the 1880s, the General Council and officials working in the Paris Bureau of Public Assistance initiated a program that created state-run vocational schools for children in departmental custody. Although the schools were at first restricted to the children in the department's Service des Enfants Moralement Abandonnés, caring for older, "morally endangered" children, admissions were soon opened to wards from the foundling service, or Service des Enfants Assistés, as well. Between 1882 and 1893, the department founded five schools designed for the professional education of its wards, four of them reserved for boys. These schools provided training in horticulture, furniture-making, printing, agriculture, and maritime labor. The fifth, the Ecole professionnelle d'Yzeure, opened in 1888, was designed to train adolescent girls in domestic arts and the skills necessary to high-quality professional needlework.

The founding of the Ecole d'Yzeure would raise many troubling questions about the state's moral and fiscal investment in training young women to earn their keep as skilled workers destined for the urban labor market. Its history, a tale of an institution defined and ultimately undone by the uneasy fit between the discursive frame of state assistance and the cultural and social construction of feminine labor in an urban context, illuminates the spaces between the broad vision of state child-rearing and the efforts to realize that vision in a particular instance. It suggests the degree to which the cultural understanding of sexual difference obstructed efforts to create synthetic and inclusive structures of care or education. It demonstrated the radical disjunction between the productive worker of the future, raised and protected by a benevolent state, and the woman worker, whose moral and physical health would appear to be put in jeopardy by the very same state.

The question of the state's role in training its wards for life as adult wage-earners provides a revealing example of the manner in which irreducible sexual difference shaped the state's overlapping projects of protective intervention, utopian social reconstruction, and the containment of social danger. If a significant aspect of the state's role as substitute parent was to oversee the vocational education of its wards, how did the recognition or suppression of gendered work-identities shape its policies? What happened when administrators encountered the contradiction between the need to prepare female children for adulthood and the wider discursive frame which valued only the creation of the productive (male) worker? How, in short, did difference operate in the context of a state-supervised transition from childhood to an adult realm of wage-earning independence? How did the state's management of the shift from childhood to *woman*hood affect the interests of *la patrie?*

In the Parisian Service des Enfants Assistés, official policy dating from the Napoleonic era dictated that upon reaching the age of twelve, the majority of state wards would be placed in agrarian service, generally as fieldworkers or domestic help.[13] When able-bodied children reached this threshold, the state ceased its payments to their rural foster families, and a regional administrator sought waged apprenticeships for them, usually with other farming families in the provinces.[14]

Officials were well aware, however, that not all state-assisted children could be absorbed into the agricultural sector. The 1811 decree mandated that those children who could not be placed in agricultural positions should be apprenticed, "boys with laborers or artisans; girls with housewives, seamstresses or other female workers or in factories and mills." Throughout the nineteenth century, this founding decree directed the placement of children "unsuited" for agriculture and farm life. Even after decades of industrial transformation, the basic contours of the Napoleonic placement policy endured.

When the Third Republic began its massive reinvestment in

assistance to children in the 1880s, agricultural apprenticeships and rural domestic service continued to predominate in the placement tables, and officials celebrated the physically and morally salutary effects of rustic life.[15] Indeed, given the late-nineteenth-century concern over the depopulation of the countryside, the government's interest in settling marginal urban children in the provinces took on a new urgency. For those children whose character or physical constitution appeared to disqualify them from field labor or the heavy domestic service required in the farm household, the Service des Enfants Assistés maintained the tradition of seeking apprenticeships in manufacturing or artisanal production. In this pursuit, officials were guided by the principles of gender-appropriate labor enumerated in the original decree.

Yet France in the 1880s could hardly be compared to France of 1813, nor could the cultural valences attached to labor at the turn of the nineteenth century compare to those in circulation near the century's end. Over the course of the intervening decades, the lives and morals of the urban poor and laboring classes increasingly preoccupied middle-class philanthropists, hygienists, and social critics. Indeed, "the social question" became one of the dominant motifs in nineteenth-century literature and politics.[16] Similarly the understanding of "work" and the increasingly complex category of "worker" came to be laden with political, social, and cultural meaning derived from a century of social unrest, revolutionary uprisings, and increasingly self-conscious labor militancy.[17]

If waged labor in the city aroused social critics' anxiety in a general sense, the labor of poor and working-class women attracted an even more intense kind of scrutiny. Early nineteenth-century industrial, political, and cultural transformations placed the laboring woman at the center of the discourse on the consequences of industrial capitalism, in France and elsewhere. Indeed, the middle of the century witnessed an explosion of literature attempting to explain a category increasingly seen as deviant, or at the very least, as discomfitingly anomalous: the woman worker.

According to Joan W. Scott, the category of "woman worker" stood in uneasy opposition to the "naturally" masculine category of "worker" in mid-nineteenth-century French social and economic thought; "woman worker," especially as it was exemplified in the female industrial laborer and the needleworker, signified the moral ills of both industrial capitalism and "modern" urban society.[18] No doubt the radicalism displayed by working women under the Paris Commune added a political edge to late-century fears that urban waged labor destroyed women's virtue and rendered them a threat to the moral fiber of society as a whole.[19] When the administrators of the early Third Republic came to reconsider the state's obligations in preparing the workers of the future, the problem of women's work was firmly situated in the context of a powerful critique of "modern" urban life and its influence on the poor and laboring classes.

By the early 1870s it was thus no simple thing to suggest that the state ought to prepare any of its female wards for waged labor outside of agriculture or rural domestic service under the supervision of the peasant *patron*. In the critiques of the 1850s and 1860s, the image of the woman worker had undermined the moral legitimacy of industrial capitalism. At the same time, among conservative observers who laid moral responsibility at the feet of the laboring classes themselves, the deviancy associated with the category of "woman worker" appeared to demonstrate laboring women's intrinsic moral incapacities.

Under the early Third Republic, the question of moral responsibility took an unprecedented form as experiments in state-run vocational education for abandoned and endangered girls brought the disquieting figure of the urban woman worker into the arena of government. In embracing the professional education of young needleworkers as an affair of state, officials in the Bureau of Public Assistance unwittingly forged a link between the immorality associated with the woman worker and the moral legitimacy of state assistance to children. It was in the context of these debates and institutional experiments that public officials confronted the most disturbing aspects of the disjunction between the figuration of the laboring woman and the mandate to create the soldier-worker-citizen of tomorrow from the state-assisted child of today. As these officials would discover, the implications would impinge as much on the everyday operation of assistance to children as they would on the forging of social policy or the tooling of political rhetoric.

Members of the Seine's General Council and Public Assistance administrators in Paris could not have been unaware of the economic and moral critiques of work in the clothing trades that had been proliferating with the intensification of social inquiry over the course of the century. Whatever their political stripe, contemporary observers agreed that women who attempted to earn their living by their needles were destined to a life of poverty, desperation, and eventually, prostitution.[20]

Reaffirming the Napoleonic principle of creating industrial workers, and especially professional needlewomen, from those girls unsuited for provincial farm life raised troubling new issues for authorities in the last quarter of the nineteenth century. First, the women workers in question were not independent adults but underage girls who had no family other than the metaphorical family embodied in the administrative bureaucracy and image of the parental state. How could public authorities, acting in their parental capacity, simultaneously protect these children from the ills of modern life and prepare them for a trade renowned for its corrosive effect on feminine morals? On both a practical and ideological level, training female wards-of-state to earn their living as needlewomen thrust the administration into the eye of the storm. Most importantly, it burdened the state itself with a degree of moral responsibility in the corruption of women workers hitherto attributed only to capital itself.

The moral risks were raised even further by concerns about the origin of these children, concerns that were also marked by the irreducibility of sexual difference. Whether or not they had been born out of wedlock, all children abandoned into the care of the state carried the stigma of illegitimacy. In the new science of criminology, moreover, late-nineteenth-century experts isolated both social environment and inherited proclivities as the root of deviance among both men and women, although they stressed women's greater vulnerability to suggestion, and hence, to learned vice.[21] The potential for reproducing the unmarried mother's sins, however, appears to have devolved strictly upon the female child; popular opinion cast girls in the care of the Service des Enfants Assistés as the embodiment of the feminine vices that had led to their mothers' pregnancy and their own abandonment.[22] Exposure to the temptations of urban life and labor, officials feared, might easily stimulate the latent moral deviancy so deeply embedded in the female ward's character and lead her to reproduce her mother's trajectory of delinquency and degradation.

If administrators and social observers at times expressed sympathy for the wards of the state, they were nevertheless bound into a discursive frame that insisted upon abandoned girls' special proclivities to moral transgression and depravity. Inherited desires and tastes attracted them to vice; the double moral weakness of their sex and social class left them open to the invitation to deviancy proffered by the urban milieu. Zola's rendering of the transmission of corruption in *L'Assommoir* and *Nana* provides an apt crystallization of the fears surrounding the female ward-of-state: every one of them was a potential Nana, driven by genealogy and social milieu to re-enact the demoralizing primal scene in which her mother had played the starring role. It would only take exposure to the degrading atmosphere of the workshop, as Zola put it in the case of Nana's debut as a artificial flower-maker, to provide "the finishing touch."[23]

What then would it mean for the state to recognize and encourage its female dependents' participation in the urban wage economy? Could the state transform young girls into adult women workers without exposing them to the moral and economic "dangers" that had brought their own mothers to unwed parenthood and the abandonment of their offspring? Was there a way, in other words, for urban waged labor to serve as a "natural" and healthy alternative to agrarian service without compromising the moral integrity of both the assisted girl and the administration?

One of the most significant efforts to resolve these questions came in the General Council of the Seine's 1884 decision to create a school designed exclusively for training of female wards-of-state in domestic arts and needlework. The training provided was to be primarily professional, that is, it was to prepare girls to enter the Parisian labor market as highly skilled workers upon the completion of their studies at the age of eighteen. In addition, pupils would be schooled in elementary domestic skills, and would run the Ecole d'Yzeure's laundry and kitchen.

Early enthusiasm ran high among officials, who saw in the creation of vocational schools for abandoned and morally endangered children the potential both for high caliber professional formation and strict moral supervision.[24] From the beginning, however, competing visions blurred the fundamental identity of the school, its population, and its mission. Besides creating skilled needleworkers, the school was to have initiated a new era in the secular institutional reform of insubordinate and potentially criminal girls. In another view, it would be the institutional haven for girls deemed too "delicate" for the physical demands of farm service. And finally, although this function was only rarely mentioned in the annual reports, it would house the girls from the Service des Enfants Assistés and the Service des Moralement Abandonnés who had been categorized as *idiotes* or mentally-handicapped.[25]

Within the department's administrative imagination, the specters of feminine congenital weakness did battle with the desire to train an elite corps of craftswomen, selected on the basis of their special talents. In both cases, the creation of an alternative to agricultural labor and life in the peasant household was marked by the insistence that there was something far more pathological about these girls than there was about male state wards or their fellow female wards who remained on the farms.

The amalgam of correcting the deviant and educating the talented marked the early structure of the Ecole d'Yzeure as well as its philosophy. When the school opened its doors in 1887, it housed two services: a reform ward and a professional school. Candidates for vocational training were drawn exclusively from the Service des Moralement Abandonnés, while the reform school served both the Moralement Abandonnés and the Enfants Assistés. In 1891 the department transferred the reform school to Paris, leaving to the Ecole d'Yzeure the sole function of training female wards in the production of fine linens and clothing. Soon thereafter administrators opened the program to girls from both services and new workshops were added. The increased stress on vocational training in the 1890s in turn stimulated efforts to professionalize the school's instructional staff; the department began to stage public competitions in Paris to select "expert" professional needlewomen who could also provide documentary proof of their "moral integrity."[26] By the end of 1891, the staff of the Ecole d'Yzeure included a director, four primary school teachers, and three vocational instructors.[27] The population climbed from the first class of ninety-three to an annual average of almost three hundred students by the middle of the decade.[28] Although only a tiny portion of the department's population of wards, the number far exceeded the student bodies at the Seine's other industrial schools reserved for male wards-of-state.[29]

With the professionalization and expansion of the Ecole d'Yzeure came the insistence that the school adhere to rigorous standards of recruitment and training. According to the General Council's report from 1895, the Ecole d'Yzeure chose its students from among female wards of the Seine, aged ten to thirteen, who possessed "good characters, a certain minimum level of education, and who show[ed] an aptitude for needlework." Most of all, the department stressed the recruitment of "virtuous" and "talented" girls who were also of "delicate constitution," that is, too weak for agricultural occupations. The students remained at the school, and under direct supervision of departmental administrators, until the age of eighteen. For some wards, then, the period of training could last for eight years, although five years was more typical.

No sooner was the foundation of intensive vocational education laid, however, than doubt about the viability of the school's aims appeared in departmental records and inspection reports. News of the dismal conditions confronting former students filtered back to the Ecole d'Yzeure before the end of the 1880s. Shaken, administrators and departmental officials began to ask themselves whether the school could ever successfully fulfill its mission of transforming girls of fragile physical and moral constitutions into self-sufficient workers. Even as they celebrated the new institution and called for its expansion, Seine authorities began to express their fears that no amount of training could counteract the misfortune and vice endemic in Paris. The question of whether the Ecole d'Yzeure's lengthy apprenticeship program in the needle trades was worth the budgetary "sacrifices"—as contemporary reports put it with increasing frequency—forced administrators to define institutional success and failure in explicitly gendered terms. Both the images of success and failure rested upon culturally contingent, and often contradictory, understandings of women as productive workers and experiencing subjects.[30]

Although department officials appeared to direct much of their attention to the harsh material and economic conditions that greeted the graduates of the Ecole d'Yzeure in Paris, they bound these concerns into a broader moral critique that focused on the interior transformation of the young women themselves. Most of all this critique centered on the acquisition of new tastes and habits that might serve as the internal engine to demoralization. In contemporary representations of women needleworkers, tastes acquired in the course of their daily exposure to the seductions of city life often predicated moral undoing. An inquiry on labor conditions published by the Chamber of Deputies in 1881 included the opinion of the Paris prefect of police on the subject of young women workers, material desire, and prostitution. "The life they lead," contended M. Camescasse, "and the examples they run across quickly give them a taste for luxury that grows with every passing day and pushes them to seek ways to satisfy these unnatural needs. At that point they need money, which they procure however they can."[31]

Here too, anxiety about the particularly "tainted" moral constitution of the female ward-of-state, her intrinsic disposition to vice, and the state's complicity in exposing her to temptations lent a unique pitch to administrative fears about demoralizing desires. Returning *une petite parisienne* to the city, that is, to the scene of her sinful conception and early degrading experience, seemed to many to be the deliberate and inevitable undercutting of the state's investment in re-education and moralizing supervision. "[F]or some of our pupils," the report of 1896 reads, "there is a real danger in placement in Paris or its environs."[32]

Critics also argued that the program of professional training constituted a double assault on the familial basis of feminine virtue. Recruitment for the Ecole d'Yzeure appeared to rupture the tenuous family ties established between the girls and the foster families that had raised them in childhood. Once loosed in Paris, these wards-of-state lacked even the most fragile of familial structures that bound other working-class women into more apparently resilient structures of mutual surveillance. As one councilor remarked in his 1910 report on the school, "It is hardly desirable to see the young girls from our provincial bureaus, for whom we have reforged families in the countryside, swelling the multitude of young girls *sans famille* in Paris."[33] Deprived of family care at least twice in their lives—once as a result of abandonment by biological parents, and once when they were removed, sometimes against their will, from their present foster families for professional training at the Ecole d'Yzeure—the young seamstresses and embroiderers sent to Paris seemed doubly endangered in a culture where proper parental or familial supervision seemed the only sure rampart against vice.

Ironically, the fear that the Ecole d'Yzeure's graduates were not able to lead the lives of virtuous self-sufficient workers in Paris was layered over a deeper anxiety about the implications of the program's potential for success. Equipping young women for a life of urban wage-earning independence, beyond the reach of familial or administrative supervision, challenged the very moral codes that had brought the school into existence. It assimilated women workers too closely to the model of the universal male worker, whose capacity for earning and social independence entitled him—at least in principle—to participate in the civic life of the nation.

The state's programs for training girls as high-quality seamstresses thus conjured only compromised images of success and devastating images of failure. An effective professional transformation might yield a self-sufficient wage-earner, a status difficult to reconcile with nineteenth-century notions of womanhood. On the other hand, unsuccessful training would yield a young woman unable to earn her living "honestly," a woman who would sully the state's reputation and squander its investment in her education by turning to prostitution in times of economic hardship. Neither the independent, skilled woman worker nor the casual prostitute could easily be worked into the prognostic fantasy of honest men and brave soldiers.

In practice, officials need not have worried that the school would prove too successful in the forging of an independent female labor elite. Early investigations revealed that very few of the girls trained in the needlework ateliers at Ecole d'Yzeure managed to find employment that made use of their expertise or provided a comfortable income. The General Council's report on the school from 1892 showed that of the twenty-nine students who left that year, not one had been placed as a seamstress or needleworker.[34] The figures from 1896 show little change; twenty-two of the thirty-eight girls who left the school left before the completion of any professional training at all after they had been deemed "unsuited" for the program. Of the others, only three found work in the needle trades, and these were girls retained by the Bureau of Public Assistance as sous-maîtresses in the Ecole d'Yzeure's own workshops. The situation in the mid-1890s prompted one member of the General Council to question not only the school's feeble achievements, but the administration's own complicity in transforming young girls into an economically and morally vulnerable class of urban workers: "Will we be assured of finding jobs in keeping with the tastes and habits that we have given these girls whom we spirited away from common labor and the limited horizon of agricultural life?"[35]

Complaints about the school multiplied further after the turn of the century, even as the administration documented a definite increase in the number of girls who found their way to the professions for which they had been prepared.[36] Indeed, the improved placement record only deepened the administration's moral concerns. One inspector for the Enfants Assistés concluded in 1908 that Paris promised no future to these girls, and that there was little point in continuing a program that forced the state to endanger their physical and moral health. Another inspector railed the following year that it was impossible for the former pupils of the Ecole d'Yzeure "to earn their livings . . . under suitable conditions."[37] In short, the more wards the school placed in Paris, the more departmental officials felt the onus of creating a category of laborer whose experiences threatened not only her own moral status, but the moral foundation of the state's parental identity.

By 1914 the Ecole d'Yzeure loomed in the vision of its creators—and their successors—as an unnerving monument to their conceptual and practical failure. During the war the school suspended its training programs while the buildings were used as an army hospital. In 1918, with the lease on the property at Yzeure expired, the General Council proposed that a reduced version of the school be transferred to a site in the suburbs of Paris.[38] In the same report, the General Council made a final attempt to defend the school against the calls for its closure. Relocation, reform, and modernization, council members claimed, would put an end to the complaints of the inspectorate and the departmental prefect. Along with investing in a new site for the school, the report concluded, "we must raise the level of instruction, orienting it in such a manner that our pupils might occupy those desirable positions that are already—and more than ever before—available to women."[39]

Critics saw no solution to the program's intrinsic flaws,

however, and renewed their lobby for dismantling the program altogether. Departmental inspectors, far less lenient towards the school than the General Council, announced their unanimous condemnation of the Ecole d'Yzeure in a letter to the departmental prefect, drafted in April 1921:

> [it] had been clearly established that the pupils of this school, apprentice *lingères, couturières,, corsetières,* and *brodeuses,* have not been able to earn their living honorably after five or six years of training: the uselessness of the establishment consequently becomes evident. It is regrettable that the opinion of the inspection committee was not heard, for far too many girls, abandoned children at the start, could have been spared the most cruel disillusionment, while considerable expense could have been avoided.

The inspectors further objected to the proposition to transfer the Ecole d'Yzeure to Paris, repeating their earlier complaints about the malevolent influence of urban experience: "the young girls designated to benefit from professional education would there be exposed to temptations of all kinds."[40]

For the inspectors, tracing the careers of the graduates of Yzeure had revealed a most horrifying truth: the desire to produce elite craftswomen, respected for their skill and duly recompensed, had in reality produced a corps of underemployed women workers, even more prone to bodily and moral disintegration than their working-class sisters. Establishing a delicate balance between the goal of economic and moral self-sufficiency—the conceptual touchstone of the department's public apprenticeship programs—and the social subordination and moral protection so important in the "proper" education of young women, had proven to be an impossible task.

Despite evidence that departmental officials continued to debate the future of the Ecole d'Yzeure into the 1920s, historical accounts of the school become vague after the war. Albert Dupoux, an official historian of the Paris Bureau of Public Assistance, remarks rather cryptically that the Ecole d'Yzeure simply "disappeared" in 1918, along with several other vocational schools that had fallen into disuse or had proven too costly for the department to maintain after the war. According to Dupoux, only the printing and horticulture schools for boys survived both world wars, becoming in the 1950s "excellent vocational training centers" and the "pride of the administration."[41]

After a last warning on the school in 1921, the departmental inspectorate appears to have imposed its own silence on the fate of the Ecole d'Yzeure and the project of institutional apprenticeship for girls in the care of the state. For its part, the General Council seems to have issued no further reports on the school after 1918. In other twentieth-century internal histories of the Bureau of Public Assistance, moreover, the Ecole d'Yzeure is entirely absent, effaced by the "more successful" experiments in the professional education of boys.[42] A trace of the Ecole d'Yzeure does appear in a slim pamphlet issued in 1958.[43] Alongside photos celebrating the newly modernized printing and horticultural schools for boys, the pamphlet includes photos of the new Ecole Henri Mathé, as the Ecole d'Yzeure had been renamed after the turn of the century. According to the text, the new school devoted itself exclusively to training mentally-disabled female wards-of-state in the most elementary domestic tasks. What was almost unspeakable in the late-nineteenth-century debates on institutional apprenticeships for female state wards thus became the ultimate *raison d'être* for the postwar incarnation of the Ecole d'Yzeure.

What are we to make of the unsettling—and profoundly gendered—silences and ellipses in the official history of the Ecole d'Yzeure and the department's attempt to create skilled and professionalized industrial workers from its female wards? What accounts for a discomfort so profound that the state's own historians and administrators could not bring themselves to conclude the story of the Ecole d'Yzeure in the twentieth century? Perhaps the contradictions that riddled the efforts to turn female wards of the state into skilled independent professionals have remained, even decades later, too difficult, too compromising, and too embarrassing for the administrative apologist to handle. The question of the state's moral complicity in exposing its own "children" to moral danger, a problem raised only in the care and education of girls, meant that the Ecole d'Yzeure could never become "the pride of the administration."

While the above must surely be true, the answer lies deeper, and returns us to the wider question of gender, the construction of assistance to children, and the Third Republic's *imaginaire d'état*.

Specifically, the "failed" experiment of the Ecole d'Yzeure and the unresolved narration of its fate in the twentieth century suggests that for those charged with representing "the state"—either as administrators or as historians—the issue of training skilled female workers shut down the dominant frame of reference for understanding public assistance to children in more general terms.

Most of all, the Ecole d'Yzeure represented the breach of the Third Republic's historical sensibilities. It interjected "woman worker" into a paradigm that consistently grounded its images of the past and the future in universalized masculine terms. We should not think that this paradigm was simply a rhetorical gesture. Instead, it provided the fundamental interpretive frame for a state bent on investing in an apparatus of assistance and education that would create the subjects of the future, subjects who would contribute to the wealth and health of the nation as a whole. "[I]n the nineteenth century," Christina Crosby argues, "'history' is produced as man's truth, the truth of a necessarily historical Humanity, which in turn requires that 'women' be outside history, above, below, or beyond properly historical and political life."[44] In the end, it was precisely this kind of gendered vision of history that structured the ideologies and practices of assistance to children in Third Republic France.

NOTES

1.   Conseil Général de la Seine [hereafter CGS], *Rapport général présenté par M. Rousselle au nom de la 3e Commission sur le service des Enfants moralement abandonnés* 1 (1894): 2. Versions of Rousselle's statement abounded in this era. Another member of the General Council of the Seine, Paul Strauss, lauded the project of state-run child protection with similar sentiments. "For the state," Strauss wrote in 1896, there could be "no enthusiasm more profitable, no expenditure more productive" than child protection, "for in rescuing the body and soul of a child, we create citizens and soldiers, a store of strength and vitality for the fatherland." Strauss, *L'enfance malheureuse* (Paris, 1896), v.

2.   In 1889 the French National Assembly enacted legislation entitling the state to deprive "morally dangerous" parents of their rights over their children. By denying any natural foundation to parental authority, particularly paternal authority, the law overturned older conceptions of the relationship between state and family, and laid the groundwork for a vision of parenthood that was purely social. See Sylvia Schafer, "Children in 'Moral Danger' and the Politics of Parenthood in Third Republic France," (Ph.D. diss., University of California, Berkeley, 1992).

3.   B. R. Mitchell, *European Historical Statistics 1750–1970* (New York, 1978),

21. See also Armengaud, "La démographie, signe et facteur: une population quasi stationnaire 1880–1914," in *Histoire économique et sociale de la France* vol. 4 ed. Fernand Braudel and Ernest Labrousse (Paris, 1979), i, 100.

4. In her essay on the Yale School of criticism, Barbara Johnson uses Wordsworth's phrase, "the child is the father of the man," to explore the discursive suppression of possible female identities in the common definition of "child" in Western culture. See Barbara Johnson, *A World of Difference* (Baltimore, 1987), esp. 34.

5. Luce Irigaray, *Ethique de la différence sexuelle* (Paris, 1984), 14 (emphasis hers). All translations are my own, unless otherwise noted.

6. See Rachel G. Fuchs, *Abandoned Children: Foundlings and Child Welfare in Nineteenth-Century France* (Albany, 1984), 64–65.

7. Other areas of public assistance did address women explicitly, mostly in the programs of aid to single mothers and in the pronatalist policies also developed under the aegis of the Third Republic. See Fuchs, *Abandoned Children*, especially chapter 2, "Attitudes and Public Policy toward the Family." See also Fuchs, "Preserving the Future of France: Aid to the Poor and Pregnant in Nineteenth-Century France," in *The Uses of Charity: The Poor on Relief in the Nineteenth-Century Metropolis*, ed. Peter Mandler (Philadelphia, 1990) and Mary Lynn McDougall, "Protecting Infants: The French Campaign for Maternity Leaves, 1890s–1913," *French Historical Studies* 13 (1983).

8. Irigaray, "The Power of Discourse and the Subordination of the Feminine," in *This Sex Which is Not One*, trans. Catherine Porter with Carolyn Burke (Ithaca, N.Y., 1985), 118.

9 See for example, Philippe Meyer's invocation and condemnation of a calculating bourgeois apparatus of state in *L'Enfant et la raison d'état* (Paris, 1977). Although his arguments are ultimately more complex than Meyer's, Jacques Donzelot makes similar gestures in *The Policing of Families*, trans. Robert Hurley (New York, 1979). See also Sanford Elwitt, *The Third Republic Defended: Bourgeois Reform in France 1880–1914* (Baton Rouge, 1986).

10. Michel Foucault's use of the term "governmentality" comes closer to providing a useful point of departure for the cultural history of the state by linking the concerns of government more closely with changes in the historical and political context. Foucault's thoughts on "governmentality" provide an important counterpoint to studies—including some of his own—that have emphasized the seamless and univocal implementation of ruling strategies. As Foucault puts it in "Governmentality," "the state . . . does not have this unity, this individuality, this rigorous functionality, nor, to speak frankly, this importance; maybe, after all, the state is no more than a composite reality and a mythicized abstraction . . . ." Foucault errs, however, in his assertion that the paradigms of family had no place in modern rationales of government, and indeed, despite his disclaimers, appears to over stress rationality in his own analysis of modern mechanisms of state. Michel Foucault, "Governmentality," in *The Foucault Effect: Studies in Governmentality*, ed. Graham Burchell, Colin Gordon, and Peter Miller (Chicago, 1991), 103.

11. In this respect, Joan W. Scott's exhortation to consider gender in the analysis of political theory and history is particularly relevant. See Scott, "Gender: A Useful Category of Historical Analysis," in *Gender and the Politics of History* (New York, 1988), esp. 48–50.

12. In 1899 the population of abandoned children enrolled in the Seine's Service des Enfants Assistés exceeded 46,000, while the department of the Rhône and the Seine-Inférieur followed with approximately 5,000 wards apiece. According to the Ministry of the Interior's statistics for 1899, the Seine's Service des Enfants Assistés accounted for 34% of the state wards in France. Ministère de l'Intérieur, Direction de l'Assistance et de l'Hygiène publiques. Bureau des services de l'enfance. *Statistique de la mortalité des Enfants Assistés (année 1899)* (Melun, 1901).

13. *Décret du 19 janvier 1811 concernant les enfants trouvés ou abandonnés et les orphelins pauvres*, reproduced in Albert Dupoux, *Sur les pas de Monsieur Vincent. Trois cent ans d'histoire parisienne de l'enfance abandonnée* (Paris, 1958), 183–186.

14. Fuchs, *Abandoned Children*, 256–257; Dupoux, *Sur les pas*, 246; and CGS, *Rapport général présenté par P. Strauss sur le service des Enfants secourus, des Enfants assistés et des Enfants moralement abandonnés* 12 (1896): 36–37.

15. See Henri Monod, *Les enfants assistés de France* (Melun, 1898), xxvi. On the relationship between the placement policies of the Paris Bureau of Public Assistance and rural depopulation, see Nancy Fitch, "'Les Petits parisiens en province': The Silent Revolution in the Allier, 1860–1900," *Journal of Family History* 11 (1986).

16. See Louis Chevalier's seminal work, *Laboring Classes and Dangerous Classes in Paris during the First Half of the Nineteenth Century*, trans. Frank Jellinek (Princeton, 1973). On the construction of social problems in the discourse of philanthropy and moral economy, see Katherine A. Lynch, *Family, Class, and Ideology in Early Industrial France: Social Policy and the Working-Class Family, 1825–1848* (Madison, 1988).

17. See the wide-ranging essays in *Work in France: Representations, Meanings, Organization and Practice*, ed. Steven Laurence Kaplan and Cynthia J. Koepp (Ithaca, N.Y. 1986).

18. See Joan W. Scott's insightful analysis of this debate in mid-nineteenth-century political economy, "'L'ouvrière! Mot impie, sordide . . .': Women Workers in the Discourse of French Political Economy, 1840–1860," in *Gender and the Politics of History*.

19. On the feminist component of the Commune, see Claire Goldberg Moses, *French Feminism in the Nineteenth Century* (Albany, 1984), 189–196. See also Edith Thomas, *The Women Incendiaries*, trans. James and Starr Atkinson (New York, 1966).

20. Influential treatises on the question of women's work, poverty, and prostitution in nineteenth-century France include A. J. B. Parent-Duchâtelet, *La Prostitution à Paris au XIXe siècle*, ed. Alain Corbin (Paris, 1981); Pierre-Joseph Proudhon, *La Pornocratie*, vol. 2 of *Oeuvres complètes* (Paris, 1939); Julie-Victoire Daubié, *La Femme pauvre au XIXe siècle* (Paris, 1866); and Jules Simon's *L'Ouvrière*, 2nd ed. (Paris, 1862). On the socialist and anarchist critique of prostitution as a consequence of capitalism, see Alain Corbin, *Women for Hire: Prostitution and Sexuality in France after 1850*, trans. Alan Sheridan (Cambridge, Mass., 1990), 234–246.

21. On criminology and medical explanations of deviance, see Robert B. Nye, *Crime, Madness and Politics in Modern France: The Medical Concept of National Decline* (Princeton, 1984) and Ruth Harris, *Murders and Madness: Medicine, Law and Society in the Fin de Siècle* (Oxford, 1989). On theories of female and child

criminality, see Patricia O'Brien, *The Promise of Punishment: Prisons in Nineteenth-Century France* (Princeton, 1982).

22. Parent-Duchâtelet, for example, noted the belief common in 1836 that the majority of prostitutes were illegitimate, and that a great many of them had been abandoned at birth. His study of Paris-born, registered prostitutes suggested that the assumption was ill-founded; according to Parent, around 25% were registered as illegitimate, and 50% percent of those had been legally recognized by their fathers. Parent-Duchâtelet, *Prostitution à Paris*, 82.

23. Émile Zola, *L'Assommoir*, trans. Leonard Tancock (Harmondsworth, Eng., 1970), 248.

24. The founding of industrial schools reserved for the Seine's wards-of-state also corresponded to a wider movement in the late nineteenth century to combat the decline in apprenticeships and the accompanying shortage of skilled workers through the creation of new public and private vocational schools. See Michelle Perrot, "Les Classes populaires urbaines," in Braudel and Labrousse, ed., *Histoire économique et sociale*, 4, vol. 1, 476–477.

25. See CGS, *Rapport sur le Service des Enfants Assistés présenté par M. Paul Strauss* 27 (1883), for the department's outline of its project. See also Archives du département de la Seine et de la ville de Paris [hereafter ADS], series D.1 x4, 1886, Procès verbaux de la Commission des Enfants Assistés.

26. CGS, *Rapport présenté par M. Navarre au nom de la 3e Commission sur l'Ecole professionnelle d'Yzeure et le transfert de l'Ecole de réforme à la Salpêtrière* 75 (1891): 2.

27. CGS, *Rapport présenté par M. Navarre au nom de la 3e Commission sur l'Ecole professionnelle d'Yzeure* 34 (1892): 1.

28. CGS, *Rapport par M. Astier au nom de la 3e Commission sur l'école professionnelle et ménagère d'Yzeure* 27 (1896): 2.

29. In contrast, the Seine maintained around 45 boys at its horticultural school in 1893, and about one hundred at the printing and furniture-making school at the end of 1892. Administration générale de l'Assistance publique à Paris, *Notice historique et statistique sur l'Ecole d'Horticulture de Villepreux (Seine-et-Oise) de 1882 à 1894* (Montrévrain, 1894), 17, and CGS, *Rapport présenté par M. Champoudry au nom de la 3e Commission sur l'école professionnelle d'Alembert* 22 (1893): 1.

30. Many of the more general charges against the Ecole d'Yzeure were part of a larger turn-of-the-century skepticism about the utility of any state vocational school reserved exclusively for assisted children, male or female. The most common theme in these attacks was the high cost of institutional apprenticeship. CGS, *Rapport* 75 (1891).

31. France, Chambre des Députés, *Procès verbaux de la commission chargée de faire une enquête sur la situation des ouvriers de l'industrie et de l'agriculture en France et de présenter un premier rapport sur la crise industrielle à Paris* [1881], 330.

32. CGS, *Rapport* 27 (1896): 4.

33. CGS, *Rapport* 38 (1910): 3.

34. CGS, *Rapport* 34 (1892): 2.

35. CGS, *Rapport* 34 (1895): 5.

36. The 1910 report on the school noted that the girls trained at the Ecole d'Yzeure—now the Ecole Henri Mathé—had finally gained a good reputation in Paris, and could be placed in workshops with relative ease, particularly in linen,

embroidery, and corsetry workshops. CGS, *Rapport au nom de la 3e Commission sur le projet de budget pour 1911...: école Henri Mathé à Iseure* [sic] *présenté par M. E. Chausse* 38 (1910): 5.

37.   ADS D.1 S4, Procès verbaux de la Commission des Enfants Assistés, 16 December 1908 and 21 December 1909.

38.   Among the reasons given for abandoning the site in Yzeure, Seine officials included material damage sustained during the war, and the hope that moving the school closer to the city might improve post-placement contact between girls and the administration. The report also implied that since black troops had been treated at the temporary hospital in a second segregated ward, the locale might no longer be considered fit for further occupation by department wards. CGS, *Rapport au nom de la 3e Commission tendant à la liquidation de l'école Henri Mathé à Yzeure . . . présenté par M. Henri Sellier* 28 (1918): 2.

39.   *Ibid.*, 2–3.

40.   ADS D.1 X4, Procès verbaux de la Commission des Enfants Assistés, 8 April 1921.

41.   Dupoux, *Sur les pas*, 257.

42.   Thus in the centennial volume published by the Administration Générale de l'Assistance publique à Paris, the Ecole d'Yzeure is entirely omitted from the section on the history of professional education for state wards. Roger Tourtel and Jean Fayard, *Cent ans d'assistance publique à Paris, 1849–1949* (Paris, 1949).

43.   Archives de l'Assistance publique, Fosseyeux Collection 686 [Administration de l'Assistance publique à Paris], *Trois siècles d'aide à l'enfance dans le département de la Seine (1638–1958)* (n.p., 1958). Ironically the pamphlet was printed by the students at the Ecole d'Alembert, the very departmental vocational school whose existence overshadowed the Ecole d'Yzeure from its foundation.

44.   Christina Crosby, *The Ends of History: Victorians and "The Woman Question"* (New York, 1991), 1.

Three Southern Women and Freud

A Non-Exceptionalist Approach to Race, Class, and Gender in the Slave South

NELL IRVIN PAINTER

In my work on sexuality in the nineteenth- and twentieth-century South, my mind returns often to what the late Herbert Gutman used to say about Marx, but with application to Sigmund Freud: He raises some very good questions. While I have plenty of feminist company in my turn toward psychoanalysis, the Freud I am using here is not quite the Freud who has been making recent appearances.[1] As a historian of the nineteenth- and early twentieth-century United States South trained in a history project grounded in the archives, I find Freud valuable mainly as an acute observer of nineteenth-century bourgeois society, as an analyst (no pun intended) who recognized the relationship between sexuality and identity. His writing permits unusually clear views into the ways in which social, economic, and ethnic hierarchies affected households and families, for he was accustomed to dealing with people in households that encompassed more than one economic class. Such vision enriches southern studies, which is still impoverished by an exceptionalism that cannot see commonalities between the American South and other hierarchical societies that were not structured along racial lines and by a tendency to see race as an opaque barrier to feminist investigation.

My subject is the family relations that affected the richest and the poorest of antebellum southern daughters. The tragically tiny number of black daughters who would have been actually or nominally free, and the large cohort of white daughters who

This essay forms part of a new book on southern families and sexuality in the nineteenth century. Portions of this essay were originally published in a slightly different form in "Of *Lily*, Linda Brent, and Freud: A Non-Exceptionalist Approach to Race, Class, and Gender in the Slave-holding South," *Georgia Historical Quarterly* (Summer 1992) and "Introduction" to *The Secret Eye: The Diary of Ella Gertrude Clanton Thomas*, ed. Virginia Ingraham Burr (Chapel Hill: University of North Carolina Press, 1990).

would have lived beyond the reach of the aristocracy, belonged to families who were able to shelter them from predatory wealthy men and were more likely to escape the fate of the daughters under discussion here. But whether black or white, if young women lived in households in which men had access to the poorest and most vulnerable—women who were enslaved—these daughters ran gendered risks related to sexuality that did not respect barriers of class and race.

It has been no secret, then or now, that during the slavery era, owners and slaves lived on terms of physical closeness and often engaged in sexual intimacy. Yet historians have followed the lead of privileged nineteenth-century southerners who, though well aware that sex figured among the services that masters demanded of slaves, briskly pushed the matter aside. Even psychoanalysts like Abram Kardiner and Lionel Ovesey pass quickly over the repercussions of interracial sexuality on southern white families and hence on southern society generally.[2] Virtually by default, the conclusion in southern history has been that master-slave sex was a problem for the families of slaves, not the families of the masters; thus as a social phenomenon, interracial, interclass sexuality has been relegated solely to African-Americans. This is not the position I hold. Because intimate relations affected white as well as black families, I argue that such sexuality and its repercussions belong not to one race or the other, but must reside squarely in southern history.[3]

One needs only read the work of class- and gender-conscious historians of Great Britain and Europe to recognize the parallels between nineteenth-century European bourgeois societies and that of the United States society in a similar period.[4] Such usefulness is not limited to historians' insights. While it is very much in vogue with literary critics, Freudian psychoanalysis also offers thought-provoking assistance to historians, particularly on the formation of individual identity. Specifically, Sigmund Freud's "Dora" case history raises fundamental questions about the dynamics of elite families in a hierarchical society in which the employment of servants—and here I concentrate on female servants—is routine. This essay addresses the pertinence of three pieces of Freud's writing to southern society, as reflected in the histories of three southern women: Gertrude Thomas, "Lily," and "Linda Brent."

Gertrude Thomas (1834–1907) spent much of her life as a plantation mistress near Augusta, Georgia. Her journal, written over the better part of forty years, takes a long but self-censoring look into one privileged white woman's family. Gertrude Thomas was not a fictional character, but she tried to make the record of her everyday life into a portrait that fitted her ideals.

Lily is the title character of an 1855 novel by Sue Petigru King (Bowen) (1824–1875), a daughter of the very respectable Charlestonian Thomas Petigru. Having been educated in Charleston and New York, she had returned to South Carolina to pursue her career as a writer. King's protagonist, Lily, is the quintessential young plantation mistress: hyper-white, wealthy, and beautiful. Much better known today, thanks largely to the work of Jean Fagan Yellin and others, is Linda Brent, who in contrast to Lily, is a slave. Brent is both the central character and the pseudonym under which the Edenton, North Carolina, fugitive slave Harriet Jacobs (1813–1897) wrote her autobiography, *Incidents in the Life of a Slave Girl*, originally published with the help of abolitionists in Boston in 1861.[5]

If rich, white, and free Gertrude and Lily stood at the top of the antebellum South's economic and racial hierarchies, then poor, yellow, and enslaved Linda Brent lived near, but not at the very bottom. Linda, after all, has some free relations, and her grandmother, though nominally enslaved, lives in her own house in town. Things could have been much worse for Linda Brent. Gertrude's, Linda's, and Lily's stories are about women and sex; taken together with Freud's "Dora" they tell us a great deal about southern family dynamics in slaveholding households. As all three of these texts are about race and sexuality, I begin with the phenomenon of master-slave sex as I discovered it in Gertrude Thomas's journal.

GERTRUDE THOMAS'S SECRET

Although historians have not begun to quantify its incidence, we know that sexual relations between male slavemasters and female slaves were exceedingly common in the antebellum South— as in any other slave society, as Orlando Patterson points out.[6] Nineteenth-century fugitive slave narratives, such as those of Frederick Douglass and Moses Roper, and the Fisk and WPA ex-slave narratives from the 1930s, are full of evidence that masters did not hesitate to sleep with their women slaves, despite the marital status of either. Although I have not had an opportunity to pursue this hunch, I suspect that about ten percent of masters also slept or wanted to sleep with their enslaved men and boys; some mistresses may also have regarded their female slaves as objects of desire.[7] On the other side of the class and racial continuums from the Frederick Douglasses and Moses Ropers, nineteenth-century white women—southerners and observers—penned and sometimes published criticisms of the institution of slavery based on what they perceived as the demoralization of white men who engaged in adultery and/or polygyny.

I began to draw my own conclusions as I concentrated on the journal of Ella Gertrude Clanton Thomas, published in 1990 as *The Secret Eye*.[8] Thomas was wealthy, educated, and white, and she began keeping a journal in 1848, when she was fourteen years old, and stopped writing definitively in 1889, when she was fifty-five. Although born into an immensely wealthy, slave-owning family, she married a man who was a poor manager. Her husband, Jefferson Thomas, succeed financially as a planter before the Civil War, thanks to unpaid labor and continual financial help from Gertrude's father. But her father died in 1864, and their slaves were emancipated in 1865. After the war the Thomases entered a long cycle of debt that sent Gertrude into the paid labor force as a teacher. Her earnings kept the family afloat economically, but poverty imposed great strains. This journal, therefore, chronicles a life of privilege before the Civil War, the trauma of supporting the losing side, the loss of the labor and prestige that slavery had assured, and the chagrin of downward mobility. Thomas joined the Woman's Christian Temperance Union in the 1880s and became a suffragist in the 1890s. She died in Atlanta.

Initially I appreciated this journal for its value as a primary source for the study of the social history of the South, for which Thomas is an excellent witness. Extraordinary as is the historical source, however, the journal works on yet another level that is characterized by the keeping of secrets, lack of candor, and self-deception and that psychoanalysis is well-equipped to explore. What Thomas tried to hide in her journal offers glimpses into persistent tensions over gender and sexuality in the South and, ultimately, into the nature of nineteenth-century southern society.

The Thomas journal contains a hidden layer of secrets that is murky, personal, and highly gendered. There are actually two great secrets in the journal, one of which, Jefferson's drinking, Gertrude did succeed in hiding. The other proved too painful to suppress entirely. Whereas the surface of this text presents a southerner of a certain class at given historical junctures, a less straightforward message also emerges, though it is not so easy to decipher. The veiled text, less bounded chronologically, concerns families and gender, and it contains and reveals a great secret that is relatively timeless: adultery.

Even when she is strongest and most outspoken, Thomas draws a veil across certain realities of her life that she shared with large numbers of other plantation mistresses. Like them, she tries not to see. But unlike the great majority of her peers, Thomas left a huge, magnificent journal. Her writing hints—through what psychologists call "deception clues" (cues that something is being withheld) and "leakage" (inadvertent disclosure) of highly-charged material—that some important truths remain obscured.[9]

Both leakage and deception clues are associated with the phenomenon of self-deception, the concealment of painful knowledge from the self. The line between deception of her readers (her children) and self-deception is not entirely clear in the Thomas journal, for Thomas's concept of her audience varied over the many years that she wrote. At times she addresses her children, at other times her God. In the later years she speaks with remarkable candor to her journal as a confidante (herself). Drawing the line between deception and self-deception may not be an indispensable task here, for as observers as disparate at the sociologist Erving Goffman and the poet Adrienne Rich point out, the intention to mislead others quickly becomes the misleading of the self.[10]

The most obvious deception clue is one of Thomas's favorite refrains. Four times between 1852 (the year in which she married) and 1870 she cites this poem (or alludes to it by quoting the first line) by the Georgia poet Richard Henry Wilde:

> There are some thoughts we utter not.
> Deep treasured in our inmost heart
> Ne'er revealed and ne'er forgot.[11]

In addition, the intensity of portions of the writing manifests Thomas's uneasiness over certain subjects (e.g., competition between women, the dual sexual standard), without going to the heart of her distress. The most important deception clues begin with the entry of 2 June 1855, in which Thomas says: " [T]here are some thoughts we utter not and not even to you my journal ... yet there are some moments when I must write—must speak or else the pent up emotions of an overcharged heart will *burst* or *break*. . . . With a heart throbbing and an agitated form. How can I write?" Thomas cites "one of the most exciting conversations I have ever held. A conversation which in a moment, in a flash of the eye will change the gay, thoughtless girl into a woman with all a woman's feelings" and the "chilling influence (it may be of disappointment) to wonder at the wild tumultuous throbbings of early womanhood." She says that she is troubled by something.

I have never succeeded in decoding this confusing entry entirely, for the language is more than ambiguous; these phrases lead in two separate directions at once. Thomas's language echoes other women's private descriptions of infatuations at the same time that it represents Thomas's own language of disappointment. When she writes of "all a woman's feelings" elsewhere in the journal, she speaks of chagrin rather than fulfillment. Neither this entry nor those around it provides clues as to the cause(s) of her agitation. But she clearly manifests great anxiety over the contents of a conversation that takes place when her first child is eighteen months old. Moreover in two other entries in the same season, she speaks of the "bitter agony" and the bitterness of "taunts and expressions" that are the lot of married women.

Several years later Thomas begins to explicate her concerns in what I call her leakage entries, in which she inadvertently reveals that certain matters are significant to her. The lengthy, intense entry of 2 January 1859 deplores miscegenation, which she acknowledges as matter "thought best for [white] women to ignore." Thomas castigates white men of uncontrolled, animal passions who buy mulatto slave women for sex. In general, Thomas had a very low opinion of southern white men's morals, but bachelors' fortunes were not uppermost in her mind.[12] Rather, she laments the effect of miscegenation in "our Southern homes." While she believes that white men are more degraded by slavery (i.e., the miscegenation that accompanies the institution) than blacks, her main preoccupation is with white families.

A young mother worrying over slavery's pernicious effect on children, Thomas points away from her own nuclear family and toward the setting in which she was herself a child: her parents' household.[13] She also mentions "others," whom she does not name, who are equally guilty. Thomas deplores interracial sex as a violation of the racial hierarchy, but she is aware that the significance of the miscegenation she has in mind exceeds mere race mixing. It is also sex outside of marriage, so that someone worth worrying about in her father's household and in the household of "others" had violated one of the Ten Commandments. As a devout Christian who knew that there was a heaven and a hell and that the sins of the parents were liable to be visited upon the children, she worried "upon whom shall the accountability of their [the illegitimate children's] future state depend."

By January 1865 the combined strains of the war, her father's death, and the impending Confederate defeat brought Thomas's anxieties closer to the surface. She writes at length about competition between women. Finally, in 1869, she writes of her son, Turner, a mulatto plowboy, and his mother who is only slightly darker than Turner's mother.

With this entry, much of Thomas's impassioned writing falls into place. Gertrude Thomas worried about competition between women because it was a bothersome part of her own life as a daughter and a wife. Thus her long, fervent comments on the effect of slavery on white families and on black women's usurpation of the places of white wives now appear as commentary on her own family's tragedy. She believed that her father had had children and that her husband had had a child outside their marriages. It is possible, though far from certain, that whatever unspeakable thing distressed her when her first child was a baby was the discovery that her husband was sleeping with someone else.

Pulling all these leakage entries together, I conclude that the great secret of Gertrude Thomas's journal is something that she experienced as adultery. As a devout, nineteenth-century Methodist, she was deeply concerned with matters of moral rectitude and divine retribution. At the same time, however, she reacted to her husband's sexual relations with a slave as people have traditionally responded to adultery—with jealousy, anger, and humiliation, not with the placid assurance of racial superiority.

This should come as no surprise, as some of the best known observations about antebellum southern society make more or less the same point. Abolitionists—who are currently out of favor with historians as analysts of southern society—routinely pilloried slaveowners for the sexual abuse of mulatto women.[14] Female visitors to the South criticized slavery for its deleterious effect on white men's morals. In the 1830s Harriet Martineau spoke of the plantation mistress as "'the chief slave of the harem.'" Fredrika Bremer in the 1850s coined a famous phrase about slaves of mixed ancestry—the "white children of slavery"—which Thomas quotes in her journal. And Mary Chesnut wrote of the mulatto children present in every slaveholding household. Gertrude Thomas was far, very far, from alone.[15]

The intense hurt and anger in Thomas's entries on competition between women and sexual relations between slaveowners and slaves indicate that she experienced her husband's action as a breach in her marriage. Yet there may be an alternative and more appropriate definition of the phenomenon that Thomas deplored.

The pattern of slaveowning married men's sexual relations with women to whom they were not legally married was widespread, and these nonlegal relationships sometimes endured—like marriages. Seen another way, Thomas may have been party to a social pattern that she did not recognize and for which anthropologists use the term "polygyny." It may well have been that men like Jefferson Thomas, more than regularly committing adultery, were establishing something like polygynous marriages. Gertrude does not say how long Jefferson's relationship with his slave-partner lasted, whether it was a fling or might qualify as a marriage. Evidence from the journal supports at least a suspicion that the relationship may have endured from 1855 to 1870, perhaps even until 1880, but it is far from conclusive.[16] The stresses that Gertrude reports in her marriage—Jefferson's irritability, his refusal to give her moral support, his withdrawal from intimacy—could as easily represent the human cost of financial ruin as an expression of the distance between partners that accompanies extramarital relationships.

There can be no well-founded representation of the circumstances that led to the conception of Jefferson Thomas's outside child, but other cases are clearer. James Henry Hammond, a prominent antebellum South Carolina statesman, for instance, had two slaves who were, in effect, multiple wives. Southern court records are full of litigation over which set of families might inherit from men who had had children by more than one woman.[17]

Thomas's unwillingness to spell out what was taking place in her marriage hints by indirection at her husband's adultery. Her South pretended not to see slave wives, whose existence was a sort of elephant in the living room of family secrets.[18] Secrecy, the very heart and soul of adultery, is much of what makes adultery toxic to marriages, families, and, ultimately, society. Of itself, secrecy stifles intimacy and rigidifies relationships, even when partners are not so deeply religious as Gertrude Thomas.[19]

In the early nineteenth century Harriet Martineau understood that adultery places enormous strains on families, and modern scholarship makes the same point. Adultery breaks the pact of sexual exclusivity in marriage and undermines the betrayed spouse's trust in the other. The consequences of such ruptures could not always be confined to the private sphere. James Henry Hammond believed, with good foundation, that his wife's angry reaction to his taking his second slave wife ruined his political career.[20]

Adultery also subverts the social order by weakening the most fundamental social relationship upon which procreation and socialization depend. Adultery breeds moral and sexual ambivalence in children, who vacillate between the outraged virtue of the betrayed parent and the adulterous parent's indulgence in sin. Ultimately adultery creates chaotic inheritance patterns, which in the antebellum South meant that fathers were liable to own and sell their children. Lillian Smith, a perceptive twentieth-century southern observer of her region, grasped the way that secrets, miscegenation, sin, and guilt combined to endow white southerners with a terrible fear of impending disaster. Smith would have agreed that southern society, riven by so many instances of bad faith, was pathological.[21]

According to the ostensible mores of her society, Gertrude Thomas was the superior of nearly everyone in it. She was a plantation mistress in a society dominated by the 6 percent of white families that qualified as planters by owning twenty or more slaves. She was an educated woman at a time when only elite men could take higher education for granted. And she was white in a profoundly racist culture. Yet neither Gertrude Thomas's economic or educational attributes nor her social status protected her from what she saw as sexual competition from inferior women. From Thomas's point of view, white men saw women—whether slave or free, wealthy or impoverished, cultured or untutored, black or white—

as interchangeable sex partners. She and other plantation mistresses failed to elevate themselves sufficiently as women to avoid the pain of sharing their spouses with slaves. The institution of slavery, which assured female slaveowners social prestige, also gave them sexual nightmares. The effects of the victimization of slave women could not be contained, for (otherwise) privileged women like Gertrude Thomas felt that their husbands' adultery intruded into their own as well as their slaves' families.

Some of the most interesting evidence of this pattern comes from fiction, which, considering the subject, should not be surprising. Most respectable nineteenth-century people retreated—or attempted to retreat—behind the veil of privacy, rather than reveal their actual patterns of sexuality, whether in their homes, in their letters, or in their journals. The very ability to conceal the rawer aspects of the human condition, an ability that we sum up in the term privacy, served as a crucial symbol of respectability when the poor had no good place to hide. Nonetheless the topic of interracial sexuality was of enough fascination to reappear in fiction under various disguises. Taking my cue from Gertrude Thomas, who was hypersensitive about sexual competition between women, I began to pursue sexuality through the theme of competition. Tracked in that guise, southern fiction reveals some interesting manifestations.

LILLY

Sue Petigru King sounded themes that occur in the work of several white southern women writers, such as Caroline Hentz, Grace King, and Willa Cather. For example, Cather's final novel, *Sapphira and the Slave Girl* (1940), is precisely and openly about a white woman's perception of sexual competition between herself and a Negro woman. In its racial candor, *Sapphira* is exceptional. More often the competition between women is not about individuals with different racial identities, but about two white characters who are color-coded in black and white. While I realize that European writers such as Walter Scott and Honoré de Balzac used light (blond) and dark (*la belle juive*) female characters symbolically, Ann Jones, Mary Kelley, and Jane Pease, scholars familiar with southern writers, corroborate my view that nineteenth- and early twentieth-century white southern women writers were singularly fascinated by competition between light and dark women. While most publications by these women followed the usual theme of a young woman's quest for autonomy and her eventual marriage to a good man, they also echo Gertrude Thomas's fixation on female rivalry.

The author Sue Petigru King is no longer very well known, but she loomed large in Gertrude Thomas's literary world and was known in Great Britain. William Thackery, one of Britain's most celebrated authors, visited her on a trip to the United States. In the mid-nineteenth century King published several novels which repeatedly stress themes of jealousy and competition between women, the best-known of which is *Lily*, published in 1855.

Very briefly, *Lily* is the story of Elizabeth Vere, whom her father calls "Lily" because she is "as white as any lily that ever grew." Over the course of the novel's plot, Lily goes from age seven to seventeen. King describes her heroine with words like "white," "pure," "innocent," "simple," and "lovely." The character with whom King pairs Lily is her cousin, Angelica Purvis. Angelica is also a rich white woman, but King focuses on the blackness of her dresses and the intense blackness of her hair. At one point, King contrasts Lily, who "seemed made up of light and purity," with Angelica, who "was dark, designing, distracting." Angelica is exotic; King describes her as an "Eastern princess" and calls her looks "Andalusian." Whereas Lily is pure, Angelica is passionate, evil, voluptuous. Angelica says of her attractiveness to men: "I am original sin . . ."[22] At the age of seventeen, Lily is engaged to her first great love, Clarence Tracy, a childhood friend who is a graduate of Princeton. Despite all her goodness, however, Lily is not rewarded with love, for Clarence is crazy in love with Angelica, who is married.

On the face of it, the most obvious theme in *Lily* is competition between two white women, which the less virtuous is winning. But race hovers in the very near background. First, these ostensibly white competitors are color-coded in black and white. Then, as though to make the point conclusively, King abruptly introduces a new character, Lorenza, at the very end of the novel. Lorenza is Clarence's Negro mistress. On the night before Lily's wedding, a jealous Lorenza murders Lily.

King leaves nothing to guesswork in this novel, and to hammer home her message, she also addresses her readers directly. Her point is the same made by Mary Chesnut in her Civil War diary: that southern planter husbands repaid their wives' faithful virtue with base infidelity. Wealthy southern men married young, pure, rich, white girls like Lily, then left them for mistresses tinged by blackness, whether of descent or intimation. King sums up Mary Chesnut's conviction and Gertrude Thomas's fears: "It is not the woman most worthy to be loved who is the most loved." This conclusion is echoed in the writing of Sigmund Freud.

In 1912 Freud discussed exactly that phenomenon in his second contribution to the *Psychology of Love:* "On the Universal Tendency to Debasement in the Sphere of Love." Freud appraised the practical results of "civilized morality" and the sexual double standard from the standpoint of middle- and upper-class men who were susceptible to psychosomatic impotence with women of their own class. Freud said, making King's point: "Where such men love they have no desire and where they desire they cannot love."[23]

In *Lily*, the pure, young, rich, white daughter is the most dramatic loser in the southern sexual sweepstakes. In this interpretation of southern sexuality, the motif is competition between women and the victims are wealthy white women. Writers from the other side painted a disturbingly similar, yet differently shaded portrait.

LINDA BRENT

While many exslave narrators discuss master-slave sexuality, the most extended commentary comes from Harriet Jacobs, who, writing under the pseudonym Linda Brent, tells of being harassed by her master for sex from the time she was thirteen. Her character, Linda, becomes the literal embodiment of the slave as sexual prey in the testimony of slaves.

Harriet Jacobs depicts puberty as a "sad epoch in the life of a slave girl." As Linda Brent becomes nubile, her master begins to whisper "foul words in my ear," which is the kind of act whose consequences Freud comprehended and that we term sexual harassment. Jacobs generalizes from Linda's predicament and says that "whether the slave girl be black as ebony or as fair as her mistress"—she, the slave girl, is sexually vulnerable. This vulnerability robs her of her innocence and purity. Hearing "foul words" from her master and angry and jealous outbreaks from her mistress, the slave girl, in Jacob's phrase, becomes "prematurely knowing in evil things." The more beautiful she is, the more speedy her despolation. Beauty, for Linda Brent and young women like her, is no blessing: "If God has bestowed beauty upon her, it will prove her greatest curse."[24]

Incidents in the Life of a Slave Girl is of great interest in this discussion because Jacobs confronts the sexual component of servitude so straightforwardly. She recognizes, too, that slaves and owners interpreted the situation very differently. Jacobs dedicates an entire chapter of *Incidents* to "The Jealous Mistress." Here and elsewhere, Jacobs maintains that mistresses whose husbands betrayed them felt no solidarity whatever with their slaves. Like other exslave narrators, Jacobs could ascertain the view of slaveowning women but emphatically did not share their conclusions. Writing as Linda Brent, Jacobs supplies a key word: "victim," and recognizes that it is a matter of contention between slave and mistress.

White women, black women, and black men all resented deeply white men's access to black women. But the comments from the two sides of the color line are contradictory: where white women saw sexual competition—with connotations of equality— black men and women saw rank exploitation that stemmed from grossly disparate levels of power. Moses Roper, his master's child, relates the story of his near-murder, shortly after his birth, by his father's jealous wife. Frederick Douglass also noted that slaveowning women were distressed by the bodily proof of their husband's adulteries.[25]

For Jacobs as for other exslave narrators the prime victim was the slave woman, not the slaveowning woman, no matter how slaveowning women perceived the situation. So far as slaves were concerned, slaveowners' sexual relations with their women slaves constituted one of several varieties of victimization of slaves by men whose power over their slaves was absolute. Slaves of both sexes were oppressed by class and by race, and women slaves suffered a third, additional form of oppression stemming from their gender. Slaves were victims several times over, and extorted sex was part of a larger pattern of oppression embedded in the institution of slavery.

H arriet Jacobs and Gertrude Thomas provide examples of the family dynamics of cross-class adultery. Located in very different places within the complicated families of slavery, each explicates the deleterious effects of adultery within their households. Like Jacobs and Thomas, Sigmund Freud, in his analysis of "Dora," recognized the damage that the father's adultery did to the daughter.

"DORA"

In the "Dora" case, Herr K, had made sexual advances toward "Dora," Ida Bauer, who had overheard Herr K's propositioning a servant woman in exactly the same phrases that he used with Bauer. Entangled emotionally with several women, Bauer identified (at the least) with Frau K, who was her father's mistress, and with the servant. She also felt as though she were being made a pawn in an adulterous game between her father and the Ks. When Ida Bauer's father took her to Freud in October 1900, after she had tried to commit suicide, Freud was already anxious to try out his ideas.[26]

Freud had been thinking about hysteria for several years and had worked out his notions in letters to his close friend and regular correspondent, Wilhelm Fliess. These comments are exceedingly helpful to me, particularly in observations that Freud enclosed with a letter dated 2 May 1897. Here Freud notes that children, even very young babies, hear things that later become the raw material for fantasies and neuroses. Accompanying this letter was "Draft L," which includes a paragraph on "The Part Played by Servant Girls."

In Draft L, Freud echoes his society's assumption that the poor young women who worked in bourgeois households were "people of low morals" because they were likely to become sexually involved with the men and boys of the household. Here Freud was echoing the commonest of common knowledge about black people in the South. But whereas Freud identified morals with class, white southerners saw low morals as a racial characteristic of African Americans. For my purposes, however, this comment about morals is not the crucial point of Freud's failed analysis of Ida Bauer. For me Freud's most useful observation relates to the critical importance of servants in the psychological and hence social dynamics of the families in which they work. Although Freud thought mainly of the ramifications of the situation on the family of the employers, servants, too, as we saw with Linda Brent, felt the effects of adulterous—should I add incestuous?—family dynamics.

Freud wrote to Fliess that in households in which servant women are sexually intimate with their employers, the children— and here I believe he means the female children—develop an array of hysterical fantasies: fear of being on the street alone, fear of becoming a prostitute, fear of a man hidden under the bed. In sum, says Freud, "There is tragic justice in the circumstance that the family's head's stooping to a maidservant is atoned for by his daughter's self-abasement."[27]

Freud underscores the degree to which women in a household are emotionally intertwined, for he observed that "Dora" identified with the servant whom her would-be lover had tried to seduce. Observing situations in which race was not a factor, Freud understood that the very structure containing class and gender power dynamics is virtually Foucauldian in its leakiness. No class of women remained exempt from a degradation that aimed at the least of them. Just as Gertrude Thomas saw that her adulterous father and husband treated rich and poor and black and white women as interchangeable sexually, Freud saw there was a "part played by servant girls" and an object connection between "Dora" and her father's mistress. A recent Freud scholar, Hannah Decker, put her finger on the phenomenon that poisoned young women's lives in Freud's Vienna and that also characterized the nineteenth-century South: the careless sexual abuse of *das süsse Mädel*—the sweet young thing.[28]

Freud's letters to Fliess, "On the Universal Tendency to Debasement in the Sphere of Love," and especially the "Dora" case analysis, show that "Dora's" predicament is reflected in both *Lily* and *Incidents in the Life of a Slave Girl*, but in somewhat different ways. Linda Brent is more directly comparable with "Dora," for she is the object of unwanted sexual advances, as was young Ida Bauer. The case of Lily Vere is less obvious, for she is the daughter of "Draft L," of "The Part Played by Servant Girls." Lily is the daughter whose affective value is lowered by the existence of the sexually vulnerable servant class and the allure of enticing dark/ Negro women like Angelica and Lorenza. While Linda Brent is a clear victim of her society's hierarchies of race and gender, Lily, unloved by her fiancé and murdered by his servant lover, is victimized as well. Her fiancé, Clarence, is the very figure of the Freud patient suffering from psychically-induced impotence.[29]

CONCLUSION

Listening to these southern women's stories and taking Freud to heart leads to two conclusions: First, that historians of the United States South have sheltered too long in southern exceptionalism and let an intellectual color bar obstruct their grasp of the complexity of gender roles within households that were economically heterogeneous. Lily and Linda Brent, two examples of a spoilation of young women that is no respecter of race or class—underscore both the sexual vulnerabilities and the psychological interrelatedness of southern daughters. Second, Freud points the way toward an understanding that families and societies cannot designate and thereby set apart one category of women as victims. The victimization spreads, in different ways and to different degrees. But where historians have been prone to construe southern family relations within watertight racial categories, the stories of Gertrude Thomas, Lily, and Linda Brent pose complicated new questions whose answers do not stop at the color line.

Historians have wanted to reach a single conclusion that would characterize the relationship between slaveowning and slave women in the antebellum South: *Either* slave women were at the bottom of a hierarchical society, as the exslave narrators testify, *or* all southern women were, finally, at the mercy of rich white men. The relationship between black and white women through white men deserves to be named, for slavery often made women of different races and classes into co-mothers and co-wives as well as owners and suppliers of labor. The question is whether there should be one name or, corresponding to the number of races involved, more than one.

So far no historian of southern women has given more than a chapter or its equivalent to interracial sexuality and the gender relations that flowed from it, but the work is coming along. The older, full-length studies of race and gender in the antebellum South by Deborah Gray White, Catherine Clinton, and Elizabeth Fox-Genovese and the newer work that builds upon them all tend toward use of one concept to characterize relations within extended southern households: oppression. Deborah Gray White, in *Ar'n't I a Woman*, stresses the "helplessness" and "powerlessness" of slave women vis-à-vis slaveowners and in American society in general. Conceding that white women and black men may have envied black women, White nonetheless views black women at the bottom of a malevolent system that disempowered all women, even those who were rich and white. She places slave women at the negative end of a continuum of power, on which white women also occupied positions of relative powerlessness and exploitation.[30]

Viewing matters from the other side of the class/race divide, Catherine Clinton, in *The Plantation Mistress*, also acknowledges a "parallel oppression of women, both white and black." But where Deborah White cites instances of aggression on the part of white women against black, Clinton stresses plantation mistresses' roles as nurturers, mediators, and nurses. Clinton speaks of a patriarchy, in which rich white men possessed slaves of both sexes as they possessed their own wives. In *The Plantation Mistress*, slaveowning women do not appear in hierarchical relationships with slave women. Rather than portray slaveowning women as rulers of their workers, Clinton sees white male masters as the font of all power and all evil.[31]

In *Within the Plantation Household*, Elizabeth Fox-Genovese departs from the view of black and white women's parallel exploitation that White and Clinton evoke. Stressing the spacial and emotional intimacy in which many slave and slaveholding women lived in plantation households, Fox-Genovese softens the domination of the master. She prefers the term "paternalism" to Clinton's "patriarchy," because paternalism carries an air of "legitimate domination," which was how slaveholding men viewed their role. (Let us not quibble about whether slaveowners should be allowed to chose the words we historians use to characterize them a century and a half later.)

Fox-Genovese stiffens the authority of slaveowning women over their female slaves, providing theoretical and empirical arguments for a somewhat ambiguous but clearly hierarchical relationship between women of different races and classes. Rather than see masters as the proximate wielders of power, Fox-Genovese shows that slaveholding women and slave women were cognizant of who held the power between them and who could inflict the greatest violence with impunity. To make her point, Fox-Genovese enumerates instances of violence and minimizes slaveholding women's abolitionist leanings. For her, slaveholding women who saw themselves as victims of the kind of adultery that the slave system allowed were simply mistaken.[32]

Clinton's more recent essays reveal the pathologies of planter families in which rape and adultery distorted descent and parental attachment. While "Caught in the Web of the Big House" glimpses the ways in which owner-slave rape affected mistresses, the emphasis still falls mainly on the tragedy of the direct victim of assault: the slave woman. "Southern Dishonor," Clinton's spiked critique of both southern historiography and slavery's brutal system of reproduction, announces themes and works-in-progress in the study of sexuality and slavery. Martha Hodes's 1991 Princeton dissertation and Mary Frances Berry's 1991 presidential address to the Organization of American Historians further enrich the historical literature by revealing the complexities of southern sexuality.[33]

So far, this work, though intriguing, stops short of completing the investigation of the relationship between southern families, society, and history. If feminist history has taught us anything in the last two decades, it is that important private matters become important historical matters. The example of the South Carolina fire-eater, James Henry Hammond—whose emotional turmoil following his wife's deserting him when he took a second slave wife so incapacitated him psychologically that he missed an important secessionist meeting that would have bolstered his sagging political career—makes the point. Hammond's wife serves as a reminder that Gertrude Thomas's preoccupation—competition—needs to reenter the equation, or historians risk missing much of the psychodrama of southern history. Focusing on one part of the picture, even if more compatible with present-day understandings of relations of power, flattens out the inherent complexity of southern history. If historians do not acknowledge that wealthy white women saw themselves as victims, as the losers in a competition with women who though black and poor and powerless seemed somehow more attractive, we miss a vital dimension of southern history that helps explain the thorniness of women's contacts across the color line well into the twentieth century. We must acknowledge the existence of two ways of seeing, even while we keep our eyes on fundamental differentials of power.

What my approach means for southern history is a renunciation of a single "The South" way of thinking. For me there is seldom a "The South," for simple characterizations eliminate the reality of sharp conflicts over just about everything in southern culture, slavery most of all. Saying that "The South" was proslavery (or, later, prosegregation) equates the region with its rulers and annihilates the position of at least one-third of its inhabitants. As a labor historian with a keen sense of the historical importance of all groups of people within a society (not simply the prestigious, published, and politically powerful) I insist on going beyond neglectful characterizations in the singular. Recognizing the complex and self-contradictory nature of southern society, I can rephrase my conclusions about the study of southern history succinctly: Southern history demands the recognition of complexity and contradiction, starting with family life, and therefore requires the use of plurals; and though southern history must take race very seriously, southern history must not stop with race.

Notes

1.   I am coming to Freud's writing from a direction that is different from that of the literary critics and most Lacanians. Although Freud's work is the starting place for object relations theory, it, too, would be more useful to me than certain Lacanians (notably Jane Gallop, whose insights are valuable here) if object relations analysts were not so relentlessly mid-twentieth-century-middle class. The family structure that objects relations scholars—such as Nancy Chodorow—envision is strictly nuclear, whereas many nineteenth-century southern families included parental figures who were not related to children by birth.

2.   Abram Kardiner and Lionel Ovesey, *The Mark of Oppression: Explorations in the Personality of the American Negro* (New York, 1951).

3.   I should add that family relations also affect more than women and girls; men and boys deserve—and will ultimately receive—a far larger place in this piece of work in progress than they currently occupy.

4.   E.g., Leonore Davidoff, "Class and Gender in Victorian England: The Diaries of Arthur J. Munby and Hannah Cullwick," *Feminist Studies* 5 (Spring 1979) and Maria Ramas, "Freud's Dora, Dora's Hysteria," in *Sex and Class in Women's History*, ed. Judith L. Newton, Mary P. Ryan, and Judith R. Walkowitz (London, 1983).

5.   Sue Petigru King Bowen, *Lily* (New York, 1855) and Jean Fagan Yellin, *Incidents in the Life of a Slave Girl, Written by Herself, by Harriet A. Jacobs* (Cambridge, Mass., 1987). Although I am aware the controversy surrounding the designation of genre of *Incidents*, I am treating it here as autobiography.

6.   Orlando Patterson, *Slavery and Social Death: A Comparative Study* (Cambridge, Mass., 1982), 50, 229, 230, 261.

7.   Hortense Spillers makes some tantalizing observations in this regard in

"Mama's Baby, Papa's Maybe: An American Grammar Book," *Diacritics* 17 (Summer 1987).

8. Virginia Burr, ed., *The Secret Eye: The Journal of Ella Gertrude Clanton Thomas, 1848–1889* (Chapel Hill, 1990).

9. Paul Ekman, "Self-Deception and Detection of Misinformation," in *Self-Deception: An Adaptive Mechanism?*, ed. Joan S. Lockard and Delroy L. Paulhus, (Englewood Cliffs, 1988), 231–232. Building on Sigmund Freud's observations that individuals provide nonverbal clues that undermine what they are saying, psychologists have usually looked for deception clues and leakage in the realm of nonverbal communication, which, of course, is not available in the present case. Thomas, however, provides verbal clues and verbal leakage that undermine conventions that she expresses in her writing.

10. Erving Goffman, *The Presentation of Self in Everyday Life* (Garden City, 1959), 81; and Adrienne Rich, *On Lies, Secrets, and Silence: Selected Prose 1966–1978* (New York, 1979), 188.

11. After writing the entry for 4 November 1852, in which she explained Jefferson's illness that postponed their wedding and quoted the first line of the poem twice in three sentences and added that "there are some emotions too powerful for words . . ." Thomas did not write again until 8 April 1855.

12. In the 12 May 1856 entry she includes the following cryptic comment on men's morality: "were that faith [in her husband] dissipated by *actual experience* then would be dissolved a dream in which is constituted my hope of happiness upon earth. Of course between a husband and wife, this is (or should be) a forbidden subject but to *you* my journal I would willingly disclose many thoughts did I not think that the prying eye of curiosity might scan these lines."

13. Thomas writes of her father's "estate," which would indicate a larger place than the Clanton household. Virginia Burr, Thomas's great-granddaughter and the editor of the Thomas journal, says: "Thomas, in referring to 'so many' mulatto children 'growing up on Pa's estate, as well as others,' includes Turner Clanton's entire estate of five plantations and the Clanton household. In that context, it is highly probable that resident overseers contributed to the mulatto population. Turner Clanton was, without doubt, guilty of miscegenation to some degree." [Virginia Burr to Nell Irvin Painter, 2 April 1989] I believe, however, that Thomas would not have been so disturbed had she had not suspected her father. Hence I understand "Pa's estate" here to mean the Clanton household.

14. E.g., Harriet Beecher Stowe, *A Key to Uncle Tom's Cabin; Presenting the Original Facts and Documents upon Which the Story Was Founded. Together With Corroborative Statement Verifying the Truth of the Work* (Leipzig, 1853), 63, 142–143, and L. Maria Child, *An Appeal in Favor of Americans Called Africans* (New York, 1836, republished, 1968), 23–24. Historian Ronald G. Walters quotes abolitionists who wrote of the antebellum South as "ONE GREAT SODOM" and of the male slaveowner as one who "totally annihilates the marriage institution." Ronald G. Walters, "The Erotic South: Civilization and Sexuality in American Abolitionism," *American Quarterly* 25, no. 2 (May 1973): 183, 192.

15. Harriet Martineau, *Society in America*, vol. 2 (New York, 1837), 112, 118; Fredrika Bremer, *Homes of the New World; Impressions of America*, vol. 1 (London, 1853), 382; C. Vann Woodward and Elisabeth Muhlenfeld, *The Private Mary Chesnut: The Unpublished Civil War Diaries* (New York, 1984), 42 (18 March 1861).

See also Deborah Gray White, *Ar'n't I a Woman?: Female Slaves in the Plantation South* (New York, 1985), 27–47; Catherine Clinton, *The Plantation*

Mistress: Woman's World in the Old South (New York, 1982), 203–204, 210–222; James
Hugo Johnston, *Race Relations in Virginia and Miscegenation in the South 1776–1860*
(Amherst, 1970), 165–190, 243; Kenneth M. Stampp, *The Peculiar Institution: Slavery
in the Ante-Bellum South* (New York, 1956), 350–361; Eugene D. Genovese, *Roll,
Jordan, Roll: The World the Slaves Made* (New York, 1974), 413–429; and Bertram
Wyatt-Brown, *Southern Honor: Ethics and Behavior in the Old South* (New York,
1982), 307–324; Marli Frances Weiner, "Plantation Mistresses and Female Slaves:
Gender, Race, and South Carolina Women," (Ph.D. diss., University of Rochester,
1986), 131–139, 177–190; bell hooks, *Ain't I a Woman: Black Women and Feminism*
(Boston, 1981), 26–41; Angela Y. Davis, *Women Race and Class* (New York, 1981),
25–29, 173–177; Elizabeth Fox-Genovese, *Within the Plantation Household: Black and
White Women of the Old South* (Chapel Hill, 1988), 325–326.

16.   In December 1870 Thomas draws a parallel between herself, Hester
Prynne of *The Scarlet Letter*, and African-American women who bear mixed-race
children, and in November 1880 she writes of her cross to bear.

17.   Clinton, *The Plantation Mistress*, 213–221.

18.   See Ann Taves, "Spiritual Purity and Sexual Shame: Religious Themes
in the Writings of Harriet Jacobs," *Church History* 56 (1987): 65–66.

19.   Herbert Fingarette, in his classic *Self-Deception* (London, 1969), explains
the tactic of not spelling out or hiding uncomfortable truths (especially 43–50).
Fingarette's not spelling-out is analogous to Jean Paul Sartre's *mauvaise foi*, which is
translated as "bad faith," in the context of self-deception. Jean-Paul Sartre, *Being
and Nothingness: An Essay on Phenomenological Ontology*, trans. Hazel E. Barnes,
(New York, 1967), 47–56. The terms "toxic," "toxicity," and "spoiled" are Annette
Lawson's, in *Adultery: An Analysis of Love and Betrayal* (New York, 1988), 12, 30–31,
53. See also Sissela Bok, *Secrets* (New York, 1982), 25, 59–72. A recent southern
autobiography, Sallie Bingham, *Passion and Prejudice: A Family Memoir* (New York,
1989), exemplifies the pernicious effects of not telling the truth within a family.

20.   Carol Bleser, ed., *Secret and Sacred: The Diaries of James Henry Hammond,
a Southern Slaveholder* (New York, 1988), 170, 134–244, 254–269.

21.   See Lawson, *Adultery*, 10, 35, 56–59, 221, 260; and Philip E. Lampe, ed.,
Adultery in the United States: Close Encounters of the Sixth (or Seventh) Kind (Buffalo,
1987), 3–9, 13. Sue M. Hall and Philip A. Hall, "Law and Adultery," in *Adultery in
the United States*, point out that adultery is often cited as a reason for denying child
custody. An adulterer appears to be unfit to care for children and unable to serve the
child's best interests (73–75). Thomas discusses parents who own or sell their own
children on 2 January 1859. Lillian Smith, *Killers of the Dream*, revised ed. (New
York, 1961), 83–89, 121–124.

22.   King (Bowen), *Lily*, 206, 227–228. W. J. Cash also utilizes Spanishness to
hint at the blackness within white southerners. See W. J. Cash, *The Mind of the South*
(New York, 1941), 25.

23.   King (Bowen) *Lily*, 278. *Sigmund Freud: Collected Papers*, trans. Joan
Riviere (New York, 1959), 4, 207. According to Freud, well-brought-up women
who have been taught that sex is distasteful and who reject their sexuality tend to
be inexperienced, inhibited, and frigid in marriage. This means that their husbands, who also regard the sex act as polluting, relate to their wives more as judges
than as joyous physical partners. Hence only love objects who seem to these men
to be debased—prostitutes, women of the lower class—can inspire in them full
sensual feelings and a high degree of pleasure. This explains why these men keep
lower-class mistresses (207, 210–211).

24. Harriet A. Jacobs, *Incidents in the Life of a Slave Girl Written by Herself*, ed. Jean Fagan Yellin (Cambridge, 1987), 27–28, 33.

25. Moses Roper, *A Narrative of the Adventures and Escape of Moses Roper from American Slavery*, 5th ed. (London, 1843), 9–10, quoted in Frances Smith Foster, *Witnessing Slavery: The Development of Antebellum Slave Narratives* (Westport, Conn., 1979), 78; and Frederick Douglass, *Narrative of the Life of Frederick Douglass an American Slave* (Boston, 1845), 4, quoted in Foster, *Witnessing Slavery*, 79.

26. See Jane Gallop, "Keys to Dora," in *The Daughter's Seduction: Feminism and Psychoanalysis* (Ithaca, N.Y., 1982), 137, 141–145, 147; Elisabeth Young-Bruehl, ed., *Freud on Women: A Reader* (New York, 1990); Jim Swan, "*Mater and Nannie: Freud's Two Mothers*," *America Imago* 31, no. 1 (Spring 1974); Hannah S. Decker, *Freud, Dora, and Vienna 1900* (New York, 1991); Maria Ramas, "Freud's Dora, Dora's Hysteria," in *Sex and Class in Women's History*, eds. Judith L. Newton, Mary P. Ryan, and Judith R. Walkowitz (London, 1983); and Mary Poovey, "The Anathematized Race: The Governess and *Jane Eyre*," in *Uneven Developments: The Ideological Work of Gender in Mid-Victorian England* (Chicago, 1988).

27. Jeffrey Moussaieff Masson, *The Complete Letters of Sigmund Freud to Wilhelm Fliess, 1887–1904* (Cambridge, Mass., 1985), 241.

28. Decker, *Freud, Dora, and Vienna 1900*, 109.

29. See also Freud's "'Civilized' Sexual Morality and Modern Nervous Illness" (1908) and *Civilization and Its Discontents* (1930), in which he surveyed the what he saw as the psychosexual dysfunctions associated with civilization. In "'Civilized' Sexual Morality" Freud makes some observations that might be useful in southern history: "In her [the girl's] mental feelings [as she marries] she is still attached to her parents, whose authority has brought about the suppression of her sexuality; and in her physical behaviour she shows herself frigid, which deprives the man of any high degree of sexual enjoyment. I do not know whether the anaesthetic type of woman exists apart from civilized education, though I consider it probable. But in any case, such education actually breeds it . . . In this way, the preparation for marriage frustrates the aims of marriage itself." In Young-Bruehl, ed., *Freud on Women*, 176.

30. Deborah Gray White, *Ar'n't I a Woman*, 15–17, 27–28, 58.

31. Catherine Clinton, *Plantation Mistress*, 6–15, 35, 222.

32. Elizabeth Fox-Genovese, *Within the Plantation Household*, 29–30, 34–35, 43–45, 63–64, 313–315.

33. "Caught in the Web of the Big House: Women and Slavery," in *The Web of Southern Social Relations: Women, Family, and Education*, ed. Walter J. Fraser, Jr., R. Frank Saunders, Jr., and Jon L. Wakelyn, (Athens, Ga., 1985), 19–34; "'Southern Dishonor': Flesh, Blood, Race, and Bondage," in *In Joy and in Sorrow: Women, Family, and Marriage in the Victorian South, 1830–1900*, ed., Carol Bleser (New York, 1991), 52–68; Mary Frances Berry, "Judging Morality: Sexual Behavior and Legal Consequences in the Late Nineteenth-Century South," *Journal of American History* 78 (December 1991): 835–56; Martha Hodes, "Sex Across the Color Line" (Ph.D. diss., Princeton University, 1991); Eugene Genovese, "'Our Family, White and Black': Family and Household in the Southern Slaveholders' World View," in Bleser, ed., *In Joy and in Sorrow*, 69–87, grasps the reality of slaveholders' ideology of the family almost as though to substitute it for reality and without following its significance in family relations.

Moments of Danger
Race, Gender, and Memories of Empire

VRON WARE

> *To articulate the past historically does not mean to recognise the "way it really was."* . . . *It means to seize hold of a memory as it flashes up at a moment of danger.*
> Walter Benjamin, *Illuminations,* 1977

I have taken this brief extract from Benjamin and borrowed its vivid imagery as a means to introduce my own argument about race and gender in historical memory. I was immediately drawn to it because the act of seizing hold of a memory conveyed something of the urgency that I had felt in writing my book *Beyond the Pale.*[1] I was intrigued too by the phrase "moment of danger" and the possibilities of hijacking it to explore my preoccupations with the contemporary politics of race and gender, an area fraught with tensions of one kind or another.

This essay arises out of a concern to understand how categories of racial, ethnic, and cultural difference, particularly between women, have been constructed in the past, in order to explore how these categories continue to be reproduced in more recent political and ideological conflicts. Such a project necessarily involves a consideration of the ways that feminist historiography has so far dealt with questions of difference. To put it another way, has "women's history" provided feminism with sufficient theoretical or historical evidence to make sense of ideas about racial and cultural difference today? My response to this question would be that until very recently feminist theory relating to the writing of history has tended to emphasize questions of gender and their

---

Walter Benjamin, "Theses on the Philosophy of History," in *Illuminations* (London, 1977), 257. I would like to thank Paul Gilroy for pointing me towards Benjamin and for helpful discussions held in the course of writing this essay.

articulation with class with the result that issues of "race" have been overlooked. In 1988, for example, Joan Scott wrote that:

> The realization of the radical potential of women's history comes in the writing of histories that focus on women's experiences *and* analyze the ways in which gender constructs politics and politics construct gender. Feminist history then becomes not the recounting of great deeds performed by women but the exposure of the often silent and hidden operations of gender that are nonetheless present and defining forces in the organization of most societies. With this approach women's history critically confronts the politics of existing histories and inevitably begins the rewriting of history.[2]

This is not to say that Scott herself has overlooked questions of "race," either in her critique of the politics of existing histories or in her outline of the "radical potential" of women's history. It is rather that her descriptive phrase "often silent and hidden operations" could be applied just as well to other kinds of social relations in addition to gender, and the claim would have been all the more powerful if she had been able to be more explicit about "race" and ethnicity as other kinds of "defining forces" in women's lives.

Although I am writing specifically about British history and taking into account the relatively recent impact of colonialism and decolonization, the general argument I am making is intended as a contribution to debates in feminism also taking place in the United States. British and North American women have been communicating, exchanging ideas, and organizing transnationally for over 150 years. In the United Kingdom both black and white feminists have looked to the United States for enlightenment about how to understand and talk about the relationships between race and gender that were intrinsic to the foundation of the women's movements there. A growing number of books on these problems by African-American feminists like bell hooks, Angela Davis, and June Jordan and white feminists like Adrienne Rich have been lifelines for many of us. But this body of work does not often address the specific relationships between black and white women in Britain, where we are struggling to understand the effects of postimperial experience and to create a politics in these conditions. Nor does it address the particular awkwardness, silences, discomfort, and anger that have made themselves felt in political interaction between black and white feminists in Britain as a result of our postcolonial predicament.

WHITENESS

Before going on to discuss the "radical potential" of a women's history which addresses race as well as gender and class, it is important to recognize that racial domination is a system that positions or constructs everyone, albeit in different ways. Focusing on ideas about whiteness and the various constructions of white racial identity can offer new avenues of thought and action to those working to understand and dismantle systems of racial domination.[3] However, in a society habituated to dominant ideologies of white supremacy it is often easier for people who fall in the category "white" to see themselves as merely "normal" and therefore without a racialized identity.

I encounter a small illustration of this process not many yards from my front door. There is a thriving women's gym in my neighborhood that has as its logo a sketchily drawn female body, fit, healthy, and strong. Although the gym is located in an ethnically mixed neighborhood, for some strange reason the figure is tinted an unmistakably pale pink, the kind of color that is labeled "flesh" in children's paint boxes. Whenever I see it I marvel at what is communicated by this sign which implies that athletic femininity is linked to having pale skin. I have no doubt that the management of the gym would be outraged if anyone were to suggest that they were trying to deter "brown-skinned" members. I don't want to speculate on the unconscious thought processes behind this particular example, but it can serve to highlight a way of ignoring the symbols of "race" which can cause bitterness and resentment. The pallor of the image doesn't say anything explicitly derogatory about black women, but it still manages to reinforce the assumption that to be white in this society is to be normal, implying that anything else is abnormal, strange, or just invisible.

Answering the problem posed by the image means moving away from a position that identifies "race" as a matter of exclusive concern to black people, and something that rarely impinges on the lives of whites. This is not to advocate that people begin to think of their whiteness as a positive or even neutral attribute, nor to fall into the trap of reifying whiteness and, thereby, missing the processes involved in maintaining and renewing it as a subject position. In talking about the social construction of whiteness it is also important to acknowledge that it certainly has not been invisible to those identified as black. As bell hooks writes: "black folks have, from slavery on, shared in conversation with one another 'special' knowledge of whiteness gleaned from close scrutiny of white people. Deemed special because it was not a way of knowing that has been recorded fully in written material, its purpose was to help black folks cope and survive in a white supremacist society."[4]

It has also occurred to me that the sign at the gym could be read as a small metaphor for the way that contemporary feminism has routinely dealt with differences between and among women. Feminism is supposed to appeal to women everywhere, inspiring us into collective action to improve our lives and to change society. Instead, too many women have been excluded or left by the wayside feeling unwelcome, invisible, and unaccounted for by the representation of a sisterhood that was apparently "white." Of course, "race" was not the only issue to divide women during the last decade, but it has certainly presented feminists with one of the most complex puzzles. As Elizabeth V. Spelman explains in her book *Inessential Woman:*

> Because women live in a world in which there is not only sexism but racism, classism, and other forms of oppression, some of the differences among women carry with them differences in privilege and power. Such differences may become problematic for the privileged women as the occasion for fear, shame and guilt. In such circumstances the 'problem of difference' is really the problem of privilege.[5]

Spelman goes on to describe how some feminists have tried to theorize questions of difference in ways that compound the problems of privilege and exclusion. She suggests that the language used in such discussions often "reveal[s] the privileges meant to be called into question. What am I really saying when I say something like 'Feminist theory must take differences between women into consideration,' or 'Feminist theory must include more of the experiences of women of different races and classes'?" Her critique of the language often used to discuss these questions—terms such as "include" or "take into consideration"—shows how many feminists are interested in notions of difference from choice rather than necessity. It is too easy for women occupying privileged positions in race and class hierarchies to assume that it is for them to invite other women to join them in feminist politics, and that parity can be achieved merely by acknowledging that they are somehow "different." In my view, an examination of the construction of whiteness, and in particular white femininity, can shift these debates away from an obsession with difference toward the less fashionable concept of relational connectedness. For ideas about what constitutes white femininity are constructed in relation to those about black femininity, and vice versa. The different elements in this system of race and gender identity have no intrinsic meaning. They work only in and through differentiation. Furthermore, the task of uncovering and making connections between these different constructions may lead to a more useful understanding of the social relations of both race and gender.

In order to figure out how ideas about black and white femininity are expressed today, it helps to consider how these categories have been produced historically. This means adopting a perspective on history that takes into account not just gender and class but ideologies of racial difference as well. In many ways, this is precisely what black women and other women of color have been doing in the process of developing a feminist politics that reflects their priorities. The last ten years has seen a growing body of work on historical constructions of black womanhood, some of which inevitably discusses the relationship between ideologies of deviant and normative, black and white, femininity. For instance, in her book on African-American women novelists, *Reconstructing Womanhood*, Hazel Carby writes that

> [i]t is also necessary to situate narratives by black women within the dominant discourse of white female sexuality in order to be able to comprehend and analyze the ways in which black women, as writers, addressed, used, transformed, and, on occasion, subverted the dominant ideological codes.[6]

In an essay on the representation of black female sexuality in the "cultural marketplace," bell hooks emphasizes the effect of nineteenth-century racism in shaping contemporary perceptions of black women in the United States. In the context of British history, black feminists have also dealt with the deconstruction of imagery of black women through an understanding of race, class, and gender relations, recognizing that in a racist society it would be totally inadequate to discuss images of nonwhite women and men without considering ideas about race. Pratibha Parmar, for example, has argued that the representation of Asian women in Britain cannot be divorced from the social and political relations that sustain racism:

> Specific images of Asian women are mobilized for particular arguments. Commonsense ideas about Asian female sexuality and femininity are based within, and determined by, a racist patriarchal ideology. If women are defined differently according to their race, the ideology of femininity is constructed as a contradiction for all women: they are both mothers who service husbands and children, and also desirable sexual objects for men.[7]

What Parmar terms "commonsense ideas" encapsulates a whole discourse on Asian femininity produced over several hundred years of European contact with the Asian subcontinent. Her use of this phrase reinforces the way that assumptions and prejudices about cultural difference can be so deeply rooted in a dominant culture that they appear to be self-evident or even "natural."

The recognition that the lives of women of color are inescapably prescribed by definitions of race as well as gender can also be applied to women who fall in the category "white." In other words, any feminist historian wanting to adopt a perspective on race and gender ought to use the example of black feminist criticism as a model. Leaving aside for a moment the theoretical difficulties of identifying the combined effects of racism and female subordination on the lives of nonblack women, there is also the problem of finding the historical evidence with which to begin constructing a history of ideas about white womanhood, in Britain at least. This is largely because women's history and feminist history has been silent on race, even in the context of the British Empire,[8] while histories of racism and of black settlers in Britain have too often failed to address questions of gender. Although black people have figured in the lives of white British women from the early days of the antislavery movement through the colonial period to the present, the extent of British feminist interest in that encounter has generally been limited to tales of English women as intrepid travelers, pioneers, missionaries, memsahibs—that is, women as interesting individuals, pioneers of sexual equality, and symbols of protofeminist autonomy. Their sometimes eccentric femininity and adventurous sexual politics are effectively highlighted against a vaguely defined exotic background. Meanwhile, where racism is discussed in British historiography the focus has been the particularity of black lives and the development of pseudoscientific thought about racial difference. The frequent omission of gender in these histories conveys another dimension of the invisibility of black women, this time in accounts provided both by whites and by black male writers. This absence, which has been more robustly challenged in the context of the United States, also stems from a failure to comprehend that racial domination is a system that works partly in conjunction with gender as well as class.

CRITICAL INTERFACE

This new mode of feminist historiography that I am proposing is not simply a matter of bringing a history of black people or of racism alongside what is already known about women's history, or of inserting gender into existing accounts of race and class. Applying a perspective of race, class, and gender to historical enquiries should effectively transform interpretations based on either race and class or class and gender. The antislavery movement, whose history has suffered from this division of historiographical labor, coincided with a period of tumultuous social change in Britain. Studies of women's abolitionist work have so far mainly been restricted to a limited "women's contribution" style of enquiry,[9] but the evidence these studies offer can also be used with other material to speculate both on the changing dynamics of social, economic, and political relations within Britain and on the development of gendered national identities in the mid-nineteenth century. As Catherine Hall has argued:

> In the debates over slaves or freed blacks, English men and women were as much concerned with constructing their own identities as with defining those of others, and those identities were always

classed and gendered as well as ethnically specific. Furthermore, their capacity to define those others was an important aspect of their own authority and power.[10]

The language of female antislavery tracts, although frequently formulaic and rhetorical, nonetheless reflects how mainly middle-class women saw the relationship between their own "racial," sexual, and political identities, and, therefore, how they understood and constructed their Englishness, Scottishness, Welshness, or Irishness in relation to other groups of people.

I would also argue that a historical perspective that takes into account race, class, and gender is essential in analyzing the highly complex web of social relations found in colonial societies. The conventional documentary sources relating how white women passed the time in those societies do not necessarily contribute to an analysis of how those societies reproduced themselves, whereas prizing apart the social relations that connected white women to white men as well as to black women and men is likely to shed more light on the mechanics of power and domination under colonialism. This is an area that is beginning to be explored by historians of colonialism. Anne Laura Stoler refers to the poverty of a social documentary approach in her substantial essay "Carnal Knowledge and Imperial Power":

> As a critical interface of sexuality and the wider political order, the relationship between gender prescriptions and racial boundaries is a subject that remains unevenly explored. Recent work on the oral history of colonial women, for example, shows clearly that European women of different classes experienced the colonial venture differently from one another and from men, but we still know relatively little about the distinctive investments they had in a racism they shared.[11]

Stoler's essay is a prime example of the mileage to be gained by examining the "critical interface of sexuality and the wider political order" in the context of colonial societies. This extract hints at the possibility that some aspects of this interface may be too easily neglected at the expense of others. Her recognition that European women led very diverse lives under colonialism sits oddly with her assumption that they all shared a common, uniform racism, even though they might have had different kinds of investment in it. In my view, "racism" is perhaps too much of a blanket term which can obscure the contradictory positions that many found themselves in. What seems more interesting are the forms of opposition and resistance that a significant number of colonial women devised precisely to disassociate themselves from diverse forms of racial dominance. An exploration of this area could only enrich the project of trying to analyze "the relationship between gender prescriptions and racial boundaries."

Oral History

Stoler's reference to oral history is extremely relevant here because it provides an opportunity to examine the complex relationship among different kinds of memories and thus the processes by which certain histories are remembered.[12] First, the oral history of colonial life compiled from British women's experiences, for example, raises questions about the way in which women remember differently from men. In a study of "social memory," James Fentress and Chris Wickham observe that "women's life histories give less, or different, space to 'public' history than men's do, for the simple reason that women were less involved in it, or involved in ways that created different sorts of perspectives."[13] Second, it is impossible for personal memories not to be disturbed or in some way affected both by collective memories and, more significantly here, by different cultural representations of the colonial period, whether in literature, film, or television. The different processes involved in the formation of a social, historical memory of Empire reveal how the past can be both reinvented to fit the present, and the present to fit the past.

In the course of making a television documentary on the role of white women living under the Raj, entitled *Hilda at Darjeeling*, my collaborator Mandy Rose and I found that by asking a set of questions designed to uncover the complexities of race, class, and gender in British colonial society, we received a fascinating range of replies that convinced us of the contradictory nature of "racism" itself. We quickly began to see that our five interviewees, who were selected initially on the grounds of having a critical reflexive relationship to their colonial experiences, all saw themselves as being opposed to and in some cases free from racial prejudice as well as being critical of many aspects of colonial power; yet a (filmed) group discussion ran into vehement argument when one of the women stated a view that the others perceived to be "racist."

Despite the fact that one of the most repeated statements made by the interviewees in describing their very diverse lives was "that's just how it was," it is important to recognize ways in which oral history can offer interpretations of the past that are strongly influenced by hindsight. As Luisa Passerini argues in her study of Italian fascism and popular memory: "In the first place, memory resorts to tricks and leaps over time."[14] In her examination of the periods between 1919–1921 and 1943–1945 she goes on to say that

> [t]he mental leap from one great moment of social tension and collective identity to the other, is not, however, just a way of keeping quiet about the 20 years locked away between these two high points. It is already an historical interpretation in its own right, a way of redeeming something from the defeat. For the subjects who survived, what happened afterwards is inextricably bound up with what happened then.

This process of interpretation of past events is central to my discussion of historical memory and colonialism. If it is still possible to assemble an oral history of colonial societies with black and white, male and female participants, then how are historians to account for the effects of almost forty years of political and cultural expression of the aftermath of colonialism as well as the admittedly less significant impact of feminism? For instance, the implications of endorsing opinions or behaviors that are now thought to be "racist" are now entirely different; with hindsight have come powerful emotions such as guilt, regret, anger, shame, and a sense of loss, and these feelings are not confined to the former colonizers.

In piecing together fragments of evidence about how different colonial societies were sustained, oral historians also have to examine the role of cinema, television, and literature in shaping both individual and collective memories of the past. There is a particularly rich tradition, stretching back to the seventeenth century, of fictional writing about colonialism which continues today in the works of writers like Ruth Prawer Jhabvala.[15] Within this there are genres particularly popular with female readers. In our discussions with the forty subjects originally interviewed for *Hilda at Darjeeling,* we discovered that M. M. Kaye's *Far Pavilions* was a favorite novel read by most of the women. In a less escapist vein, Paul Scott's *Raj Quartet*, first published in 1971 and adapted for television in 1984, was thought to be a very fair description of life in India under the Raj in the years leading up to independence.

The televising of Scott's work under the title *Jewel in the Crown* coincided with the release of a number of lavish film productions set in the British Empire. Films like *Heat and Dust, A Passage to India, Out of Africa,* and *White Mischief* proliferated in the 1980s, and while I am not concerned here with the reasons for this, these cultural representations of colonialism play a significant role in shaping social memory, both for individuals and for the dominant culture as a whole. I find it useful here to consider the role of "imperialist nostalgia," an expression used by Renato Rosaldo to discuss "the curious phenomenon of people's longing for what they themselves have destroyed."[16] His essay on this subject was inspired by his anger at the enthusiastic reception given to films that portray white colonial societies as "decorous and orderly":

> Hints of these societies' coming collapse only appear at the margins where they create not moral indignation but an elegiac mode of perception. Even politically aware North American audiences have enjoyed the elegance of manners governing relations of dominance and subordination between the 'races.' Evidently, a mood of nostalgia makes racial domination appear innocent and pure.

The cultural expression of imperialist nostalgia reflected in high budget films and TV series inevitably has the effect of stirring the memories of those who experienced life in the old Empire. This will obviously influence the compilation of oral histories, especially if they concern either the British Raj or East Africa, the location for many of these dramas. Individuals may respond to questions about their experience of colonialism with direct comparisons, often denouncing the fictional representation as in some way false or unrealistic. Our experience in probing the sexual relations between white women and Indian men, for example, led us to conclude that the representation of interracial desire and transgressive sex frequently found in both colonial literature and film did not necessarily correspond to our interviewees' experience of everyday life. On the other hand, those who learn about the "decorous and orderly" nature of colonial societies solely through these fictionalized forms will conclude that "that's just how it was."

FRAMEWORKS

While the relationship between representation and experience involves a complex debate not particularly relevant here, this brief discussion of the complexities of historical memory returns me to the Walter Benjamin quote with which I began. What is the racial component of these "moments of danger" for women in our contemporary lives and what are the postcolonial memories that illuminate them? How is feminist history to begin to analyze the historical representations of empire produced in the present and so diffuse the danger, transforming the tension for more constructive purposes? But first, given the inadequacies of existing histories, how are feminist historians to construct a framework in which to explore the crucial "relationship between gender prescriptions and racial boundaries" in the past, to borrow Stoler's phrase once again? I have addressed these questions in some detail in *Beyond the Pale* where I examine three significant moments or periods in nineteenth-century British history. Here I intend to summarize the reasons why I was drawn to these particular narratives and to describe the recurring themes which enabled me to connect the different strands of historical material that I came across.

My first theme is the link between feminism and black struggles against racial domination. This takes as its starting point the British antislavery movement which spanned the period from the 1820s to the 1860s, a period of intense social and political radicalism and reform. The emergence of the American women's rights movement out of abolitionism prompted this investigation, although the evidence for making this link in the British context appeared far more tenuous at the outset. The fact that most British abolitionists lived hundreds of miles away from the site of slavery and had very little contact with black people gave the movement a different kind of impetus than its counterpart in North America. Added to this, the specific economic, social, and political forces within each country influenced both the composition of the antislavery movements and the image of abolitionism as a political or moral activity. However, the discovery of a handful of radical women in Britain who endeavored to make connections between their own situation as women and the lives of black slaves either in the Caribbean or in the southern states of America was sufficient basis to explore wider connections between the movements for black emancipation and women's rights. Early feminists, for example, drew heavily on the language of bondage and freedom in their arguments for sexual equality, using metaphors which had a very different and far more urgent resonance then from the more watered down and rhetorical meanings they were inevitably to acquire after the abolition of racial slavery in the Western world. This type of connection between these parallel struggles against domination can be usefully explored throughout the histories of feminism and black politics to the present day, bearing in mind, of course, that neither struggle is homogeneous and that black women's lives complicate the apparent division between the two.

The second theme is the development of feminism in a racist society—that is, a society structured by domination of race, gender, and class. This theme emerged as an important element of my discussion about the potential of feminism as a radical political movement, since the historical evidence I uncovered suggested that so many of the problems associated with "race" and feminism were direct legacies of Empire. As feminism began to develop during the second half of the nineteenth century, it seemed highly relevant to inquire into the forces that influenced it as a movement, particularly the effects of imperialism. The political activities of two Englishwomen both engaged in social reform movements in colonial India—Annette Ackroyd and Josephine Butler—provided a rich opportunity to explore how middle-class women who identified themselves as feminists in Britain made both theoretical and practical links with women living under a different system of male domination that was configured by colonial rule thousands of miles away. Ackroyd traveled to India to start a school for Indian girls at the invitation of the Brahmo Somaj, an Indian reform movement dedicated at that time to the spread of education throughout the country. Her copious notebooks and diaries provide various insights into her motives for going, her reactions to people she met, and her frustrations with the project itself. They offer a rare chance to read into the mind of someone formed by radical politics from childhood yet incorporated into imperialist ways of thinking and situating herself in the world that posed more difficult and complex questions than she could answer. Butler, on the other hand, never actually traveled to India, but expended a good deal of energy campaigning on behalf of the Indian prostitutes servicing British troops. It proved an interesting exercise to compare the lives of the two women, looking at their motives for wanting to work with or on behalf of women in the Empire, how they dealt with cultural difference, how they explained the subordination of women in relation to colonial domination, and finally their definitions of femininity itself.

English feminists writing about the position of Hindu and Muslim women in India revealed ways in which they positioned themselves in relation to nonwhite, non-Christian femininity, and also how they contributed to enduring constructions of Asian femininity as passive, mute, submissive, and wronged. In doing so they also defined aspects of their own femininity that derived from their position as English women, Christians, wives, and daughters. It was not necessary for these women to describe or even see themselves as being "white" since their complex relationship to the dominant imperial culture allowed them to feel part of a superior racial and cultural order without advocating an explicitly white supremacist position. In this context it is important to explore the different meanings of Englishness and whiteness and to consider the impact of gender on nationalist ideologies that fused the two together. This case study of Annette Ackroyd and Josephine Butler exposes the contradiction faced by many Victorian feminists: in their zeal to uplift women of other cultures and to free them from tyrannical patriarchal customs they were in fact supporting the imperial project of liberalizing and "bringing light" to heathen peoples. This contradiction has survived uneasily throughout the history of Western feminism.

The third theme on which I focused was the instrumentality of white women, either active or passive, in different forms of racism. Here a campaign against lynching provides the most stark example of white female complicity since it reveals how racial terror is spread in the name of defending the honor of white womanhood. In 1893 the writer and activist Ida B. Wells came to Britain at the invitation of Catherine Impey, editor of a journal dedicated to the eradication of racial prejudice. There followed an extraordinary episode in the history of British anti-imperialist politics as the two women set out to form a campaign against lynching in the American South, traveling up and down the country giving lectures and interviews. Wells returned the following year to give a more comprehensive tour. Her radical analysis of lynching as a form of economic and political repression in part drew its strength from her conviction that the routine killing of black men was legitimized by stories of rape and sexual assault of white women. The crux of her argument was that this legitimation was made possible by the ideological construction of the pure white woman, a development of the plantation mistress figure in days of slavery and of the bestial nature of black manhood, a more recent invention developed in response to black emancipation in the reconstruction period. Following on from this, Wells was also able to provide evidence that where there had been consensual liaisons between black men and white women before the lynchings, the friendship had often been initiated by the woman.

Close investigation of the papers relating to the British campaign reveals that serious disagreements broke out among some of the women who claimed publicly to support it, all of which hinged on the question of female sexual autonomy. Analyzing these conflicts meant probing into a range of different (and sometimes feminist) definitions of femininity current at that time. In turn this uncovered varying positions on white supremacy—implied as well as overtly stated.

The fourth theme is related to the previous one since it addresses some of the ways in which British women sought to challenge what they saw as racial prejudice or exploitation of black people by whites. This theme offers a crucial site for examining the relationship of those women to the various constructions of white femininity in operation and the effects of their rejecting or disavowing those ideals. The involvement of Catherine Impey and other white women committed to exposing the construction of an ideal white womanhood that legitimized racial terror undoubtedly helped to give the campaign its radical edge. Just as they needed Ida B. Wells to supply both the analysis and the evidence of firsthand experience, so she needed their support if she was not to be dismissed as an angry and unreasonable African-American woman who dared to speak against the sanctity of white women.

The final organizing theme was the search for connections or intersections among systems of domination, a theme to which I have alluded earlier and which can also be illustrated by the discussion of lynching. Here the construction of white woman-hood involves retaining white women in a particular state of subordination to white men; the white woman is cast as innocent victim, vulnerable in her moral purity, requiring protection from (black) men by (white) men. This pattern of racial domination provides constructions of black masculinity (and femininity) that cast black men as predators threatening the safety of white women. A similar pattern may be discerned in more recent accounts of criminality in the inner cities. It could be said that women, especially white women, are kept in a state of fear as potential victims of black male violence which affects their right to use public space. Authoritarian modes of policing ensure that black males are harassed if not forcibly removed from public space in the name of upholding law and order.[17]

Seeing that some racialized constructions of masculinity and femininity recur over and over again it becomes important to locate founding moments when they were produced and nodal points when they were given added vitality. Two major rebellions in the mid-nineteenth century precipitated intense debates con-cerning the safety of white women in the Empire. Both marked significant points in the development of imperialist ideology, and both influenced subsequent governmental policy as well as social relations in the colonies. One was the First National Uprising in India in 1857, also known as the Indian Mutiny, in which, accord-ing to popular belief, thousands of English women and children were slaughtered by ruthless Indian rebels; the other was the Morant Bay Uprising which took place in Jamaica in 1865. Catherine Hall, who has written about the latter in a discussion of the formation of ethnic and gendered identities of the English middle classes, points out that the specter of the Indian Mutiny haunted many of the commentators on the Jamaican insurrection, particularly in their evocation of the dangers posed for Englishwomen by unruly black men.[18] Both rebellions were brutally crushed by English forces, their repression partly sanctioned by a desire to avenge the honor of white women and to protect their lives.

REMAKING THE PAST

In the final part of this paper I want to recount two contemporary stories that recode and reactivate these older, deeper structures of feeling about white women and Empire. In doing so, I hope also to give some substance to the idea of "moments of danger" and to demonstrate how memories of the past can transform understandings of current events.

Both accounts revolve around gruesome forms of violence carried out against women by men from countries once colonized by the British. In both there is a distraught parent battling against official apathy and interminable bureaucracy. Given these ingredients, it is hardly surprising that the British media should have followed both events so closely, and in some cases, so salaciously. These tragedies have also received slightly longer-lasting treatment at the hands of journalists who have written books about their personal involvement in the investigations, works that may be found anywhere from feminist book catalogues to airport book stalls under the category "true crime."[19]

The first narrative concerns a young, white, English woman called Julie Ward who "fell in love" with Africa as an intrepid tourist. After traveling to East Africa with an overland safari group, she set up home with expatriates in Nairobi, eking out her money so that she could make expeditions into the country to pursue her hobby of photographing wild animals. On the eve of her return to England she disappeared. It was later discovered that she had been mysteriously killed as she drove on her own through a game reserve. Her story is about her father's attempts to prove that she had been raped and murdered by park rangers and to find the culprit in the face of apparent political apathy and intrigue in a former British colony, protective of its image as a tourists' haven. Julie Ward's death took place in 1988, but her father's pursuit of justice still continues five years later. In June 1992 he called for a fresh investigation after the acquittal by the Nairobi Supreme Court of two game rangers on murder charges.

Without wanting to diminish the tragedy endured by Julie Ward and those who knew her, it is worth looking more closely at some of the elements of the narrative that received attention from the press. Here was a white woman—by all accounts a likable and attractive person—traveling on her own in the African wilderness, a landscape described by one journalist writing about the case as a "place of primordial natural savagery."[20] The bizarre claim by the local police that wild animals had feasted on her (white) body was immediately disproved by the discovery of half of her denim-clad leg near the charred remains of a fire. However, the first pathologist's report which stated that the leg had been severed from the body with a sharp instrument was swiftly rewritten under pressure from Kenyan officials to allow the possibility of her death among wild animals to persist as long as possible. John Ward, Julie's father, who was present at the scene shortly after the first remains were found, has described his battle with Kenyan authorities in minute detail in his book *The Animals Are Innocent*. His role in confronting endless officials with evidence that he had prepared with the help of his own lawyers has allowed the media to speculate on the wiles of an independent black African country resisting interference from white Englishmen telling them how to run their business. In his racy account of the murder inquiry, Michael Hiltzik, a journalist for the *Los Angeles Times*, devoted several chapters to the history of colonial rule in Kenya which includes an attempt to portray the social relations of class and race in Nairobi. His evocation of Karen Blixen's *Out of Africa* in his own descriptions of the landscape provides further confirmation that colonialism does indeed provide a lens through which the mystery of Julie's murder is being viewed, almost thirty years after independence.

At the center of the second narrative were Zana and Nadia Muhsen, two sisters from Birmingham, England. At the ages of fifteen and fourteen they were taken on vacation to their immigrant father's homeland in North Yemen, only to be married off to boys scarcely older than themselves and held virtual prisoners in a remote mountainous area. Their father disappeared with the money he earned from this exchange, while their mother—who was not of Yemeni origin—tried in vain to get British officials to send a rescue party. In this incident, media interest was focused by *The Observer*, a liberal Sunday newspaper respected for its international coverage, which dispatched a female journalist and a male photographer to find the young women and bring out the story seven years after they had first disappeared. The reporters were instructed not to try to rescue the pair because they would be shot, but from the moment that they met them they were convinced that it was their duty to remove them from such a "backward" culture and inhospitable environment. For one thing, the sisters begged Eileen MacDonald, the journalist, to take them away, recounting grueling details of the deception that led to their forced marriages and resulting children. MacDonald evidently took on the task as a kind of personal crusade, writing a book-length report on her experiences traveling through North Yemen and her investigations into the bureaucratic diplomacy that led eventually to Zana's visit to England. Her book, entitled *Brides for Sale?*, powerfully expounds on the iniquities of patriarchy, attempting to take the girls' point of view throughout. North Yemen is seen as a country offering a bleak and unrewarding life for women, where the Western female traveler has to conform to restricting codes of dress and behavior in order not to attract the wrong sort of attention. The book ends on a bewildered note, however, as Zana is flown back to England to be reunited with her mother, but instead of expressing gratitude for her release she tries aggressively to convert her saviors to Islam, saying she didn't want to be a British woman.[21] Readers are left with the impression that something had gone terribly wrong with the mission and that it was likely that both of the young women would remain in North Yemen, from choice. The book ends bitterly by saying: "Zana's father is rejoicing. The Yemeni community have taken him to their hearts. It is them against Britain."

This narrative that I have condensed from a longer and more complex account is in some respects substantially different from the Julie Ward murder. Though they hold British citizenship, these young women are not white, and the chief villain was their own father. The worst violence and deception took place in the immigrant community in Birmingham, a colony within the workshop of the old Empire, rather than in a postcolonial society struggling to assert its independence from British domination. Unlike Julie

Ward, Zana and Nadia Muhsen lived to describe their terrifying experiences and to imagine what it would be like to escape, even though they were to develop ambivalent feelings about their former home. However, the point is not to try to connect the fate of these three young women but to consider how a feminist analysis would interpret the symbolic meanings that these narratives of culture and conflict may have in contemporary British society—a feminist analysis that is alert to the historical relationship between "gender prescriptions and racial boundaries."

WILD MEN AND ANIMALS

As I have already said, both countries implicated in these "moments of danger" were former British colonies. This provides a direct link with the imperial past and means that neither country can be free of its associations with colonialism. By looking at the images of white femininity produced in these narratives it is possible to show how social memories of this past affect the way in which they are read today. This is not a simple, straightforward process, but a question of "seizing hold" of these fragmentary images as they occur in order to understand why the narratives continue to mediate important political questions. Julie Ward, alone and vulnerable in her broken-down jeep, allegedly fell victim to the uncontrollable lust of black men, a point made by the judge at the trial of the park rangers accused of her rape and murder when he referred to the fact that one of the possible culprits who had escaped prosecution was "fond of white women."[22] The history of ideas and associations governing this particular couplet—black man and white woman—means that the encounter cannot easily be stripped of its racialized and mythologized meanings. However, Julie's vulnerability is complicated by her act of driving unaccompanied through a game reserve. This suggests an element of foolhardiness, a readiness to trust the natives if trouble should arise. Here, the image of white femininity ties into those repeatedly found in colonial fiction, typified by Adela Quested in *A Passage to India*, whose trusting curiosity of the Indian landscape and its inhabitants ended in disaster of a different kind.[23] But Kenya is the land of safari rather than strange gods, a country routinely depicted in both travel brochures and fashion photography as being curiously empty of human inhabitants and cultures, save those whose native costume elevates them to the same exotic status as the wild animals roaming the reserves. Kenya provides the ideal backdrop for constructing an image of the white woman as explorer, suggesting strength, independence, a touch of androgyny, and even eccentricity, her vulnerability underscored by her proximity to lions, rhinos, and Masai warriors. This construction stems partly from tales of colonial figures such as Isak Dinesen and Beryl Markham,[24] and is constantly revitalized by glossy articles aimed at women in magazines such as *Vogue*[25] and *Elle* as well as travel features in the pages of the so-called "quality" press. By chance there happened to be such a spread in a Sunday newspaper the very week in which I completed this essay—coinciding (a genuine coincidence, I believe) with reports of the final verdict in the murder trial. The travel feature was entitled "Wild about Kenya" and was introduced by the following sentences: "Kenya can still offer the authentic African experience. Angela Palmer samples some animal magic." The first paragraph referred directly to the country's tarnished image as a tourist haven, delicately avoiding mention of the recent spate of assaults on tourists by local bandits:

> Poor Kenya: mention its name and the cynic will tell you it's finished—overrun by tourists packed into giraffe-print minibuses, forever shoving zoom lenses into the faces of bewildered animals. Not surprisingly, this image outrages the old Kenya hands, and none more than one Primrose Stobbs, an aristocratic excolonial farmer who is now a formidable force with Abercrombie and Kent, the African travel specialists.[26]

The article continues with an account of the better class of safari travel being offered by Ms. Stobbs, full of sightings of rare birds and animals. The country itself does not merit a mention nor do its inhabitants, although there is the inevitable accompanying picture of the author astride a camel, watched over by two Masai men. The caption reads: "Ride on the wild side: the author keeps her feet well away from creepy-crawlies."

This kind of double-entendre in which indigenous peoples are constructed as a form of wildlife, sometimes exotic and protected, sometimes threatening and dangerous, is highly relevant to this reading of the Julie Ward story. While fashion and travel literature constructs the Masai as wild people whose presence merely adds to the fascination of the landscape, in the reporting of the Ward case they are depicted more ominously as living beyond the realm of civilization, untouched by the requirements of modern rationalism and hence justice. Giving his final verdict after the eighteen-week trial, the judge criticized the London detectives sent out to investigate the case, saying that they "forgot they were dealing with young Masai tribesmen from the wilderness."[27] To coincide with the end of the trial *The Times* sent out a reporter to find out "the truth." Equipped with a translator and claiming to be sympathetic to the accused, the journalist found it difficult to get a "straight answer":

> "They say they don't gossip, and that's the truth—it's considered beneath them to talk about the affairs of other people," the translator said. A wall of silence? The Masai closing ranks to protect one of their own, as if obeying a mafia code? No wonder the policemen from London found it baffling in the bush.[28]

Where the bestial Africans roam through a wild landscape, the presence of animals also serves to highlight aspects of the white woman's femininity. The cover of her father's book—pointedly called *The Animals Are Innocent* in an implicit suggestion that the people must, therefore, be guilty—bears a large photograph of Julie smiling happily with a chimpanzee in her arms. Donna Haraway has written at length about such images and the complex range of meanings suggested by this particular pairing of white woman and primate.[29] The juxtaposition of the title with this photograph—which has become the standard image used to portray Julie in the press—effectively conveys the English woman's innocent and harmless fascination with wild animals and her ability to get close to them. This acts as a sinister reminder that it was this easygoing trust which was betrayed in her encounter with the wild men from the bush.

Articles of Clothing

The versions of white femininity that I have identified in the Julie Ward narrative are constructed mainly in relation to black men, animals, and landscape. Turning now to the second narrative,

I want to show how the representation of the Muhsen sisters' ordeal involves direct comparisons between different kinds of femininity as well. In *Beyond the Pale* I have suggested that, historically, the status of women in a culture has often been read as an index of relative civilization, and that the figure of the white Christian woman contrasts favorably with the image of downtrodden, submissive, oriental, invariably Muslim, female.[30] This discourse has a profound effect on the way the story of the Muhsen sisters has been told in the British press. After all, the girls were virtually kidnapped, removed from one country where women are supposed to be liberated, and stranded in another where they were forced to live almost as slaves to men. The point is not that any criticism of Yemeni men is racist, but that a feminist analysis must be sensitive to the way in which such stories can feed existing racist ideas about Islamic cultures.

The image of white liberated femininity in this story is provided by the journalist Eileen MacDonald, whose subjective account of the rescue operation provides its own commentary on cultural and ethnic difference among women. Her story is reminiscent of Annette Ackroyd's passage to India over one-hundred years earlier in that they both set out to liberate Eastern women from their tyrannically patriarchal menfolk but in doing so found themselves recoiling from elements of a culture that they could not comprehend.[31] MacDonald's venture is symbolic of a kind of feminism; her book has been recommended on the Women's Book Club mailing list, a well-known and widely circulated feminist mail order catalogue operating in Britain.

Like many commentators on non-Christian societies, including Ackroyd, MacDonald focused on dress as a significant mark of cultural difference, clearly expressing her irritation at the limitations imposed on her own sartorial style when visiting North Yemen:

> I still found it uncomfortable being stared at by the men. I was hardly wearing a revealing bikini, after all. Because of the Foreign Office instruction to bring warm clothes, I had two pairs of thick cord trousers, and a pair of cotton trousers. I was wearing these, with boots of all things, in temperatures approaching 90 degrees Fahrenheit. I also wore a long blouse, buttoned to the neck, and had sunglasses on. Pretty safe, I would have thought.[32]

But MacDonald only found out later on that people continued to stare at her because her shirt was tucked into her trousers. She went on to complain: "I got very fed up being touched, stared at and shouted at by men. The women, I noticed, would turn away their heads with a sort of scandalised sneer." In passages like these, the reader, assumed to be British, is invited to share the writer's impatience with a society that appears to sanction the inhuman treatment of women by men, symbolized by the obligation to wear veils and "tent-like" dresses. At various points in the book MacDonald draws attention to the clothes worn by the Muhsen sisters as a way of marking their passage from "modern" Western culture to a "backward" Islamic one. Before packing her holiday clothes in Birmingham, Zana, the older girl, was told by their father that "Yemen is open to Western ideas about dress"; when she arrived in Taiz and went to stay with some relatives she interpreted the fact that they kept talking about her in corners as being a sign of curiosity at seeing "a Western girl in her pencil skirt and blouse."[33] The morning after her first traumatic night as a married woman, "Zana's own clothes were taken away, and her mother-in-law pointed to a pile of Arab clothes and a head-dress."[34] When the British journalists first saw the sisters several years later, they saw "the girls covered from top to toe in Arab dress, their faces hidden by veils."[35] The first sight of Zana on her arrival back in England was of "a girl in white Arab clothes, including a veil."[36] Within hours of her reunion with her mother and MacDonald herself she announced "I want to go back to Taiz and get a job. I will visit England when I want to. I am not sure I want to be a British woman anyway. I don't like the short skirts; it's disgusting."[37]

The English woman's emphasis on dress as an index of women's subordination evokes countless other travel narratives that record encounters between Europeans and "the Orient." Written as a breathless account of her mission as a journalist, and, therefore, full of subjective observations which provide atmosphere and suspense, her report manages to reinforce ideas about the backwardness of Arab cultures through repeating certain stereotypes of masculinity and femininity. It is interesting to compare her reactions to those of Annette Ackroyd, whose Victorian sensibilities are greatly offended by the clothing worn by her Indian benefactor's wife: "She sat like a savage who had never heard of dignity or modesty—her back to her husband, veil pulled over her face—altogether a painful exhibition—the conduct of a petted foolish child it seemed to me, as I watched her playing with her rings and jewels."[38]

It is evident from the start that MacDonald had little time for Arab men, which again has the effect of confirming her own position as the liberated, independent, white woman. At several points she is exasperated when Yemenis make assumptions about her relationship to the male photographer, Ben Gibson, who is accompanying her: "All conversation was directed towards Ben. When I spoke he was given amazed looks as if he was expected to keep me silent. We were, everyone assumed, man and wife, in spite of having different surnames. It would be unthinkable that we should travel together unless we were married."[39]

This kind of comment, made with undisguised hostility toward Arab men, reminds me again of Annette Ackroyd's more openly judgmental observations. After attending an open-air meeting in Calcutta Ackroyd wrote:

> I do not think there were three women amongst the crowd, and certainly I was the only lady. In consequence of the infrequent appearance of a woman the people looked at me with profound amazement, and for the first time I realised how uncivilised are their notions about women. I read it in their eyes, not so much in the eyes of those who looked impertinently at me, for this is an expression not unknown to civilisation! as in the blank wonder with which most scrutinised me.[40]

MacDonald and Gibson ran into trouble when they tried to take photographs of women, despite having had it explained to them that it was considered bad for a woman to allow having her picture taken, especially by a stranger. Since their assignment included a "general piece on the sort of society the girls were living in," the intrepid journalists had to use speed and guile to snatch the visual material they considered relevant. The reader is incorporated into attempts to persuade their various escorts that they are innocent tourists, art students, or even doctors, anything but journalists. Their deceit in the name of tracking down the Muhsen sisters (not to liberate them initially, but to interview them) is justified by the representation of Yemeni men as accomplices in the subordination of all Yemeni women. The image of Arab masculinity both in the immigrant community in Birmingham and in Yemen is constructed as duplicitous, irrational, prone to violence, and extremely dominating of women. MacDonald's book also portrays Yemeni men as objects of ridicule. In one passage, for example, she recounts how a tense situation was averted by handing round a quantity of *qat*, described as: "the mild narcotic which everyone from government minister to peasant chews in Yemen, and which we had brought with us. When it was handed round, the steady chewing began, making the men look like so many Popeyes, with their bulging cheeks."[41]

References to *qat* as a factor that explains the irrational behavior of the men crop up frequently in the book. In this last extract, MacDonald describes in a tone of utter disgust a journey through the mountains with an escort:

> His driving had become less good, though he seemed full of beans. One or two sharp mountain bends had been taken at break-neck speed—presumably the effect of qat. He kept adding more leaves to his mouth, but not spitting out those he already had in there. Occasionally he would spit out of the windows. Throughout Yemen we saw dried green liquid on the ground, the result of the population's chief pastime.[42]

The irony of MacDonald's book is that it ought to have ended with the Muhsen sisters returning thankfully to a liberated lifestyle in Birmingham, rescued by an English woman from a life of submission to uncivilized men. Instead there is only the bleak speculation that the young women will be "lost" in either country, their experience of two such different cultures having ruined all prospect of happiness in both. This ending manages to throw up some of the complexity that was absent in the actual narrative, for it finally, though implicitly, recognizes that life in Britain for a working-class, Muslim woman might not be much of an improvement on life in an Islamic society.

CONFRONTING THE DANGERS

In order to be alert to these multilayered images of femininity inherited from the past, feminism needs to reconstruct histories of ideas about women with a perspective that takes in not just the shifting parameters of gender itself, but also the interrelated concepts of ethnic, cultural, and class difference. The danger that arises from overlooking the "often silent and hidden operations" of racial domination throughout women's histories poses a threat to the survival of feminism as a political movement. For it is partly through returning to the past that we are able to understand how those categories of difference between women and men, white and nonwhite, have emerged and how, why, and where they continue to retain significance today.

A feminist politics that is equipped to identify ways in which images of femininity activate contemporary political questions is also able to confront other kinds of danger. Ideas about Arab cultures, for example, that I have discussed briefly through the narrative of the Muhsen sisters, play a part in reinforcing stereotypes that affect the lives of Muslim migrants or settlers within Britain and constantly appear in public discourses on racism and cultural difference. No doubt some of those ideas about the barbarity of Arab men were also instrumental in securing support for the British and American forces during the Gulf War, when distaste for certain kinds of Arabness reached new heights. Likewise, notions of black masculinity, constructed in relation to black and white femininity, help to shape perceptions of black men as marauders, protocriminals, or rioters, whether in Britain's inner cities, South Africa, or South Central Los Angeles. If feminism is to fight for the legitimacy of its critical perspectives, then it must be able to intervene in debates about contemporary politics with a historically informed and "antiracist" perspective. In Britain, at least, the future of feminism depends on it.

NOTES

1. Vron Ware, *Beyond the Pale: White Women, Racism and History* (London and New York, 1992).

2. Joan W. Scott, *Gender and the Politics of History* (New York, 1988), 27.

3. Here I see my work being in dialogue with other recent explorations of whiteness such as David R. Roediger, *The Wages of Whiteness: Race and the Making of the American Working Class* (London and New York, 1991); Ruth Frankenberg, *White Women, Race Matters: The Social Construction of Whiteness* (Minneapolis, forthcoming); and bell hooks, *Black Looks: Race and Representation* (London, 1992), especially chapter 11, "Representations of Whiteness in the Black Imagination."

4.   hooks, *Black Looks*, 165.

5.   Elizabeth V. Spelman, *Inessential Woman: Problems of Exclusion in Feminist Thought* (London, 1988), 161–162.

6.   Hazel V. Carby, *Reconstructing Womanhood: The Emergence of the Afro-American Woman Novelist* (New York and Oxford, 1987), 20–21.

7.   Pratibha Parmar, "Hateful Contraries: Media Images of Asian Women" in "Critical Decade: Black British Photography in the 80s," *Ten.8* 2, no. 3 (1992): 54.

8.   Despite Anna Davin's classic study of imperialism and motherhood which discusses connections between racist ideologies and social policy towards English women: see Anna Davin, "Imperialism and Motherhood," *History Workshop Journal* 5 (Spring 1978): 9–65.

9.   See, for example, L. Billington and R. Billington "'A Burning Zeal for Righteousness': Women in the British Antislavery Movement, 1820–1860" in *Equal or Different: Women's Politics 1800–1914*, ed. Jane Rendall (New York and Oxford, 1987), although this essay does attempt to address the relationship between abolitionism and feminism. Clare Midgeley's recent book *Women against Slavery: The British Campaigns 1780–1870* (London, 1992) represents a substantial effort to break out of this narrow focus on women's role in the antislavery movement.

10.   Catherine Hall, *White Male and Middle Class: Explorations in Feminism and History* (Cambridge, Eng., 1992), 209.

11.   Anne Laura Stoler, "Carnal Knowledge and Imperial Power" in *Gender at the Crossroads of Knowledge: Feminist Anthropology in the Postmodern Era*, ed. Micaela di Leonardo (Berkeley and Oxford, 1991), 55.

12.   James Fentress and Chris Wickham, *Social Memory* (Oxford and Cambridge, Mass., 1992), 89–90.

13.   *Ibid.*, 140–141.

14.   Luisa Passerini, *Fascism in Popular Memory: The Cultural Experience of the Turin Working Class* (New York and Cambridge, Eng., 1988), 67–68. I am grateful to Barbara Taylor for referring me to Passerini's work.

15.   Robin W. Winks and James R. Rush, eds., *Asia in Western Fiction* (Manchester, Eng., 1990).

16.   Renato Rosaldo, *Culture and Truth: The Remaking of Social Analysis* (Boston, 1989), 68–87.

17.   In *Beyond the Pale* I have developed this argument at greater length; see 4–11. For a more detailed account of the social construction of black criminality, see Paul Gilroy, "Lesser Breeds without the Law" in *There Ain't No Black in the Union Jack: The Cultural Politics of Race and Nation* (Chicago, 1991).

18.   Hall, *White, Male and Middle Class*, 282–285.

19.   Michael A. Hiltzik, *A Death in Africa: The Murder of Julie Ward* (London, 1991). The writer was at the time the Nairobi Bureau Chief of the *Los Angeles Times*. Julie Ward's father, John Ward, also wrote a book, called *The Animals Are Innocent: The Search for Julie's Killers* (London and New York, 1991). Arising from the other story was Eileen MacDonald's *Brides for Sale? Human Trade in North Yemen* (Edinburgh, 1988). MacDonald was a journalist working for The *Observer* newspaper in London.

20.   Hiltzik, *A Death in Africa*, 4.

21.   MacDonald, *Brides for Sale?*, 207–211.

22.   The *Guardian* (Manchester) 30 June 1992.

23.   Jenny Sharpe, *Allegories of Empire* (Minneapolis, forthcoming).

24.   Isak Dinesen's autobiography was immortalized in the film *Out of Africa* starring Robert Redford and Meryl Streep; Stanley Crouch has written an essay eulogizing the aviator Beryl Markham, calling her "a mulatto by culture instead of by blood." Stanley Crouch, "African Queen," in *Notes of a Hanging Judge* (New York and Oxford, 1990), 146. Markham's eventful life is also to be the subject of a high-budget film.

25.   See, for example, the feature in *Vogue* [U.K.] (December 1991).

26.   *Observer*, 28 June 1992, 44–47.

27.   *Guardian*, 30 June 1992.

28.   The *Times Saturday Review* (27 June 1992), 6.

29.   Donna Haraway, "The Promise of Monsters," in *Cultural Studies*, ed. L. Grossberg et al. (New York and London, 1992), 307.

30.   Ware, *Beyond the Pale*, 11–17.

31.   *Ibid.*, part three, 117.

32.   MacDonald, *Brides for Sale?*, 86–87.

33.   *Ibid.*, 28–29.

34.   *Ibid.*, 32.

35.   *Ibid.*, 9.

36.   *Ibid.*, 204.

37.   *Ibid.*, 207.

38.   Ware, *Beyond the Pale*, 139.

39.   MacDonald, *Brides for Sale?*, 76.

40.   Ware, *Beyond the Pale*, 146.

41.   MacDonald, *Brides for Sale?*, 11.

42.   *Ibid.*, 88.

Gender in the Critiques of Colonialism and Nationalism
Locating the "Indian Woman"

MRINALINI SINHA

K umkum Sangari and Sudesh Vaid's excellent analysis of the
historical processes which reconstituted patriarchy in colonial
India provides both a definition and an example of the potential of
feminist historiography. They provide a definition of feminist historiography that goes much beyond an exclusively "women's history." According to Sangari and Vaid, "a feminist historiography
rethinks historiography as a whole and discards the idea of women
as something to be *framed* by a context, in order to be able to think
of gender difference as both structuring and structured by the wide
set of social relations."[1] Hence they argue, on the one hand, that
feminist historiography is neither a choice, as in the choice of an
area or field of study, nor a simple inclusion of women, nor an
evaluation of their participation in particular movements, but
rather a mode of questioning that must undergird all attempts at
historical reconstruction. On the other hand, they also suggest that
"patriarchies are not . . . systems either predating or superadded to
class and caste but are intrinsic to the very formation of, and
changes within, these categories."[2] Feminist historiography, conceived in these terms, recognizes that all aspects of reality are
gendered and that the very experience of gender changes according to race, class/caste, nation, and sexuality.

This double move is also being reflected in feminist theory in
general. This is evident, for example, in the bid to go beyond the
simple enumeration of gender, race, class/caste, nationality, and
sexuality, as parallel or co-equal axes along which oppression,
identity, and subjectivity are organized, to a recognition of the

This article draws from my earlier discussion of the *Mother India* controversy. See
"Reading *Mother India*: Empire, Nation, and the Female Voice," *Journal of Women's
History* (forthcoming).

ways in which these axes are mutually determining and necessarily implicated in one another. For, as Chandra Mohanty puts it, "no one 'becomes a woman' (in Simone de Beauvoir's sense) purely because she is female. . . . It is the intersections of the various systemic networks of class, race, (hetero)sexuality and nation . . . that position us as 'women'"[3] This, according to Teresa de Lauretis, marks the crucial shift in feminist consciousness brought about by the interventions made by women of color and lesbians. It has led, she suggests, to a redefinition of the feminist subject as "not [just] *unified* or *simply divided* between positions of masculinity and femininity, but *multiply organized* across positionalities along several axes and across mutually contradictory discourses and practices." This recognition of the interrelatedness and co-implication of various other categories, such as race, class, nation, and sexuality, in gender and in one another, has made possible the redefinition of the "feminist subject . . . as much less pure, as indeed ideologically complicitous with 'the oppressor' whose position [the feminist subject] may occupy in certain sociosexual relations (though not in others), on one or another axis."[4]

It is from within the challenges of feminist historiography as defined by Sangari and Vaid, and the redefinition of the feminist subject as outlined by Teresa de Lauretis, that I pose the problem of locating "Indian womanhood" and the politics of feminism in colonial India. I will approach this question through a discussion of a particular historical controversy in India, occasioned by the 1927 publication of the American-born writer Katherine Mayo's *Mother India*.[5] *Mother India* was ostensibly an exposé of the condition of women in India. Although Mayo's book focuses on the various inequities imposed upon women, such as child marriage and premature maternity, by a patriarchal Hindu culture, it includes a more wide-ranging discussion of India's various social, economic, and political ills, for which Mayo held Hindu culture responsible. Mayo arrived at the conclusion that far from being ready for political self-determination, India needed the continued "civilizing" influence of the British. Her connections with the official British propaganda machine quickly discredited Mayo's credentials as a champion of women's issues in India. For nationalists, however, *Mother India's* attack on the political and cultural project of Indian nationalism, made under the pretext of a discussion of the

condition of women in India, could not be left unchallenged.[6]
Indeed, the book generated a tremendous controversy, the impact
of which was felt in India, Britain, and the United States.

My interest in this particular controversy as an Indian feminist
grew out of an earlier effort to reconstruct the Indian woman as
subject in the debate in which both sides used the Indian woman as
the object of their starkly opposed evaluations of Indian society.
My attempt was to highlight the contributions of individual women
and of the women's movement in India to the *Mother India* debate.
Here, I return to my earlier reading of the emergence in this
controversy of what Sarojini Naidu and her other middle-class/
upper caste contemporaries identified as the "authentic voice of
modern Indian womanhood"[7] in order to explore the particular
discursive strategies by which a subject position was created en-
abling the Indian woman to speak. I will explore the opportunity
that such a reading offers for locating the Indian woman and the
politics of middle-class Indian feminism.

My earlier inclination had been simply to read women's responses, following Joanna Liddle and Rama Joshi's analysis of the
women's movement in India, as naturally occupying a space from
which both male nationalist patriarchy and imperialist-feminism
could be critiqued in order to disrupt imperialist-nationalist invo-
cations of the Indian woman in the *Mother India* controversy.[8]
However the responses of the individual women and of the organized women's movement were not readily amenable to such an
analysis. A nationalist critic of imperialism and/or imperialist-
feminism could very easily interpret the women's responses as a
triumph of the general nationalist critique of *Mother India*. For a
feminist critic of nationalism, however, the women's responses
could be read just as easily as a co-optation of Indian women by
nationalist politics.[9] Such possible interpretations proved to be
inadequate in one crucial way. To paraphrase Chandra Mohanty,
reading women's responses simply in terms of their "achievements"
or their "failures" in relation to some ideal effectively removes
them and the ideal from history, and freezes them in time and
space.[10] I was forced to recognize that any interpretation that
hoped to historicize women's responses or the ideals against which
they are measured must refuse to take as given or self-evident either
the gender politics of colonialism and nationalism which framed

the *Mother India* controversy or the self-constitution of the Indian woman herself in women's responses to the controversy. Such a reading would have to take into account both the historical context which made possible the identity of the Indian woman and the particular strategies by which women learned to speak in the voice of the Indian woman.

The historical context in which the identity of the Indian woman emerged has been written about extensively, but comparatively little work has been done on women's own self-constitution within this context.[11] Here, therefore, my efforts to locate Indian womanhood and the politics of middle-class Indian feminism in the *Mother India* controversy will shift between a survey of some recent scholarship on the gender politics of colonialism and nationalism and an examination of the voice of Indian womanhood itself. This survey in no way pretends to be exhaustive, but touches primarily on those issues that may enhance a reading of Indian women's voices in the *Mother India* controversy. I will return to the responses of Indian women themselves via a brief discussion of gender in some critiques of colonialism and nationalism in India.

Chandra Mohanty's introduction to *Third World Women and the Politics of Feminism* identifies three symptomatic characteristics of imperial rule: the ideological construction and consolidation of white masculinity as normative, and the corresponding racialization and sexualization of colonized peoples; the effects of colonial institutions and policies in transforming indigenous patriarchies and consolidating hegemonic middle-class cultures in metropolitan and colonized areas; and the rise of feminist politics and consciousness in this historical context within and against the framework of national liberation movements.[12] These aspects of imperial rule mark both Mayo's *Mother India* and the imperialist-nationalist controversy following the book's publication. I will briefly make a note of some of these elements in the framing of *Mother India* and the subsequent controversy, but will focus mainly on the impact of imperial rule on the emergence of a hegemonic middle-class Indian culture and its implications for the mobilization of women in the *Mother India* controversy.

Ann Stoler, in an article on the colonial cultures of French Indochina and the Dutch East Indies, makes the important point that the very categories of "colonizer" and "colonized," essential for the exercise of imperial authority, were never stable, but needed to be secured through various policies and practices that constructed and regulated particular, historically specific, gendered, and racialized identities.[13] Stoler's analysis has implications for understanding why the construct of the "manly Englishman" as the liberator of helpless Indian women and other oppressed groups becomes such a crucial element in Mayo's defense of imperial rule. Mayo's use of such old colonial stereotypes as the enlightened and reform-minded British official and the indolent and selfish Indian male who was the nemesis of helpless Indian women, however, also limited her discussion of Indian women. Consequently, in *Mother India* the Indian woman appears either as the object of the benevolent salvation of British imperialists or the object of the Indian male's cruel and barbaric practices.

Various scholars have also pointed out the collusion between imperialist and indigenous patriarchies in nineteenth-century debates over the "woman's question" in India. Lata Mani's and Uma Chakravorty's analyses of debates about women in social-reform and protonationalist movements in India have provided illuminating insights into the simultaneous proliferation of discourses about women and their surprising marginalization in these same discourses.[14] Lata Mani's study of the official discourse on the regulation and the eventual abolition of the practice of widow immolation (*sati*) in the early nineteenth-century clearly demonstrates that women were seldom the major concern of the various groups in this debate; instead, women were merely the sites on which competing views of tradition and modernity were debated. The legacy of these nineteenth-century debates about women was felt in many ways in the *Mother India* controversy. The understanding of tradition and modernity, for example, that framed the responses to child marriage and early sexuality were particularly colonial constructs; the arguments for and against the practice of child marriage were made, as Lata Mani has so brilliantly identified, in the context of the early nineteenth-century debate over *sati,* on the basis of a selective, textualized construct of Hindu culture and tradition. In such a context, the debate over child-marriage reforms shifted attention from the historical and material conditions for such practices to an evaluation of Indian culture. Both imperialists and nationalists invoked the position of the Indian woman to buttress their opposing evaluations of Indian culture. Uma Chakravorty, for example, has demonstrated that the upper caste/class concept of the Indian/Arya woman was crucial to the modern re-invention of traditions for the protonationalist and nationalist project of national regeneration. Not surprisingly, therefore, the image of the Indian woman featured prominently in the *Mother India* debate: both sides invoked her in their battle over the nature of "India."

The image of the Indian woman as simply the object of imperialist-nationalist debates, however, was further complicated by the broader nationalist agenda. The re-articulation of middle-class Indian womanhood had been necessary for the emergence of a new middle-class public and private sphere in colonial India; this same ideal of womanhood also offered a space for the mobilization of middle-class women themselves. The significance of the ideal of womanhood to the consolidation of a hegemonic middle-class culture has been examined by several scholars. Sangari and Vaid, drawing upon the works of Partha Chatterjee and Sumanta Banerjee, suggest that the definition of Indian womanhood was closely tied to the class polarization that accompanied the development of the middle-class, and to the anxieties of colonial nationalism. Sumanta Banerjee argues that the need for sharper differentiation between the classes provided the context for the regulation of women's popular culture in the nineteenth century, and for the creation of a new public space for the respectable *bhadramahila,* (new, educated middle-class woman) who was now defined in opposition to women from the lower economic strata.[15]

According to Partha Chatterjee, a re-articulation of Indian womanhood was crucial in the resolution of the "constitutive contradiction" in the formation of an Indian identity.[16] The central problem for Indian nationalism, he suggests, was the problem of modernizing the nation on Western terms while at the same time retaining an essential national identity as the basis for a political claim to nationhood. Nationalist thought dealt with this contradiction by distinguishing the spiritual from the material and the inner from the outer. Nationalists could now afford to imitate the West in the outer or material sphere while retaining the spiritual or the inner sphere as an "uncolonized space" wherein the essence of Indianness could be located. This dichotomy was related, he suggests, to the socially prescribed roles for men and women. Women as the guardians of the inner or spiritual sphere of the nation were now regarded as the embodiments of an essentialized "Indianness."

The re-articulation of the Indian woman for the self-definition of the nationalist bourgeoisie provided the context for the "modernizing" of certain indigenous patriarchal modes of regulating women in orthodox Indian society.[17] Although the critique of orthodox indigenous patriarchy did afford a limited agenda for the emancipation and self-emancipation of women, its emancipatory politics was severely constrained within the modernizing project of Indian nationalism. The models for modernization, for example, drew upon notions of bourgeois domesticity and the ideals of Victorian womanhood introduced via British rule in India; yet they were crucially modified to suit the particular needs of the nationalist bourgeoisie. Dipesh Chakrabarty suggests, drawing upon Chatterjee's work, that the "originality" of the Indian middle class' project of modernization was constituted by the nationalist "denial of the bourgeois private": the cultural norm of a patriarchal, patrilineal, patrilocal extended family was counterposed to the bourgeois patriarchal ideals of companionate marriage.[18] This reconfiguration of the middle-class "home," he suggests, was part of the history of the development of the modern individual in India. Indeed, it was central in marking the difference between what was "Indian" and what was "European/English."

We can see the impact that nationalist modifications of bourgeois domesticity had on the construct of the Indian woman in Chakrabarty's analysis of the word "freedom" in debates about women's education in nineteenth-century India. He suggests that while freedom in the West was defined as the right to self-indulgence, freedom in India was defined as the capacity to serve and obey voluntarily. Hence, unlike the ultrafree Western/Westernized woman who was selfish and shameless, the "modern" Indian woman was defined as educated enough to contribute to the larger body politic but yet "modest" enough to be unself-assertive and unselfish.[19] The ideological construct of the modern Indian woman as "superior" to orthodox, uneducated women, to women of the lower castes/class, and to the Western/Westernized woman was key to the emerging social order in India, characterized by the consolidation of the nationalist bourgeoisie. At the same time, however, the construct of the modern Indian woman also created the climate both for women's reforms and for women's entry, under male patronage, to the male-dominated public sphere. The impact of this was evident in the unprecedented mobilization of middle-class women on behalf of the Gandhi-led nationalist movement, as well as in the all-India women's organizations and movements in the early twentieth century.

The question that we might legitimately raise at this point is that, given the ideological structures of domination outlined above, how can any reading of women's responses, as those in the *Mother India* controversy, hope to reconstruct the Indian woman as the subject of the controversy? In other words, do the ideological constructs that condition women's participation predetermine the nature of women's responses and make any interrogation of the consciousness and agency of women themselves irrelevant? I contend that a focus on the voice or the agency of women themselves does not have to be opposed to an examination of the ideological structures from which they emerged. I take as my model Joan Scott's suggestion for a mode of analysis that interrogates and relativizes the history by which subjects are produced, instead of constructing subjects by describing their experience in terms of an essentialized identity. According to Scott, identities are not timeless or fixed, but are learned in particular historical moments. Hence, as she puts it, "it is not individuals who have experience, but subjects who are constituted through experience." Such a mode of analysis allows us to focus on the consciousness or experience of individuals, not as "incontestable evidence [or] as an originary point of explanation," but as a historical event itself in need of explanation.[20] After Scott, I focus on women's responses during the *Mother India* controversy, not because they make visible the voice of the modern Indian woman that was always there, simply waiting to be expressed, but because these responses make visible the particular strategies by which a subject position was created, in a certain historical moment, from which the Indian woman could speak.

The question of the Indian woman's voice was clearly critical to the narrativization of the *Mother India* controversy. In the midst of the controversy, for example, *The Times* of London carried a piece with the provocative title: "Indian Women: Are They Voiceless?"[21] Indian nationalists were happy to be able to give a resounding no to that question. The male author of *Sister India*, a book written in response to Mayo's *Mother India*, reported, with barely concealed satisfaction, that while Mayo considers herself a champion of women in India "the women of India have held meetings in every part of India and have unanimously protested against *her* descriptions of their troubles."[22] Prominent women leaders, such as Sarla Devi Chaudhrani, Latika Basu, and Jyotirmoyee Ganguly, were conspicuously present at the large protest meetings held against the book.[23] In separate women's meetings, such as the Mahila Samitis in Bengal and similar women's associations all over the country, women met to discuss the "insult" to Indian womanhood contained in *Mother India*. Fairly typical of resolutions passed at such meetings was one proposed by Mrs. Mirza Ismail at the Mysore Women's Education conference. The resolution declared Mayo's book to be "at variance with the ideals of Indian womanhood, which inspire Indian women to lead much happier lives than appear to be led by women of other countries."[24] Similarly, Maya Das's letter compared the nature and extent of the sexual exploitation of women in Britain unfavorably with the situation in India, provoking a long controversy in the *Pioneer*, a semi-official British newspaper in India.[25] Books written by women in response to *Mother India* also expressed feelings of nationalist outrage against Mayo. Chandravati Lakhanpal's *Mother India Ka Jawab* (A Reply to Mother India) and Charulata Devi's *The Fair Sex of India: A Reply to Mother India* pursued a line of argument also found in the numerous books written by men. Lakhanpal's, for instance, was a *tu quoque* response; she focused on the "depraved sexuality" of Western societies just as Mayo had focused on sexual practices in India.[26] Charulata Devi, on the other hand, made no mention of Mayo or any of the points raised in *Mother India*, but simply provided sketches of eminent Indian women that countered Mayo's dismal portrait.[27]

The voices of women in India alluded to above may be read as contributing to the general nationalist outrage against *Mother India*. Of particular interest to me, however, are the discursive strategies through which a subject position was created for the Indian woman to speak. I turn, therefore, to the strategies that enabled the emergence of an "authentic voice of modern Indian womanhood." I will begin by examining the different strategies exemplified in the responses of four women: Cornelia Sorabji, Uma Nehru, Sarojini Naidu, and Dhanvanthi Rama Rau. My aim in analyzing the array of positions represented by these women is to identify the particular conditions that enabled a so-called distinctive Indian woman's position on the controversy—a position to be contrasted not only with the imperialist/imperialist-feminist positions, but also with the allegedly gender-neutral nationalist positions. I will also explore the emergence of a politics of middle-class Indian feminism in this context.

CORNELIA SORABJI

Cornelia Sorabji was the only Indian woman who had been cited at some length in *Mother India*. Sorabji and Mayo maintained a warm relationship, through private communications, for years after the *Mother India* controversy. Yet Sorabji's complicated attitude toward Mayo's imperialist project precluded any possibility for the emergence of an Indian woman's position critical of either indigenous or imperialist patriarchy. At the time, Sorabji was one of the leading female legal practitioners in India and had developed a considerable reputation as the legal advisor to orthodox Hindu women in *purdanashin* (veiled seclusion).[28] Sorabji's main interest in the women's question was in social service, embodied in her scheme for an Institute for Social Service in India. Her role models came from an earlier generation of strong female reformers, such as Pandita Ramabai, Ramabai Ranade, and her own mother, Francina Sorabji. She was also an ardent supporter of the female ascetic Mataji Tapashwini who had started a school for women along orthodox Hindu lines in Calcutta.[29] Sorabji herself adopted a cautious, or even conservative, attitude toward female reform; she, for example, often defended the practice of *purdah* among upper-caste Hindu women. As a self-confessed loyalist of the British Raj, she was particularly skeptical of the new generation of women activists who, according to Sorabji, were advocating overly hasty political and social reforms for women. These women, in turn, regarded Sorabji as far too "individualist" and far too critical of India.[30]

Despite Sorabji's close ties to Mayo and her prominence as an advocate for social reform in India, she remained a shadowy figure

in the debate over *Mother India*. Apart from a review of *Mother India*
which appeared in the Calcutta-based newspaper *The Englishman*,
Sorabji's views on the book were confined to private communications to Mayo and to a handful of British women in Britain.[31] Even
Mayo's efforts to portray Sorabji as an example of the "enlightened" woman's position in India came to naught. Sorabji was
forced to write to Mayo's secretary, Henry Field, urging him to
request that Mayo refrain from using Sorabji's name in public. She
later wrote to Mayo directly requesting that Mayo write to the
Indian press absolving her of any complicity in the writing of
Mother India. Mayo's disclaimer along these lines appeared in the
Calcutta *Statesman* and in the Swarajist newspaper, *The Forward*.[32]
Sorabji's sensitivity no doubt had been prompted by the flurry of
criticism directed against her from nationalist quarters in India.
She was publicly denounced at nationalist meetings held to protest
Mayo's book. *The Forward* accused Sorabji of supplying Mayo with
all her ammunition against India, while C. S. Ranga Iyer, a Swarajist
member of the legislative assembly, denounced Sorabji in his *Father
India*, written as a rejoinder to *Mother India*. Iyer had described
Sorabji's work, from which Mayo had quoted extensively, as the
"vaporings of an unbalanced and unstructured mind."[33] Even Sorabji's
younger sister Dr. Alice Pennell had disagreed with her sharply on
her evaluation of Mayo's politics and on Mayo's contributions to
the cause of Indian women. The most hurtful attack, one which
Sorabji herself recorded with great bitterness, came from the
young women graduates of the Federation of University Women in
India, of which she was honorary president. The younger university women in India circulated a virulent petition, behind Sorabji's
back, attacking her for her conciliatory stand toward Mayo's *Mother
India*.[34]

   If Sorabji's public position in the controversy was fraught, her
private position was equally problematic. Even though Sorabji had
praised Mayo for writing about the condition of women in India,
she was, at first, careful to distance herself from Mayo's general
political conclusions. This was in essence the position she had
adopted both publicly, in her review of *Mother India*, and in her
private communications with Mayo in which she expressed regret
that Mayo had not eschewed all "politics." She even advised Mayo,
although to no avail, to change the title of her book in subsequent

editions so that it did not appear as an indictment of all of India or of Indian political aspirations.[35] As an advocate of social reform, Sorabji's initial concern was to use the controversy as an opportunity to draw attention to the need for a social service institute in which the conditions of women could be discussed in a less charged political atmosphere. This position, however, was abandoned quickly in favor of an antinationalist and pro-imperialist position. Later Sorabji, acknowledging her secret collaboration with Mayo, saw her role in the controversy only as a "Scarlet Pimpernel," who supplied Mayo with information for her subsequent anti-Indian books. Sorabji's direct collaboration with Mayo, however, had to be kept a secret because, as she herself acknowledged, her association with such anti-Hindu diatribes, like that in Mayo's subsequent book *The Face of Mother India*, might end up alienating Sorabji's Hindu wards.[36]

Sorabji's role in the Mayo controversy was marked by contradictions and shrouded in secrecy. Sorabji found it impossible, from a position of support for Mayo and her imperialist politics, to articulate a subject position for/by the Indian woman in the controversy. Even Sorabji's initial sympathy for the Indian woman as the object of benevolent salvation, either by the British or by her own Institute for Social Service, provided only a limited appeal for an Indian women's position in the controversy. Her subsequent endorsement of Mayo's pro-imperialist politics, moreover, caused her to abandon all efforts at trying to describe a space from which the Indian woman could become the subject of the controversy. The only other Indian woman to be cited in *Mother India*, Mona Bose, had recognized the impossibility of speaking either for or as an Indian woman from within Mayo's pro-imperialist politics. Bose, therefore, publicly denied the views that were attributed to her in *Mother India*.[37] In contrast, Sorabji learnt through bitter experience that her pro-imperialist defence of Mayo could not provide a subject position from which the Indian woman could address either the British or male nationalists in India.

UMA NEHRU

For very different reasons, Uma Nehru also failed in her efforts to articulate a subject position for the Indian woman in the *Mother*

India controversy. Although Nehru was an uncompromising critic of certain patriarchal assumptions in male nationalist discourse, she responded to Mayo's book from the general nationalist perspective. Indeed, her response to *Mother India* reflected the power of the nationalist discourse to contain even those voices that were critical of its particular nationalist resolution of the women's question. Nehru long had been a powerful advocate for women's rights through her articles in the Hindi journal *Stri Darpan* (*Women's Mirror*), edited by her sister-in-law Rameshwari Nehru. Her articles had addressed the hypocrisy of male nationalist discourse in prescribing models of ideal Indian womanhood for modern Indian women that were drawn from the legendary figures of Sita-Sati-Savitri.[38] Not surprisingly, Nehru was considered as far too "Westernized," even in the anglicized Nehru family into which she was married.[39] Yet, in the imperialist-nationalist controversy over *Mother India*, Nehru responded to Mayo from the allegedly unmarked position of the "Indian."

Nehru's *Mother India Aur Uska Jawab* is a Hindi translation of Mayo's book meant, most probably, for Hindi-speaking women.[40] In the preface Nehru writes that her aim is "to use this book meant to insult us to instill pride among us." Her translation of *Mother India* was preceded by an imaginary dialogue with Mayo. *Mother India Aur Uska Jawab* was true to Nehru's earlier reservations about the nationalist ideal of modern Indian womanhood: it refrained from invoking the glorious tradition of Indian womanhood in responding to Mayo's criticism of the position of women in India. Deprived of the countervailing argument about the ideals of Indian womanhood, however, Nehru's dialogue with Mayo deals largely with the political and economic issues raised in *Mother India*. Nehru avoided discussing the particular implications of Mayo's book for the women's question. She missed, for instance, the opportunity to respond to Mayo's taunt to India's women leaders. In her second book on India, *The Slaves of the Gods*, Mayo had written that her aim was "to awaken [Indian women's] intelligent patriotism and the consciousness of [their] men, by making inescapable the contrast between, on the one hand, florid talk of devotion and 'sacrifice' poured out before an abstract figure, and, on the other hand, the consideration actually accorded to the living woman, mother of the race."[41] Nehru's desire to present a strong nationalist argument against *Mother India*, even though she was herself critical of the attitudes towards women in male nationalist discourse, led her to avoid a detailed discussion of the special emphasis that Mayo had placed on women's issues in her attack on India. Nehru's critique of *Mother India*, therefore, was made from the supposedly neutral, or nongendered, position of the Indian nationalist: it could not become the site for the elaboration of the gendered subject position of the Indian woman.

Sarojini Naidu

Ironically, the consolidation of a distinct Indian woman's position in the controversy could occur only within the male nationalist discourse. This is evident in the response of Sarojini Naidu, one of the most prominent women in the nationalist and the women's movements of the time. Naidu, by combining "modern" political activism with "traditional" Indian roots, embodied the nationalist ideals of middle-class Indian womanhood.[42] Her response to the *Mother India* controversy reflects the ways in which the Indian woman could arrogate a subject position for herself from which to address both the British and the male nationalists in India. In one of Naidu's earliest responses, she referred to *Mother India* only to urge Indian men to give up their prejudices against women and to educate their wives, mothers, and sisters if they sincerely wished to neutralize the impact of Mayo's book. Mayo would later use extracts from this speech to endorse her own views about the hypocrisy of male nationalists.[43] Yet there was no mistaking Naidu's sharp criticism of Mayo's imperialist politics. Her telegram to the famous Calcutta Town Hall meeting, organized by the nationalist Mayor J. N. Sengupta, summed up her attitude towards Mayo: "The mouths of liars rot and perish with their own lies, but the glory of Indian womanhood shines pure and as the morning star."[44] Unlike some of her male colleagues, however, Naidu's main concern was not to prove that oppressive practices against women did not exist in India, but to show that the women of India were capable of redeeming themselves.

Naidu's invocation of the glorious ideals of Indian womanhood and her elaboration of the nationalist Sati-Savitri model for the Indian woman did not simply reflect a co-optation by male nationalist discourse, but was also critical in legitimating the interventionary practices of Indian women themselves. Naidu's challenge to Mayo was directed at the latter's right to speak for Indian womanhood. Naidu stated this in no uncertain terms in her 1928 Kamala Lectures at the Calcutta University Senate in a speech on the "Ideals of Indian Womanhood":

> The women of India should answer all those who come in the guise of friendship to interpret India to the world and exploit their weakness and expose the *secrets of the home* [my emphasis], with the words "whether we are oppressed, treated as goods and chattels and forced on the funeral pyres of our husbands, our redemption is in our hands. We shall break through the walls that imprison us and tear the veils that stifle. We shall do this by the miracle of our womanhood. We do not ask any friend or foe in the guise of a friend, to come merely to exploit us while they pretend to interpret, succor and solace our womanhood."[45]

The accent on the "secrets of the home" in Naidu's speech signals the ambivalence at the heart of the identity of the Indian woman. On the one hand, her speech recalls the nationalist effort at reformulating the new middle-class "home" as an insulated space in which patriarchal authority remained intact and, on the other, its vigorous arguments for the potential of Indian woman's own agency in correcting the roots of their domination also leave open the possibility of challenging the patriarchal closure of the "home" as a site for women's struggle.

Naidu's intervention demonstrates that although the nationalist ideal of the Indian woman ensured that middle-class women's entry into the public space was under male patronage, the same ideal also enabled a relatively liberal space for women at least partly of their own making. The popular representation of the nation as Mother India as well as the figure of the Indian woman as the essence of Indianness had also opened up new arenas for women's activism. The potential of such an ideal was evident in the radical claim that Naidu, as a prime example of the "new woman" in India, had the unique distinction of representing, not only the Indian woman, but the entire Indian nation. Gandhi, for example, would recognize Naidu's claim as the unofficial ambassador for India/Indian women. In the wake of the *Mother India* controversy,

he was persuaded to send Naidu to the United States as the
spokesperson for India and the Indian woman. Officially Naidu
was a representative of the All India Women's Conference at the
Pan-Pacific Women's Conference in Honolulu, but as her extensive
lecture tour demonstrates, her trip was meant to educate the
American people about the "real" Mother India.[46] Naidu lectured
in the United States on "The Interpretation of Indian Womanhood" and "The Political Situation in India," topics on which she
seemed uniquely qualified to speak. As the symbolic figure of
nationalist India and of Indian women, she hoped to dispel the
image of an unregenerate patriarchal Indian nationalism and of the
downtrodden Indian woman found in Mayo's book. Therefore, she
felt no compulsion to debate the specifics of the book with a
Western audience.[47] Despite the sustained efforts of Mayo and her
supporters to discredit Naidu as simply a mouthpiece for Gandhi,
her trip was an immense public relations success, especially with
the more liberal u.s. women's organizations.[48] Indeed, it was precisely because Naidu had offered a strategy for articulating the
Indian woman's position within male nationalist discourse that she
was able to appropriate a unique subject position for the middle-
class Indian woman in the *Mother India* controversy.

How does a discourse of the Indian woman as a figure of
essentialized Indianness, however, enable a subject position for the
"Indian woman"? To recall Partha Chatterjee's analysis, the modern Indian could create a subject position from which to address
the British only by elaborating an ahistorical and essentialized
notion of Indian womanhood. Chatterjee, for example, argues that
a marked "*difference* in the degree and manner of westernization of
women, as distinct from men" was essential for the subject position
of the Indian.[49] However, the entry of women into the male-
dominated public sphere in the early twentieth century made it
increasingly difficult to maintain this essential difference in the
westernization of women, and created new demands on the gendered subject position of the Indian. In the context of rapid
westernization of women, modern/westernized women, like Naidu,
could, through service to the nation, also appropriate a subject
position from which to address the West as Indian. They did this by
positing an essential difference in the degree and manner of westernization of the truly modern Indian woman, as distinct from the

merely westernized Indian woman. The essential difference lay in the fact that the modern Indian woman, unlike her merely westernized counterpart, claimed "traditional" ideals of Indian womanhood *on behalf of the modernizing project of nationalism.* Naidu's strategy of negotiation in the *Mother India* controversy, therefore, reflected the particular conditions under which even the modern/westernized woman could address the West as Indian. This particular moment of an Indian female subjectivity, however, rested on an uneasy resolution of the modern Indian woman as both subject and as object of the nationalist discourse of essentialized Indianness.

DHANVANTHI RAMA RAU

Dhanvanthi Rama Rau's interventions in the Mayo controversy further illustrate how a subject position for the modern Indian woman was assigned within male nationalist discourse. Rau's contributions to the controversy lay in her struggle to establish the claim of Indian women and their organizations, against the rival claims of Western women's organizations, as the legitimate crusaders for the rights of all women in India. The argument for the special role of the modern Indian woman received its legitimacy from a nationalist discourse that papered over the very real class/caste contradictions in the particular imagining of the national community.

Following *Mother India*, women's organizations, especially in the United States and in Britain, demonstrated a great interest in the "upliftment" of women in India. In the United States it was the more conservative women's groups, like the Daughters of the American Revolution, which openly endorsed Mayo's book, and started a fund for the helpless child brides of India.[50] More direct intervention on behalf of the women in India was left to British women's organizations, especially under the direction of Eleanor Rathbone. Rathbone acknowledged a "great tidal wave of responsibility" for the helpless women of India.[51] As an imperialist, Rathbone was equally impressed by the political implications of Mayo's revelations in *Mother India*. Rathbone, therefore, urged Mayo to issue a cheaper edition of her book to be distributed among members of the Labour party in Britain which "badly need the corrective of [*Mother India*] because of their tendency to espouse self-government anywhere."⁵² In response to Mayo's description of women in India, Rathbone petitioned the British parliament to appoint two members of the National Union of Societies for Equal Citizenship (NUSEC), of which she was president, to the parliamentary commission, popularly known as the Simon Commission. This all-white commission was later boycotted in India by all the major political parties and by the all-India women's organizations for its exclusion of Indians and of women. Rathbone's proposal to the commission, as it was about to undertake an inquiry into the political conditions in India, was that British women appointed to the commission could provide information about that part of Indian society "hidden behind the veil." Rathbone's scheme, however, was met with skepticism from some Indian women. The wife of a distinguished Muslim leader from India wrote to the London *Times*, "Indian women are not voiceless. They received the franchise, and those among them who are able and willing to take advantage of it are aware of the needs of their own people."⁵³

The most sustained criticism of Rathbone's efforts to get British women's organizations to assume responsibility for the women of India, however, came from Dhanvanthi Rama Rau, an active member of three of the all-India women's organizations. Rathbone, inspired by the revelations made in Mayo's book, had organized two large conferences in London on "Women in India." At the second conference, which was held in Caxton Hall on 7 and 8 October 1929, Rau attacked the remarks of the various speakers at the conference as variations of the "white man's burden," and hotly "disputed the right of British women to arrange a conference on Indian social evils, when all the speakers were British and many of them had never even visited India."⁵⁴ On the request of some prominent British feminists, Rathbone was forced to provide Rau a platform to present her views to the conference. In her speech Rau outlined the work being done in India by Indian women's organizations and reiterated that British women could give only moral support: the practical work had to be done in India and by Indians. Despite the interventions of Rau and other Indian women, the resolution that British women's organizations had a special responsibility for Indian women was passed with only a few Indian women present dissenting. Sir M. F. Dywer, a former British official in India, concluded that the "great meeting of British Women's Association" held at Caxton Hall could do much good to improve the status of Indian women because, at present, the "Hindu women [themselves] were Dumb."[55]

Although frustrated by the outcome of the conference, Rau did not leave unchallenged the claim that British women's organizations had a special responsibility for the condition of women in India. Rau, along with some British and Indian women associated with the Lyceum Club in London, wrote a letter to the *Times* accusing Rathbone's conference for promoting "racial cleavage." She boldly reiterated that while "India welcomes co-operation [she] will not tolerate any form of patronage or philanthropy which will rob her of her self-esteem."[56] Rau's various interventions served to attack the patronizing politics of Western women's organizations, and to secure recognition for the role of the modern Indian woman as the true representative of all her oppressed sisters in India. Henceforth, Rathbone and the NUSEC would be forced to work through the modern Indian woman as the representative of the women of India.

The consolidation of the nationalist bourgeoisie in India allowed the women of this class to emerge as the true champion of all women in India. Hence the modern Indian woman came to be seen as the liberator of all other women in India. To paraphrase Dipesh Chakrabarty's observations made in a slightly different context, the Indian woman, as a member of the modernizing elite, stood for an "assumed unity called the 'Indian people' that is always split into two—a modernizing elite and a yet-to-be-modernized peasantry."[57] Within the modernizing project of nationalism, therefore, the modern Indian woman was also always the subject of modernity, the transmitter of the fruits of modernization to all other women in India. The self-constitution of the "Indian woman," as simultaneously the subject and the object of nationalist discourse, however, exemplifies the contradictions in the subject positions available to women in all patriarchies.[58]

THE WOMEN'S MOVEMENT

The particular history of the self-constitution of the Indian woman in nationalist discourse also had implications for the politics of middle-class Indian feminism. The political struggles of the

Indian women's movement in the *Mother India* controversy provided an arena for middle-class Indian women's engagement with feminism. For the fledgling women's movement, the controversy afforded an opportunity to consolidate a feminist agenda for women's issues. Women activists and the women's movement, therefore, admitted the urgent need for the reform of women's position in India, even as they challenged Mayo's description of the Indian woman in *Mother India*. Kamala Sathianadhan, editor of the *Indian Ladies Magazine*, wrote:

> We honor Miss Mayo for her courage in not caring for resentments and accusations; we congratulate her on her public spirit in "shouldering the task" of "holding the mirror" to that part of the human race which is a "physical menace" to the world; we do not question her ability or her cleverness in writing this book; but we do deny her the presumption that she is "in a position to present conditions and their bearing," and we do not for a minute admit her "plain speech" as the "faithful wounds of a friend": for she is no friend of ours.[59]

Women's organizations carefully distanced themselves from Mayo's imperialist propaganda, but used the attention that the controversy created to facilitate their own campaign for child-marriage reform and other legislation for women. The Women's Indian Association (WIA), a pioneer of the all-India women's movement, issued the following statement on Mayo's book: "while we repudiate the book as a whole we must turn every ounce of our zeal towards the rooting out of those social evils which are undoubtedly in our midst."[60] At Triplicane in Madras, the association organized the largest protest meeting of women against the book. This meeting was chaired by Dr. Muthulakshmi Reddy, the first Indian woman to be nominated to the Provincial legislatures. The meeting passed the following two resolutions: first, it denied that "Indian womanhood as a whole is in a state of slavery, superstition, ignorance and degradation which Miss Mayo affirms"; and, second, they called upon the legislative assembly and legislative council to enact measures that would legally prohibit child marriage, early parentage, enforced widowhood, dedication of girls to temples, and "commercialized immorality." This was also the position of the *Stri Dharma* (Woman's Duty), the paper of the Women's Indian Association.[61]

An episode at the annual meeting of the Indian National Social Conference held on 27 December 1927 indicates the context in which women activists conducted their successful campaign for child-marriage reform.[62] At the conference prominent men and women, while advocating the urgent need for child-marriage reform, denounced Mayo's *Mother India*. Only one speaker introduced a discordant note. S. N. Arya, the only representative from the Non-Brahmin Youth League present, referred to Mayo as a champion of women's reform in India. Pandemonium broke out at the mention of her name. Arya's comments, despite the pro-imperialist politics which he shared with some groups in the Non-Brahmin Movement of the 1920s and 1930s, served to question the consensus over women's issues secured within the upper caste/class politics of the nation-state.[63] The politics of the nation-state, however, also privileged the understanding of women of dominant classes/castes on women's reforms, and allowed the middle-class women's movement to set the agenda for women's reform in India. Dr. Muthulakshmi Reddy, who chaired the conference, persuaded the delegates to ignore Arya's disruption and redirected their attention to women's reform.

The issue around which the all-India women's organizations mobilized in the *Mother India* controversy, that of the upper caste/class child-bride rather than the underpaid *dhai,* or midwife, also mentioned in Mayo's book, reveals the elitist character of the early women's movement. It also reveals, however, the special conditions under which women's organizations could conduct a successful political campaign for women. The issue of child-marriage reform was not fundamentally opposed to the "modernizing" efforts of the social reform and nationalist movements. The legacy of such male-sponsored reforms meant that the women's movement could mount a campaign for the modernization of the Indian home by urging child-marriage legislation without necessarily attacking male authority in the home. Rameshwari Nehru, for example, who was active in the campaign for child-marriage legislation, considered herself to be an advocate of women's rights, but not an advocate of sexual equality in the home. She wrote: "I do not think that the home should be made a forum for women's battles."[64]

This should not, however, make us overlook the contributions of the women's organizations in getting child-marriage legislation passed in the face of governmental indifference and orthodox male opposition. The women's movement had an uphill battle to gain recognition for their own contributions in getting child-marriage legislation passed in India. The issue of child-marriage reform had been a major concern of the women's movement in India even before the publication of *Mother India*. The very first meeting of the All-India Women's Conference (AIWC) held in Poona in 1926 had committed its support, not only to a bill on the age of consent— then languishing in the legislative assembly partly due to official indifference, but also to the eventual abolition of child marriage in India. The Mayo controversy speeded up the women's demand for child marriage reform.[65] On 11 February 1928 a delegation of nineteen members of the AIWC led by the Rani of Mandi met the viceroy and leaders of all the major Indian political parties to urge the passage of the Sarda Bill in the legislative assembly. The delegation also secured the appointment of one of its members, Rameshwari Nehru, to the age-of-consent committee appointed by the government on 25 June 1928. Rameshwari Nehru later wrote that it was in dealing with private bills on age-of-marriage and consent that the government had appointed this committee. Significantly, she made no mention of the publicity created by the Mayo controversy.[66] The report of the committee, which Mayo later used to write her sequel to *Mother India* and to validate the claims of her previous book, testified to the need for marriage reforms.[67] Women witnesses to the committee meetings were among the strongest advocates for the abolition of child marriage.

Following the report of the age-of-consent committee, women activists launched a lobbying effort with Indian legislators and British officials to ensure the passage of the Sarda Child-Marriage Bill. Kamaladevi Chattopadhyay, on behalf of the AIWC, orchestrated the work of getting support for the bill from Indian legislators in Delhi. Dhanvanthi Rama Rau, as secretary of the Child-Marriage Abolition League, worked among the wives of British government officials urging them to persuade their husbands to support the child-marriage legislation.[68] On the day of the final debate on the Sarda Bill in the legislative assembly, approximately 300 AIWC activists attended to ensure support of the measure. The AIWC would later see the passage of the Child-Marriage Restraint Act in 1929 as a triumph of their own fledgling organization.

Yet the contributions of the Indian women's movement in

getting child-marriage reform in India did not receive automatic recognition. International opinion, for example, gave all the credit for the appointment of the age-of-consent committee and the passage of the Sarda Bill to Mayo's *Mother India*. The *New York Times* even carried a piece entitled "Miss Mayo's Book on India Gets Action on Child Marriage."[69] Mayo and her supporters were in great part responsible for popularizing the view that Indians had been shamed into supporting legislative reforms for women as a result of her brave exposé in *Mother India*. A letter which Mayo received from India chided her for taking credit for the passage of the child-marriage legislation:

> speaking for every woman in India, I want to say to you that when you claim for yourself the credit of an "attempt to raise the marriage age of females," because the u.s., as you explain, had accepted your book as truth—that you have betrayed yourself into a perfect illustration of what Dr. Besant, Dr. Tagore, Gandhi and others have called your perversion of facts. Such attempts have been going on for a number of years now.[70]

It should come as no surprise that the women actually involved in the campaign for child-marriage legislation make little or no mention of the role of Mayo or *Mother India* in getting the legislation passed.[71]

It is in the act of constructing themselves as the agents or subjects in the discourse about Indian women that we can locate the origins of middle-class Indian women's activism. Indian feminism emerged in the context of middle-class women's challenge to orthodox indigenous patriarchy. The very success of this challenge, however, also strengthened the new nationalist patriarchy and the class/caste stratification of Indian society. This ambivalence has led some scholars, like Kumari Jayawardena, to the pessimistic conclusion that the nationalist struggle did not permit "a revolutionary feminist consciousness" in India.[72] Yet this desire for a "pure" feminist consciousness or agency serves, in the end, to remove the feminist subject from the history of her production within interconnected axes of gender, race, class/caste, nation, or sexuality. A more useful way of locating middle-class Indian feminism is offered in Sangari and Vaid's observation that "nowhere can or have reforms been directed at patriarchies alone, but they have also been involved in re-aligning patriarchy with social stratification (both existing and emerging) and with changing political formations."[73]

As R. Radhakrishnan points out, Sangari and Vaid's observation has the potential for the reconceptualization of historiography as a whole. According to Radhakrishnan, implicit in Sangari and Vaid's comment, is the recognition that the categories of gender, race, nationality, sexuality, or class can neither be made to speak for the totality nor for one another, but are rather relationally implicated in one another. This notion of "relational articulation," he suggests, makes a feminist, nationalist, or class-based historiography, pursued entirely from within itself, highly questionable.[74] Discrete feminist, nationalist, or class-based historiographies arbitrarily fix the boundaries of the "totality" or the total social formation that is the object of their study according to the different priorities that each assigns to gender, nation, or class as distinct categories. Radhakrishnan's notion of a truly critical historiography, however, suggests a new understanding of "totality," not as the product of fixed or given boundaries, demarcated by distinct categories, but as the product of several different relational articulations. Hence, Sangari and Vaid's feminist historiography, conceived within such a radical rethinking of "totality," does not claim to offer a new and improved paradigm for the flawed nationalist understanding of India, but locates its challenge clearly within that nationalist paradigm even as it critiques its very terms.

This reconceptualization of historiography not only emphasizes the need to historicize the conditions in which politics and identities emerge, but also draws attention to the writing of history itself as an interventionary practice that recreates the past for the present. It, therefore, opens up new possibilities for conceptualizing the problem of locating the Indian woman and the politics of middle-class Indian feminism. For example, such a reconceptualization enables me, as an Indian feminist, to see my reading of the "Indian woman" and middle-class Indian feminism in the *Mother India* controversy as not just a retrieval of some lost historical past, but as an intervention in the historical present. The range of women's responses in the *Mother India* controversy indicates that there was nothing necessarily inevitable or predetermined about the voice of the modern Indian woman. In fact, the particular discursive strategies that gave rise to the subject position of the "modern Indian woman" and the politics of middle-class Indian feminism were produced by, and meant to intervene in, a certain historical moment.

This understanding of the historical specificity of the Indian woman allows us to recognize an ideological continuity in the contemporary re-articulation of the Indian woman as the figure of some essentialized identity. In recent years, various communalist and nativist movements in India have engaged in constituting and reconstituting the Indian/Hindu woman as subjects and as objects of virulently antidemocratic discourses.[75] By insisting on historicizing the identity of the Indian woman, we can begin to critique the implications of the resurgence of an essentialized and ahistorical identity, divorced from the political and economic contexts in which it is produced and which it helps sustain.

NOTES

1. Kumkum Sangari and Sudesh Vaid, "Recasting Women: An Introduction" in *Recasting Women: Essays in Indian Colonial History*, ed. K. Sangari and S. Vaid (New Brunswick, N.J., 1990), 2–3.

2. *Ibid.*, 1.

3. Chandra Talpade Mohanty, "Cartographies of Struggle" in *Third World Women and the Politics of Feminism*, ed. C. Mohanty, A. Russo, and L. Torres (Bloomington, 1991), 12–13.

4. Teresa de Lauretis, "Displacing Hegemonic Discourses: Reflections on Feminist Theory in the 1980's," *Inscriptions* 3/4 (1988): 136.

5. Katherine Mayo, *Mother India* (New York, 1927).

6. For a detailed study of Mayo's imperialist politics, see Manoranjan Jha, *Katherine Mayo and India* (New Delhi, 1971).

7. The actual quotation is from the foreword, written by Sarojini Naidu, one of the most famous Indian women of the time, for a collection of essays by Indian women, Evelyn C. Gedge and Mithan Choksi, eds., *Women in Modern India, Fifteen Papers by Indian Women Writers* (Bombay, 1929).

8. See Joanna Liddle and Rama Joshi, "Gender and Imperialism in British India," *South Asia Research* 5, no. 2 (November 1985): 147–165.

9. This tendency of evaluating women's mobilization in India along one or another of these lines is referred to in Geraldine Forbes, "The Politics of Respectability: Indian Women and the Indian National Congress" in *The Indian National Congress, Centenary Hindsights*, ed. D. A. Low. (Delhi, 1988), 54–97.

10. Chandra Mohanty, "Cartographies of Struggle," 5–6.

11. For some exceptions, see Himani Bannerji, "Fashioning a Self: Educational Proposals for and by Women in Popular Magazines in Colonial Bengal," *Economic and Political Weekly* 26, no. 43 (26 October 1991): WS50–WS62 and Susie Tharu and K. Lalitha, "Literature of the Reform and Nationalist Movement" in *Women Writing in India*, vol. 1 (New York, 1991), 143–186. Also useful are Susie Tharu, "Women Writing in India," *Journal of Arts and Ideas*, 20–21 (March 1991):

49–66; and Lata Mani, "Cultural Theory, Colonial Texts: Reading Eyewitness Accounts of Widow Burning" in *Cultural Studies*, ed. Lawrence Grossberg, Cary Nelson, and Paula Treichler. (New York, 1992), 392–408.

12.   Chandra Mohanty, "Cartographies of Struggle," 15.

13.   See Ann Stoler, "Making Empire Respectable: The Politics of Race and Sexuality in 20th Century Colonial Cultures," *American Ethnologist* 16, no. 4 (November 1989): 634–660. Also "Rethinking Colonial Categories," *Comparative Studies in Society and History* 31, no. 1 (January 1989): 134–161.

14.   Lata Mani, "The Production of an Official Discourse on Sati in Early 19th Century Bengal," *Economic and Political Weekly* (April 1987): 32–40 and "Contentious Traditions: The Debate on Sati in Colonial India," *Cultural Critique* 7 (1987): 119–156. Uma Chakravorty, "Whatever Happened to the Vedic Dasi? Orientalism, Nationalism and a Script for the Past," in Sangari and Vaid, eds., *Recasting Women*, 27–87.

15.   Sumanta Banerjee, "Marginalization of Women's Popular Culture in Nineteenth Century Bengal," in Sangari and Vaid, eds., *Recasting Women*, 127–179 and *The Parlour and the Streets* (Calcutta, 1989). For the following discussion, I have drawn from Sangari and Vaid, "Recasting Women: An Introduction," 1–26.

16.   Partha Chatterjee, "The Nationalist Resolution of the Women's Question" in Sangari and Vaid, eds., *Recasting Women*, 233–253 and "Colonialism, Nationalism and Colonized Women: The Contest in India," *American Ethnologist* 16, no. 4 (November 1989): 662–683. For Chatterjee's analysis of Indian nationalist thought in general, see *Nationalist Thought and the Colonial World: A Derivative Discourse?* (London, 1986).

17.   Sangari and Vaid in "Recasting Women: An Introduction" distinguish between what they call the "modernizing" of gender relations in the social reform and nationalist movements and the "democratizing" of gender relations in mass peasant movements, 19–24.

18.   Dipesh Chakrabarty, "Postcoloniality and the Artifice of History: Who Speaks for 'Indian' Pasts?" *Representations* 37 (Winter 1992): 17.

19.   *Ibid.*, 11–14.

20.   Joan Scott, "The Evidence of Experience," *Critical Inquiry* 17 (Summer 1991): 773–797.

21.   The article, written by a British doctor who had served in India, was reprinted in the Calcutta *Statesman* (30 March 1928), 8.

22.   World Citizen [S. G. Warty], *Sister India: A Critical Examination of and a Reasoned Reply to Miss Katherine Mayo's "Mother India"*, (Bombay, 1928), 143.

23.   See *Bombay Daily Mail* 5 September 1927 in India vol. 2 in folder no. 207, series 4, box 37, *Katherine Mayo Papers*, manuscript group no. 35 at Sterling Memorial Library, Yale University [Henceforth: *K. M. Papers*]. For details of this meeting see *Bengalee*, (6 September 1927), 3.

24.   Cited in *Indian Social Reformer* in India vol. 2 in folder 207, series 4, box 37 in *K. M. Papers*. For some examples of the women's protest meetings held all over India see the report of the protest of "ladies" at Noakhali in *Amrita Bazar Patrika*, 17 September 1927, 5; Lahore "ladies" protest, *Amrita Bazar Patrika*, 13 December 1927, 10; protest of Comilla Mahila Samiti Meeting, *Bengalee*, 8 September 1927, 3. Several other protest meetings were reported in the *Statesman*, *Bengalee*, and *Amrita Bazar Patrika* during the period September to December 1927.

25.   For the exchange occasioned by Maya Das's letter, see *Pioneer*, 5 May

1928; 10 May 1928; 18 May 1928; and 31 May 1928 in India vol. 3 in folder no. 207, series 4, box 37, *K. M. Papers.*

26.   Mrs. C. Lakhanpal, *Mother India Aur Uska Jawab* (Dehradun, 1928). I was unable to trace this book; however, I had access to a brief translation of the book in a letter from Wolsey Haig to Mayo's secretary, Henry Field, Letter, dated 22 June 1928 in folder no. 47, series 1, box 6, *K. M. Papers.* Although Haig declares the book to be poorly written, the Indian papers give it a more favorable review. See *Bombay Daily Mail,* 14 January 1928 in India vol. 3 in folder no. 207, series 4, box 37, *K. M. Papers.*

27.   Charulata Devi, *The Fair Sex of India* (Calcutta, 1929).

28.   Mayo had quoted from Cornelia Sorabji's *Between the Twilights* (London, 1908). Biographical information on Sorabji is available in her prolific writings; see especially *India Calling: The Memoirs of Cornelia Sorabj* (London, 1934); *"Therefore": An Impression of Sorabji Kharshedji Langrana and his wife Francina* (Humphrey Milford, 1924); and *Susie Sorabji: Christian-Parsee Educator of Western India* (London, 1932). For a brief sketch of Sorabji's early career, also see Mrs. E. F. Chapman, *Sketches of Some Distinguished Indian Women with a Preface by the Marchioness of Dufferin and Ava* (London, 1891), 121–138.

29.   See Cornelia Sorabji, "The Position of Hindu Women Fifty Years Ago," in *Our Cause: A Symposium of Indian Women,* ed. Shyam Kumari Nehru (Allahabad, 1938). Also Letter from Sorabji to Mayo, dated 29 January 1927, in folder no. 36, series 1, box 5, *K. M. Papers.*

30.   For Sorabji's views on this matter see her *The Purdanashin* (Calcutta, 1917) and *India Recalled* (London, 1936). For critical assessments of Sorabji by her female contemporaries, see Margaret Cousins, *Indian Womanhood Today* (Kitabistan, 1941), 145; Kamaladevi Chattopadhyay, *Indian Women's Battle for Freedom* (New Delhi, reprinted 1983), 51; and for Kamala Sathianadan's view, see Padmini [Sathianadan] Sengupta, *The Portrait of an Indian Woman* (Calcutta, 1956), 41.

31.   Cornelia Sorabji, "Mother India—The Incense of Service: What Sacrifice Can We Make?" *Englishman,* part 1, 31 August 1927, 6–9 and part 2, 1 September 1927, 6–9.

32.   Letter from Sorabji to Mayo, dated 21 November 1928 in folder no. 50, series 1, box 7, *K. M. Papers.* Mayo's letter to the *Statesman* appeared on 5 March 1929, 18.

33.   C. S. Ranga Iyer, *Father India: A Reply to Mother India* (London, 1928 reprint), 72–73. Ramananda Chatterjee, editor of the *Modern Review,* addressed a large gathering of Indians at which he accused Sorabji of providing Mayo with all her information on India, *Bengalee,* 8 September 1927, 3; *Amrita Bazar Patrika,* 15 November 1927, 5.

34.   Letter from Sorabji to Mayo, 10 June 1928, in folder no. 47, series 1, box 6, *K. M. Papers.* For Alice Pennell's position, see the letter from Miss Hotz to Mayo, dated 1 January 1936 in folder no. 78, series 1, box 10, *K. M. Papers.*

35.   See letters from Sorabji to Mayo, dated 6 September 1927 and 1 September 1927 in folder no. 38, series 1, box 5 and letter of 10 June 1928 in folder no. 47, series 1, box 6, *K. M. Papers.*

36.   Katherine Mayo, *The Face of Mother India* (New York, 1935); letter from Sorabji to Mayo, dated 2 May 1935 in folder no. 75, series 1, box 9, and 31 December 1935 in folder no. 76, series 1, box 10, *K. M. Papers.*

37.   Bose's denial appeared in an article written by a British Y.M.C.A. official, in the *Indian Witness*, 7 September 1927 cited in Henry Field, *After "Mother India"* (New York, 1929), 140. For Mayo's concern about Bose's denial, see letter from Mayo to Ellen Stanton, 17 December 1927 in folder no. 41 and Moyca Newell [Mayo's partner] to Col. Baltye, 25 February 1928 in folder no. 43, series 1, box 6, *K. M. Papers.*

38.   For a discussion of Nehru's journalistic contributions see Vir Bharat Talwar, "Feminist Consciousness in Women's Journals in Hindi, 1910–1920" in Sangari and Vaid, eds., *Recasting Women*, 204–232. See also Uma Nehru, "Whither Women" in S. K. Nehru, ed., *Our Cause*, 403–419.

39.   Nehru was married to the journalist Shyamlal Nehru, uncle of the famous Jawaharlal Nehru. For an assessment of Nehru as too "westernized" see Vijaylakshmi Pandit [Uma Nehru's niece by marriage], *The Scope of Happiness: A Personal Memoir* (New York, 1979), 194–195 and interview with Indira Gandhi [Nehru's grand niece] in Promilla Kalhan, *Kamala Nehru: An Intimate Biography* (Delhi, 1973), 133.

40.   *Miss Mayo ki "Mother India" (Sachitra Hindi Unuwad) jis me Srimati Uma Nehru likhit "Bhumika" tatha paschimi samajyawad ke vishay me "Miss Mayo se do do bate"* (Allahabad, 1928).

41.   Katherine Mayo, *Slaves of the God* (New York, 1929), 237.

42.   For a discussion of Naidu in these terms, see Geraldine Forbes, "The Women's Movement in India: Traditional Symbols and New Roles," in *Sectarian, Tribal and Women's Movements* vol. 2 of *Social Movements in India*, ed. M.S.A. Rao (Delhi, 1979), 149–165; and Meena Alexander, "Sarojini Naidu: Romanticism and Resistance," *Economic and Political Weekly* 20, no. 43 (26 October 1985): ws68–ws71.

43.   Naidu's speech was reported in the *Times* (London), 5 September 1927, 5. For an extract of Mayo's interview in which she quotes from Naidu's speech, see folder no. 38, series 1, box 5, *K. M. Papers.*

44.   For Naidu's telegram to the Calcutta meeting, see *Forward*, 7 September 1927 in India vol. 2 in folder no. 207, series 4, box 37, *K. M. Papers.*

45.   Quoted in the *Statesman*, 24 January 1928, 6. See also *Hindu*, 24 January 1928 in India vol. 2 in folder no. 207, series 4, box 37, *K. M. Papers.*

46.   See *Statesman*, 30 January 1929, 10.

47.   For Naidu's refusal to discuss Mayo in the U.S., see Tara Ali Baig, *Sarojini Naidu* (New Delhi 1974), 99–100; and Padmini Sengupta, *Sarojini Naidu* (Bombay, 1966), 209–211.

48.   Naidu's triumphant U.S. trip is covered in the *New York Times*, 14 October 1928, 14; 28 October 1928, 6; and 3 March 1929, 15. For the efforts of Mayo and her supporters to sabotage Naidu's reception in the U.S. see Letter from Sutton to Mayo, dated 22 September 1930 in folder no. 56 in series 1, box 8, *K. M. Papers.* Also see the publication of Henry Field's [Mayo's secretary], *After "Mother India,"* with its unfounded charge that Naidu had attempted to bribe an American woman who had been killed in a Gandhi-led demonstration in Bombay.

49.   Chatterjee, "The Nationalist Resolution," 243.

50.   Mayo was now seen as an authority on Indian women in some women's circles abroad; she was invited by the League of Nation's Fellowship Branch to head the Indian delegation on Child Health. See letter from Miss Gail Barker, dated 9 September 1927, in folder no. 38, series 1, box 5, *K. M. Papers.* For the Daughters

of the American Revolution, and other conservative women's groups' support for Mayo, see the Colony Club meeting of women's groups in the U.S. held on 27 November 1927, letter from Field to Mrs. Henry Loomis, 19 October 1927, in folder 39, series 1, box 5; copy of the resolutions passed at this meeting, see folder 42, series 1, box 6, *K. M. Papers*.

51. Rathbone's sense of "responsibility" for the condition of women in India is discussed in Barbara Ramusack, "Cultural Missionaries, Maternal Imperialists, Feminist Allies: British Women Activists in India 1865–1945," *Women's Studies International Forum* 13, no. 4 (1990): 309–321. For the significance of the condition of women in India for the self-identity of British feminism in the nineteenth century, see Antoinette Burton, "The White Woman's Burden: British Feminists and 'The Indian Woman' 1865–1915," *Women's Studies International Forum* 13 no. 4 (1990): 245–308.

52. Letter from Rathbone to Mayo, 24 August 1927, in folder no. 37, series 1, box 5, *K. M. Papers*.

53. Mrs. I. Ameer Ali's letter to the *Times* is quoted in *Statesman*, 14 December 1927, 12. Ali's letter also provoked a response from a "Rani of India" who argued that women behind the veil were indeed voiceless.

54. The second two-day conference was reported in the *Times*, 8 October 1929, 9 and 9 October 1929, 9. The report of the conference in the *Statesman* appeared under the heading "Indian Women Lively," 9 October 1929, 9. The details of the conflict between Rathbone and Rau is discussed in Mary D. Stocks, *Eleanor Rathbone: A Biography* (London, 1949), esp. 137 and Dhanvanthi Ram Rau, *An Inheritance: The Memoirs of Dhanvanthi Ram Rau* (London, 1977), esp. 170–172.

55. See his "Mother India-Swaraj and Social Reform," *Fortnightly Review* 122, no. 633 (2 January 1928): 182.

56. Letter signed by Dhanvanthi Rama Rau, Hannah Sen, and others appeared in the *Times*, 22 October 1929, 12. Rathbone's reply was published on 24 October 1929, 12. A letter supporting Rathbone's complaint that Indian women were politicizing women's issues appeared under the name Eva Mary Bell on 31 October 1929, 10.

57. Chakrabarty, "Postcoloniality and the Artifice of History," 18.

58. This point has been made in the context of discourses about nineteenth century property and marriage legislation in Britain in Rosemary Hennessey and Rajeshwari Mohan, "The Construction of Women in Three Popular Texts of Empire: Towards a Critique of Materialist Feminism," *Textual Practice* 3, no. 3 (Winter 1989): 323–359.

59. Quoted in Sengupta, *The Portrait of an Indian Woman*, 179–180.

60. The statement of Margaret Cousins, an Irish woman and pioneer of the all-India women's organizations, on behalf of the WIA, was quoted in the *Indian National Herald* 17 September 1927 in India vol. 2 in folder no. 207, series 4, box 37, *K. M. Papers*.

61. For the report of the WIA protest meeting, see *Hindu*, 29 September 1927 in India vol. 2 in folder 207, series 4, box 37, *K. M. Papers*.

62. The events of the meeting have been reconstructed from the *Bombay Daily Mail*, 27 December 1927 and the letter-to-editor in the *Hindu*, 12 January 1927 in India vol. 3 in folder no. 207, series 4, box 37, *K. M. Papers*.

63. For a background of the Non-Brahmin movement, see Gail Omvedt,

Cultural Conflict in a Colonial Society: The Non-Brahmin Movement in Western India, 1873–1930 (Poona, 1976).

64. See Rameshwari Nehru, *Gandhi is My Star: Speeches and Writings of Smt. Rameshwari Nehru*, comp. and ed. Somanth Dhar (Patna, 1950), 52.

65. For a history of child-marriage and age-of-consent reforms, see Geraldine Forbes, "Women and Modernity: The Issue of Child Marriage in India," *Women's Studies International Quarterly*, 2 (1979): 407–419. For a general history of the AIWC, see Bharati Ray, *Women's Struggle: A History of the All India Women's Conference 1927–1990* (New Delhi, 1990).

66. Rameshwari Nehru, "Early Marriage," in Nehru, ed., *Our Cause*, 256–267.

67. Katherine Mayo, *Volume 2* (London, 1931).

68. See Kamaladevi Chattopadhyay, *Inner Recesses, Outer Spaces: Memoirs* (New Delhi, 1986), 113–117 and Rau, *An Inheritance*, 151.

69. See *New York Times*, 10 February 1928, 13. Papers in Britain, like the *Edinburgh Evening News*, 10 February 1928; *Star*, 10 February 1928; *Reynolds Illustrated News*, 12 February 1928; among others, gave sole credit to Mayo's book, see Great Britain vol. 2 in folder no. 207, series 4, box 38, *K. M. Papers.* The view continues today; see the biographic entry on Mayo by William E. Brown Jr. in vol. 30 of *Encyclopedia of American Biographies*, 20, *K. M. Papers.* Historians also continue to differ in their evaluations of Mayo's contribution to women' reform; William W. Emilsen, "Gandhi and Mayo's *Mother India*," *South Asia* 10, no. 1 (1 June 1987): 69–82 credits Mayo with the reform, ignoring entirely the women's movement in India. R. K. Sharma, *Nationalism, Social Reform and Indian Women: A Study in the Interaction between the National Movement and the Movement of Social Reform among Indian Women 1921–1937* (Patna, 1981), 198–212, argues that Mayo had no role in getting reform legislation passed.

70. Letter from Blanche Wilson, no date, in folder no. 42, series 1, box 6, *K. M. Papers.*

71. For some examples, see Jahan Ara Shahnawaz, *Father and Daughter* (Lahore, 1971), 97–98; Hansa Mehta, *Indian Women* (Delhi, 1981), 63; Amrit Kaur, *Challenge to Women* (Allahabad, 1946), 5; and the collection of essays in Kamaladevi Chattopadhyay et al., eds., *The Awakening of Indian Women* (Madras, 1939).

72. Kumari Jayawardena, *Feminism and Nationalism in the Third World* (London, 1986), 107–108. This point has been made in Mary John, "Postcolonial Feminists in the Western Intellectual Field: Anthropologists and Native Informants?" *Inscriptions* 5 (1989): 49–74.

73. Sangari and Vaid, "Recasting Women: An Introduction," 19.

74. R. Radhakrishnan, "Nationalism, Gender and Narrative," in *Nationalisms and Sexualities,* ed. Andrew Parker et al. (New York, 1992), esp. 79–82.

75. The importance that such questions hold for our sense of the contemporary historical situation in India is spelled out in Kumkum Sangari, "Introduction: Representations in History," *Journal of Arts and Ideas* 17 and 18 (June 1989): 3–7. For an excellent example of the currency of the Indian/Hindu woman in some contemporary communal discourses in India, see Tanika Sarkar, "The Woman as Communal Subject: Rashtrasevika Samiti and Ram Janmabhoomi Movement," *Economic and Political Weekly* 26, no. 35 (31 August 1991): 2057–2062.

Theorizing Deviant Historiography

JENNIFER TERRY

I find myself for a moment in the interesting position of not knowing whether what I have to say should be regarded as something long familiar and obvious or as something entirely new and puzzling. But I am inclined to think the latter.
—Sigmund Freud, "Splitting of the Ego in the Defensive Process," 1938

The forces operating in history are not controlled by destiny or regulative mechanisms, but respond to haphazard conflicts. They do not manifest the successive forms of a primordial intention and their attraction is not that of a conclusion, for they always appear through the singular randomness of events.
—Michel Foucault, "Nietzsche, Genealogy, History," 1977

At what price can subjects speak the truth about themselves as mad persons? . . . How can the truth of the sick subject be told?
—Foucault, "Critical Theory / Intellectual History"

Feminist Theoretical Lineages of Deviant Historiography: A Retrospective Preface

The following essay was originally composed for one of the earliest conferences on queer theory.[1] To relocate the essay in the present volume, I want to signal how feminist theoretical debates over two complex and fruitful terms—identity and experience—implicitly informed its original composition. These terms pose particular problems for the disciplinary framework of women's history and perhaps for feminist politics in general, as well as for the emerging field of queer history. An impressive array of feminist theorists have taken on these two terms, examining in detail how

Thanks to Ann-Louise Shapiro for editorial suggestions, and to Jacqueline Urla, Nasser Hussain, Teresa de Lauretis, Patricia White and Donna Haraway for emotional, political, and intellectual support. This essay appeared in a slightly different form in *differences: A Journal of Feminist Cultural Studies* 3, no. 2 (1991): 55–74. Reprinted by permission.

they are constructed and how they operate, including both what these terms enable and what they constrain, in the strategic articulation of feminist political claims and in the writing of history.[2] To go back over such immense theoretical territory is too large a task here, but I do want to suggest several bridge points between debates over these terms within feminist theory and the terms of the emerging field of queer theory where the following essay is primarily situated.

In a brilliant summary of generative contradictions within U.S. feminist theory, Elizabeth Weed warns that identity and the writing of any identity in terms of narrative coherence represents a lure which limits or fixes a set of possibilities which "can secure the individual and the rational subject in their place with all the political fragmentation and isolation that implies."[3] Instead, Weed argues for "another kind of intervention" aimed at "displac[ing] questions of coherence and origin to interrogate the effects of [the subject's] own constitution."[4] Weed's intervention, though not directly focused upon historical work, signals a crucial operation in writing a *history of difference*, and avoids the rigid boundary-drawing now embedded in identity-based projects. Through this interrogation, the critical scope of history is broadened to look, not at women or gay people or African Americans per se, but at the analytic categories and social systems of race, gender, class, and sexuality which, through dividing practices, construct these subjects as well as their heretofore unmarked opposites. Weed's strategy would lay bare the operations by which "women," "people of color," and creatures identified as "lesbians" and "gay men" are discursively produced, as opposed to taking them as given objects or essential, embodied perspectives from which to tell or "experience" history. In the following essay, I attempt to theorize such an intervention for analyzing the historical production of a class of subjects called (sexual) deviants.

To a significant degree, what we might call the historiography of difference gains its power from the very tendency within women's history upon which Weed focuses her critique: the idea of *identity* as a stable quality shared by women across historical periods. Questions of silence and invisibility animated the "hidden from history" model which launched the field of women's history in its early days. And this model necessarily relied upon some idea of a stable or essential group called "women" who could be discovered,

excavated, and restored to speech and visibility from the obscurity
of the past of "His Story." But even in its most popular form,
"herstory" came to be not simply an additive to "history," but
carried the seeds of a radical critique of existing historiography. As
Joan Scott has noted, it "occasioned a crisis for orthodox history"
by multiplying stories and subjects as well as by showing that
history, like other fields of inquiry, is written from the perspective
of its author, carrying with it the vision and blind spots of that
point of view.[5] This meant that there was no single or narrow truth
about history, and in retrospect we can see that the crucial differences offered by historical accounts of women are among the most
valuable consequences of this decentering of orthodox history.
However, women's history, to a substantial degree, did not refuse
the idea of accuracy and truth, provided one furnished adequate
and reliable evidence to support one's claims and took into account
the lives lived at the margins of social power. Despite, then, the
limitations embedded in this adherence to conventions of accuracy,
it would be hard if not impossible to imagine theorizing a history
of difference without the ambitious and crucial projects that placed
women at the center of historical analysis, and thus began to
unsettle sacred aspects of traditional historical inquiry.

Turning to the second critical term, "experience," it is clear
that, in feminist theory in general and women's history in
particular, the term has taken on a great deal of power as a tool for
arguing that histories that emanate from the universal standard of
generic Man are themselves partial. Invoking "women's experience" has been a way to empower women in history (both women
historians and their subjects) by privileging a different perspective
from "Man's experience." Again, Weed, glossing the work of Paula
Treichler and Denise Riley, cautions against the trap of viewing
"experience" as authentic evidence upon which to ground theory
and politics.[6] Treichler notes that the "I" in the enunciation of
autobiographical "experience" privileges the individual, a vestige
of bourgeois humanism that reenacts the subject/society opposition and places other ways of approaching history outside the realm
of critical analysis. And, further, when it is a "we" which is
enunciated, a host of seductive but profoundly homogenizing
mechanisms are brought into play.

Revolutionary criticism generated by feminists of color in the early 1980s raised crucial questions about these homogenizing moves as they played out in many instances where "women's experience" in its unmodified form was invoked. This very important intervention came in the form of Lorraine Bethel's crucial question: "What Chou Mean *We*, White Girl"?[7] Political and theoretical crises over the claims of women's collective experiences, particularly across racial differences, demanded a greater sophistication among feminist theorists and historians to clarify what qualifies as experience, for whom and when.

Scott, in her particular critique of the use of "experience" as evidence in historical work, points to several assumptions upon which historians rely when they take stock of "lived experience."[8] Scott's critique is perhaps most useful for rethinking some of the limitations of social history, for many social historians fall back on a notion of experience as that which is *real*, existing prior to discourse or interpretation, and thus constituting the raw material to provide an authentic basis for the historian's account. "Experience" in these terms is transparent; that is, merely *lived* by its subjects and *discovered* by the historian. In her critique, Scott attempts to show how this use of experience as bedrock evidence masks the historian's decisions about what qualifies as evidence in any given account. Beyond this, the assumption that experience is transparent "fixes" the subject as authentic, self-knowing, and self-expressive in a holistic humanist fashion.

This foundational category of experience clearly influenced Charles Tilly in defining the broad parameters of social history as a field that examines how the masses of ordinary people lived the big shifts in history.[9] This approach offered a generation of historians the means for interpreting various kinds of events at various strata of social organization. Thus, it also provided a strong impetus to historians attempting to locate women in history. Women's history, in its close relationship to other projects in social history, has been interested in the relationship between the subjective feelings of women (individually and in collectivities), and the larger historical and social fields in which they were situated. Thus, the "lived experience" of women is commonly invoked in relation to massive structural shifts in society, the family, the economy, the state, and the world. Not only do women become authentic

subjects in the historical process, but their experience is presumed
to be prediscursive, existing as something that can be used for the
reconstruction of reality by the historian in much the same way
that the subjects "lived" it. An additional problem results in the
formulation of collective experience where differences within and
among subjects in the collectivity are elided rather than traced.
And while "experience" affords a way of endowing historical
actors with agency, it is an agency grounded in the notion of the
realm of a *real* outside of discursive construction, as if "experience"
were an essential and boundable truth, knowable and livable prior
to interpretation.

Scott is concerned with getting historians to see the discursively constructed nature of "experience" as they invoke it, noting
how it operates in the production of different classes of subjects.
Her critique can be extended to a tendency within gay and lesbian
history and theory. There, too, "experience" is commonly invoked
as a way to make one's case stronger, especially through appropriations of biographical sources. In these kinds of histories, the
historical actor's experience is tied to consciousness and self-
knowledge, and used to produce an authoritative account in which
the historian claims a position more akin to that of a scribe.

However, this understanding of experience has been a persistent and central problem for scholars researching the place of
lesbians and gay men in history. In most cases, the particular
predicament posed to queer historians pertains to source material
itself. The evidence of experience in an overwhelming number of
accounts of lesbianism and male homosexuality is, in fact, inscribed
within the clinical and pathologizing mechanisms that brought the
deviant subject into being and induced it to speak. In other words,
reconstructing lesbian and gay experience entangles the historian
in discursive analyses of pejorative labels, medical diagnoses, and
penological categorizations of homosexual subjects. Of course, the
deviant subject is neither isomorphically interchangeable with, nor
totally encompassing of, the subjectivities of "lesbians" and "gay
men;" the deviant subject occupies a particular position in a
discursive and historiographic field.[10]

It is this subject position—that of the deviant subject—which
I am interested in theorizing as part of the larger project of
developing a history of difference. In those sources that render or

effect the *deviant subject*, we find an even more unmistakable example of how experience is not merely mediated, but constructed through discourse. Again, I would agree with Scott's general claim that experience is never prediscursive or transparent. But I am interested in how the process of reading for deviance which is implied in constructing a genealogy of "lesbians" and "gay men" problematizes the evidence of experience in particular ways, driving Scott's point home with a vengeance. A practical problem of having little "raw material" or authentic "experience" that is not already configured in pejorative medical, psychiatric, penal, or religious discourses leads to a theoretical problem highlighted in queer history which Foucault summed up in a question: "How can the truth of the sick subject be told?"[11]

Queer historians in most cases do not have the illusion of direct recourse to lives and experiences of their subjects in the past to the same degree that women's historians, especially in the early days of the discipline, believed themselves to have (although even there a shift in optics was necessary in order to locate the spheres in which women "lived"). In practical and theoretical terms, historians of homosexuality had to come to terms with the fact that their subjects often spoke only through adversarial doctors, police, and clergy. There can be no illusion of transparency or unmediated access to the subjects' essential experience nor, ultimately, to the experience of the authority who fashions subjects as deviant in medical records or police files. In psychiatric accounts that spawn the homosexual as a deviant species, the humanist hopes of restoring the deviant to full personhood (even in fictitious terms) are dashed in a dramatic fashion because the apparatus that produces his or her subjectivity is predicated on a diagnosis of pathology. In quite literal terms, the doctor dictates the subjects' words and experiences. There can be no deviant experience outside of discourse (or, for that matter, outside of diagnosis). This predicament, brought out in bold relief in queer history, is a point I try to make in my discussion of *deviant subjectivity* which follows, and a point I regard as crucial for any project in the history of difference.

As the terms *identity* and *experience* have been increasingly problematized, we now find a vexing but productive tension in theory and methods within several different branches of cultural and social history. This tension revolves around the critical question of what should be or can be the central category of historical analysis. Should it be *identity* ("women," "African Americans," "lesbians" or "gay men")? Or should it be the *system(s)* by which differences are constituted? Again, we can gain insight by surveying some of the debates within women's history and ethnic history in order to sketch out directions for queer history. Today in women's history, for example, attention to women in various pasts has spurred scholars on to an interrogation of the systems by which gender differences have been constituted and propelled. Though some skeptics complain that this slide from "women's history" to "gender history" represents a return to telling men's stories at the expense of women's, the radical potential of gender history lies in its ability to trace how inegalitarian power relations between "women" and "men" have been produced and enforced historically in order to demolish these relations now. Gender becomes a "useful category" *not* because it recuperates women to humanist dignity (thus "fixing" them once again), but because it threatens to interrupt radically the existing oppressive terms of gender difference.[12] Similarly, one could interrogate race *as a system* with particular operations that produce all modern subjects—whether they are "people of color" or "white people"—and shift the terms away from a merely additive model of telling the history of black people, for example, to a critical and deconstructive approach which examines how racial differences are produced. Again, the radical potential is in seeing how racism is produced in order to take it apart.

These questions and disciplinary tensions are relevant to the emerging fields variously called lesbian and gay studies, sexuality studies, and queer theory. Here too we find a tension between, on the one hand, making *queer* an identity which grounds intellectual production and political positioning, and, on the other hand, making *sexuality* a "useful category" from which to construct a history of difference. Perhaps because of its historical emergence after significant disciplinary inroads were made by social historians, lesbian and gay history has had an accelerated journey to the kind of theoretical and methodological tensions existing in "women's history" today.[13] A strong critique of transhistorical and transcultural essentialism vis-à-vis sexual identity appeared in early works in the history of sexuality, which placed questions of identity and experience under critical scrutiny and argued for the historical specificity of gay and lesbian identity formation.[14] Even so, as in women's history, we find examples of lesbian and gay history aimed at recuperating or claiming gays in distant pasts.[15] This approach has been unsettled by a shift toward focusing on how normative and deviant sexualities get defined, and are thus enabled to set the terms in relation to which all kinds of subjects are constrained to exist. A history of *difference* thus becomes a history of *deviance* in the piece that follows, signalling the mechanism by which the norm is always silently and visibly constructed through a noisy, anxious, and flamboyant fixation on the deviant.

Yet there remain theoretical and political differences among historians of homosexuality as to whether one must posit at least a provisionally coherent lesbian or gay identity which can be identified in the past, or if one should trace the conditions by which the myriad identity positions of the *homosexual* as well as the *heterosexual* came into being and operate. Again, among some practitioners of lesbian and gay history, we find a political and intellectual worry that lesbian and gay history will be subsumed in a larger history of sexuality which would focus its gaze on heterosexuality and, in the process, bury the particular conditions and stories of same-sex lovers. It is my own belief that historiographic practices that expose the means by which both "homosexuals" and "heterosexuals" are produced constitute interventions in the reproduction of inegalitarian and homophobic relations of difference, and will in fact *require* the telling of queer stories, many of which involve (intentional and unintentional) resistances, accommodations, and strategic appropriations of the mechanisms by which deviant subjects are produced.

I assume, in the following piece, that Weed's caution about the lure of identity and narrative coherence is as important for the nascent field of queer theory as it is for feminist theory. I take from Gayatri Spivak the suggestion that in tracing the history of subalternity—whether it be of "women" or of "queers"—one must look for difference rather than stable categories of identity. In other words, deconstructive historiography strategically mobilizes constructed identities ("women," "men," "heterosexuals," "lesbians," "subalterns") in order to watch their *diachronic construction* through systems of binary opposition. This is what I have attempted to sketch out in what follows.

Theorizing Deviant Historiography

The work of an historian of the present is today a form of political activism. I write as a historian of homosexual subjectivity—which is to say, as a historian of our presence under the present circumstances of widespread homophobia. I do not attempt to correct the historical record through locating great or even common homosexuals in the past in order to reconstruct their effaced stories, for such a project would presume that the subject of homosexuality is essentially transhistorical and transcultural. Instead I look for the conditions that make possible, and those that constrain, the emergence and vitality of "lesbians" and "gay men" who populate our present. This is a project in theorizing new historiographic practices for tracing *deviant subject formation*. In the following pages, I explore theoretical possibilities for the development of *deviant historiography*—a method for mapping the complex discursive and textual operations at play in the historical emergence of subjects who come to be called lesbians and gay men. I begin first by considering the methodological utility of Foucault's *effective history* and Gayatri Spivak's deconstruction for contending with the predicament of historical elision and pathologization faced by homosexual subjects. I then deploy these strategies in order to explore the production of a counterdiscursive *deviant subjectivity*, forged in conflict with medico-scientific discourses that pathologize homosexuality. Finally, I conclude with some speculations on a future agenda for deviant historiography.

The New Archivist of (Sexual) Deviance

The territory of historical interpretation is charged with power not only to decide upon the important elements of a story—"the events" and "the actors"—but to emplot these elements according to certain narrative designs that bind the moment in question and deliver truth at the point of narrative closure.[16] Foucault disrupts this grand delivery of truth through his reading of Nietzsche's notion of genealogy. In contrast to the ideal continuity of traditional history which fixes a series of events into a truthful story of the past, Foucault's *effective history* is attentive to the ruptures and discontinuities in history; it is "without constants."[17] By *effective history* Foucault is not suggesting a more efficient or instrumentally useful kind of history (as the term's translation into English might suggest). To the contrary, he is interested in thinking about genealogy as a process that takes stock of *effects*. *Effects* are the most acute manifestations of events, often where and when they appear to be most in contradiction or resistance to rationalistic sequencing. They disrupt the seduction of (historical) narrative in its desire for the climactic truth which is the product of resolution enjoyed in the afterglow of achieved textual tumescence.[18] Genealogy allows a dissociation that deconstructs coherent historical truth-telling; it "refuses the certainty of absolutes" and is "capable of shattering the unity of man's being" which relied on a version of the past for its coherence and dominance.[19]

This kind of historical method is an interventionist strategy useful and necessary to those positioned in the margins of dominant accounts. It is, however, more than a deconstruction of traditional history. It involves what Foucault calls "historical sense"— a strategic awareness of points of emergence or "possibilities" existing at particular historical moments in the formation of particular discourses. It traces the conditions whereby marginal subjects apprehend possibilities for expression and self-representation in a field of contest. This genealogical method allows us to theorize a counterdiscursive position of history-telling which neither fashions a new coherence, nor provides a more inclusive resolution of contradicting "events." It is *not* an alternative narrative with its own glorious tumescence peopled by previously elided but now recuperated Others. *Effective history*—that is, a history concerned with effects—exposes, not the events and actors elided by traditional history, but the *processes* and *operations* by which these elisions occurred.

The topography of effective history is a "place of confrontation but not . . . a closed field offering the spectacle of struggle among equals. It is a 'non-place,' a pure distance, which indicates that the adversaries do not belong to a common space."[20] Gilles Deleuze, in reading Foucault, talks about the new archivist who sees effects neither in a vertical hierarchy of propositions stacked on top of one another, nor in clean horizontal relationships between phrases that seem to respond to one another. Instead the new archivist "will remain mobile, skimming along in a kind of diagonal line that allows him [*sic*] to read what could not be apprehended before."[21] Effects are like shrapnel in a discursive battle. They are not to be forged into a new functioning story but remain as evidence of the violence of dominant discourses. They are traces of the unremitting and carefully crafted terms of hegemonic accounts which structure conditions of marginality for certain subjects who are marked as Others. Effects are deviant fragments which fall outside these accounts.

The new archivist of deviance, from oppositional subject positions in the historiographic field, looks not only for how subjects are produced and policed, but for how they are resistant and excessive to the very discourses from which they emerge. I am not suggesting a privileged vantage point above the discursive traffic. On the contrary, the new archivist is on the street, in the thick of things, occupying a mobile subject position. Subject positions are population points on the map of effective history, constituted through various modes of meaning production and contingent upon discursive power relations. They are places from which to see, think, and act. A subject is the occupant of a subject position situated as such through discourse, or, more precisely, through the relay or relation between hegemonic and counter discourses.

The notion of subject positions created by and through discourse has produced compelling theoretical and political possibilities both for understanding the various intersecting and contradictory positions particular individuals might occupy at particular moments in heterogenous social fields,[22] and for performing a *diagnostics of power*.[23] Social fields are the very matrices of power in which subject positions are staked out and subjects circulate. What Deleuze draws out of Foucault is the radical potential for a modality of historiographic activism taken up by the new archivist who, from a position of deviance, finds effects that exceed the truth-telling of narrative history, and thus exposes the processes of deviant subject formation.

Spivak raises the crucial problem faced by genealogists of marginality who are methodologically constrained to search for subaltern consciousness in elite history, those accounts of the past which simultaneously constitute the dominant historiography and the history of dominance.[24] In analyzing the predicament of developing a subaltern history of British colonial rule, Spivak says that if we stay strictly within the terms of traditional historiography, we have only the elite accounts of what happened. The apparatus of colonial rule provides the sources from which to make a narrative history which poses as truth. In this way, the search for subaltern consciousness in the past relies on the dominant account, not only for source material, but also for tracing how these sources constructed the very conditions of subalternity. Because the subaltern subject is, in this textual sense, produced by the dominant historical account, it cannot be understood independent of the documentary evidence of the elite. Conversely, in this strictly textual sense, the elite, within traditional historical accounts, is itself a textual effect, the residue of the subaltern upon which it is reliant for its very definition. To destabilize such an account and, thus, to locate subaltern agency, Spivak suggests a subversive reading strategy from *within* the dominant account which questions how this account establishes itself as "truthful." By this operation, an archivist/reader reveals that the dominant account is never fully capable of containing the subaltern it launches, nor fully able to stabilize itself.

Throughout her discussion, Spivak is deconstructing the notion of self-consciousness in a broader sense but holding onto the strategic discursive position called the "subaltern" in order to illuminate the violent qualities of elite historiography. Acknowledging that "history" is both textual practice and textual product, she proposes that we read against the grain of these accounts. The power to expose the partiality of the dominant account and, thus, destabilize it is generated from the counterdiscursive position of the subaltern. But instead of looking for another *identity* ("the subaltern"), the reader watches for *difference* within textual operations of elite accounts.

Spivak's method of reading for difference is useful for considering the recently named identities of "homosexual," "lesbian," and "sex pervert" which were produced and elaborated through the medico-scientific and criminological discourses in the late nineteenth and throughout the twentieth centuries in the West. Deconstructive historiographic strategies proposed by Spivak and Foucault are indeed useful, though not for the discovery of great gays in history whose essence travels across historical and discursive formations and whose coherent stories must be told. "Alternative" historical narratives claiming to recuperate the truth of homosexuality strive for a kind of respectability, a restoration, a coherence, an identity which is illusory. For Spivak, the notion of a coherent and autonomous subaltern subject whose history can be disentangled from colonial accounts is preposterous; similarly, a lesbian and gay history which hopes to find homosexuals totally free of the influences of pathologizing discourses would be a historiographic optical illusion. At best, we can map the techniques by which homosexuality has been marked as different and pathological, and then locate subjective resistances to this homophobia.

In theorizing the complexities of deviant historiography, we cannot overlook the problem of sources. Three main dilemmas exist for historians interested in researching homosexuality:

1. Materials documenting the discrete identities of "lesbians" and "gay men" are specific to certain places and periods. Recent works tracing the cultural and historical construction of sexuality raise critical questions about the imposition of sexual identities from the Euro-American present to the past and to different cultures around the world.[25] One cannot simply "find" homosexuals everywhere.

2. Much of the material written by lesbians and gay men has been destroyed through homophobic vandalism, effacement, and suppression. Thus, we are left with few accounts that offer us representations of sexuality produced by those living at the sexual margins.

3. Many of the extant historical materials concerning homosexuality and lesbianism are overwhelmingly pejorative and oppressive accounts of sin, criminality, or pathology. While it may be depressing to think that these account for the largest number of sources on homosexuality from the late nineteenth century until at least the beginning of the homophile movement, these sources are ripe for the destabilizing strategies of reading for difference. They constitute the hegemonic discursive field for watching the conflictual interplay between scientists, doctors, police, and clergy on the one hand, and deviants on the other.

When examining such accounts of homosexuality, we would

do well to heed Spivak's strategic refusal of *identity* in favor of *difference*, or for my purposes here, *deviance*. The new archivist is a reader-against-the-grain who recognizes traces of deviant subjects revealed through conflict within dominant accounts. Instead of positing a fixed deviant subject position, the archivist finds a provisional position corresponding to a discursively fashioned, outlawed, or pathologized sexual identity—the location from which a resistant historiography can be generated.

The Production of Deviant Subjectivity

Through a process of what I call *vengeful countersurveillance,* I am interested in exposing the ways we have been constituted as deviant subjects and, most importantly, in locating how we have spoken back against the terms of a pathologizing discourse that has relied upon us parasitically to establish its own authority. By *deviant subjectivity* I mean the process by which a position or identity-space is constructed discursively by sexology and medicine and strategically seized upon by its objects of study, who, in their processes of self-inquiry, are at moments compliant and at other moments resistant to pejorative or pathologizing characterizations of themselves by doctors.[26]

I look for texts that feature homosexual subjects engaged in their own investigation of how they came to desire others of the same sex. These texts reveal historical actors asking what I call *questions of the self*, questions, we might say, of modern homosexual identity: "Who am I?" "How did I come to be this way?" "How and why am I different?" "Is there something wrong with me?" These instances of self-interrogation are often embedded in published psychiatric case histories which allow the archivist to watch the complex interplay between doctors and homosexuals as both attempted to make sense of diverse forms of desire.

As an archivist of deviance, I am presently scrutinizing a particular medico-scientific study of homosexuality conducted in New York City during the late 1930s to chart episodes in the production of deviant subjectivity.[27] This study, sponsored by the Committee for the Study of Sex Variants, is particularly interesting to examine because it involved an extraordinary combination of diagnostic probing techniques. Using methods ranging from anthropometry to psychoanalysis, the study was situated in a

precarious epistemic space between a scopic regime aimed at finding
deviance on homosexuals' bodies, and a quasi-psychoanalytic method
used to interrogate subjects for signs of perversion in their psyches.
The study was generated prior to the emergence of a visible
political gay and lesbian movement, and prior to an organized
opposition to the homophobia within the medical profession.
Therefore, it can be read as an antecedent to our overtly political
emergence because it features "sex variant" subjects engaging in
conflict over the medicalization of homosexuality.

The published report, entitled *Sex Variants: A Study of Homosexual Patterns*, contains over a thousand pages of case histories of
eighty men and women who voluntarily participated in this extensive study.[28] The volume also has several appendices including "The
Gynecology of Homosexuality" which features detailed sketches
of lesbians' genitals. Subjects were given pseudonyms in order to
protect their true identities. In an effort to determine how "sex
variants" were different from the "general population," the subjects were put through an assembly line of expert examinations:
they were interviewed by psychiatrists, examined by various spe-
cialists, photographed, x-rayed, and given a standardized test for
measuring their levels of masculinity and femininity. On the basis
of these various *modalities of objectification*, researchers concluded
that certain psychological and physical patterns distinguished sex
variants from "adjusted" heterosexuals.

Working with this text, I have found many nodal points in
relation to which a resistant subjectivity emerged. Rather than
craft these nodal points into a coherent story about gay and lesbian
life in the 1930s, I use them to locate the sites of conflict, tension,
and resistance between the doctors and the subjects. Following is a
sampling of nodal points of contest, or "relays," which demonstrate processes operating in the production of deviant subject
formation. As you will see, the case histories reveal complex
operations of power within the pathologizing discourse. Watch as
the "sex variants" intervene in the terms of homosexual representation:

RELAY 1: DESIRE IN EXCESS/MOUNTAINS OF LESBIAN FLESH

The doctor begins the case study with a "general impression"
summarizing his initial survey of the subject, noting any unusual

signs that might be related to "sex variance." He notes aggression, excessive size, masculine gait, and forcefulness in the female subjects and weakness, insecurity, flamboyance, and mincing gait in the male subjects. While these were taken as signs of sex inversion, the doctor was baffled when subjects or their lovers boasted about these anomalies or excesses. Furthermore, he did not know what to make of the subjects' descriptions of their lovers as both "feminine" and "aggressive," or "masculine" and "sensitive" since these couplings were seen as fundamentally impossible. Here we witness the interplay between the psychiatrist, Ursula W. and Frieda S.:

> DOCTOR: Ursula is a short, stocky woman of thirty-two who heaves broad shoulders as she swaggers into a room. After expressing her regret that she had agreed to participate in this study, she gradually . . . talked easily and freely. She was much interested in the various examinations and asked many questions. . . . She smoked one cigarette after another, stopping every now and then to hitch up her dress as though she were wearing trousers.[29]

The doctor's authority rests on the subject's complicity in the research. He registers anxiety over her size and the confidence of her gestures. He establishes Ursula as deviant in relation to proper conventions of gender by remarking on her discomfort in a dress.

Elsewhere the doctor gives his impression of Frieda, Ursula's lover:

> DOCTOR: Frieda is a small woman of twenty-eight whose long black hair is graying. She has the pallor, softness, and the general timidity in bearing of an oriental woman. . . . Frieda's artistic productions have attracted attention because they are so masculine. For many years her work was believed to be that of a man. . . . She is a thorough feminist with intense sex bitterness.[30]

Taking distance from the subject, the doctor describes her as foreign, by virtue of her timidity, but goes on to suggest that this outward demeanor of shyness and femininity is a veil over her (true) interior virility which manifests in her sculpture. He then suggests that this is a signifier of her pathological refusal to accept the subordinate position of woman ("sex bitterness").

We go back to Ursula's case history to hear her waxing expansive about her desire for Frieda, strategically deploying clinical terms like "femininity" and "aggressiveness" which she knows the doctor is using in his attempt to make sense of lesbian desire.

URSULA: . . . I found Frieda, the grandest person in the world. She's tiny and very feminine, a fine artist, very virile and aggressive, my equal in aggressiveness and not at all possessive. . . . Love is a form of madness—every part of the body becomes beautiful—caressing and kissing all parts of the body. This is the greatest love of my life. . . . My sex life has never caused me any regrets. I'm very much richer by it. I feel it has stimulated me and my imagination and increased my creative powers.[31]

Ursula refuses the standard opposition between femininity and aggressiveness. The researchers were very curious about how lesbians, in particular, had sex. Hence, in responding to the direct question of how she experienced pleasure, Ursula refused the centrality of genitals, thereby territorializing the lesbian body as capable of polymorphous desires and satisfaction. Furthermore, she narrates her lesbian desire in relation to creative powers, explicitly negating the tragic or pathological definitions of homosexuality.

Meanwhile, Frieda produces a counterdiscourse under the voyeuristic scrutiny of the curious doctor, emphasizing her desire for a mannish woman and reveling in Ursula's excessiveness:

FRIEDA: At twenty-six I found Ursula, a woman I am actually in love with. . . . According to [my friends] she is a big, bold, mannish, fat woman who heaves into a room like a locomotive under full steam. . . . To me this force, this energy, this bigness and boldness are tremendously attractive. My admiration for bulk is such that I really enjoy getting into bed with this mountain of flesh. . . . She is 100 percent masculine, both mentally and physically. . . . I am convinced I will never again be interested in a man. I'm sure I would like to spend the rest of my life with Ursula.[32]

Mountain of flesh, indeed. Unapologetically, Frieda claims her love of mannishness and bigness in women, not men. We can almost hear Frieda chuckling at the doctor's shocked expression.

Not surprisingly, in his closing summary of Frieda's case, the doctor pathologizes Frieda's desire for Ursula by reducing it to an obsession:

DOCTOR: Having thus disposed of men there was nothing left [for Frieda] but the conquest of virile women, of those who had the force, strength and bulk she lacked. . . . She had developed a strange obsession for flesh. Ursula, a big, bold, mannish, fat woman, has satisfied her desires.[33]

He attempts to contain both Frieda's and Ursula's confidence and desires by casting these as pathological symptoms. Thus he reveals not only his inability to comprehend lesbian desire but any leg-pulling on the part of the subjects seems to have gone over his head.

RELAY 2: HOMOSEX MADE EXPLICIT

The subjects were asked to describe their adult sexual desires and to explain in detail what kinds of sex practices and partners they preferred. In this portion of the psychiatric interview, con-frontations were more intricate and embedded in the pathologizing discourse as subjects spoke back in anticipation of the doctors' desire to define the normal and the abnormal at the expense of the subjects. Here we witness the subjects narrating their homosexual desire with a vengeance, being campy, boisterous, and genuinely curious about themselves. They often seized the opportunity to be iconoclastic according to what they imagined would most scandal-ize the doctors: some told stories of promiscuity, intergenerational sex, and affairs with married men and women.

As if to warn the doctor that she has no intention of being "cured" or reformed out of lesbianism, Myrtle, a black vaudevil-lian, traces her precocious desires, embracing them as nearly pri-mordial and crucial to her health and well-being:

MYRTLE: I can't remember when I wasn't interested in women. When I was six I used to stand on the fence and look admiringly at all the women who passed. Even earlier than that I had a lively curiosity about the bodies of little girls. When I was eight I tried to have sex with a little girl. I've played with little girls since I was big enough to raise a hand to pat them and I ain't never gonna stop! . . . Titty calms me. If I can't have it every day I get evil.[34]

Anticipating the psychiatrist would make a predictable link between her lesbianism and maternal desire, Irene described the ecstasy of sex with a lesbian lover whom she could treat as her "son" by day but at whose passionate mercy she would be by night. Here we see a subversive lesbian spin on the family romance:

IRENE: [A] girl twenty-eight years old wished herself on me. . . . For a year she wore boys' clothes and I introduced her as my son. That satisfied my maternal complex. She was powerful and aggressive as far as sex was concerned but in everything else she was completely childish. At night she was a giant and in the day a little child. . . . She was an insatiable little wench and I was burned up most of the time. I wanted so much to play with this youngster that I didn't care whether I worked or not. We stayed in bed for two or three days at a time, repeating our sex play. I never before knew what real sex excitement was. . . . I never knew that anybody could set up a current of electricity such as this girl did in me. And I loved her little soft hand as well as her mouth.[35]

In the framework of the study, the terms *active* and *passive* roughly corresponded to masculinity and femininity. However, again and again the male and female subjects deployed these terms and altered their meanings. We find instances of the subjects describing their sexual preferences, not only in terms of homosexual partner choice, but in terms of the mode or position they most enjoyed. Hence, the explicit narrativizations of sex introduced possibilities unforeseen by the doctors. Not only did men claim passivity and women claim activity, but some subjects expressed a fluid or contextually specific desire to be passive one moment, and active the next. This fluidity confused the researchers who had not adequately separated the complexities of gender from those of sexual orientation or sexual mode.

In an inversion of gender that radically alters the terms of heterosexuality, Susan's sexual mode choice takes precedence over her lesbian object choice when she expresses a desire to have sex (as a "man") with an effeminate homosexual man she imagines to be a "woman":

SUSAN: I feel very safe going places with [a homosexual man]. . . . Somehow in the last year I've had some desire for this boy. He excites me passionately but I never think of having intercourse with him. I do enjoy hugging and kissing. It's the first time I would be intimate with a boy. . . . He's rather effeminate. . . . I feel I would like to make love to him, to lie on top of him. I wouldn't tell him but I think of him as a woman.[36]

In characteristically myopic fashion, the doctor reduces the complexity of Susan's desire to experiment with this man to a matter of convenience and capitulation to social conventions:

DOCTOR: [Susan] wonders whether for the sake of companionship and conventionality she shouldn't marry an effeminate homosexual man.[37]

Clinical voyeurism about homosexual sex gave subjects the opportunity to articulate their desires vividly. In this way, they deployed the power of representing the pleasures of homosexuality and lesbianism, in opposition to the essential constraints of conventional heterosexual and gender arrangements.

RELAY 3: GIRLS ON TOP

The most remarkable instances of confrontation between the female subjects and the doctors occur where the subject claimed, as many of them did, that she could do anything a man could do but better. This is particularly highlighted in lesbians' descriptions of their deft love-making techniques and their remarkable genitals. They are easy to spot in the text because they stir in the doctors a mixture of anxiety, curiosity, terror, and disbelief.

> MYRTLE: As I started going with women [my clitoris] enlarged itself. [It] enlarges when I get steamed up. . . . I insert my clitoris in the vagina just like the penis of a man. . . . Women enjoy it so much they leave their husbands. My clitoris natural is two inches long. Enlarged it's three inches and the thickness of a little finger. I think it's grown half an inch in the past year. I'll have to get a jock strap if it gets much more. . . . While a woman is going down on me I visualize myself as a man and I talk as if I was a man. I say, "Ain't that a good dick? O baby, ain't that good."[38]

Linking race with lesbianism, the psychiatrist notes that "Myrtle's rapport with other women is typical of many homosexual negro women." In an attempt to reassert control over the terms of representation, he simultaneously discounts her claim to sexual superiority by casting it as merely subjective: "With her enlarged clitoris she *says* she is able to produce orgasms in other women."[39]

Moving from the psychiatrist's couch to the gynecologist's examining table, we again find the clitoris inciting clinical fascination and distress, especially in the case of Susan, another black subject, who boasted that she was capable of penetrating her female partners when her clitoris was "erect."

> SUSAN: She [her first lover] would lie on top and rub the clitoris. Her clitoris was not well developed but mine was—about one inch— twice as much as the average. When I realized what it was all about I thought I should take the active part. . . . It's more pleasure and more complete when I'm taking the active part. I like girls who have

lots of experience. It saves a lot of trouble. I like girls who are naturally that way, not curiosity-seekers. Some of them are white. I have no preference. The relations last longer when I'm active. Usually it's about twenty minutes but if the other girl wants to stop I do, to prolong the period before the orgasm. I think they are fond of me because of my large clitoris. I think that's the chief reason. They comment upon it. They whisper among themselves. They say, "she has the largest clitoris."[40]

The doctors were fixated on Susan's clitoris, amazed at her confidence in claiming that she pleased her lovers better than men could. Through life-sized sketches, the doctors attempted to represent visually the action of the clitoris in its so-called "excursions" up and down. In countering Susan's bold claim, they even went so far as to draw the "infeasibility" of clitoral penetration.

In the sketches, Susan's race was frequently noted in connection with the dimensions of her clitoris. Elongated clitorises were noted in several of the African-American lesbian subjects, echoing the common racist representation of the atavistic black man with an unusually long penis. The link, in the white imagination, between blackness and hypersexuality is this time made through the clinical reading of female genitals. These women, through their strategic signification of the clitoris as powerful, appropriated the popular belief that black people were unusually well-endowed and sexually more desirable.

This relay back and forth between Susan and the doctors provides the opportunity for effective history as we watch the operation of power in a discursive field. While the "real woman" to whom the pseudonym "Susan" is assigned remains inaccessible to us, we can locate the subject-effects of this conflictual exchange between the clinical questions posed by the doctors and the subject's powerful response which strikes at one of their greatest fears: the woman who threatens to render men sexually insignificant.

Far from coming to any clear conclusions about the problem of homosexuality, this particular scientific inquiry unleashed explicit narrativizations of lesbian sex and homosexuality between men the likes of which had not yet been heard and which were not fully comprehended by the researchers. The *Sex Variants* study is unusually rich for watching the contest between deviant subjects and the apparatus that constructed them as such. These queer subjects could not be reduced to a medicalized identity; on the contrary, while they participated in this scientific study that assumed from the outset that they were not normal, they were never docile victims. They deployed interventionist strategies within and against a medical discourse in relation to which the subjects— frequently with humor, anger, excess, and irony—asked questions of the self and at the same time eluded the determined and finally frustrated gaze of the doctors.

Differences Among Deviant Subjects

There are irreducible differences in the experiences of lesbians and gay men which raise problems for theorizing them as a unity. These differences are reflected in the source material for tracing the emergence of lesbian subjectivity as distinct from gay male subjectivity. While many aspects of the hidden-from-history hypothesis pertain to gay men as well as lesbians, accounts of lesbianism and male homosexuality are shaped by different kinds of historical elision, different conditions of visibility, and different strategies of resistance. The project of deviant historiography involves mapping these differences.

When it comes to straight notions of homosexuality, images of gay men are most often conjured. Generally speaking, the homosexuality of men is more explicitly documented in the archive in everything from novels to police reports of public sex arrests for sodomy. A persistent problem for historians of lesbianism is to find evidence of its very existence, and particularly of its sexually explicit forms. Even more difficult is locating sources about lesbianism produced by lesbians themselves. Lesbians have not had much of a public sexuality. The policing of lesbianism, like female sexuality in general, has taken a more micropolitical form, focused on enforcing proper gender behavior in the private realm. Lesbians are often seen more as a threat to the family than a threat to the streets, through their rejection of the subordinate role of wife and through their refusals to procreate (at least in conventional terms). Women are less often arrested for "unnatural acts." And on those rare occasions, they confuse the phallocentric police and lawmakers who basically cannot believe that sex between women is *really* possible. Debates over the unnaturalness of male and female homosexuality have led to a quagmire of legal definitions in which lesbianism is usually treated like a misunderstood step-sister. There is no definition of homosexuality on the law books in the United States that is not based primarily on male same-sex practices. And since there is nothing women do together sexually that is singled out by law, lesbianism is cryptically defined through poorly adapted analogies. So, we must ask, how does the public nature of (male) homosexuality render a kind of visibility that lesbianism does not?

The problematic of historical elision is central to the theorization and deployment of deviant historiography. It raises a number of complex and important questions for the political expression of deviant subjects. Since the homophile movement of the 1950s, struggles over visibility and representation form the basis of lesbian and gay political theory and practice in the United States. *How* we are represented, *why* we are represented, and *if* we are represented are central issues of contemporary homosexual politics and identity. We are still in the midst of challenging a legacy of pathology in relation to which we have been constrained to exist. However, as I have tried to suggest, deviant subjectivity is itself evidence of our power, not victimhood.

Gender and sexuality are not the only systems by which differences are marked between and within homosexual subjects. Race, ethnicity, age, and class also structure understandings of homosexuality within both dominant and marginal discourses. The idea of a coherent, full identity that is marked only by homosexuality has been unsettled by the cultural production of lesbians and gay men of color, whose work enacts the multiplicities and contradictions of living at the intersection of many different marginal subjectivities.[41] Deviant historiographers are now confronted with crucial questions about the different ways pathological discourses and historical elision have operated to construct different homosexualities in relation to stratifications of race, gender, class, and age: What are the dangers of assuming that the stamp of pathology is influential and determinative of all homosexual subjectivities? Does resistance to the pathologizing discourse occur differently among different subjects? Specifically, how has the medicalization of homosexuality influenced the conditions of lesbian and gay subjectivity among people of color? Similarly, we must ask how the pathologization of male homosexuality shapes the terms of lesbian subjectivity. And what particular social and historical contextualizations ought we to take into account when tracing the genealogy of what has been called the "remedicalization" of homosexuality, the AIDS epidemic? How do lesbians fit into this remedicalization and how does this influence the terms of lesbian subjectivity? Finally, how can we articulate an activist deviant historiography in the "war of representation" being waged through the epidemic and its spin-off crises of homophobic censorship, rampant antigay and antilesbian discrimination, and intensified queer bashing? I suggest these questions as part of a theoretical agenda for deviant historiography in the present and future.

Subjects in deviant positions are required, as a matter of survival, to have the ability to see and know the rules of the center as well as those of the margins. They are in the complicated position of having to negotiate the intricate and contradictory relationships between, for example, the rules of the courtroom and the semiotics of the street, the conventions of the clinical confession and the limitations to self-knowledge, the demands of the desiring body and the probabilities of risk. Deviant subjects are engaged in a *process* of living in a system of epistemic relay between authoritative knowledge and "experience," and between past and future. Deviant subjects do not set the terms of this in-betweenness—they confuse them.

Teresa de Lauretis has theorized a subject of feminism who is both inside and outside of the ideology of gender, having a strategic awareness of its complex relationship to Woman (the representation) and women (the social subjects). De Lauretis' emphasis on the *processual* character of this subject recalls the figure of the deviant subject who is in a dynamic and contestatory relationship with pathology. Like the subject of feminism, the deviant subject operates in relation to pathological representations on the one hand, and the social subjects called "lesbians" and "gay men," on the other. And like the mobile archivist, neither de Lauretis' subject nor the deviant subject is fixed in one spot, but instead each watches from multiple and changing vantage points.[42]

Foucault observed that the naming of sexual deviance into diverse categories of the *abnormal* was itself the method used for constructing (and therefore attempting to stabilize) that which came to stand for the *normal*. In an ironic way, "deviance" is central to the narrative history of the *normal*. But the subject-effects or traces of counterdiscourse that are excessive to the dominant historical account are deviant in another sense of the term: they are deviant in relation to the moral and political agenda of normalization intrinsic to the dominant account. So while *deviance as a taxonomic mode* is crucial to writing a "traditional history" (of proper heterosexuality), *deviance as a counterdiscursive mode* is marginal, or apparent only in effects, when it is embodied or strategically engaged by counterdiscursive (deviant) subjects. Like the subject of feminism, deviant subjects are inside and outside of the ideology and history of heterosexuality, engaging in the construction of a genealogy of survival.

The concept of *deviant subjectivity* allows the new archivist to look for and analyze operations of lesbian and gay subject formation in relation to pathologizing discourses. This historiographic practice does not cleanse homosexual subjects of characteristics that could be called "self-hatred" or "self-degradation," replacing them with utopian and heroic qualities like "liberated" and "self-determining." To demand of lesbians and gay men unmitigated and uncomplicated self-understandings, historically or in the present, is to ignore our agony of living in the margins of a deeply homophobic culture. What I have tried to propose here is not only a way of reading and understanding history against the grain of heterosexual hegemony, but a way of conceptualizing and enacting subjectivities forged in process through multiple resistances to systematized homophobia. These subjectivities are neither static nor contained; they are effects in the history of the perilous present.

NOTES

1. An earlier version of this article originally appeared in "Queer Theory: Lesbian and Gay Sexualities," *differences* 3, no. 2 (Summer 1991): 55–74.

2. For example, see Hazel Carby, *Reconstructing Womanhood: The Emergence of the Afro-American Woman Novelist* (New York, 1987); Teresa de Lauretis, "Semiotics and Experience," in *Alice Doesn't: Essays in Feminism, Semiotics, Cinema* (Bloomington, 1984), 158–186; Chandra Talapade Mohanty, "Feminist Encounters: Locating the Politics of Experience," *Copyright* 1 (198?): 30–44; Donna Haraway, *Simians, Cyborgs and Women: The Reinvention of Nature* (London, 1991); Denise Riley, *"Am I That Name?": Feminism and the Category of "Women" in History* (Minneapolis, 1988); Denise Riley, "A Short History of Some Preoccupations" in *Feminists Theorize the*

Political, ed. Judith Butler and Joan W. Scott (New York, 1992), 121–129; Joan Wallach Scott, "'Experience,'" in Butler and Scott, eds., *Feminists Theorize the Political,* 22–40; Elizabeth Weed, "Terms of Reference," in *Coming to Terms: Feminism, Theory, Politics,* ed. Elizabeth Weed (New York, 1989), xi-xxxi.

    3.   Weed, "Terms of Reference," xxi.

    4.   *Ibid.,* xxi.

    5.   Joan Scott, "'Experience,'" 24.

    6.   Weed, "Terms of References," xiv, referring to Paula Treichler, "Teaching Feminist Theory," in *Theory in the Classroom,* ed. Cary Nelson (Urbana and Chicago, 1986) and Denise Riley, "Does Sex Have A History? 'Women' and Feminism," *New Formations* 1 (Spring 1987).

    7.   Lorraine Bethel, "What Chou Mean *We,* White Girl? or the Cullud Lesbian Feminist Declaration of Independence (Dedicated to the Proposition that All Women Are Not Equal, i.e. Identical/ly Oppressed)," *Conditions: Five* 2, no. 2 (Autumn 1979): 86–92.

    8.   Scott, "'Experience.'"

    9.   Charles Tilly, "Retrieving Europeans' Lives," in *Reliving the Past: The Worlds of Social History,* ed. Olivier Zunz and David Cohen (Chapel Hill, 1985), 11–52.

    10.   Denise Riley has argued similarly that the category of "women" is neither self-evident, transhistorical, nor prediscursive. Historians of homosexuality are certainly not the only ones whose privileged subjects are embedded within discourses that construct them as inferior to the unmarked generic norm. However, beyond acknowledging that both *women* and *queers* are categories or subject positions that have historically specific and changing meanings, we might ask how a medico-diagnostic label such as *homosexual* or *sexual deviant* differs from the normalized social label *woman.*

    11.   Michel Foucault, "Critical Theory/Intellectual History" in *Michel Foucault: Politics, Philosophy, Culture: Interviews and Other Writings 1977–1984,* ed. Lawrence D. Kritzman, trans. Jeremy Harding (New York, 1988), 30.

    12.   Joan Wallach Scott, "Gender: A Useful Category of Historical Analysis" in *Coming to Terms: Feminism, Theory, Politics,* ed. Elizabeth Weed (New York, 1989), 81–100.

    13.   The case of working-class history may be closer in kind to gay and lesbian history than to women's history since scholars of both working-class and gay history now qualify that their privileged subjects—the worker and the homosexual—emerged out of particular historical and cultural locations (i.e., were not transhistorical). Scholars in both these fields of history generally agree that individuals who performed similar acts of work or sex in earlier periods were not "workers" or "homosexuals" since these identities were products of capitalist and epistemological systems of the modern West, and only make sense in those terms. In fact, a productive dialogue among theorists of difference has lead to a critique of essentialist homogenous categories of *women* and *people of color* in histories of gender and race. The privileged subjects of these histories can be radically contextualized, unsettling the transhistorical tendency which would otherwise lump Antigone together with Hilary Clinton as two Anglo-European white women, Cleopatra with Frederick Douglass as two people of African descent, and Marie Antoinette with Martina Navritalova as two lesbians.

14.   For example, see Jeffrey Weeks, *Coming Out: Homosexual Politics in Britain from the Nineteenth Century to the Present* (London, 1977); Jeffrey Weeks, *Sex, Politics and Society: The Regulation of Sexuality since 1800* (London, 1981); Jeffrey Weeks, *Sexuality and Its Discontents: Meanings, Myths and Modern Sexualities* (London, 1985); Jonathan Ned Katz, *Gay/Lesbian Almanac: A New Documentary* (New York, 1983); Michel Foucault, *The History of Sexuality: An Introduction,* trans. Robert Hurley (New York, 1980).

15.   Lillian Faderman, *Surpassing the Love of Women: Romantic Friendship and Love between Women from the Renaissance to the Present* (New York 1981); John Boswell, *Christianity, Social Tolerance, and Homosexuality* (Chicago, 1980).

16.   Hayden White, "Interpretation in History," in *Tropics of Discourse: Essays in Cultural Criticism* (Baltimore, 1978), 51–80.

17.   Michel Foucault, "Nietzsche, Genealogy, History," in *The Foucault Reader,* ed. Paul Rabinow (New York, 1984), 87.

18.   Teresa de Lauretis' theorizing of (male) desire as a motor of narrative provides a useful way of thinking about the libidinal drive toward narrative closure in historical writing. Her illustration of this motor, particularly in Sophocles' myth of Oedipus, shows Woman to be both the landscape and the penultimate oasis of (phallic) story telling before Man is returned to (him)self. The historiographic tumescence and climax to which I refer here relies on this aspect of the structure of de Lauretis' theory not to make a feminist point per se (about Woman as vehicle for Man's return to Self by way of Other) but to argue that the laws of (narrative) desire rule out contradictory fragments that do not fit the closure of a traditional historical account. The libidinal drive to closure is also the political imperative of securing the dominant subject in his place when the traditional historian lays down the pen after writing "The End." I am interested in what does not cohere and who is willfully put outside or subordinated to the service of the subject of such a (dominant) account. Teresa de Lauretis, "Desire in Narrative," in *Alice Doesn't: Essays in Feminism, Semiotics, Cinema* (Bloomington, 1984), 103–157. For an analysis of the moralizing agenda of historical narrativity see Hayden White, "The Value of Narrativity in the Representation of Reality," in *The Content of the Form: Narrative Discourse and Historical Representation* (Baltimore, 1987), 1–25.

19.   Foucault, "Nietzsche, Genealogy, History," 87.

20.   *Ibid.,* 84–85.

21.   Gilles Deleuze, *Foucault,* trans. and ed. Sean Hand, forward by Paul Bove (Minneapolis, 1988), 1.

22.   See Gloria Anzaldua, *La Frontera/Borderlands: The New Mestiza* (San Francisco, 1987); Teresa de Lauretis, "Eccentric Subjects: Feminist Theory and Historical Consciousness," *Feminist Studies* 16, no. 1 (1990): 115–150; Lauretis, "The Technology of Gender," in *Technologies of Gender: Essays on Theory, Film, and Fiction* (Bloomington, 1987), 1–30; Donna Haraway, "A Manifesto for Cyborgs: Science, Technology, and Socialist Feminism in the Late Twentieth Century," in *Simians, Cyborgs and Women,* 149–182; Donna Haraway, *Primate Visions: Gender, Race and Nature in the World of Modern Science* (New York, 1989); Audre Lorde, *Zami: A New Spelling of My Name,* (Watertown, Mass., 1982).

23.   Anthropologist Lila Abu-Lughod proposed this idea when she argued that analyzing resistances within a given social field allows us to chart the mechanisms of power operative between the dominant and the subordinate subject

positions. Lila Abu-Lughod, "The Romance of Resistance: Tracing Transformations of Power through Bedouin Women," *American Ethnologist* 17, no. 1 (1990): 41–55.

24.   Gayatri Chakravorty Spivak, "Subaltern Studies: Deconstructing Historiography," in *In Other Worlds: Essays in Cultural Politics* (New York, 1988), 193, 202–207.

25.   Barry Adam, "Pasivos y Activos en Nicaragua: Homosexuality Without A Gay World," *Out/Look* 1, no. 4 (Winter 1989): 74–82; Ramon A. Gutierrez, "Must We Deracinate Indians to Find Gay Roots?" *Out/Look* 1, no. 4 (Winter 1989): 61–67; Katz, *Gay/Lesbian Almanac* (1983); Richard G. Parker, *Bodies, Pleasures and Passions: Sexual Culture in Contemporary Brazil* (Boston, 1991).

26.   My notion of "deviant subjectivity" derives from Foucault's reverse discourse the idea that deviants make use of their own pathologization, and, thus, they are neither "outside" of pathology nor outside of power. But I also want to stress that the deviants' clash with medicine is not entirely dependent on the medical discourse for its enunciation. Much of this conflict comes from lesbian and gay subcultural practices which may overlap with the pathologizing discourse but whose origins, implications, and effects are locatable partially outside the hegemonic formations of science and medicine in a homosexual "underworld." Foucault, *The History of Sexuality*, 101.

27.   Jennifer Terry, "Lesbians under the Medical Gaze: Scientists Search for Remarkable Differences," *Journal of Sex Research* 27 (1990): 317–340; Jennifer Terry, *Siting Homosexuality: A History of Surveillance and the Production of Deviant Subjects (1935–1950)*, (Ph.D. diss., University of California at Santa Cruz, 1992).

28.   George W. Henry, *Sex Variants: A Study in Homosexual Practices* (New York, 1948).

29.   *Ibid.,* 808.

30.   *Ibid.,* 700.

31.   *Ibid.,* 814–815.

32.   *Ibid.,* 706–707.

33.   *Ibid.,* 710.

34.   *Ibid.,* 782, 778.

35.   *Ibid.,* 757.

36.   *Ibid.,* 915–916.

37.   *Ibid.,* 918.

38.   *Ibid.,* 783.

39.   *Ibid.,* 776 (emphasis mine).

40.   *Ibid.,* 913–914.

41.   See, for example, the essays and fiction of Samuel Delaney; fiction and poetry of Gloria Anzaldua, Essex Hemphill, Audre Lorde, and Jewelle Gomez; the video and cinematic work of Richard Fung, Marlon Riggs, and Pratiba Parmer; the cultural criticism of Kobena Mercer; and the social theory of Jackie Goldsby, Barbara Smith, and Tomas Almaguer.

42.   Lauretis, "The Technology of Gender," 9–10.

NOTES ON CONTRIBUTORS

Ava Baron is a professor of sociology at Rider College. She is currently (1993–1994) a member at the Institute for Advanced Study in Princeton where she is completing her book *Men's Work and the Woman Question: The Masculinization of Printing, 1830–1920.* She is the editor of *Work Engendered: Toward a New History of American Labor* (Cornell University Press, 1991). Her research on gender and work in printing, sewing, and the legal profession and on gender equality and the law has also been supported by fellowships from the National Endowment for the Humanities and the Bunting Institute of Radcliffe College.

Judith M. Bennett is a professor of history at the University of North Carolina at Chapel Hill. The author of *Women in the Medieval English Countryside* (1978) and co-editor of *Sisters and Workers in the Middle Ages* (1989), she is currently completing a study of women and brewing in England between 1200 and 1600.

Marilyn A. Katz is a professor of classics and women's studies at Wesleyan University. She has published a number of articles on women in ancient Greece and in ancient Greek epic poetry and is the author of *Penelope's Renown: Meaning and Indeterminacy in Homer's* Odyssey (Princeton, 1991). She was a founding member of the Women's Classical Caucus of the American Philological Association, and has served as the chairperson of the Columbia University Seminar on Women and Society, and as the coordinator of the Wesleyan University women's studies program.

Regina Morantz-Sanchez is a professor of history at UCLA. She teaches women's history, history of the family, the social history of medicine, and selected topics on gender, race, and class. She has published widely on the history of women physicians in the United States and is the author of *Sympathy and Science: Women Physicians in American Medicine.* She is currently studying the emergence of gynecological surgery in the nineteenth-century United States.

NELL IRVIN PAINTER, the Edwards Professor of American History at Princeton University, is the recipient of numerous fellowships and honors, including a Guggenheim fellowship, the Candace Award of the National Coalition of One Hundred Black Women, and a National Endowment for the Humanities fellowship. At present she is completing a biography of the black feminist abolitionist Sojourner Truth which will be published by W. W. Norton. Her most recent book is *Standing at Armageddon: The United States, 1877–1919*.

SYLVIA SCHAFER is an assistant professor of history at the University of Wisconsin—Milwaukee where she teaches European social history and women's history. She is currently completing a book on the problem of "moral danger," the family, and the state in nineteenth-century France.

ANN-LOUISE SHAPIRO teaches in the history department and in the women's studies program at Wesleyan University and is an associate editor of the journal *History and Theory*. She is the author of *Housing the Poor of Paris, 1850–1902* and of numerous articles on female criminality in late nineteenth-century Paris. She is currently completing a book, *Breaking the Codes*, about the meanings of female criminality in the context of the cultural renegotiations of the *fin-de-siècle*.

MRINALINI SINHA is an assistant professor of history at Boston College. She is completing a manuscript entitled *Manliness: A Victorian Ideal as Colonial Policy in Late Nineteenth-Century Bengal*.

BONNIE G. SMITH teaches history at Rutgers University and writes on gender and the professionalization of historical writing. Among her books is *Changing Lives: Women in European History since 1700*, published in 1989 by D. C. Heath.

CAROLYN STEEDMAN teaches in the department of arts education at the University of Warwick. She is the author of *The Tidy House; Landscape for a Good Woman; Childhood, Culture and Class in Britain: Margaret McMillan, 1860–1931*; and *Past Tenses: Essays on Writing, Autobiography and History*. She is currently working on the idea of childhood in eighteenth- and nineteenth-century thought.

JENNIFER TERRY is an assistant professor of comparative cultural studies at Ohio State University. She is co-editor with Jacqueline Urla of *Deviant Bodies*, which is soon to be published by Indiana University Press, and is working on a manuscript entitled *Siting Homosexuality: A History of Surveillance and the Production of Deviant Subjects (1935—present)*.

VRON WARE is a lecturer in cultural geography at the University of Greenwich in London. She is the author of *Beyond the Pale: White Women, Racism and History* (Verso, 1992).